Tort Law in Ireland

Tort Law in Ireland

By

John Tully
LLB, LLM, Barrister (Middle Temple), PGCE, PG Cert

CLARUS
PRESS

Published by
Clarus Press Ltd,
Griffith Campus,
South Circular Road,
Dublin 8.

Typeset by
Deanta Global Publishing Services

Printed by
Sprint Print,
Dublin

ISBN
978-1-905536-69-6

Disclaimer
Whilst every effort has been made to ensure that the contents of this book are accurate, neither the publisher nor authors can accept responsibility for any errors or omissions or loss occasioned to any person acting or refraining from acting as result of any material in this publication.

For Val

PREFACE

Tort law is a core subject for all undergraduate law courses in Ireland and is an essential element of legal practice. Written primarily with the student in mind, this book aims to provide a comprehensive and accessible account of tort law in Ireland by outlining the fundamental principles of the subject in a clear and succinct manner, making it a valuable introductory or supplementary text for this vital area of legal education.

As part of *The Core Text Series* this book seeks to introduce the reader to the key principles of tort law with a clear and concise explanation of the law in an easy-to-use format. As tort law is almost entirely based upon case law, the facts of many of the most important cases have been included, placing legal principles into their factual contexts. The clear layout, sub-headings, and intended learning outcomes at the beginning of each chapter, ensure that the subject-matter is accessible and easy to navigate. This first edition is fully up-to-date to reflect recent developments in the law, including consideration of new cases on privacy, economic loss, nuisance, vicarious liability, standard of care, occupiers' liability and more.

This text can be used both as an ongoing revision and reference source to provide extra support to students throughout their studies. The use of diagrams, tables, flow-charts and summaries is intended to reinforce the information and provide quick visual cues for the understanding of key points contained in the text. It is also hoped that the book will provide a sound foundation to this important area of undergraduate study and will act as a stepping-stone to other recently published leading texts, such as *Torts in Ireland* by Eoin Quill, *Tort Law in Ireland* by Paul Ward, and, what is widely regarded as the definitive text on Irish torts, *Law of Torts* by Bryan McMahon and William Binchy – a work described by Mr Justice Hogan as "magisterial".

Readers will notice that I have used the generic pronoun "he" in some instances instead of "he or she". This is deliberate and has been done for style purposes only. The repeated use of the latter can sometimes affect the flow of passages, detracting somewhat from their clarity. Similarly,

I have used the singular "they" or "them" in some instances for the same style reasons. For all the elegance and sophistication of the English language, it does not provide us with personal pronouns that can refer to someone – as opposed to something – without identifying whether that person is male or female. Hence the use of "he" or "they" or "them" in sections of text where the repeated use of "he or she" or "he and she" would appear awkward and clumsy.

My hope is that this book will inspire students to consider further and deeper study of this fascinating area of law.

John Tully
29th September 2014

ACKNOWLEDGMENTS

I would like to express my sincere appreciation to my colleagues in the Department of Humanities at the Institute of Technology, Carlow, in particular those involved in the organisation and delivery of the LL.B programme: Margaret Crowley, Marian Egan, Allison Kenneally, Maebh Maher, Pauline McHugh, Sadhb Reddy, Yvonne Scully and Ivan Sheeran. I am especially grateful to David McCartney of *Clarus Press* without whose hard work and encouragement this book would simply not have appeared. Sincere thanks also to Val, Joe, Liam and Ruby for their patience and forbearance. Any errors or omissions are mine and mine alone. I have attempted to state the law as at 1 August 2014.

John Tully
29th September 2014

CONTENTS

TABLE OF CASES

TABLE OF LEGISLATION

Statutory Instruments

UK Acts

Other

GLOSSARY

Chattel: An item of property other than freehold land, including tangible goods (chattels personal) and leasehold interests (chattels real)

Conversion: A tort which is committed by a person who deals with chattels not belonging to him in a manner which is inconsistent with the rights of the owner; there must be an intention to deny the right of ownership on the part of the wrongdoer

Corporation: An entity that has legal personality, i.e., that is capable of enjoying and being subject to legal rights and duties

Corporator: One who is a member of a corporation; a corporator is not in general liable personally for any act of the corporation

Damage: Loss or harm, physical or economic, resulting from a wrongful act

Damages: Money compensation for loss suffered by a person owing to the wrong of another

Defendant: An individual, company, or institution sued or accused in a court of law

Defender: Used in Scotland for *defendant*, as the name of the party opposite a *pursuer* in civil actions

Detinue: A tort which consists of the withholding of goods from the person who was immediately entitled to their possession; an action in detinue will be taken by a person who claims the specific return of goods wrongfully detained or their value and damages for their detention

Hard law: Binding instruments of law enforceable by the courts, e.g., statutes, statutory instruments, common law rules

Injury: Harm, damage, wrong, or injustice

Inominate tort: Unnamed tort (e.g. the tort in *Wilkinson v Downton*)

Liquidated damages: Money compensation for loss suffered by a person owing to the breach of contract of another which is fixed and ascerained in the contract

Locus standi: The right to be heard in court proceedings ("standing")

Loss: See *Damage*

Misfeasance: An otherwise lawful act performed in a wrongful manner

Next friend: A person through whom a minor plaintiff or plaintiff lacking capacity sues; next friends will usually be relatives

Nominate tort: Named tort (e.g. negligence, trespass, defamation)

Nonfeasance: Failure to perform an act that is required to be done

Official Referee: In England, a person, normally a judge attached to the High Court who is empowered to try certain cases, esp where a detailed examination of accounts or other documents is involved

Plaintiff: A person who brings a case against another in a court of law

Promisee: A person to whom a promise is made

Promisor: A person who makes a promise

Pursuer: Equivalent to *plaintiff* in Scots law

Reversionary interest: Any right in property the enjoyment of which is deferred

Reversioner: A person who possesses the reversion to a property

Soft law: Non-binding codes of conduct, declaratory statements, principles without specific obligations, administrative circulars or memorandums

Strict liability: A legal obligation or duty which is independent of fault

Testator: A person who has made a will or given a legacy

Tort: A civil wrong other than breach of contract

Tortfeasor: A person who commits a tort

Tortious: Constituting a tort/of or relating to a tort

Unliquidated damages: Unascertained damages to be determined by the court

Vendor: A person or company offering something for sale

THE NATURE AND FUNCTIONS OF TORT LAW

Learning Outcomes

Upon completion of this chapter, the reader should be able to:

- Explain the nature of tort law and the tort system;
- Discuss the aims of tort law in compensating for wrongs;
- Appreciate the distinction between tort law and other areas of law;
- Comprehend the specific functions of individual torts and their internal rules;
- Explain the role of insurance in the tort system;
- Distinguish between common law torts and "Eurotorts".

A. What is Tort Law?

Winfield's classic definition of tort law is:

> "Tortious liability arises from the breach of a duty primarily fixed by law; such duty is towards persons generally and is redressable by an action for unliquidated damages." (Winfield, *The Province of the Law of Tort* (1931), 92)

Tort law, therefore, could be described as the area of civil law which provides a remedy for a party who has suffered the breach of a protected interest. The word itself is derived from the Latin "tortum", meaning twisted or wrong.

Tort law deals with a wide range of activities and many different types of loss. It covers such obvious things as negligent or intentional personal injury, damage to goods or invasion of land. It also deals with such things as the protection of a person's good name, the prevention of unfair trading, or the control of pollution.

It is important to bear in mind, however, that not all interests are protected by tort law. Accordingly, a person could suffer loss owing to the conduct of another person for which the law does not provide a remedy. This situation is described as *damnum sine injuria esse potest* ("there can be damage without injury"). This refers to a situation where a plaintiff, who has suffered damage in consequence of the act of another, may not be entitled to recover compensation because the defendant's act was not in law wrongful. This could arise in respect of injuries caused wholly accidentally in, for example, contact sports like rugby, or damage done by way of competition in trade. For instance, if I open a small grocer's shop on the high street and later a large food retail chain lawfully opens a branch next door, I may suffer loss of business and reduced profit, but that loss is not recoverable in tort because no "legal wrong" has been committed by the retail chain.

Possibly the most litigated of all torts is negligence. This tort covers a wide range of human activity. It deals with carelessly causing injury to the person, to chattels and, in some circumstances, economic interests. A road traffic accident is an example of an event which could give rise to an action in negligence; or medical accidents which give rise to personal injury in the course of the treatment of illness.

In relation to economic interests, the courts in both England and in Ireland have struggled to lay down clear parameters as to when economic injury caused through negligent advice is compensatable. For example, should a person be able to sue for a negligently written reference which means that they do not get a job they have applied for? Or should a referee, in a soccer match for example, be allowed considerable freedom to express a personal opinion?

Tort law defines the obligations imposed on one member of society to his or her fellows and provides a range of remedies for harms caused by breach of those obligations. Tort law is often considered to be primarily concerned with "corrective justice" — that is, the circumstances in which a wronged party is able to obtain recompense or reparation from the wrongdoer. Accordingly, the success, or otherwise, of tort law is often judged by how successful it is at compensating those who suffer wrongs. Since most actions in tort have as their principal objective monetary compensation for loss inflicted on the plaintiff by the defendant, a critical question that frequently arises is: "who should bear the cost?" Should the cost lie where it falls: on the plaintiff? Or is the conduct of the defendant such that the law should transfer the loss to him? In the tort of negligence, as with many other torts, determining who bears that cost is a core issue.

But tort law is not only concerned with monetary compensation. It provides remedies for many different types of loss or harm. In cases such as road traffic accidents, injuries in the workplace, and medical accidents, the remedy sought by the plaintiff is likely to be damages. Tort also deals with disputes between neighbours about the use of land. If enjoyment of land is interfered with by noise or smells which are deemed to be unreasonable, this will constitute the tort of nuisance. In such circumstances, rather than seeking an award of monetary compensation, the plaintiff may request that the court grant an injunction, which is an order restraining the defendant from continuing to interfere with the plaintiff's enjoyment of his land.

B. The Aims of Tort Law

As mentioned, the primary objective of tort law is to compensate. The purpose of compensation is to seek to put the plaintiff into the position that he would have been in had the tort not occurred. Tort law also has two subsidiary objectives:

- Deterrence —awareness of possible tort liability may lead to more care being taken and generally raise standards in a particular field of activity, thereby preventing future loss. Insurance and punitive damages exercise opposing influences upon this objective;
- Justice—recognition that a wrong has taken place and that this must be acknowledged and corrected. This is of particular significance in torts that are actionable without proof of damage. For example, in an action for false imprisonment the plaintiff may not be entitled to significant compensation but instead require recognition of the breach of his right to liberty

The traditional approach of tort law has been to ask whether a loss that B has suffered should be shifted to A. If A were at fault, the answer would usually be to shift that loss from innocent victim B to wrongdoer A. There is, however, another view. By spreading the loss from an individual victim to the many that benefit from the activity that has caused it, the loss is more easily — and more fairly — borne. The employer whose worker is injured can spread the loss through raising the price of his product. The same argument applies where his product injures a consumer. This concept of *loss distribution* is, for example, advanced as a justification for the vicarious liability principle which makes an employer answerable for the torts committed by those who work for him.

Loss distribution is reinforced by insurance. The owner of a vehicle can readily insure — and indeed is required by law to insure — against the risk of his negligently inflicted harm on third parties. The insurance premium that he pays will fall short of the amount payable in damages for a typical road traffic accident. Yet, in this way, the aggregate cost of all road accidents is distributed among all properly insured drivers.

However, the type of loss distribution described here which is achieved through insurance can militate against another objective of tort law: *deterrence*. The imposition of liability in tort operates not only to transfer the relevant loss from the wronged to the wrongdoer, but also to deter others from committing such wrongs in the first place. Tort law is very effective at deterring tortious conduct. The more a person commits a tort, the more he will have to pay in damages. A good example is the imposition of strict liability on manufacturers of defective products. This encourages them to maintain the highest standards of safety in their products in order to avoid liability.

It is, however, possible to overstate the effect of deterrence. There will be many instances where the wrongdoer's conduct is not deliberately harmful. The conduct which gives rise to the harm may merely have been inadvertent. In these cases, it is difficult to see how the wrongdoer could have been deterred.

C. Tort and Contract

The principle underpinning a contractual obligation is that, rather than being imposed by law, it is negotiated by the two parties. Accordingly, the obligations in a contract are owed to the specific two parties to the contract, not to persons generally. In contrast, in the tort of negligence, the duties and matching rights therein have evolved out of the operation of the common law, supplemented in some instances by statute, rather than by agreement. Such duties and rights tend to be applied to the population in general. All road users, for example, have a duty not drive carelessly and injure other road users; and all road users have a right to seek a remedy in tort if that duty towards them is breached.

The distinction between tort and contract can be seen in the different limitation periods that apply to the respective actions. Remoteness of damage is not determined in the same way in tort and contract. As we have seen, the object of damages in tort is to compensate the plaintiff by restoring him to the position he was in before the tort was committed: whereas in contract, loss of expectations and loss of profit may be allowed, since the object of compensation in contract is to put the plaintiff into the position he would have been in had the contract not been breached.

But, it is also clear that the distinction between tort and contract is not absolute. For example, in cases of pure economic loss caused by negligent misstatement, the plaintiff may have a choice of bringing his action in either tort or contract.

D. Tort and Criminal Law

The primary distinction between tort and criminal law concerns the nature of their objectives. The main objective of the criminal law is to enforce the law by punishing those who break it. The main objective of tort law, on the other hand, is to enforce the law by compensating those who suffer damage when a right is interfered with. In general, criminal law seeks to punish, whereas tort law seeks to compensate.

In tort law, the principal focus is on the loss or damage suffered by the plaintiff, rather than upon the individual personality and motivation of the criminal defendant. As we have seen in relation to contract, the distinction between tort and criminal law is not absolute either. There will be circumstances, such as in defamation cases, where tort law allows punishment of defendants through the use of punitive damages. This type of award can be made under the Defamation Act 2009. Similarly, the criminal courts now have powers to award compensation to victims of crime through compensation orders. Such orders were introduced by s 6 of the Criminal Justice Act 1993. This provision allows the court, on conviction of any person for an offence, instead of or in addition to dealing with that person in any other way and "unless it sees reason to the contrary", to make a "compensation order", requiring the convicted person to pay compensation in respect of any personal injury or loss resulting to another from the offence.

In addition, some wrongs will constitute crimes as well as torts. For example, the torts of assault, battery, and public nuisance can be prosecuted as criminal offences as well as being the basis for civil actions in tort.

E. Competing Interests within Tort Law

Many of the interests protected by law are competing interests. For example, with the tort of nuisance, one resident may complain that the volume of his neighbour's music is so loud that it amounts to an interference with his use and enjoyment of his home. On the other hand, the neighbour may argue that it is he who is suffering the wrong, in that he has the right to play music in the privacy of his own home without interference from his neighbours. In a case such as this, the role of the court is to apply the law of tort in order to determine which of these competing interests should receive legal protection under the tort of nuisance. Similarly, the competing interests of protecting one's reputation and recognising another's right to freedom of expression are matters which must ultimately be balanced by the court in applying the rules of the tort of defamation.

F. The Role of Insurance

There is little doubt that insurance schemes have had a significant influence on tort litigation in recent years. This is not just the case in Ireland. The United Kingdom and North America have all experienced the influence of insurance in the context of litigation. It is particularly relevant in circumstances where professional persons are sued in negligence. For example, in *Smith v Bush* [1990] 1 AC 831, Lord Griffiths said:

> "There was once a time when it was considered improper even to mention the possible existence of insurance cover in a lawsuit. But those days are long past. Everyone knows that all prudent, professional men carry insurance, and the availability and cost of insurance must be a relevant factor when considering which of the two parties should be required to bear the risk of a loss."

Here, Lord Griffiths was giving expression to one of the key functions of tort law which is to spread the cost of losses efficiently and fairly throughout society. In many cases, it may be either too difficult or impossible to prove fault on the part of the defendant, or there may simply be no one to blame. One possible answer to this might be the introduction of no-fault liability schemes. In the UK, consideration was given to this possibility by the Royal Commission on Civil Liability and Compensation for Personal Injury (1978), but its recommendations, although limited, were not implemented. New Zealand did implement a wide-ranging no-fault scheme in 1974, which in recent years, has been subject to some modification and restriction. There appears to be no appetite for this approach in Ireland.

A person who suffers injury may benefit from private insurance in a number of ways. First, he may have an insurance policy of his own for which he pays a regular premium which covers him for such risks. Such policies are known as *personal accident* or *first-party* policies. They are normally taken out by the insured person for accidental injuries which they personally may suffer. The insurance company is the second party. In addition, a person who injures another person may have a liability policy that covers the risk that they, the insured person, will become liable in law to the person they have injured. Under s 56 of the Road Traffic Act 1961, owners of motor vehicles are obliged by law to carry such third-party insurance. This has been the case since 1933. Many people take out "comprehensive" policies which cover them for injuries to themselves or to others. Such policies are, in effect, combined *liability* and *personal accident* policies in respect of vehicle use.

There are cases where innocent third parties receive personal injuries as a result of being struck by a motor vehicle for which there is no valid insurance at the time of the accident. Persons so injured may recover from the Motor Insurers Bureau of Ireland (MIBI). All injuries suffered in the course of "hit and run" accidents are covered. Paragraph 6 of the agreement provides that payments will be made by the MIBI "for personal injury or death … caused by the negligent use of a vehicle in a public place, where the owner or user of the vehicle remains unidentified or untraced".

One innovation to tackle the rising level of insurance premiums in Ireland was the creation of the Personal Injuries Assessment Board (PIAB). It was established in 2004 by the Personal Injuries Assessment Board Act 2003. It is now called the Injuries Board. It is a statutory body with the task of assessing compensation in most cases of personal injury where liability is not contested. The claimant must submit to the procedure and cannot initiate a claim in court without the Injury Board's authorisation. This does not apply to medical negligence claims. Proceedings are conducted entirely on paper. There is no oral hearing. Claimants can receive assistance from the Injury Board's own telephone advice line, but if they wish to be represented by their own solicitor they can be, but at their own expense. The parties can choose whether to accept or reject the Injury Board's assessment of the compensation. If both accept, it has the same legal effect as a court judgment. If either party rejects the assessment, the case can be pursued through the courts in the normal way. This reform aims to allow the resolution of personal injury claims quickly and without the legal expenses and expert fees frequently associated with traditional tort litigation.

G. The European Union Dimension and "Eurotorts"

Ireland has been a member of the EU (the EEC as it then was) since 1 January 1973. EU law, since then, has had full legal force within the State. The Member

States of the EU are under Treaty obligations to ensure that all EU law has full effect within their respective territories. Sometimes, however, Member States fail to implement EU law, depriving their citizens EU rights. In *Francovich v Italian Republic* [1993] 2 CMLR 66, the European Court of Justice held that failure by a Member State to implement an EU directive designed to create rights in respect of particular individuals would give rise to a claim in damages on the part of those individuals *against the State*. The Court set out three conditions which had to be met before there would be a right to compensation:

(i)   the directive should entail the grant of rights to individuals;
(ii) it should be possible to identify the content of those rights on the basis of the provisions of the directive; and
(iii) there must be a causal link between the breach of the State's obligation and the harm suffered by the injured parties

The significance of the *Francovich* decision was that the EU legislation in question was not directly effective. This meant that, in the absence of an action against the State, there would have been no one against whom an action could have been brought. But in the later case of *Brasserie du Pecheur SA v Germany* (Case C-46/93) [1996] ECR 1-1029, the European Court made it clear that the *Francovich* principle applied equally where the legislation *is* of direct effect. This opened the way for the Court, in subsequent cases, to find that the *Francovich* principle also applied where the breach of EU law entailed a legislative act (not merely an omission), where the national courts failed to observe EU law and in respect of administrative decisions.

The conditions under which the State might incur liability for its acts or omissions contrary to EU law were stated by the European Court in *Brasserie du Pecheur SA v Germany*. Accordingly, before a Member State can be held liable, a national court must find that:

(i)   the relevant rule of EU law is one which is intended to confer rights on individuals;
(ii) the breach must be sufficiently serious;
(iii) there must be a direct causal link between the breach and the loss complained of.

It is for each Member State's own legal system to determine, in accordance with the rules of national law on liability, how the State must make reparation for the harm caused by the failure to implement EU law. The failure of a Member State to implement EU law in such circumstances is referred to as a "Eurotort". In *Tate v Minister for Social Welfare* [1995] 1 ILRM 507, the Court characterised the government's failure to implement a directive as a tort. This approach was endorsed in *Coppinger v Waterford County Council* [1986] 2 ILRM 427. In that case, the plaintiff was injured when he drove his car into a stationary tipper truck owned by the defendant County Council. The plaintiff's injuries were more serious than they otherwise would have been because the defendant's truck was not fitted with an under-run protection barrier. An EU directive required that Member States make such barriers compulsory. Ireland, however, in its implementing legislation, wrongly exempted tipper trucks of the type involved in the accident. The Court confirmed that Ireland's failure to properly transpose the directive into Irish law was a tort.

Table Outlining the Major Torts

Tort	Description
Negligence	The breach of a legal duty of care whereby damage is caused to the party to whom the duty is owed. It is the doing by a person of some act which a reasonable and prudent man would not do or the omission to do something which a reasonable and prudent man would have done. For actionable negligence there must be (a) a duty of care between the parties; (b) a failure to observe the required duty of care; and (c) reasonably foreseeable damage suffered.
Trespass to land	Intentionally or negligently entering, or remaining on, or directly causing anything to come into contact with, land in the possession of another, without lawful justification
Trespass to the person – assault	The unlawful direct interference with a person; the threat of, or attempt to apply, force to another which puts that other in reasonable apprehension that immediate violence will be inflicted upon him
Trespass to the person – battery	The unlawful direct interference with a person; the direct touching of the person of another, however slightly, with hostile intention or against the other person's will
Trespass to the person – false imprisonment	The unlawful direct interference with a person; the unlawful and total restraint of the personal liberty of another whether by constraining him or compelling him to go to a particular place or confining him to a prison or police station or private place or by detaining him against his will in a public place

Private nuisance	The unlawful interference with another's servitude or the unauthorised use of a person's own property which causes damage to the property of another or interferes with another's enjoyment of his property
Public nuisance	An act or omission which causes injury to, or materially affects the reasonable comfort and convenience of the public, or a section of the public
Defamation	The publication of a defamatory statement concerning another without just cause excuse, whereby he suffers injury to his reputation
The tort in *Wilkinson v Downton*	The wilful commission of an act calculated to cause injury to the plaintiff by indirect means

Negligence: Duty of Care

Learning Outcomes

Upon completion of this chapter, the reader should be able to:

- Trace the development of the duty of care in negligence in Ireland and England;
- Describe the key features and internal rules of the duty of care;
- Discuss the role of the duty of care in the negligence equation;
- Distinguish between the concepts of foreseeability and proximity;
- Identify public policy considerations taken into account by the courts in determining the existence of a duty of care;
- Analyse how the courts assess the nature of fairness, justice and reasonableness in the context of duty of care;
- Appreciate the potential for the application of human rights principles to negligence claims.

A. What is Negligence?

Negligence is a breach of a legal duty to take care which results in damage to the plaintiff. It is the doing by a person of some act which a reasonable and prudent person would not have done in the particular circumstances, or the failure to do something which a reasonable and prudent person would have done in the particular circumstances. To maintain an action in negligence there must be:

(a)   a duty of care between the parties;
(b)   a breach of that duty;
(c)   damage which was reasonably foreseeable; and
(d)   a causal link between the breach and the damage.

Figure 2.1

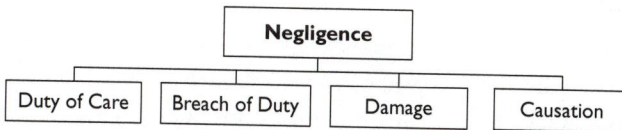

Negligence nowadays occupies a central position in the law of tort. It is the most commonly litigated of all torts, but it was not always so. Historically, many actions in nuisance and trespass were once based upon negligent conduct. Over time, a wide range of situations in which negligence was the common element became subsumed under the "action on the case": these would now be described as negligence actions. It was not until around 1825 that there developed a separate and discernible tort of negligence. There existed then only what amounted to a list of factual situations where the victims of careless conduct might recover damages. Actions on the case for negligence became more and more common throughout the nineteenth century, probably because of a significant increase in negligently inflicted injuries through new inventions and developments, such as the railways and industrial machinery and equipment.

This chapter deals only with the first of the ingredients of negligence mentioned above: the duty of care. The other ingredients are dealt with in later chapters.

B. Duty of Care: Historical Development

Initially, the courts tended to limit the plaintiff to a claim under a contract and preclude attempts to rely on an obligation which might arise under a contract to which the plaintiff was not a party. This was the effect of the doctrine of privity of contract which was generally necessary to enable one person to sue another in contract. Then, as now, no one could sue on, or be sued on a contract to which he or she was not a party. In other words, a contract cannot impose liability on a stranger. In the early part of the nineteenth century it was possible for a contracting party to sue the other party to a contract for breach of a tortious duty imposed by law. Also, it was possible, in certain circumstances, for a stranger to a contract to sue for injury caused by negligent behaviour which was done pursuant to a contract. An example might be a pedestrian injured by the negligence of a coachman. There was an expectation that parties to a contract would protect their interests by incorporating appropriate warranties into the contracts in question. Most cases that came before the courts related to the liability of manufacturers or suppliers of defective goods or equipment, but, as we have seen, only those who were parties to the contract could secure a remedy. This meant that a third party who suffered loss and damage as a consequence of a breach of a warranty in a contract between two other parties, could not obtain redress before the courts.

In *Winterbottom v Wright* (1842) 10 M & W 109, for example, the plaintiff entered into a contract with the Postmaster General to drive a mail coach. The coach had been supplied by the defendant to the Postmaster General under a contract which provided that during the term of the contract the coach was to be kept in a safe and secure condition. The coach collapsed. The plaintiff was thrown from his seat and was injured. He alleged that the defendant "negligently conducted himself, and so utterly disregarded his aforesaid contract and so wholly neglected and failed to perform his duty in this behalf". The Court, however, found for the defendant. Lord Abinger CB said:

> "I am… of the opinion that the defendant is entitled to our judgment… Here the action is brought simply because the defendant was a contractor with a third person; and it is contended that thereupon he became liable to every body who might use the carriage… There is no privity of contract between these parties; and if the plaintiff can sue, every passenger, or even any person passing along the road, who was injured by the upsetting of the coach, may bring a similar action. Unless we confine the operation of such contracts as this to the parties who entered into them, the most absurd and outrageous consequences, to which I can see no limit, would ensue… There is… a class of cases in which the law permits a contract to be turned into a tort; but unless there has been some public duty undertaken, or a public nuisance committed, they are all cases in which an action might have been maintained on the contract…"

It is clear that the Court in this case was concerned about what we would now call the "floodgates" argument. In other words, if liability were imposed in this case, it might open the door to countless other claims in similar cases leading to a major expansion in the scope of the then very limited duty. It was clearly an unsatisfactory situation where the common law would allow a claim by a pedestrian injured by the negligent driving of a coachman, but not a claim by the coachman himself who was injured by the negligent maintenance of the coach. The courts thought in terms of a general rule of no liability, to which only limited exceptions were made, for example, in respect of articles dangerous in themselves or (later) articles which were dangerous due to defective manufacture. In *George v Skivington* (1869) LR 5 Ex 1, for example, the second plaintiff purchased from the defendant a hair wash for his wife, the first plaintiff. She was injured by the product when she used it. The Court of Exchequer held that the wife had a good cause of action notwithstanding the fact that there was no fraud and the case did not appear to fit into any of the exceptions to the general rule of no liability in tort in such cases. Kelly CB expressly stated that the action was not in contract, so no issue of breach of warranty arose. An action on the case was brought for "unskilfulness and negligence in the manufacture of [the product] whereby the person who used it was injured".

As we have seen, the duty to take care, which was originally linked to contractual relationships, widened its reach throughout the nineteenth century. On a case-by-case basis a duty was found to exist owing to the relationship between the parties, for example that of employer and employee. However, attempts to set down a more general concept of duty, such as in *Heaven v Pender* (1883) 11 QBD 503, failed. In that case, the plaintiff was painting a ship when one of the ropes holding up the staging on which he was working broke. He fell and was injured. The staging had been erected by the defendant dock owner under contract with the plaintiff's employer. It was found that the rope which failed was unfit for use at the time it was supplied by the defendant. Lord Esher (Brett MR then) had attempted to enunciate a general principle defining when a duty of care existed. He said:

> "[W]henever one person is by circumstances placed in such a position with regard to another that everyone of ordinary sense who did think would at once recognise that if he did not use ordinary care and skill in his own conduct with regard to those circumstances he would cause danger or injury to the person or property of the other, a duty arises to use ordinary care and skill to avoid such danger."

Lord Esher's approach was rejected by the other two judges in the case. They confined their reasoning to the particular facts before them. Some time later, the House of Lords in *Derry v Peek* (1889) 14 App Cas 337 affirmed that there was no general principle of liability for negligent misstatements causing monetary loss; and in *Le Lievre v Gould* [1893] 1 QB 491 Lord Esher again attempted to state a general principle of duty of care on the basis of physical proximity between the plaintiff and the defendant. He said:

> "*Heaven v Pender* ... established that, under certain circumstances, one man may owe a duty to another, even though there is no contract between them. If one man is near to another, or is near to the property of another, a duty lies upon him not to do that which may cause a personal injury to that other, or may injure his property. For instance, if a man is driving along a road, it is his duty not to do that which may injure another person whom he meets on the road, or to his horse or his carriage. In the same way it is the duty of a man not to do that which would injure the house of another which he is near..."

Le Lievre v Gould concerned a negligent statement made by a surveyor. Lord Esher accepted that *Heaven v Pender* would not apply in such a case. He said: "Such negligence, in the absence of a contract with the plaintiff, can give no right of action at law or in equity". The courts continued to resist the idea of a general principle of a duty of care in negligence. This can be seen in *Black v Lake & Elliott Ltd* (1912) 107 LT 533 where Lord Sumner said: "the breach of the defendant's contract with A to use care and skill in and about the manufacture or repair of an article does not of itself give any cause of action to B when he is injured by reason of the article proving to be defective". All that changed with *Donoghue v Stevenson*.

C. *Donoghue v Stevenson*

The facts of *Donoghue v Stevenson* [1932] AC 562 are as follows. At about 8.50 pm on 26 August 1928, Mrs May Donoghue went to a café owned by Francis Minchella. The café was known as the Wellmeadow Cafe, Wellmeadow Road, Paisley. A friend of hers bought a bottle of ginger beer and an ice cream. The bottle was made of opaque glass. Mr Minchella poured part of the contents into a tumbler containing the ice cream. Mrs Donoghue drank some of this and the friend then poured the remainder of the ginger beer into the glass. It was said that a decomposed snail floated out of the bottle. Mrs Donoghue claimed that she suffered shock and gastroenteritis. She claimed £500 in damages from the manufacturer of the ginger beer, David Stevenson of Paisley. Mrs Donoghue argued that a manufacturer of products was liable in negligence to a person injured by the product. The defendant, however, claimed that there could be no liability as there was no contract between himself and Mrs Donoghue. The contract was with the wholesalers, not with her. The House of Lords held that such a defendant could be liable to such a plaintiff in negligence on the basis that the defendant manufacturer had been under a duty of care not to cause her, the end user of the product, injury. This decision included the "neighbour principle". It was set out by Lord Atkin in the following terms:

✳ "The rule that you are to love your neighbour becomes in law, you must not injure your neighbour; and the lawyer's question, Who is my neighbour? receives a restricted reply. You must take reasonable care to avoid acts or omissions which you can reasonably foresee would be likely to injure your neighbour. Who then, in law, is my neighbour? The answer seems to be — persons who are so closely and directly affected by my act that I ought reasonably to have them in contemplation as being so affected when I am directing my mind to the acts or omissions which are called in question."

The decision in *Donoghue v Stevenson* is significant for two reasons. First, it established a new category of duty: namely, that of a manufacturer of goods to the eventual user of those goods. Second, it removed any doubts as to whether the tort of negligence was capable of further expansion. The case also removed the application of the doctrine of privity of contract to negligence cases. In other words, the existence of a contract between the defendant and a third party did not prevent the defendant owing a duty to the plaintiff in tort in relation to the performance of that contract. The House of Lords, therefore, distinguished *Winterbottom v Wright* on the basis that the plaintiff in that case had sought to found his claim on the defendant's breach of contract with a third party — not his breach of an independent tortious duty owed directly to the plaintiff himself. *Donoghue* also established the "neighbour principle", which, although not forming part of the *ratio* of the case, did introduce into the law of negligence the notion that we all have a duty to take care of our "neighbours". Lord Atkin's supreme achievement, perhaps, was placing this idea of "good neighbourliness" into a legal principle.

The existence of a duty of care is an essential requirement for a successful action in negligence. A failure to take reasonable care cannot give rise to liability if there is no duty. One notable fact in *Donoghue* was that the product (the ginger beer) was supplied in an opaque bottle. The potential significance of this was examined by the Judicial Committee of the Privy Council in *Grant v Australian Knitting Mills Ltd* [1936] AC 85. In that case, the plaintiff bought underwear from a retail shop. The defendants manufactured and supplied the article to the shop from where the plaintiff bought it. The plaintiff suffered a serious skin injury, apparently from chemicals used in the manufacture of the underwear. He sued the manufacturers in negligence, succeeding (eventually) before the Judicial Committee. One issue the Judicial Committee had to determine was whether *Donoghue v Stevenson* applied only to products which the manufacturer supplied in a sealed and opaque container (as was the case with the ginger beer in that case). The Judicial Committee ruled that the essential question was whether the product reached the consumer in the same defective condition it had been in when it left the manufacturer.

Furthermore, in *Donoghue*, Lord Atkin had stated that there should be "no reasonable possibility of intermediate examination" of the product subject to the defect. It was thought this might place a limitation on the circumstances in which a duty of care could be held to exist. The Judicial Committee in *Grant* ruled that the limitation, such as it was, only arose where there was a reasonable possibility of discovering the defect. Since the chemicals in the underwear in question could not have been detected by any examination that could reasonably have been made, the limitation did not apply. In later cases it was held that Lord Atkin's statement in *Donoghue* in relation to intermediate examination did not create a separate requirement of liability: see *Griffiths v Arch Engineering Co Ltd* [1968] 3 All ER 217. Liability, therefore, could arise even if a third party did have a reasonable opportunity of inspecting the product. The possibility of intermediate examination, it would appear, is more likely to be a matter for the law on causation than duty of care. Although *Donoghue v Stevenson* was at first considered to be confined only to cases involving defective products, over time the circumstances in which a duty of care could be recognised moved further and further away from the facts of the case itself.

D. Duty of Care: English Developments

Overview

Following *Donoghue v Stevenson*, the courts in a number of key cases used and adapted the concept of duty care in ways which at first expanded and later contracted the tort of negligence. In *Hedley Byrne & Co Ltd v Heller & Partners Ltd* [1964] AC 465 the House of Lords recognised the possibility of negligence liability in respect of negligent misstatements where the defendant voluntarily assumed responsibility for the accuracy of the statement made to the plaintiff in circumstances where a special relationship existed between both parties and the plaintiff placed reliance on the accuracy of the statement. Subsequently, in *Home Office v Dorset Yacht Co* [1970] AC 1004, the House of Lords came close to accepting that the "neighbour principle" was the sole criterion for determining whether or not a duty of care arose. In that case, young offenders in the custody of the prison authorities escaped from a weekend outing and damaged the plaintiffs' yacht. The plaintiffs claimed that the defendant owed them a duty of care in respect of the actions of the young offenders held in their custody. The House of Lords held by a majority of 4 to 1 that the Home Office owed a duty of care to the plaintiffs. It recognised that in so doing it was extending the neighbour principle established in *Donoghue v Stevenson* into circumstances which were novel for two reasons. First, the wrong against the plaintiff had not been committed directly by the defendant but by a third party. Any liability of the defendant would then be based upon an omission — that is, the defendant's failure to control the actions of the boys. Second, the defendant was a public authority and thereby was subject to statutory and resource constraints. Lord Reid said:

> "The time has come when we can and should say that ... [the neighbour principle] ought to apply unless there is some justification or valid explanation for its exclusion."

This trend continued with the seminal case of *Anns v Merton London Borough Council* [1978] AC 728. There, plans for a building were deposited with the defendant local authority for approval. The plaintiffs alleged that the defendant negligently allowed the construction of the building on inadequate foundations as a result of which cracks appeared due to subsidence. This resulted in loss to the plaintiffs. Lord Wilberforce set out a two-stage test for duty of care:

> "Through the trilogy of cases in this House — *Donoghue v Stevenson* [1932] AC 562, *Hedley Byrne & Co Ltd v Heller & Partners Ltd* [1964] AC 465, and *Dorset Yacht Co Ltd v Home Office* [1970] AC 1004, the position has now been reached that in order to establish that a duty of care arises in a particular situation, it is not necessary to bring the facts of that situation within those of previous situations in which a duty of care has been held to exist. Rather the question has to be approached in two stages. First, one has to ask whether, as between the alleged wrongdoer and the person who has suffered damage there is a sufficient relationship of proximity or neighbourhood such that, in the reasonable contemplation of the former, carelessness on his part may be likely to cause damage to the latter — in which case a *prima facie* duty of care arises. Secondly, if the first question is answered affirmatively, it is necessary to consider whether there are any considerations which ought to negative, or to reduce or limit the scope of the duty or the class of person to whom it is owed or the damages to which a breach of it may give rise."

In applying this two stage test, the court might ask the following questions:

(1) Was the harm to the plaintiff foreseeable, so bringing him within the "neighbour principle"?

(2) If so, was there any valid policy reason to deny the existence of a duty to the plaintiff?

The effect of this approach was that once the plaintiff established foreseeability of damage a duty of care was presumed to exist unless the defendant could successfully rebut it on policy grounds. The role of policy in setting the limits of the duty of care was emphasised by Lord Wilberforce in *McLoughlin v O'Brian* [1983] 1 AC 410 when he said: "at the margin, the boundaries of a man's responsibilities for acts of negligence have to be fixed as a matter of policy". That case concerned liability for psychiatric harm and, in the course of his judgment, Lord Scarman appeared to suggest that foreseeability of damage ought to be the sole test for the existence of a duty of care. He thought that policy limitations, if there were to be any, should be a matter for Parliament.

Following the decision in *Anns*, the categories of negligence widened substantially. Liability in negligence had by 1983 expanded to include psychiatric harm (*McLoughlin v O'Brian*) and pure economic loss as was the case in judgments such as *Junior Books Ltd v Veitchi Co Ltd* [1983] AC 520. *Junior Books* is considered to be the "high water mark" of the expansion of the duty of care in negligence in the post-*Anns* era. There, the defenders were engaged as subcontractors to lay a floor in the pursuer's factory. There was no contractual relationship between the parties. The main contractors were not involved in the proceedings. The pursuers alleged that the floor was defective, though not dangerous, and that this was due to the negligence of the defenders. The pursuers claimed that they had suffered damage totalling some £207,000, which was the cost of replacing the floor and various other items of consequential loss. The House of Lords held that the pursuer's allegations disclosed a cause of action in negligence. The legal basis of the decision is not entirely clear. The case has been criticised for blurring the lines between contract and tort and for imposing liability in the law of negligence for pure economic loss which was not, and is not, apart from the *Hedley Byrne* principles, generally recoverable in English law. *Junior Books* has not been followed (or, for that matter, overruled) in England and appears to be confined to its own particular facts.

Judicial disapproval with the expansion of the duty of care in England became clear from 1984 onwards. This led to a retreat from *Anns*, which brought the tort of negligence back to a more category-based approach. The first case which marked this retreat was *Governors of the Peabody Donation Fund v Sir Lindsay Parkinson & Co Ltd* [1985] AC 210. In that case, a development company sued a local authority for the financial loss suffered by an inadequate drainage system, the plans for which the company alleged the authority had negligently approved. The House of Lords denied a remedy. They demanded that the plaintiff identify policy grounds upon which a duty of care should arise and why the defendant should be made responsible for loss occasioned to the plaintiff. Lord Keith said of the *Anns* test:

"There has been a tendency in some recent cases to treat these passages as being themselves of a definitive character. This is a temptation to be resisted in determining whether or not a duty of care of a particular scope was incumbent on the defendant. It is material to take into consideration whether it is just and reasonable that it should be so."

The retreat from *Anns* continued. In *Leigh and Sullivan Ltd v Aliakmon Shipping Co Ltd* [1986] AC 785, Lord Brandon made two observations in respect of Lord Wilberforce's two-step test. The first was that it did not provide, and could not have been intended to provide, "a universally applicable test of the existence and scope of a duty of care in the law of negligence". The second was that:

"Lord Wilberforce was dealing with the approach to the questions of the existence and scope of a duty of care in a novel type of factual situation which was not analogous to any factual situation in which the existence of such a duty had already been held to exist. He was not suggesting that the same approach should be adopted to the existence of a duty of care in a factual situation in which the existence of such a duty had repeatedly been held not to exist."

In *Curran v Northern Ireland Housing Co-ownership Association Ltd* [1987] AC 718 it was observed that *Anns*:

"may be said to represent the high-water mark of a trend in the development of the law of negligence by [the] House [of Lords] towards the elevation of the 'neighbourhood principle' ... into one of general application from which a duty of care may always be derived unless there are clear countervailing considerations to exclude it."

In *Yuen Kun Yeu v Attorney General of Hong Kong* [1988] AC 175 the Judicial Committee of the Privy Council subjected *Anns* to significant reinterpretation. There, a statutory officer, the Commissioner of Deposit-taking Companies, registered as a deposit-taker a company which subsequently went into liquidation. As a result, the plaintiffs lost money. They alleged that the Commissioner knew or ought to have known that the affairs of the company were being conducted fraudulently, that he had failed to exercise his statutory powers of supervision so as to ensure that the company complied with its obligations and that he should either never have registered the company or should have revoked its registration. The Judicial Committee held in favour of the Commissioner. Although the Commissioner's function was to protect depositors the characteristics of the case were such that a denial of duty was justified: the loss was economic in nature; the plaintiffs were unascertained members of a huge class of persons depositing money with various Hong Kong financial institutions; there was therefore no "special relationship" with the Commissioner; the loss in question had been caused by the wrongful act of a third party; there was no general duty to confer protection against such loss; the Commissioner simply did not have the resources or the legal power to control the day-to-day operations of many companies operating within the Hong Kong jurisdiction such that a duty of care could reasonably and practicably be imposed on the Commissioner in a way that would prevent fraudulent activity being carried out by those determined to do so. The Judicial Committee said

> "that for the future it should be recognised that the two-stage test in *Anns* is not to be regarded as in all the circumstances a suitable guide to the existence of a duty of care"

and that the test had "… been elevated to a degree of importance greater than it merits, and greater perhaps than its author intended".

The duty of care was narrowed further in *Hill v Chief Constable of West Yorkshire* [1989] AC 53. In that case it was claimed that the negligence of the police caused the death of Jacqueline Hill, the last victim of the "Yorkshire Ripper", Peter Sutcliffe. Applying the *Anns* test, the House of Lords held that no duty of care had been owed to her. Although death as a type of damage was foreseeable there was insufficient proximity between the police and Miss Hill. She was no more identifiable as a potential victim than any other young woman in the relevant geographical area. Moreover, there were key policy arguments which indicated that the police, in their role in the investigation and prosecution of crime, should not be subject to a duty of care in respect of potential victims. Such an approach could give rise to "defensive policing" and adversely affect the efficiency of the police force. It was clear that the courts were taking the view that foreseeability of harm alone was not enough to create a duty of care. Although foreseeability of harm to the plaintiff was a precondition of liability, proximity of relationship between the plaintiff and defendant was also required. This echoed back to the concept of "neighbourhood" which Lord Atkin had first enunciated in *Donoghue v Stevenson*.

Ultimately, in *Caparo Industries plc v Dickman* [1990] 2 AC 605 and *Murphy v Brentwood District Council* [1991] 1 AC 398, the House of Lords adopted a different approach with *Murphy* overruling *Anns*. These decisions of the House of Lords made it clear that the law of negligence would no longer develop by broad strides, based on general principles, but would proceed cautiously by way of close analogy with cases that had gone before.

Caparo concerned the liability of an auditor for financial loss suffered by investors. The plaintiffs were shareholders in Fidelity plc and after the accounts for 1984 (which were audited by the defendants) were published, they purchased further shares, ultimately making a takeover bid which was successful. They alleged that they had relied on the accounts for 1984 which should have shown a loss of £465,000 rather than a profit of £1.3 million. The House of Lords held that the defendant auditors owed no duty to the plaintiffs. There were two grounds for this decision. First, there was insufficient proximity between the plaintiffs and the defendants. Second, the accounts were produced for the purpose of informing the members of the company in order to assist the members (i.e. the shareholders) in directing the company and not for the purpose of advising the shareholders as to further speculation on the company's shares. Lord Bridge characterised the new approach in this way:

> "Whilst recognising … the importance of the underlying general principles common to the whole field of negligence, … the law has now moved in the direction of attaching greater significance to the more traditional categorisation of distinct and recognisable situations as a guide to the existence, the scope and the limits of the varied duties of care which the law imposes. We must now… recognise the wisdom of the words of Brennan J in the High Court of Australia in *Sutherland Shire Council v Heyman* (1985) 60 ALR 1, where he said:
>
> > 'It is preferable… that the law should develop novel categories of negligence incrementally and by analogy with the established categories, rather than by a massive extension of a prima facie duty of care restrained only by undefinable "considerations, which ought to negative, or to reduce or limit the scope of the duty or the class of person to whom it is owed"'."

In summary, the House of Lords held in *Caparo* that a duty of care may now be imposed if three requirements are satisfied:

(1) the plaintiff must be reasonably foreseeable (bearing in mind the kind of harm involved);
(2) there must be a relationship of proximity between the plaintiff and the defendant; and
(3) it must be fair, just, and reasonable in the circumstances for a duty of care to be imposed on the defendant.

Foreseeability

If the plaintiff is unforeseeable, there can be no duty of care owed to him. The defendant must owe a duty to the particular plaintiff in question. This means that the plaintiff must be in the zone of foreseeable danger. The reference in

Donoghue v Stevenson to "neighbours" does not refer to a relationship of physical closeness, but one of foresight, because my neighbours are "persons who are so closely and directly affected by my act that I ought reasonably to have them in contemplation". The idea is illustrated in *Palsgraf v Long Island Railroad Company* 162 NE 99 (NY 1928). The plaintiff, Helen Palsgraf, was waiting on the platform for a train to Rockaway Beach. Another train stopped and two men ran to get it. A guard pushed one of them from behind to help them in. In doing so he dislodged a parcel which turned out to contain fireworks. The parcel fell onto the railway tracks and exploded. The explosion was alleged to have upset some scales some distance away which fell and struck the plaintiff, injuring her. The New York Court of Appeals found for the defendant. It might well have been that the defendants were negligent in respect of the man carrying the package, but there was no duty owed to the plaintiff. Cardozo CJ said that "proof of negligence in the air so to speak will not do." The plaintiff, he thought, must have an original and primary duty owed to her, and not one simply derived from a wrong to someone else, and that "the orbit of the danger as disclosed to the eye of a reasonable vigilance is the orbit of the duty." In other words, the fact that a duty was owed by the guard to the men he was pushing onto the train did not necessarily mean that a duty was owed to the plaintiff. She was outside the orbit of the risk, and therefore was an unforeseeable plaintiff.

Similarly, in *Bourhill v Young* [1943] AC 92, the plaintiff was found to be unforeseeable. There, a pregnant woman sustained nervous shock after witnessing the aftermath of a serious road traffic accident. She gave birth to a stillborn child about a month later. Lord Russell said that a duty of care "only arises towards those individuals of whom it may reasonably be anticipated that they would be affected by the act which constitutes the alleged breach". More recently, in *Maguire v Harland and Wolff* [2005] EWCA (Civ) 1, the wife of a man who worked for the defendants and who came into contact with asbestos, sued when she contracted mesothelioma as a result of washing his work clothes which had been contaminated. Even though it was accepted that a duty was owed to the husband, no duty was owed to the wife because, at the time (the 1960s), it was not foreseeable that anyone could contract mesothelioma from such a low level of exposure from "secondary" contact with asbestos. Accordingly, the Court ruled that she was an unforeseeable plaintiff.

An example of a foreseeable plaintiff is *Haley v London Electricity Board* [1965] AC 778. In that case, the defendants dug a trench in the street under statutory authority. The trench presented a clear hazard to pedestrians. The defendants took some measures to ensure the safety of passers-by, but these measures were sufficient only for sighted persons. The plaintiff, who was blind and walking alone, suffered serious injury when he tripped over a long hammer which was left lying on the ground by the defendants. The House of Lords held that the defendants should have taken reasonable care for the safety of all persons using the highway. This included the blind and those otherwise disabled. Their Lordships took the view that just because blind persons constitute only a small percentage of the population that does not make them unforeseeable. Lord Reid said:

> "We are all accustomed to meeting blind people walking alone with their white sticks on city pavements...I find it quite impossible to say that it is not reasonably foreseeable that a blind person may pass along a particular pavement on a particular day."

Proximity

The second limb of the *Caparo* test is the requirement for proximity between the plaintiff and defendant. There is, inevitably, a degree of convergence between the concepts of reasonable foreseeability and proximity. Lord Wilberforce's two-step approach in *Anns* had appeared to treat proximity as a mere synonym for foreseeability. That is, there would be a relationship of proximity if harm was foreseeable. The modern approach, since *Caparo*, is to treat proximity as a separate and distinct requirement for establishing a duty of care. The effect of this was to reverse the expansion of duty situations which had been set in motion by *Anns* by placing an additional hurdle in the way of the plaintiff seeking to establish a duty of care. It is now clear that all cases of negligence need the requisite level of "proximity" between the parties. That is, there must be a sufficient level of relationship between the plaintiff and defendant. In personal injury cases or cases involving damage to property, this requirement will usually be satisfied by foreseeability. However, in cases involving other types of harm, such as psychiatric injury or pure economic loss, closer relationships between the parties will be necessary to establish liability.

The concept of proximity is important in omissions cases. Generally, where there is no prior relationship between the parties, an omission to act will not constitute negligence, however foreseeable the harm to the plaintiff might be, and however physically proximate the parties are. For example, a passer-by who stands and watches a child drown in a shallow pool is not under a duty not to harm the child. In other words, there will be no positive duty to act. The passer-by will not be liable for failing to intervene to save the child, even though he could do so with little risk to himself. A school teacher supervising a child on a school outing would, of course, be in a different position. There would be a relationship of proximity in that case. Similarly, a general practitioner who has accepted a person as a patient and who then later negligently omits to treat him would be under a positive duty to act.

The concept of proximity can be illustrated in the English Court of Appeal's decision in *Goodwill v British Pregnancy Advisory Service* [1996] 1 WLR 1397. In that case, the defendants carried out a vasectomy on a man. Three years later he entered into a sexual relationship with the plaintiff. Knowing that he had had a vasectomy, the couple did not use contraception. The plaintiff became pregnant and gave birth to a child. The vasectomy had spontaneously reversed. This can occur in a small number of cases. The plaintiff claimed that the defendant owed her a duty of care and was negligent in failing to warn her partner that the vasectomy could reverse. Her claim was struck out. Peter Gibson LJ suggested, *obiter*, that if the man had been the plaintiff's husband, and if the doctor had known that the vasectomy was to be as much for her benefit as the patient's, the defendant might have owed a duty of care to the plaintiff. But without any such connection between the doctor and the woman there could be no duty. This is because the plaintiff would merely have been a member of an indeterminate class of women with whom the man might have had a sexual relationship during his lifetime. Therefore, the plaintiff's relationship with the defendant was insufficiently proximate for a duty to be imposed.

Fair, Just and Reasonable

This is the third element of the *Caparo* test. This is the element under which policy factors are considered by the English courts. Policy factors have always been considered in the formulation of the duty of care and have been expressed in a wide variety of ways. The question to be addressed by the court is this: is it in the interests of public policy objectives to impose a duty of care on this defendant in respect of this plaintiff? One of the key factors operating against the imposition of a duty on the basis of policy is the "floodgates" argument. In cases where there is clear foreseeability and proximity, it might not be in the public interest that a duty of care be imposed. For example, in *Hill v Chief Constable of West Yorkshire* [1989] AC 53, the mother of the last victim of the Yorkshire Ripper sued the police on behalf of the estate of her daughter for alleged negligence in failing to apprehend her killer earlier than they did. The House of Lords held that no duty was owed as there was insufficient proximity. But their Lordships also held that the action was barred on grounds of public policy. Lord Keith set out a number of policy factors which led their Lordships to this conclusion:

- the police's general sense of public duty would not be reinforced by negligence liability;
- imposing liability could lead to "defensive policing";
- the carrying out of a murder investigation is a complex task which involves decisions, often resource-dependent, on "matters of policy and discretion";

- if the police were forced to defend negligence actions this would demand time, money, manpower and would inevitably divert the police from their primary function of protecting the public;
- such negligence actions could have the effect of reopening formerly closed cases; and
- inquiries, whether they be internal or public, are a more appropriate mechanism for supervising the efficiency of the police.

Another example is *Marc Rich & Co AG v Bishop Rock Marine Co Ltd (The Nicholas H)* [1996] 1 AC 211. In that case, *The Nicholas H* was on a voyage from Chile to Italy. Cracks appeared in her hull. She came into port in Puerto Rico. A Mr Ducat surveyed the ship. He was employed by NKK, a classification society, whose function was to certify ships as seaworthy for the purposes of insurance. Such societies are independent non-profit-making organisations. Mr Ducat initially recommended permanent repairs. The shipowners objected. Mr Ducat was persuaded to allow temporary repairs and he negligently allowed the ship to proceed on its voyage. The ship put to sea again with temporary welds. The welds failed, the ship sank and the cargo was lost. The claim by the cargo owners against the shipowners was settled for the amount of their limited liability of $500,000. The cargo owners then sued NKK for the remainder of their loss, $5.7 million. The House of Lords applied the *Caparo* three-step test. It concluded that NKK owed no duty of care to the plaintiffs. Although there had been proximity between the parties and foreseeability of the damage, the requirement that the duty be fair, just and reasonable had not been met. The risk between the parties had been governed by the rules of international shipping law (the "Hague Rules") and the introduction of a common law duty of care should not override those provisions. Their Lordships noted that a fine balance of risks was established by the relevant international shipping code and that the recognition of a duty of care would subvert that balance of risks with potentially adverse consequences for both marine insurance and freight costs. It was also noted by their Lordships that the imposition of a duty of care could lead to classification societies such as NKK refusing to survey high-risk vessels in the future with potentially harmful consequences for public safety at sea.

The Impact of *Caparo*

As we have seen, the House of Lords in *Caparo* approved Brennan J's dictum in *Sutherland Shire Council v Heyman* (1985) 60 ALR 1 when he said that

> "[i]t is preferable...that the law should develop novel categories of negligence incrementally and by analogy with the established categories".

This "incrementalist" approach means that the courts will develop the law of negligence on a case-by-case basis, where the facts fit into established categories where a duty of care has already been found to exist. This does *not* mean, however, that when a novel case (i.e. a new set of facts previously not considered by any court) comes before the court a duty of care will not be held to exist. It simply means that the courts will proceed cautiously in establishing new categories of duty situations, as distinct from the *Anns* approach where foreseeability could give rise to a duty situation irrespective of the facts of the particular case (subject, of course, to policy considerations).

This incrementalist approach was adopted by Hobhouse LJ in *Perrett v Collins* [1998] 2 Lloyd's Rep 255. In that case, the first defendant constructed a light aeroplane from a kit. In doing so he substituted a different gearbox but failed to change the propeller to suit. The second defendant certified the aircraft as airworthy. It was held that the inspector owed a duty to the plaintiff passenger who was injured when the plane crashed. Hobhouse LJ said:

> "[t]he overarching formula [in *Caparo*] does not affect the outcome. Established categories, with or without the assistance of [common sense and justice], provide the answer. The certainty provided by the previous authorities is not undermined...It is a truism to say that any case must be decided taking into account the circumstances of the case, but where those circumstances comply with established categories of liability, a defendant should not be allowed to seek to escape from liability by appealing to some vague concept of justice or fairness; the law cannot be remade for every case. Indeed, the previous authorities have by necessary implication held that it is fair, just and reasonable that the [plaintiff] should recover in the situations falling within the principles they have applied. Accordingly, if the present case is covered by the decisions in, or the principle is recognised by, previous authorities – and it is...we remain bound to follow them."

It would appear therefore, that Hobhouse LJ thought that the three-step *Caparo* test could be set aside in circumstances where an incremental step beyond existing authorities may be taken. It is therefore entirely legitimate and proper for the courts to increase the boundaries of negligence beyond the decided cases provided it is done incrementally. The courts will, in any event, always have recourse to concepts such as justice and reasonableness in order to set the limits of the law of negligence. Interestingly, *Marc Rich* was distinguished from *Perrett v Collins* on the grounds that the former does not apply to personal injury cases and a passenger was entitled to rely on careful certification: and the defendant (in *Perrett*) had undertaken a statutory duty for the protection of the public, rather than simply for the purposes of the insurance industry.

E. Duty of Care: Irish Developments

Overview

Lord Atkin's neighbour principle has been readily applied by the Irish courts. *Donoghue v Stevenson* was considered as early as 1944 in *Kirby v Burke and Holloway* [1944] 1 IR 207. In that case, the plaintiff's wife bought a pot of jam in a grocer's shop. The family became ill as a consequence of eating it. The plaintiff brought an action claiming damages, suing the manufacturer for negligence in manufacturing and issuing the jam for sale. The Court held that the manufacturer was bound to take specific precautions against the danger of infection to his jam from external causes before it finally left his factory. As he had not done so, and as the jam had become contaminated and caused the injury complained of, he was liable in damages. Interestingly, the Court did not specifically apply *Donoghue v Stevenson* but relied instead on the writings of Oliver Wendell Holmes in "The Common Law" Lectures III and IV (London, 1887). Gavan Duffy J said:

> "The much controverted 'Case of the Snail in the Bottle', while leaving subsidiary questions open, has settled the principle of liability on a similar issue finally against the manufacturer in Great Britain. But the House of Lords established that memorable conclusion only twelve years ago in *Donoghue v Stevenson*, by a majority of three Law Lords to two ... I was invited to assume, as a matter of course, that the view which prevailed must of necessity be the true view of the common law in Ireland. One voice in the House of Lords would have turned the scale; and it is not arguable that blameworthiness according to the actual standards of our people depends upon the casting vote in a tribunal exercising no jurisdiction over them. Hence my recourse to the late Mr Justice Holmes. His classic analysis supports the principle of Lord Atkin and the majority. And to that principle I humbly subscribe."

As we have seen, central to Lord Atkin's neighbour principle are the requirements of foreseeability of damage and proximity between the parties. In early cases, such as *Purtill v Athlone UDC* [1968] IR 205 *McNamara v ESB* [1975] IR 1, *Siney v Dublin Corporation* [1980] IR 400, and *Wall v Hegarty* [1980] ILRM 124, proximity was seen as an important factor in determining the existence of a duty of care.

Later, the decision of the House of Lords in *Anns* was followed by the Irish Supreme Court in *Ward v McMaster* [1988] IR 337. In *Ward v McMaster*, the defendant Council (Louth County Council) was empowered under s 39 of the Housing Act 1966 to make a loan to the plaintiffs for the purchase of a house. The Council was bound, before making any advance, to satisfy itself by means of a report by their valuer as to the actual value of the house and that the house provided adequate security for the loan. The authority sent out a local auctioneer and valuer to make the report on the house. He said that the house was a reasonable risk for a loan over 30 years and valued the house at about £25,000. With the aid of the loan the plaintiffs bought the house. However, when they moved in they found that it was riddled with defects. Most were concealed structural defects. They had to abandon the house and move into rented premises. The plaintiffs brought proceedings against the vendor/builder, the local authority and the valuer. The Supreme Court held that while the Housing Act 1966 did not create a private duty to take care to prevent damage to purchasers under the scheme, such a duty arose from the relationship between the parties. In addition, it was reasonably foreseeable by the defendant Council that purchasers under the scheme would not only lack the means of having their own expert examination of the house but would also rely, as the plaintiffs did rely, on the fact that the Council was investing its money in the house as a mark of its value.

The Supreme Court, in following *Anns*, interpreted Lord Wilberforce's two-step test rather differently to the way in which the English judiciary had. McCarthy J said that he preferred "not... to dilute the words of Lord Wilberforce" but he thought that a duty of care "arose" from the proximity of the parties, the foreseeability of the damage and the absence of any compelling exemption based on public policy. He also thought that any public policy exemption would have to be "a very powerful one" if it were to operate to deny an injured party his "right to redress". McCarthy J also considered the statement of Brennan J in the Australian High Court in *Sutherland Shire Council v Heyman* (1985) 60 ALR 1 that

> "the law should develop novel categories of negligence incrementally and by analogy with established categories...".

McCarthy J, was not keen on this approach. He said that this

> "verbally attractive proposition of incremental growth... suffers from a temporal defect – that rights should be determined by the accident of birth".

One possible interpretation of this is that plaintiffs should not have to wait, as a result of an incrementalist approach, until a duty of care was found to exist in a novel factual situation.

McCarthy J's approach to the duty of care was made up of the following elements: foreseeability of the damage; the proximity of the parties; and the absence of any compelling exemption based upon public policy. The plaintiff therefore had to surmount the two separate hurdles of foreseeability and proximity before the Court went on to consider if there were any public policy factors which might defeat his claim. However, the Irish courts' approach to the duty of care was altered significantly in *Glencar Explorations plc v Mayo County Council (No 2)* [2002] 1 IR 84.

In *Glencar*, the plaintiffs had been granted prospecting licences by the Minister for Energy to explore for gold in County Mayo. They spent substantial sums of money in doing so. Then, Mayo County Council adopted a mining ban in their county development plan. That plan was later held to have been *ultra vires*: see *Glencar Explorations plc v Mayo County Council* [1993] 2 IR 237. The plaintiffs sued Mayo County Council for negligence. The Supreme Court dismissed the claim on the basis that the Council did not owe the plaintiffs a duty of care.

In the course of his judgment Keane CJ said that it was "by no means clear" that *Ward v McMaster* represented an unqualified endorsement by the Supreme Court of the *Anns* two-step test. This was despite the fact that McCarthy J had expressly approved *Anns* in formulating the test for the duty of care in *Ward*. Keane CJ, however, did not consider that McCarthy J's position on the two-step test in *Anns* formed the *ratio* of the decision in *Ward*. Keane CJ took this view despite the fact that three of McCarthy J's colleagues on the Supreme Court concurred with his speech. Keane CJ formulated the test for duty of care in this way:

> "There is, in my view, no reason why courts determining whether a duty of care arises should consider themselves obliged to hold that it does in every case where injury or damage to property was reasonably foreseeable and the notoriously difficult and elusive test of 'proximity' or 'neighbourhood' can be said to have been met, unless very powerful public policy considerations dictate otherwise. It seems to me that no injustice will be done if they are required to take the further step of considering whether, in all the circumstances, it is just and reasonable that the law should impose a duty of a given scope on the defendant for the benefit of the plaintiff ..."

This appears to involve four steps which can be summarised as follows:

(1) reasonable foreseeability;
(2) proximity of relationship;
(3) countervailing public policy considerations; and
(4) whether it is just and reasonable to impose a duty of care.

In truth, there is some judicial divergence on the application of the test for duty of care in the Irish courts. Some judges treat it as a four-step test as set out above. Others apply a three-step test as in *Caparo*. Those adopting a three-step approach tend to subsume the step dealing with public policy into the requirement for fairness, justice and reasonableness. For example, in *Beatty v Rent Tribunal* [2006] 1 ILRM 164, Fennelly J summarised the test for duty of care in this way:

> "That there is a relationship of such proximity between the parties such as to call for the exercise of care by one party towards the other;
>
> That it is reasonably foreseeable that breach of the duty of care will occasion loss to the party to whom the duty is owed;
>
> That it is just and reasonable that the duty should be imposed."

Reasonable Foreseeability

Foreseeability of damage is a prerequisite for a successful claim in negligence. It is not generally a contentious issue in negligence litigation. The concept was considered in some detail in *Gaffey v Dundalk Town Council* [2006] IEHC 436. There, a child was injured when his leg became caught in a hole when the lid of a fire hydrant had been removed by an unknown person. The removal of the lid was a frequent occurrence, but the Council had never been informed of this. The Court took the view that it was not reasonable to expect the defendant Council to anticipate and guard against the possibility that the lid would regularly be removed thereby exposing children to the hazard.

In *Whelan v Allied Irish Bank plc* [2011] IEHC 544, the plaintiffs took out a loan for the purchase of lands. They had wanted a non-recourse loan only. This was not communicated to the defendant solicitors. Consequently, the defendant solicitors did not advise the plaintiffs that the loan was in fact a recourse loan. The Court held that, in the circumstances, the defendant solicitors could not reasonably have foreseen that the plaintiffs would not sign up to a recourse loan. Accordingly, the solicitors did not owe the plaintiffs a duty of care in respect of the losses they suffered as a result of taking out the loan.

Proximity

The concept of proximity concerns the relationship between the plaintiff and the defendant. If there is no "proximity" or "neighbourhood", there will be no duty of care. It is often said that reasonable foreseeability and proximity inform each other. For example, in the case of road users, the duty of care that is owed is partly founded on the fact that it is readily foreseeable that careless driving by A may result in injury to an innocent driver, B, who was unfortunate enough to be in A's vicinity. B will therefore be a reasonably foreseeable plaintiff due to the fact that he is on the same stretch of road as A at the time of A's careless driving. In other words, B's proximity, both relational and spatial, determines that he is a reasonably foreseeable plaintiff. It is clear, therefore, that a previous relationship between plaintiff and defendant is not necessary in such cases. Proximity arises by virtue of the circumstances in which the parties find themselves. In *Keogh v Electricity Supply Board* [2005] 3 IR 77 the plaintiff was injured by electric shock whilst using her telephone during a storm which damaged electrical cables in the area. She was held to be in a relationship of proximity with the defendant on the basis that she was a customer and lived in close proximity to an electricity supply pole and cables attached thereto.

In *Shinkwin v Quin-Con Ltd* [2001] 1 IR 514 the defendant was the effective sole shareholder and day-to-day manager of a company which employed the plaintiff. The defendant was held to be in a relationship of proximity with the plaintiff because he personally recruited him and personally put him to work on a machine over which he, the defendant, exercised control. In contrast, in *Fay v Tegral Pipes Ltd* [2005] IESC 34, a claim against a number of directors of a company that had employed the plaintiff was struck out due to lack of proximity: the defendants were not involved in the day-to-day running of the company.

There will normally be a relationship of proximity between a school and its pupils. In *Maher v Presentation School Mullingar* [2004] 4 IR 211, a six-year-old pupil in class received an eye injury from a pencil which had been fired towards him by another pupil using a rubber band. A relationship of proximity was held to exist between the plaintiff and defendant. In each of these three cases the degree of control exercised by the defendant over the environment in which the harm occurred is directly relevant in determining whether or not there is sufficient proximity between plaintiff and defendant.

Public bodies may or may not be in a relationship of proximity with members of the public. It depends substantially on the nature of the statutory function being exercised by them. In *W v Ireland (No 2)* [1997] 2 IR 141, the Attorney General failed to expeditiously process an extradition warrant in respect of a paedophile whose extradition to Northern Ireland was sought by the authorities there. The Court took the view that the Attorney General's statutory function under the Extradition Act 1965 (as amended) created a "public professional function". This did not create a relationship of any sort between the Attorney General and the victims of the crimes which were the subject of extradition warrants under his consideration. This position can be contrasted with *Ward v McMaster* where the statutory function in question (under the Housing Act 1966) was specifically designed to assist the class of persons to which the plaintiffs belonged.

No relationship of proximity was found to exist in *Atlantic Marine Supplies Ltd v Minister for Transport* [2010] IEHC 104. There, the plaintiff claimed that the Minister had failed to enforce legally binding measures in respect of life rafts for fishing boats which occasioned to them, as suppliers of such safety equipment, financial loss. The safety measures in question were introduced for an entirely separate purpose and did not create any relationship of proximity between the Minister and the company. By contrast, a relationship of proximity was held to exist in *Beatty v Rent Tribunal* [2006] 1 ILRM 164 on the basis that "the only parties with a direct and real interest in the outcome of the [adjudicative] proceedings" of the Rent Tribunal were the landlord and tenant. In any event, no duty of care was held to exist as the defendant was considered to have immunity from suit in negligence.

Public Policy Considerations

Public policy considerations can be invoked by the court to find that no duty of care is owed. Such considerations might be that it is not in the public interest that a duty of care be imposed. An example is *Fletcher v Commissioners of Public Works* [2003] 1 IR 465. In that case, the plaintiff, through the negligence of his employer, was exposed to asbestos dust in the course of his employment. He suffered psychiatric injury as a result of the fear of contracting asbestos-related disease later in life. He had suffered no physical injury. The Supreme Court declined to impose liability on the grounds of public policy. First, the Court took the view that it would be undesirable to award damages to plaintiffs who suffered no physical injury but whose psychiatric condition was due solely to an unfounded fear of contracting a particular disease. Second, the Court considered that to impose liability would have "implications for the healthcare field". This was based on concern that medical negligence cases might be grounded on plaintiffs' fears of contracting a particular disease as a result of having been prescribed a particular drug. Third, the Court expressed concern that there could be a proliferation claims based on fear of exposure to carcinogens in the environment which may never result in disease. United States case law was cited in respect of the latter two considerations: see *Potter v Firestone Tyre & Rubber Co* (1993) 25 Cal Rptr 2d 550 and *Temple-Inland Forest Products Corporation v Carter* (1998) 1993 SW 2d 88.

Public policy considerations have been invoked in respect of claims against public authorities like the police: see *Hill v Chief Constable of West Yorkshire* [1989] AC 53 also, see below, "The Human Rights Dimension" in respect of police duties under Human Rights law to investigate crime. In Ireland, a number of claims against the State, or State agencies such as An Garda Síochána, have failed on the basis of public policy considerations. In the following three cases we can see how public policy considerations operated to preclude the existence of a duty of care.

First, in *Lockwood v Ireland* [2010] IEHC 430, a prosecution for rape collapsed because the suspect had been arrested under an abolished power. The victim's action in negligence failed on public policy grounds. The Court considered that the imposition of a duty of care in respect of *bona fide* actions and decisions by the Gardaí in the course of criminal investigation or prosecution could be far reaching. The Gardaí might act defensively or be forced to seek legal advice constantly during the course of investigation or prosecution of crimes. This would inhibit the Gardaí's ability to carry out their public functions effectively.

Second, in *M v Commissioner of An Garda Síochána* [2011] IEHC 14, the Gardaí and the prosecuting authorities failed to process a rape allegation expeditiously. This left a 12-year-old rape victim "in limbo for six years". The Court held that the imposition of a duty of care in these circumstances could inhibit the prosecution of crime by introducing a "risk that police and prosecutors would act so as to protect themselves from claims for negligence". Furthermore, the Gardaí could find themselves having to divert resources to defend negligence actions in the courts at the expense of their primary function of fighting crime. This would not be in the public interest.

Third, in *G v Minister for Justice, Equality and Law Reform* [2011] IEHC 65, a woman was discovered dead in a house. The woman's husband was with her body. The Gardaí wanted to remove him from the scene to conduct an investigation. They took him, at his request, to the home of the plaintiff, a woman whom he knew. She agreed that he could stay in her house. He subsequently raped the plaintiff. The Gardaí had suspected that the husband had killed his wife but they did not alert the plaintiff to this possibility. She was under the impression that the woman had taken her own life. It turned out that the man had a prior conviction for rape and assault in the United Kingdom. The Gardaí did not know this at the time. The plaintiff sued for negligence. The Court characterised the actions of the Gardaí in bringing the husband to the plaintiff's house that night as "something done in the course of their investigatory functions". This appeared to be on the basis that there was nowhere else they could bring him. They could not arrest him. They had no grounds to do so at the time. Nor could they allow "him to walk the streets". In holding that no duty of care was owed, the Court stated the law in the following terms:

> "It is now clearly established in Irish Law that the Gardaí owe no duty of care in respect of actions taken in the course of their duty to investigate and prosecute crime. The absence of this duty situation arises from considerations of public policy."

In other cases, plaintiffs will not generally be entitled to maintain a claim based upon matters which are unlawful and/or disreputable. Such claims can be dismissed on grounds of *ex turpi causa non oritur actio* ("from a base cause or matter an action does not arise") or on public policy grounds. For example, in *Gayson v Allied Irish Bank plc* [2000] IEHC 9, the plaintiff, a customer of the defendant bank, claimed that an official of the bank advised him not to avail of a tax amnesty as a result of which he suffered loss. The Court dismissed the claim on a number of grounds observing that, as a matter of public policy, the courts would not hold that there was an actionable duty of care owed by the bank in the circumstances.

Fairness, Justice and Reasonableness

In *Anns v Merton* the House of Lords made explicit reference to the role of "policy" in determining whether a duty of care should be imposed. Following *Caparo v Dickman*, however, policy type matters are considered under the rubric of "fair, just, and reasonable". Many Irish decisions appear to use the concepts of "public policy" and "fair, just, and reasonable" interchangeably. Some English decisions make explicit reference to whether it is "fair and reasonable" that a duty should be imposed. *Hill v Chief Constable of West Yorkshire* and *Marc Rich v Bishop Rock Marine* are examples of this. Some Irish decisions, too, have referred explicitly to the "fairness, justice, and reasonableness" for the imposition, or non-imposition, of a duty of care in a particular case. *Beatty v Rent Tribunal* and *Hackett v Calla Associates* [2004] IEHC 336 are such examples.

In *Beatty*, Fennelly and McCracken JJ held that it would not be just and reasonable to impose a duty of care on the Rent Tribunal. Fennelly J justified this view on the basis that those who come before the Rent Tribunal had a range of other remedies available to them. This limited the possibility of their sustaining irremediable loss. In addition he thought that:

> "the existence of a remedy in damages might tend to compromise the independence of the [Rent] Tribunal by inhibiting its judgment in performing its essentially adjudicative role".

McCracken J thought that the Rent Tribunal should not have a duty of care imposed upon it because it was in the public interest that it should be able to perform its functions without the fear or threat of action by individuals.

In *Hackett*, the patron of a nightclub had been injured by security staff as they sought to quell a disturbance outside the nightclub. The patron had been involved in the disturbance. The Court took the view that it was "fair, just and reasonable that the defendants remain under the duty of care towards the plaintiff and other patrons even in the unpleasant and potentially dangerous circumstances which arose outside the premises" that night.

F. The Human Rights Dimension

In the United Kingdom, European human rights law has had an important influence on the development of the duty of care, in particular in respect of public authorities. Actions in negligence against public bodies, such as organs of government, schools and the police have, as we have seen, raised particular difficulties around the question of duty of care. Public bodies often operate under statutory authority and are subject to — sometimes severe — resource restrictions. Public policy plays an important role in such cases.

In *X v Bedfordshire County Council* [1995] 2 AC 633, for example, a negligence action was brought against a local authority social services department by the plaintiffs who claimed to have suffered damage due to a negligent failure to remove them, when children, from their abusive parents. The House of Lords held that, despite the fact that this decision-making process was justiciable, the imposition of a duty of care would not be fair, just and reasonable. The case was then brought by the plaintiffs to the European Court of Human Rights where it was heard as *Z v United Kingdom* (2001) ECHR 333. Judgment was given in favour of the plaintiffs by that Court. The United Kingdom was held not to have protected the children from inhuman or degrading treatment. This was a breach of Article 3 of the Convention. The UK was also held not to have given them an effective legal remedy for this failure. This was a breach of Article 13 of the Convention.

On 23 July 2014 the English High Court issued an interesting judgment in respect of police duties towards members of the public in *DSD and NVB v The Commissioner of Police for the Metropolis* [2014] EWHC 436 (QB). This case was taken by the plaintiffs under the UK Human Rights Act 1998. Article 3 of the European Convention on Human Rights provides as follows:

> "No one shall be subjected to torture or to inhuman or degrading treatment or punishment."

Section 8(1) of the UK Human Rights Act 1998 provides:

> "It is unlawful for a public authority to act in a way which is incompatible with a Convention right".

A "Convention right" means one of the rights and fundamental freedoms set out, *inter alia*, in Articles 2-12 and 14 of the European Convention on Human Rights. In this case, the Court held that police have a duty to conduct investigations into particularly severe violent acts, perpetrated by private parties, in a timely and efficient manner the purpose of which is to secure confidence in the rule of law in a democratic society. There had been systemic failings by the police in investigating a large number of rapes and sexual assaults perpetrated by the so called "black cab rapist" amounting to a breach of the victims' rights under Article 3 of the

Convention. Since the Court found a breach on the part of the defendant of the Article 3 "Convention right" within the meaning of s 6 and s 8 of the UK Human Rights Act, this, in principle, empowered the Court to grant a remedy.

As mentioned, the plaintiffs were among the victims of the so called "black cab rapist" (W), who over a six year period between 2002 and 2008 had committed more than 100 drug and alcohol assisted rapes and sexual assaults on women whom he had been carrying in his cab. Both DSD and NVB complained to the police, who commenced investigations, but failed to bring W to justice until 2009. As we have seen above, under the common law the police do not owe a duty of care in negligence in relation to the investigation of crime: see in particular *Hill v Chief Constable of West Yorkshire* [1989] AC 53 per Lord Keith at 63A-64A and per Lord Templeman at 65C-E; but also *Brooks v Commissioner of Police of the Metropolis* [2005] 1 WLR 1495; and *Smith v Chief Constable of Sussex* [2009] 1 AC 225.

However, in *DSD and NVB v The Commissioner of Police for the Metropolis*, after a review of the cases on liability, Green J concluded that there was established case law to show that Article 3 of the Convention imposes a duty upon the police to investigate crimes which covers the entire span of a case from investigation to trial.

Section 3(1) of the Irish European Convention on Human Rights Act 2003 provides as follows:

> "Subject to any statutory provision (other than this Act) or rule of law, every organ of the State shall perform its functions in a manner compatible with the State's obligations under the Convention provisions."

Under s 3(2), if a court finds that there has been a breach of statutory duty under s 3(1), it can award damages to an individual who has suffered injury and where no other remedy in damages is available to them. Although the obligation under s 3(1) cannot easily be compared with the provisions of the UK statute, in particular given the constitutional dimension in Ireland, it will be interesting to see if the Irish courts in the future will adopt a similar approach in respect of the granting of remedies in circumstances where there are investigative or prosecutorial failures on the part of the Gardaí.

ECONOMIC LOSS

Learning Outcomes

Upon completion of this chapter, the reader should be able to:

- Distinguish between "pure economic loss" and "consequential economic loss";
- Explain the operation of the *Hedley Byrne* principles;
- Identify factual circumstances to which the *Hedley Byrne* principles apply;
- Trace the development of the *Hedley Byrne* principles in England and in Ireland;
- Discuss the circumstances in which economic loss is recoverable outside of negligent misstatement;
- Explain the significance of the *Glencar* decision.

A. What is Economic Loss?

Economic loss is normally recoverable in negligence provided it is consequential upon physical damage. For example, the plaintiff in *Donoghue v Stevenson* could have recovered lost earnings and medical expenses suffered as a result of her injury. Although these losses would have been "economic" in nature, since they would have been consequential upon physical injury they would have been recoverable in tort. Similarly, if my car is destroyed as a result of another person's carelessness, my loss will be *economic* in the sense that my assets are diminished. But in legal terms that loss will be classified as damage to property and I will be entitled to the car's value in damages.

"Pure" economic loss, on the other hand, is not consequential upon physical damage. Such loss can come in the shape of failure to receive expected future profit or receipt of some financial benefit, or it may result from the acquisition of an item of defective property, or be due to property damage sustained by a third party. Essentially, pure economic loss involves such things as money expended and opportunities to profit lost as a result of the defendant's failure to take care. Whether economic loss is recoverable is a matter to be determined at the duty of care stage. The question asked by the court is this: does *this* defendant owe *this* plaintiff a duty of care in respect of *this* type of loss? Along with psychiatric injury, it is one of the two types of damage in which duty of care is likely to be problematic, or, for that matter, absent.

Historically, the courts have been reluctant to compensate for pure economic loss. There are a number of reasons for this:

- pure economic loss has historically been seen as the province of the law of contract, whereas tort law has been concerned with property damage, personal injury and death;
- there have been concerns about opening the "floodgates" in terms of potentially widespread liability;
- pure economic loss is intangible and may be difficult to measure.

This judicial reluctance to award compensation for pure economic loss has meant that such loss is generally only recoverable where the plaintiff can establish a "special relationship" between himself and the defendant. In practice, most economic loss claims arise as a result of negligent misstatements: however, they can, and do, arise in other contexts too, for example, through the acquisition of defective premises or products. It would be convenient, therefore, to examine economic loss under the two headings of "negligent misstatements" and "other categories of economic loss".

B. Negligent Misstatements

Three particular difficulties have arisen in relation to the imposition of a duty to avoid making negligent statements.

First, there is the difference in potential effects of careless words and careless acts. Negligent acts will generally have only a fairly limited range of impact, whereas negligent words may be widely broadcast and disseminated without the consent or foresight of the speaker. For example, a careless driver is likely only to injure those who are physically proximate to him, whereas a careless statement could, in theory, be broadcast to the whole world.

Second, negligent misstatements are, in general, likely only to inflict economic loss. Nevertheless, it is important to bear in mind that careless words can also have physical implications. For example, it will be recalled that in *Perrett v Collins* [1998] 2 Lloyd's Rep 255 the negligent certification of a light aircraft as suitable to fly resulted in physical injury to the plaintiff.

Third, historically, plaintiffs seeking a remedy in respect of economic loss resulting from careless statements faced a particular difficulty: it was that a person suffering economic loss through relying on a fraudulent statement could sue in the tort of deceit. In *Derry v Peek* (1889) 14 App Cas 337, the House of Lords held that to establish deceit the plaintiff had to prove fraud. In other words, the plaintiff had to prove that the defendant knew that his statement was untrue, or was reckless as to its untruth. Mere negligence was insufficient. However, that all changed with the landmark decision of *Hedley Byrne & Co Ltd v Heller & Partners Ltd* [1964] AC 465.

Hedley Byrne v Heller

The facts of *Hedley Byrne & Co Ltd v Heller & Partners Ltd* [1964] AC 465 are as follows. The plaintiffs, Hedley Byrne & Co, were advertising agents. They intended to engage in an advertising programme with Easipower Ltd which would cost about £100,000. They asked their own bankers, National Provincial Bank Ltd, to obtain a reference about Easipower. National Provincial wrote to the defendants, Heller & Partners, who were Easipower's bankers. They replied in a letter which said that it was "For your private use and without responsibility on the part of the bank or its officials". The letter went on to say that Easipower was a "respectably constituted company, considered good for its ordinary business engagements. Your figures are larger than we are accustomed to see". Easipower subsequently went into liquidation. The plaintiffs lost some £17,000. The plaintiffs sued Easipower's bankers, Heller & Partners, for making a negligent statement upon which they relied to their detriment. The House of Lords held that there could be a duty not to make a statement carelessly which causes only economic loss. However, in the circumstances of this particular case, the disclaimer prevented a duty arising and the defendants were not liable.

In *Hedley Byrne* the House of Lords ruled that *Derry v Peek* should be limited to its proper function of defining the limits of the tort of deceit holding it to be irrelevant to the issue of whether a duty of care arose in negligence. Their Lordships also ruled that the absence of a contract was irrelevant. Lord Devlin said:

> "[a] promise given without consideration to perform a service cannot be enforced as a contract by the promisee, but if the service is in fact performed and done negligently the promisee can recover in an action in tort."

However, *Hedley Byrne v Heller* was not a simple application of *Donoghue v Stevenson*. The neighbour principle was considered insufficient to create a duty of care in negligent misstatement cases. It should be remembered that *Donoghue v Stevenson* concerns *negligent acts*, whereas *Hedley Byrne v Heller* concerns *negligent statements*. In order for liability for statements resulting in economic loss to be imposed, there had to be a narrower test than simply one of foreseeability of the loss. If the test were too broad, the maker of a careless statement could find him or herself liable to a large indeterminate class of plaintiffs ("liability in an indeterminate amount for an indeterminate time to an indeterminate class" per Cardozo CJ in *Ultramares Corporation v Touche* (1931) 174 NE 441). Take the example of a financial adviser making a careless statement on a radio programme: he or she should not be accountable to every listener who suffers loss through relying on that negligent advice. There would have to be a "special relationship" between the plaintiff and defendant for a duty of care to arise. In other words, as the House of Lords said in *Hedley Byrne*, a plaintiff seeking to recover in respect of a negligent misstatement must establish that the statement was made within a relationship where the plaintiff could reasonably rely on the skill and care of the defendant in making the statement. In recognising the reality that people tend to be less careful about what they say than what they do, especially in informal settings, Lord Reid observed:

> "[q]uite careful people often express definite opinions on social or informal occasions, even when they see that others are likely to be influenced by them; and they often do that without taking that care which they would take if asked for their opinion professionally, or in a business."

Lord Reid also said:

> "A reasonable man, knowing that he was being trusted or that his skill and judgment were being relied on, would, I think, have three courses open to him. He could keep silent or decline to give the information or advice sought: or he could give an answer with a clear qualification that he accepted no responsibility for it or that it was given without that reflection or inquiry which a careful answer would require: or he could simply answer without any such qualification. If he chooses to adopt the last course he must, I think, be held to have accepted some responsibility for his answer being given carefully, or to have accepted a relationship with the inquirer which requires him to exercise such care as the circumstances require."

And Lord Morris said:

> "… I consider that it follows and that it should now be regarded as settled that if someone possessed of a special skill undertakes, quite irrespective of contract, to apply that skill for the assistance of another person who relies upon such skill, a duty of care will arise. The fact that the service is to be given by means of or by the instrumentality of words can make no difference. Furthermore, if in a sphere in which a person is so placed that others could reasonably rely upon his judgment or his skill or upon his ability to make careful inquiry, a person takes it upon himself to give information or advice to, or allows his information or advice to be passed on to, another person who, as he knows or should know, will place reliance upon it, then a duty of care will arise."

In essence, their Lordships recognised that cases of pure economic loss were very different from those of physical damage such as *Donoghue v Stevenson*. However, they felt that the ingredients of foreseeability and proximity could be adapted into a general principle of proximity, to be based on a "special relationship" between the parties which would give rise to a duty of care in the making of statements.

Figure 3.1

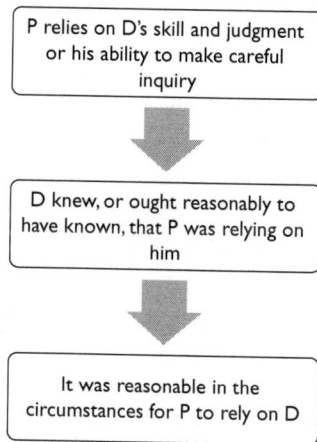

The "special relationship" under *Hedley Byrne v Heller* between plaintiff (P) and defendant (D)

Hedley Byrne Applied

The *Hedley Byrne* principles were subsequently approved by the Irish High Court in *Securities Trust Ltd v Hugh Moore & Alexander Ltd* [1964] IR 417. In that case, there was an error in the articles of association of the defendant company. A shareholder of that company requested a copy of the articles. They were sent to him pursuant to a statutory obligation. The shareholder was also the managing director of the plaintiff company. In reliance on the (inaccurate) articles of association, the plaintiff company invested money in the defendant company. They suffered financial loss as a result. The plaintiff company sued for negligent misstatement. The plaintiff's action failed because the articles of association had been supplied to the shareholder in his personal capacity only. Accordingly, there was no special relationship between the plaintiff company and defendant company. Davitt P said that it could

> "... hardly be seriously contended that the defendant company owed
> a duty to the world at large to take care to avoid mistakes and printing
> errors in the reprint of their Articles."

Hedley Byrne was again considered by the Irish courts in *Bank of Ireland v Smith* [1966] IR 646. In that case, the defendant auctioneer advertised the sale of lands in which it was stated incorrectly that the lands had been undersown with permanent pasture. In reliance on this statement, the plaintiff purchased the lands. The plaintiff argued, on the basis of *Hedley Byrne*, that an auctioneer acting for a vendor should anticipate that any statement made by him about the property he was selling would be relied upon by a purchaser. The Court rejected this proposition holding that liability could be imposed only where there was a relationship between the parties "equivalent to contract". In other words, where there was an assumption of responsibility in circumstances where, but for the absence of consideration, there would be a contract.

No duty of care was held to exist in *McSweeney v Bourke* (24 November 1980) HC where the defendant gave advice to a group of companies upon which shareholders relied. There, a group of companies were in financial difficulties. They engaged the defendant as a financial consultant to advise the group. In close consultation with the two majority shareholders, the defendant worked out a number of courses of action open to the group. One of these involved the injection of capital into the group by the two plaintiff shareholders. They made the investment and lost significant sums of money. They sued the defendant for negligent misstatement. Their claim was dismissed. The Court held that, since the defendant was advising the group of companies rather than the plaintiff shareholders personally, once he had discharged his duty of care to the group — which the Court found he had — he could not be held liable to the plaintiffs.

A duty of care was held to exist in *Wall v Hegarty* [1980] ILRM 124 where the plaintiff claimed that the defendant solicitors had negligently prepared his uncle's will, causing it to be declared invalid. As a result, he lost an expected inheritance of IR£15,000. The plaintiff claimed that the defendant solicitors owed him a duty of care in the preparation of the will and that they had failed in that duty. The Court imposed liability on the basis of the broad "neighbour" principle in *Donoghue v Stevenson*. This case is notable because the plaintiff did not place, and could not have placed, reliance on the defendant because he had no prior knowledge of the legacy. The Court in this case was willing to use general negligence principles to impose liability for pure economic loss on the defendant on the basis that he was a member of a finite group of persons who could suffer loss as a result of the defendant's negligence. The Court in *Wall v Hegarty* cited with approval the reasoning of Sir Robert Megarry in the English decision of *Ross v Caunters (a firm)* [1980] Ch 297. In that case, the Court also imposed liability on solicitors for negligently executing a will.

Similarly, in *White v Jones* [1995] 2 AC 207, liability was imposed on a firm of solicitors in relation to a will. After a family quarrel, the testator (aged 78), disinherited his two daughters, the plaintiffs. Some months later, the family reconciled. The testator then instructed his solicitors, the defendants, to draw up a new will to include legacies of £9000 to each daughter. The defendant solicitors failed to act on those instructions. The testator then died. As a result of the defendants' failure to draw up the new will, the plaintiffs did not receive their legacies. The House of Lords held that the plaintiffs could recover. Importantly, however, their Lordships did not endorse Sir Robert Megarry's approach in *Ross v Caunters*. They thought a case such as this should not be based on the neighbour principle alone. Their Lordships made it clear that a "special relationship" had to exist in the *Hedley Byrne* sense and that such a relationship will arise where the defendant assumes responsibility for providing services knowing and accepting that "the future economic welfare of the intended beneficiary is dependent on his careful execution of the task". This represents a more liberal, or "extended" *Hedley Byrne* relationship, though their Lordships made it clear that such special relationships will arise only in circumstances where the plaintiff is readily identifiable as an individual or a member of a class of persons for whom the defendant undertakes the responsibility in the performance of a particular task.

This more liberal approach can be seen in *Spring v Guardian Assurance plc* [1995] 2 AC 296. There, the plaintiff had applied for a new job. He sought a reference from his former employers, the defendants. The reference they provided was so unfavourable that his prospective employers refused to appoint him. The reference suggested that the plaintiff was dishonest. The trial judge found that the reference had been carelessly, though not maliciously, prepared and found for the plaintiff in negligence. On appeal, the House of Lords held that there had been an implied term in the contract of employment that any reference would be supplied with due care. Their Lordships also ruled in the plaintiff's favour in tort in that the defendants had assumed the responsibility to prepare the reference with care — at least in a case such as this where there was a regulatory obligation that a reference be supplied.

The fact that the defendants in *Spring* owed a duty to the recipient of the reference under the *Hedley Byrne* principles was not in doubt: but the duty claimed here was one owed to the person about whom the reference was written, not the person to whom it was sent. The application of *Hedley Byrne* in such circumstances can be justified on the basis that the financial prospects of the person who is the subject of the reference are significantly in the hands of the person who writes it. However, there was also an important policy dimension to the decision in *Spring*. The allegations of dishonesty contained in the reference were clearly defamatory. But an action in defamation by the plaintiff, given the absence of malice, would have been met by the defence of qualified privilege. Consequently, if no redress were available to the plaintiff in negligence, he would have no real prospect of redress at all.

The Impact of *Caparo*

As we have seen, during the course of the 1980s the English courts retreated from the *Anns* two-step test for duty of care in negligence and replaced it with the three-step test set down in *Caparo Industries plc v Dickman* [1990] 2 AC 605. *Caparo* was a pure economic loss case which re-examined *Hedley Byrne* liability in respect of negligent misstatements. It will be recalled that in *Caparo* the defendants were auditors who acted for Fidelity plc. They had prepared annual accounts on the strength of which the plaintiffs bought shares in Fidelity and then mounted a successful takeover bid. The plaintiffs alleged that the accounts were inaccurate showing a pre-tax profit where they should have shown a loss. Had the plaintiffs been aware of this, they would never have bid for Fidelity. The House of Lords found against the plaintiffs. The auditors owed no duty of care in respect of the accuracy of the accounts, either to members of the public who relied on the accounts to invest in the company, or to any individual existing shareholder who similarly relied on those accounts to increase his shareholding. The precise function of auditors was important. They prepare accounts, not to promote the interests of potential investors, but to assist the shareholders collectively to exercise their right of control over the company. The House of Lords held that four conditions had to be met for a defendant to be liable for economic loss resulting from negligent advice or information:

(1) the defendant must be fully aware of the nature of the transaction which the plaintiff has in contemplation as a result of receipt of the information;

(2) he must either communicate that information to the plaintiff directly, or know that it will be communicated to him (or a restricted class of persons of which the plaintiff is an identifiable member);

(3) he must specifically anticipate the plaintiff will properly and reasonably rely on that information when deciding whether or not to engage in the transaction in question;

(4) the purpose for which the plaintiff does rely on that information must be a purpose connected with the interests that it is reasonable to require the defendants to protect.

However, it was held in *Morgan Crucible Co plc v Hill Samuel Bank Ltd* [1991] Ch 295 that a duty of care could exist in a factual situation very similar to that in *Caparo* but where the financial accounts had been revealed to an identified bidder. A duty of care was held not to exist in *James McNaughton Paper Group Ltd v Hicks Anderson & Co* [1991] 2 QB 295 (CA). There, the defendant accountants became aware that the plaintiffs were considering a takeover bid of their clients. At a meeting between the two companies, the defendants were asked to confirm the accuracy of draft accounts. They did so in very general terms. The Court of Appeal found that no duty was owed to the plaintiffs. The draft accounts were not prepared for their benefit and the defendants would reasonably expect a party to a takeover bid to take independent advice and not rely exclusively on draft accounts.

Indirect Statements

It is possible under *Hedley Byrne* for indirect statements to give rise to a duty of care. This is where the statement or supply of information is made to a person other than the plaintiff. We have seen an example of this in *Spring v Guardian Assurance plc* [1995] 2 AC 296 above.

In *Smith v Eric S Bush* [1990] 1 AC 831, the plaintiff wanted to buy a house with a building society loan. The building society asked the defendant surveyors to carry out a valuation of the house. The valuation was negligently performed. The surveyor failed to notice that the chimney was not properly supported. It later fell into the main bedroom of the house. The contract for the valuation was between the building society and the defendants, although the plaintiff was obliged to pay for it. The purpose of the valuation was to protect the security of the building society and not to advise the plaintiff on the value or condition of the house, although it was foreseeable that she would rely on it. The House of Lords held that the defendants owed a duty of care to the plaintiff. This case differed from *Caparo* in that the defendants knew the identity of the plaintiff. They knew that their advice would be transmitted to the plaintiff. They also knew that the plaintiff would probably act in reliance on that advice. The plaintiff who had paid the surveyors' fees, was held to be entitled to rely on their professional skill and advice.

The Irish courts addressed the question of indirect statements in *Wildgust v Bank of Ireland* [2006] 1 IR 570. In this case, the plaintiff had obtained life cover on his own life and that of his wife from the Norwich Union Life Assurance Society to protect loan repayments to Hill Samuel Bank. The premiums on the policy were paid by direct debit from the plaintiff's account with Bank of Ireland. Due to an error, one of the premium payments was not made. As a result, the policy lapsed. Hill Samuel had been aware of the error and made enquiries at the time to Norwich Union to ensure that the monies due on that premium instalment had been paid by some other method. Norwich Union wrongly assured Hill Samuel that the policy was in order. As a result, Hill Samuel made no further contact with the plaintiff who assumed that the premium had been paid. Norwich Union subsequently refused to pay out on the policy. The plaintiff sued seeking to compel Norwich Union to pay out and/or for damages for negligent misstatement. The Supreme Court held that the proximity test in respect of a negligent misstatement included persons in a limited and identifiable class when the maker of the statement could reasonably expect, in the context of a particular inquiry, that reliance would be placed on that statement by such persons to act or not to act in a particular manner, potentially to their detriment, in relation to that transaction. The Court further held that it was obvious that an incorrect answer by Norwich Union to a query posed by the plaintiffs' banker would potentially damage the plaintiffs. This was enough to create a special relationship between the plaintiffs and Norwich Union sufficient to establish a duty of care on Norwich Union for the accuracy of its statement, even though the statement was not made directly to the plaintiffs but to a person identified with them. Moreover, the plaintiffs were, *vis-à-vis* the person giving the information, proximate neighbours who could foreseeably be damaged by the inaccuracy of the information. In addition, Norwich Union ought to have known that the information given to the plaintiffs' bankers would be relied upon by the plaintiffs and that, if the statement was incorrect, the life policy could lapse to the plaintiffs' detriment.

Public authorities can also be subject to *Hedley Byrne* principles in circumstances where they make negligent misstatements directly or indirectly. For example, in *Walsh v South Tipperary County Council* [2011] IEHC 503, the defendants carelessly and inaccurately informed landowners that a particular laneway was in the charge of the County Council. The plaintiffs subsequently purchased the land relying upon the certificate that had been supplied to a previous owner that the laneway was in the charge of the Council. Even though the negligent misstatement had not been made to the plaintiff in this case, a duty of care was held to exist. The Court took the view that it was foreseeable at the time the statement was made that it would be used by the original vendor to satisfy his purchaser and that, in turn, that statement would be relied upon by subsequent purchasers. The plaintiffs, therefore, as purchasers of the land, joined a class of persons to whom the negligent misstatement could be said to have been published. That class was capable of being defined with some accuracy at the time the statement had been made.

Liability was imposed on an auctioneer in respect of statements made to a purchaser in *McCullough v PB Gunne (Monaghan) plc* [1997] IEHC 6. This case concerned a naive married couple with no business experience. They purchased licensed premises through the defendant auctioneer which was financially disastrous for them. Given their lack of experience and the fact that they had never purchased property before, they asked the defendant's employee to "keep them straight". The defendant's employee sold their farm for them. He opened a building society account, arranged finance and found solicitors for them. The Court found that the proactive approach of the defendant's employee in assisting them, along with various statements of encouragement and reassurance, gave the plaintiffs the impression that he was "on their side". The Court made it clear that since an auctioneer is employed by a vendor to get the best price for them, the auctioneer should always make it clear that the vendor is their only client, not the purchaser. The Court found that it was just and reasonable that a duty of care be recognised.

A duty was also recognised in *McAnarney v Hanrahan* [1994] 1 ILRM 210. There, the plaintiffs bought a leasehold interest in a public house for £45,000 on the basis of two assurances given by the defendant auctioneer: first, that a bid for £54,000 had been received at auction, and second that the freehold could be purchased for £3000. Neither assurance was correct. The landlord actually sought £40,000 for the sale of the freehold (eventually settling on £30,000). The plaintiffs sued the auctioneer and his principal for negligent misstatement. The Court held that the case fell within the *Hedley Byrne* principles. A special relationship had arisen between the parties on the basis that the auctioneer had taken it upon himself to give his opinion about the purchase of the freehold when he knew, or should have known, that the plaintiffs would place reliance on his statement. By failing to take care as to the accuracy of that statement, the auctioneer breached his duty of care towards the plaintiffs.

Hedley Byrne has been held to apply in circumstances where pre-contractual negotiations induce the plaintiff to enter into a contract which he would not otherwise have entered into. For example, in *Esso Petroleum Co Ltd v Mardon* [1976] QB 801, which concerned the taking of a tenancy of a filling station the profitability of which was overstated by Esso Petroleum, Lord Denning MR stated the position thus:

> "It seems to me that *Hedley Byrne*, properly understood, covers this particular proposition: if a man, who has or professes to have special knowledge or skill, makes a representation by virtue thereof to another — be it advice, information or opinion — with the intention of inducing him to enter into a contract with him, he is under a duty to use reasonable care to see that the representation is correct, and that the advice, information or opinion is reliable. If he negligently gives unsound advice or misleading information or expresses an erroneous opinion, and thereby induces the other side into a contract with him, he is liable in damages."

The approach adopted in *Mardon* was cited by the Irish High Court in *Stafford v Mahony, Smith & Palmer* [1980] ILRM 53 in which the Court accepted that a pre-contractual misrepresentation could give rise to liability for negligent misstatement. A local authority was held similarly liable in *Darlington Properties Ltd v Meath County Council* [2011] IEHC 70. There, the local authority sold land to the plaintiff on the basis that a road would be built which would have enhanced the land's value. After the plaintiff had purchased the land, it transpired that the road could not be built because the local authority itself had already granted a planning permission making the construction of the road impossible. The Court, in deprecating the local authority's "bungling and ineptitude of a high order", made it clear that

> "a vendor, regardless of any other special relationship, is under a duty to take reasonable care to ensure that any representations made by him with a view to inducing [a] contract are accurate."

Liability under the *Hedley Byrne* principles was imposed.

Causation

It is important to bear in mind that the "special relationship" under *Hedley Byrne* goes only to establish duty of care. The plaintiff must also prove that there is a causal link between the breach and the loss suffered. This can be seen in the case of *JEB Fasteners v Marks Bloom & Co* [1981] 3 All ER 289, where it had been held that the misstatement had not motivated the plaintiff to make his loss-making takeover bid. Accordingly, defendant's breach of duty had not caused the plaintiff's loss. Causation was also found to be relevant by the Irish courts in *Carey v Independent Newspapers (Ireland) Ltd* [2003] IEHC and *Donnellan v Dungoyne Ltd* [1995] 1 ILRM 388.

C. Other Categories of Economic Loss

The Nature of Pure Economic Loss

Hedley Byrne liability for negligent misstatements is well established in both Irish and English law: but economic loss can arise in a range of circumstances other than negligent misstatement.

The English courts take the view that no duty to protect others from pure economic loss will arise however predictable that loss may be, and however just and reasonable it might appear that the defendant should bear that loss. This approach can be seen in *Murphy v Brentwood District Council* [1991] 1 AC 398, which overruled *Anns v Merton London Borough Council* [1978] AC 728. In *Murphy*, the plaintiff was a subsequent purchaser of a defective dwelling. The House of Lords classified the loss suffered by him as pure economic loss. This was notwithstanding the fact that the plaintiff's home, if not repaired, would ultimately have collapsed. Financial loss of this type is irrecoverable in England in tort whether the defendant is the builder or the local council approving the original building plans. In the absence of a special relationship of proximity, neither manufacturers of chattels nor builders of property are subject to a duty of care in relation to the quality of their work. Protection of plaintiffs in these circumstances is the function of the law of contract.

This approach can be seen in a long line of cases. In *Cattle v Stockton Water Works* (1875) LR 10 QBD 453, the plaintiff was a contractor who was employed, for a fixed sum, to dig a tunnel under a road through land that belonged to a third party. A water main belonging to the defendants was defective and caused flooding of the works. This meant that, due to delays in carrying out the work, the plaintiff lost money on his contract. The Court held that the defendants were not liable. The plaintiff's losses were economic only. Although there was physical damage, this was to the third party's land, not to the plaintiff's property.

In *Weller & Co v Foot and Mouth Disease Research Institute* [1966] QB 569, the defendant had negligently allowed the spread of foot and mouth disease. The plaintiff was an auctioneer. He suffered financial loss due to the quarantine restrictions which meant that he could not hold his weekly cattle auctions. He sued for negligence. His action failed because he had only lost profit. The defendant would, however, have been liable to compensate farmers whose livestock became infected. This was regarded as property damage.

In *British Celanese Ltd v Hunt* [1969] 2 All ER 1252 and *SCM (UK) Ltd v WJ Whittle & Son Ltd* [1971] 1 QB 337, the cutting off of electricity supplies damaged the plaintiff's machines and materials resulting in a loss of production. The plaintiffs recovered both their additional expenditure in replacing and repairing machinery and their loss of profits on the lost production run. In the latter case, the Court held that the economic loss (i.e., loss of profits) was recoverable, as it was immediately consequent on physical damage to the plaintiff's property.

In *Spartan Steel & Alloys v Martin* [1973] QB 27, the defendant negligently drove a power shovel through a cable which supplied electricity to the plaintiff's factory. This resulted in a 14 hour power cut. The plaintiff suffered losses under three heads:

- reduced value of metal which had to be removed from Furnace One before it solidified and damaged machinery;
- profit which would have been made had that "melt" been completed; and
- profit from four other future "melts" in Furnaces Two and Three which would have been made but for the lengthy power cut.

The English Court of Appeal, by a majority, held that only the first two heads justified compensation. They were treated as consequential to physical damage. The third constituted pure economic loss because it did not flow directly from physical damage to the plaintiff's property. As such, it was not recoverable.

Figure 3.2

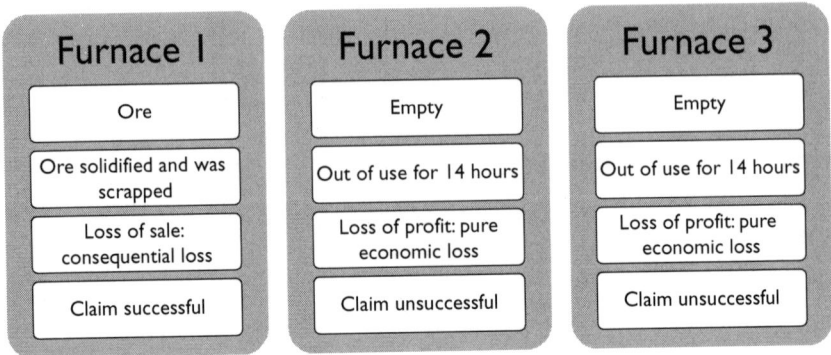

Furnace 1	Furnace 2	Furnace 3
Ore	Empty	Empty
Ore solidified and was scrapped	Out of use for 14 hours	Out of use for 14 hours
Loss of sale: consequential loss	Loss of profit: pure economic loss	Loss of profit: pure economic loss
Claim successful	Claim unsuccessful	Claim unsuccessful

Spartan Steel & Alloys v Martin

The Court of Appeal affirmed *Spartan Steel* in *Muirhead v Industrial Tank Specialities Ltd* [1985] 3 All ER 705. In that case, the plaintiff, a fish merchant, decided to buy lobsters in the summer when prices were low and store them to sell at a profit on the Christmas market. The lobsters had to be stored in tanks through which seawater was constantly pumped, filtered, and re-circulated. The pumps proved defective because the electric motors were not suitable for use in the UK. The plaintiff sued the manufacturers of the electric motors under three heads:

(1) the loss of several lobsters that died in the tanks;
(2) the costs incurred on attempts to correct the fault;
(3) the loss of profits on the enterprise.

The Court ruled that the plaintiff could recover only for the loss of his property (i.e. the dead lobsters) and any loss of profit consequent on those dead lobsters. Only that economic loss directly consequent on physical damage could be recovered in tort.

In Ireland, after examining a number of English authorities, the Court refused recovery in *Irish Paper Sacks Ltd v John Sisk and Son (Dublin) Ltd* (18 May 1972). The defendant's servants had excavated a trench on the public highway. In the course of doing so they severed a cable which supplied electricity to the plaintiff's factory. This resulted in a two-day power cut. During that time the plaintiff had to cease production at the factory. The company suffered no physical damage, only economic loss. In denying recovery, O'Keefe P said:

> "The principle to be derived from [the relevant case law] is that a
> plaintiff suing for damages suffered as a result of an act or omission

of the defendant cannot recover if the act or omission did not directly injure the plaintiff's person or property, but merely caused consequential loss."

Interestingly, the Court explicitly made no distinction between pure economic loss and physical damage in *McShane v Wholesale Fruit and Vegetables Ltd v Johnston Haulage Co Ltd* [1997] 1 IR 86. There, the plaintiff's factory was brought to a standstill by the loss of electrical power caused by a fire in the defendant's adjoining premises. The plaintiffs sued for damages for the economic loss they sustained. Relying on the test for actionable negligence in *Ward v McMaster*, the Court held that such economic loss was recoverable, even though the plaintiff did not suffer (or at least claim for) physical damage. Flood J said:

"The quality of the damage does not arise. It can be damage to property, to the person, financial or economic. The question as to whether the damage (of whatever type) is recoverable is dependent on proximity and foreseeability subject to the caveat of compelling exemption on public policy."

In general, the case law discloses two separate specific issues arising in relation to pure economic loss:

(a) dangerous defects in a product or building;
(b) non-dangerous defects in a product or building.

The question in relation to category (a) above is whether plaintiffs should be compensated for the costs of neutralising the danger to their health and safety. In *Colgan v Connolly Construction Co (Ireland) Ltd* [1980] ILRM 33 the Court held that compensation should be awarded in such circumstances. Similarly, in *Ward v McMaster* [1985] IR 29, where the plaintiffs purchased a house which had both dangerous and non-dangerous defects, the High Court compensated the plaintiffs for both categories of defect.

In relation to category (b) above, the Supreme Court in *Glencar* appeared to cast doubt over whether liability for this category of loss should ever be imposed. Liability had been imposed for this type of loss in England in *Junior Books Ltd v Veitchi Co Ltd* [1983] 1 AC 520. There, a sub-contractor with no contractual relationship with the plaintiff was held liable for pure economic loss sustained by the plaintiff for a defective, though not dangerous, floor installation. *Junior Books* was endorsed by the High Court in *Ward v McMaster*, though it has been effectively sidelined in England. The Supreme Court in *Glencar* questioned whether *Junior Books* should be followed in this jurisdiction at all.

The Constitutional Dimension

In a small number of cases recovery for pure economic loss has been considered in the context of the Constitution. In *Byrne v Ryan* [2009] 4 IR 542, the plaintiff gave birth to two children following a failed sterilisation operation. The Court awarded damages for the pain, suffering and inconvenience of pregnancy and childbirth together with special damages for extra medical expenses. A further claim in respect of the costs of rearing the two children was denied. The Court adopted the reasoning of the House of Lords in *McFarlane v Tayside Health Board* [2000] 2 AC 59 in which it rejected a claim for care costs until adulthood. In that case, their Lordships ruled, as a matter of legal policy, that it was unacceptable to award damages for the birth of a normal, healthy child to compensate for the cost of his upbringing. Considerations of distributive justice also militated against such an award. In *Byrne v Ryan*, the Court also took the view that the denial of compensation for the economic costs of rearing a child in such circumstances would be consistent with the "constitutional order which obtains in this jurisdiction" and "[t]he value which the Constitution places upon the family, the dignity and protection which it affords to human life…". In *Ahern v Moore* [2013] IEHC 72 the High Court followed the approach adopted in *McFarlane v Tayside* and *Byrne v Ryan* and unambiguously stated, in respect of the second defendant, that "[a]ny monetary expenses laid out by him come into the category of pure economic loss unassociated with injury and are [...] incapable of being recovered".

In *Hanahoe v Hussy* [1998] 3 IR 69, damages were awarded against the Commissioner of An Garda Síochána in respect of the execution of a search warrant in circumstances where members of the press had been notified by the Gardaí beforehand. As a result, a search of the plaintiffs' premises took place with members of the media present. The Court found that the information had "emanated from a Garda source". This amounted, in the Court's view, to an "outrageous interference with [the plaintiffs' privacy] and [their] constitutional rights".

The Role of Contract

As mentioned at the outset, recovery for pure economic loss was, and is, seen as the province of the law of contract. Concurrent liability in both contract and tort is, however, possible. This position was definitively established by the Supreme Court in *Findlay v Murtagh* [1979] IR 249. In that case it was recognised for the first time that the client of a solicitor may sue the solicitor in the tort of negligence as well as for breach of contract.

A particular difficulty may arise, however, where a contract purports to exclude liability in tort. This question has been examined in a number of cases. Lord Goff in the House of Lords in *Henderson v Merrett Syndicates Ltd* [1995] 2 AC 145 said that there is no sound basis for a rule which automatically restricts the plaintiff to either a tortious or contractual remedy. He also said that he did not find it objectionable that the plaintiff may be entitled to take advantage of the remedy which is most advantageous to him, "subject only to ascertaining whether the tortious duty is so inconsistent with the applicable contract that, in accordance with ordinary principle the parties must be taken to have agreed that the tortious remedy is to be limited or excluded." This approach was cited with approval by the Irish Supreme Court in *Kennedy v Allied Irish Banks Ltd* [1998] 2 IR 48 and *Pat O'Donnell & Co Ltd v Truck & Machinery Sales Ltd* (1 April 1998). In the latter case, it was said that

> "if... a contract provides — whether expressly or by necessary implication — that the defendant is not liable for a particular risk, then the law of tort should not be allowed to contradict it".

The relationship between contract and tort was also examined in *Sweeney v Duggan* [1997] 2 IR 531. In that case, the plaintiff worked in a quarry. He was injured at work. He sued the company for damages in negligence and for breach of statutory duty. He was awarded damages. The company then went into liquidation. Consequently, he could not recover all of his compensation because no employers' liability insurance was in place. He then sued the defendant personally who was the managing director and owner of the company. The plaintiff claimed that the defendant owed him a duty of care (i) to have put in place the relevant insurance or (ii) to have warned him that no such insurance was in place. The plaintiff's claim was dismissed. The Supreme Court took the view that

> "the obligation[s] as between the employer and employee in a case such as the present are to be found in contract and not in tort".

Since the company had no obligation to the plaintiff in contract, the defendant could not either. Murphy J said: "I find it inconceivable that any such duty on the part of a corporator, if it did exist, could be more extensive than that of the corporation itself".

The Impact of *Glencar*

The question of the recoverability for damages in respect of economic loss in Ireland was examined in *Glencar Explorations plc v Mayo County Council* (No 2) [2002] 1 IR 84. In the course of his judgment, Keane CJ stated that the reason why damages for economic loss — as distinct from compensation for injury to persons or damage to property — are normally not recoverable in tort is best illustrated by an example. If A sells B an article which turns out to be defective, B can normally sue A for damages for breach of contract. However, if the article comes into the possession of C, with whom A has no contract, C cannot in general sue A for the defects in the chattel, unless he has suffered personal injury or damage to property within the *Donoghue v Stevenson* principle. That would be so even where the defect was latent and did not come to light until the article came into C's possession. To hold otherwise would be to expose the original seller to actions from an infinite range of persons with whom he never had any relationship in contract or its equivalent. That, Keane CJ made clear, did not mean that economic loss is always irrecoverable in actions in tort. He noted that economic loss is recoverable in actions for negligent misstatement under the *Hedley Byrne* principles. Outside *Hedley Byrne*, economic loss was held to be recoverable in *Siney v Corporation of Dublin* [1980] IR 400 where the damages represented the cost of remedying defects in a building let by the local authority under its statutory powers. Such damages were also held to be recoverable in *Ward v McMaster* [1985] IR 29; [1988] IR 337, where the loss was represented by the cost of remedying defects for which the builder and the local authority were held to be responsible. In both cases, the loss was held to be recoverable by the Irish courts following the approach adopted by the House of Lords in *Anns v Merton*. As already mentioned, the House of Lords overruled *Anns* in *Murphy*, but the Supreme Court in *Glencar* did not overrule *Ward* in respect of recovery of pure economic loss. Keane CJ stated:

> "I would expressly reserve for another occasion the question as to whether economic loss is recoverable in actions for negligence other than actions for negligent misstatement and those falling within the categories identified in *Siney v Dublin Corporation* and *Ward v McMaster* and whether the decision of the House of Lords in *Junior Books Ltd v Veitchi Co Ltd* [1983] 1 AC 520 should be followed in this jurisdiction."

That other occasion to which Keane CJ referred has yet to present itself.

CHAPTER FOUR

PSYCHIATRIC INJURY

Learning Outcomes

Upon completion of this chapter, the reader should be able to:

- Define psychiatric injury in the context of tort law;
- Trace the development of the law relating to psychiatric injury in England and Ireland;
- Identify the principles the courts apply in recognising a duty of care in psychiatric injury cases;
- Describe the range of factual situations which can give rise to liability;
- Explain how liability for psychiatric injury can arise in the workplace.

A. What is Psychiatric Injury?

Psychiatric injury has been defined as a medically recognised condition of a sustained nature that disturbs the normal functioning of the mind. Psychiatric injury may or may not be accompanied by physical symptoms. The law requires that the plaintiff suffer legally recognised harm in the form of a recognisable psychiatric injury and not mere mental or emotional distress, such as grief, sorrow, distress, worry, anger, outrage, anxiety or disappointment: see Handford, Mullany and Handford's, *Tort Liability for Psychiatric Damage* (Lawbook Co, Sydney, 2006).

In *Hinz v Berry* [1970] 2 QB 40, [1970] 2 WLR 684 Lord Denning MR set out the broad parameters within which recovery for psychiatric injury might occur:

> "In English law no damages are awarded for grief or sorrow caused by a person's death. No damages are to be given for the worry about the children, or for the financial strain or stress, or the difficulties adjusting to a new life. Damages are, however, recoverable for nervous shock, or, to put it in medical terms, for any recognisable psychiatric illness caused by the breach of duty by the defendant."

The case law in both England and Ireland has, in the main, concerned physical events giving rise to the onset of post-traumatic stress disorder (PTSD). In Ireland, Denham J (as she then was) in *Devlin v National Maternity Hospital* [2008] 2 IR 222 held that "grief and sorrow are not a basis upon which to recover damages. There has to be a proven psychiatric illness". Although this approach does not prohibit recovery for conditions such as reactive depression which results from grief or anguish, it does limit liability to those psychiatric illnesses which are medically recognised.

B. Historical Development

Historically, the law has been reluctant to allow recovery for psychiatric injury for three main reasons:

- There was a general lack of understanding or awareness as to how the human mind worked. It was not, for example, until the 1960s the post-traumatic stress disorder (PTSD) was recognised as a form of psychiatric injury;
- It was thought that psychiatric injury was more likely to be fraudulently claimed than physical injury, which is usually visible and therefore ascertainable and more "real";
- There were policy objections to allowing recovery for psychiatric injury which threatened to open the "floodgates" to innumerable claims.

✱ Nervous Shock

Notwithstanding these concerns, the Irish courts have found in favour of plaintiffs in a number of notable cases. For example, in *Byrne v Southern and Western Ry Co* (1884) 26 LR Ir 428, the plaintiff was a superintendent in the telegraph office at Limerick Junction station on the defendant's railway. One day, the railway points had been negligently left open. As result, a train crashed into the side of the telegraph office where the plaintiff was working. He "sustained a nervous shock which resulted in certain injuries to his health". The plaintiff, in evidence, explained that he suffered no physical injury whatsoever, but did suffer "great fright and shock". The Court found in his favour and he received compensation of £325. This verdict was affirmed by the Court of Appeal.

✱ This contrasts with a decision of the Privy Council in *Victoria Railway Commissioners v Coultas* (1888) 13 App Cas 222. In that case, the plaintiff suffered severe nervous shock crossing the defendant's railway line. Her buggy became trapped on the line as a train was approaching "at rapid speed" because the gatekeeper had failed to open the opposite gates in time. The train passed close to the back of the buggy but did not touch it. The plaintiff received "a severe nervous shock from the fright, and that the illness from which she afterwards suffered was the consequence of the fright". One of the plaintiff's witnesses said she was "suffering from profound impression on the nervous system, nervous shock, and the shock from which she suffered would be a natural consequence of the fright". The Privy Council found against her, expressing concern that granting remedies to plaintiffs in such cases could give rise to circumstances in which "a wide field [would be] opened for imaginary claims".

✱ In the Irish case of *Bell v Great Northern Railway Co* (1890) 26 LR (Ir) 428 (Ex Div) a 49-year-old woman was a passenger in the defendant's train. Part of the train was decoupled and reversed at high speed down a hill. The plaintiff suffered severe shock. Her mental health was affected to such an extent that, as the medical evidence disclosed, her condition might eventually result in paralysis. She was awarded £50 at trial. On appeal, the Exchequer Division followed the Irish Court of Appeal's decision in *Byrne*, rather than the more recent decision of the Privy Council in *Coultas*. The Court took the view that it was "… immaterial whether the injuries may be called nervous shock, brain disturbance, mental shock or injury". The only question to be addressed was:

> "was the health or capacity of the plaintiff for the discharge of her duties and enjoyment of life affected by what occurred to her whilst in the carriage? Next, was this caused by the negligence of the defendants?"

The Court's recognition of the relationship between body and mind was, without doubt, progressive for its time. It is interesting to note that, even in the nineteenth century, there was some divergence between the approaches of the English courts and the Irish courts in relation to recovery for what we now call psychiatric injury.

The term "psychiatric injury" was originally referred to as "nervous shock". This was because the condition had to result from the impact of a sudden event or its immediate aftermath. If the injury was the result of any sort of prolonged exposure, to say stress or grief, it would not qualify under this category of legal claim. For example in *Sian v Hampstead Health Authority* [1994] Med LR 170 (CA), the effect on a father spending two weeks sitting by the bedside of his dying son, who had been injured due to the defendant's negligence, was not sufficient to found a claim, although the Court of Appeal adopted a more liberal approach in *North Glamorgan NHS Trust v Walters* [2002] EWCA Civ 1792. There, the Court of Appeal allowed a claim in respect of woman who suffered psychiatric injury as the condition of her child visibly worsened before her eyes when medical staff failed to diagnose that the child was suffering from acute hepatitis.

C. Developments in England and Wales

The first successful claim before the English courts came in *Dulieu v White* [1901] 2 KB 669. There, a barmaid was serving customers in a public house when she looked up and saw a horse and cart out of control, crashing through the wall of the building. She was pregnant at the time. The shock she suffered from that event caused her to suffer a stillbirth for which she recovered compensation. The Court recognised that the basis of her reaction was a reasonable fear for her own physical safety.

Following *Dulieu v White* the next significant case was *Hambrook v Stokes Bros* [1925] 1 KB 141. There, a mother suffered shock when she saw a driverless lorry roll down a hill and around a bend where it crashed. The crash occurred out of her sight but was in a place where she had recently taken her children. Her fear that they had been injured, or worse, caused her to suffer nervous shock. The Court expressed the view that if the plaintiff in *Dulieu* could recover for fearing for her own safety, it was logical that the plaintiff in *Hambrook* should be able to recover where she unselfishly feared for the safety of her children. This represented an extension in the duty of care relating to nervous shock. This led to a degree of judicial uncertainty as to where the boundaries for nervous shock recovery lay.

No doubt conscious of this, the English courts then introduced some limitations in *Bourhill v Young* [1943] AC 92. There, a pregnant woman had just stepped off a tram when she heard a collision between the defendant's motorcycle and a car, some 40 yards away on the other side of the tram. The motorcyclist died at the scene. Although the plaintiff did not see the crash itself or the body, on approaching the scene afterwards, she saw blood on the road. She claimed that the shock she experienced was responsible for the subsequent stillbirth of her baby. The House of Lords classified the plaintiff as a mere bystander who had not been in any physical danger herself. This was central to their denying that a duty of care had been owed to her by the defendant. The injury suffered by her had not been reasonably foreseeable, owing to the distance she was from the accident but also because the law expects that members of the public, in such circumstances, display a degree of "fortitude". It is important to remember, also, that the plaintiff in *Bourhill* may also have been denied a remedy because she would have been an unforeseeable plaintiff, as in *Palsgraf v Long Island Railroad* 162 NE 99 (NY 1928).

In *King v Phillips* [1953] 1 QB 42 a mother in her home heard the screams of her toddler who was playing outside. She looked out of an upstairs window to see his tricycle underneath the wheels of a reversing taxi. She sustained a psychiatric injury as a result. It was held, applying the principle of *Bourhill*, that the taxi driver could not reasonably have contemplated as a result of his negligence in reversing his taxi without looking where he was going, that he would cause psychiatric injury to the mother who was 70 yards away. Interestingly, Lord Oliver in *Alcock v Chief Constable of South Yorkshire Police* [1992] 1 AC 310 (see below) suggested that the result in *Bourhill* would be different if it was litigated today and that a court would not have any difficulty in regarding the mother's presence as foreseeable.

Primary and Secondary Victims

The English courts have made a distinction between primary and secondary victims. A "primary victim" is a plaintiff who has direct involvement in the incident and is within the range of foreseeable physical injury. There is presumed to be a duty of care not to cause them physical injury and this is extended to include a duty not to cause psychiatric injury. The courts' approach is different in relation to "secondary victims". The House of Lords discussed the distinction between primary and secondary victims in *Page v Smith* [1996] AC 155. In that case, the driver of a car was involved in a relatively minor collision. The accident was caused by the negligence of the defendant, the other driver. Although the plaintiff suffered no physical injury, he alleged that the accident caused a recurrence of chronic fatigue syndrome (ME) from which he had suffered periodically in the past. The House of Lords found for the plaintiff, holding that a duty of care had been owed to him for the type of damage suffered. The two central aspects to the decision of the House of Lords in that case are:

- psychiatric injury is not to be regarded as injury of a different kind from physical injury; and

- for the primary victim, reasonable foreseeability of physical injury is sufficient to bring with it a duty in respect of psychiatric injury.

It should be noted that the "eggshell skull" rule can be relevant in psychiatric injury, as well as physical injury, cases. The "eggshell skull" rule (or the "thin skull" rule) operates to bring the defendant within liability for injuries which are not reasonably foreseeable. When the loss suffered by the plaintiff is at least partly due to his own pre-existing vulnerability, whether that be physical, psychological or financial, the fact that it is unforeseeable will not affect the defendant's ultimate liability. The defendant "must take his victim as he finds him". In *Brice v Brown* [1984] 1 All ER 997, the Court confirmed that if psychiatric injury would have been foreseeable in a person of ordinary fortitude, then, if the plaintiff suffers excessive harm owing to the fact that he was prone to depression, recovery will be available for that further injury.

In *Vernon v Bosley* [1997] 1 All ER 577, the plaintiff's two young children were passengers in a car driven by the defendant, their nanny. The car veered off the road and crashed into a river. The plaintiff did not witness the original accident, but was called to the scene immediately afterwards. He watched unsuccessful attempts to rescue his children. These efforts failed and the children drowned. The plaintiff became mentally ill. His business and marriage failed. The defendant accepted that the plaintiff's illness was the consequence of the deaths of his children, but argued that his illness was caused not by shock, but by pathological grief due to an illness termed "pathological grief disorder". This was distinct from PTSD. The Court of Appeal made it clear that damages for ordinary grief and bereavement are irrecoverable. However, a secondary victim can recover damages for psychiatric illness where he establishes the general preconditions for such a claim and that the negligence of the defendant caused or contributed to his mental illness. Since the plaintiff in this case was able to do so, he could recover.

The House of Lords in *McLoughlin v O'Brian* [1983] AC 410 emphasised the importance of a range of factors which would give rise to a duty of care in psychiatric injury cases. There, the plaintiff was a mother who was told by telephone that her family had been involved in a serious road traffic accident. She travelled to the hospital, arriving there about two hours after the accident. All four of the family were injured. She was then informed that one of her children had died. She saw the remaining three family members before they had been properly cleaned up. There were cut, bruised, and covered in oil and blood. Though the plaintiff was a woman of reasonable fortitude, she suffered severe shock, organic depression and a change of personality. The House of Lords insisted that the plaintiff demonstrate her proximity in time and space to the traumatic events. Their Lordships found that in coming upon the "immediate aftermath" of the accident, she was well within the scope of the defendant's duty to avoid causing nervous shock. Witnessing the aftermath, they thought, was equivalent to witnessing the accident itself since nothing in the horror and trauma of the sight that she met at the hospital had changed since the accident itself.

The leading case on liability to secondary victims for psychiatric harm in England and Wales is now *Alcock v Chief Constable of South Yorkshire Police* [1992] 1 AC 310. This case arose out of the Hillsborough football stadium disaster of 1989. There, 96 football supporters were killed and another 400 injured in the spectator stands when crowd control broke down and barriers collapsed at the beginning of an FA Cup match between Liverpool FC and Nottingham Forest FC. The plaintiffs were relatives and friends of those who were caught up in the crush. All suffered psychiatric injury as a result of what they witnessed that day. None of the plaintiffs had been in any physical danger themselves. They were all secondary victims. Some had watched the events unfold on television whilst others, who were present in the ground, had feared for the safety of relatives or friends. Others had identified bodies in the mortuary some nine hours later. The House of Lords dismissed all the plaintiffs' claims.

Their Lordships set out three criteria ("the *Alcock* criteria") which are necessary for finding a duty of care to a secondary victim:

1. The plaintiff must be in a sufficiently close relationship of love and affection with the primary victim. There is a rebuttable presumption between a husband and wife and parents and children; those in other relationships must satisfy the Court that they come within this category;

2. The plaintiff must be sufficiently proximate in both time and space to the accident or its immediate aftermath. Seeing bodies in the mortuary for the purpose of identification, some nine hours after the event, was held not to be sufficiently proximate;

3. The plaintiff must suffer nervous shock through what was seen or heard of the accident or its immediate aftermath. In other words, there must be a "sudden appreciation by sight or sound of a horrifying event which violently [agitates] the mind" (per Lord Ackner). What is seen on television, or told by somebody else, is insufficiently immediate.

Determining precisely what is meant by the "immediate aftermath" can be problematic. We have seen how in *Alcock* identifying a loved one in a mortuary some nine hours after the event was held by the House of Lords not to come within the scope of the immediate aftermath. In *Galli-Atkinson v Seghal* [2003] EWCA Civ 697, a mother came upon the scene where her daughter had been knocked down by a dangerous driver. She was informed that her daughter had died. She saw her daughter's body in the mortuary some two hours later. The Court of Appeal held that the plaintiff's experience, taken as a whole, was sufficient to bring her within the definition of "immediate aftermath".

Hambrook, *McLoughlin* and *Alcock* established that the shock must come about through one's own unaided senses. There must be sight, sound or hearing of the event or its immediate aftermath. There is no liability where the plaintiff's shock is caused by being informed of the event by a third party. However, Lord Bridge in *McLoughlin* did warn against inflexibility and spoke against drawing a line in respect of witnessing the accident, presence at or near where it happened and the coming upon the aftermath, as opposed to merely hearing of it afterwards, as imposing a largely arbitrary limit of liability. He gave the following example:

> "Take the case of a mother who knows that her husband and children are staying in a certain hotel. She reads in her morning newspaper that it has been the scene of a disastrous fire. She sees in the paper a photograph of unidentifiable victims trapped on the top floor waving for help from the windows. She learns shortly afterwards that all her family have perished. She suffers an acute psychiatric illness. That her illness in the circumstances was a reasonably foreseeable consequence of the events resulting from the fire is undeniable. Yet is it right in law to deny her damages as against the defendant whose negligence was responsible for the fire, simply on the grounds that an important link in the chain of causation of her psychiatric illness was supplied by her imagining the agonies of mind and body of which her family died, rather than by direct perception of the event?"

The public policy objectives of placing limits on recovery in psychiatric injury cases, whilst understandable, can appear arbitrary and unfair. They will, no doubt, be challenged in future cases.

The Position of Rescuers

Liability towards rescuers was considered in *White v Chief Constable of South Yorkshire Police* [1999] 1 All ER 1. This case also arose out of the Hillsborough disaster in 1989. A number of police officers on duty that day brought a negligence action against the Chief Constable in respect of psychiatric illness they suffered following their experiences of the tragedy. Like the plaintiffs in *Alcock*, they were never in any physical danger. Some had been on duty in another part of the ground but were called upon to tend to the injured and dying. Others had to deal with relatives of the dead at the mortuary. All were direct witnesses of the horrific scenes. These experiences led to their psychiatric injuries.

The plaintiffs succeeded before the Court of Appeal. Foreseeability was established primarily on the basis that they were employees of the defendant. However, the House of Lords reversed that decision. Their Lordships strictly applied the *Alcock* criteria to them as secondary victims. The plaintiffs had asserted that their relationship with the Chief Constable was akin to a contract of employment. Their Lordships observed that an employer's duty to safeguard his employees from personal injury is simply part of the ordinary law of negligence. The plaintiffs' argument therefore failed because they were in no better position than normal bystanders to sue in respect of psychiatric injury simply by virtue of this relationship. Employers are unquestionably under a duty to ensure that their employees do not suffer work-related injury. However, that is subject to the requirement that the injury be reasonably foreseeable: but where the employee suffers psychiatric injury, not from anything done directly by the employer to the employee but, rather, as a result of what is done to others, he or she is to be treated in the same way as any other secondary victim. Since the police officers in question lacked the requisite close ties of love or affection with the victims, they could not succeed in their action. It is likely also that there was a strong policy dimension to this decision given the apparent unfairness of the fact that the plaintiffs in *Alcock* did not recover.

The plaintiffs in *White* also claimed that they were owed a duty in their capacity as rescuers. Prior to the decision in *White*, it appeared that rescuers would form a special category of victim for the purposes of determining duty of care for psychiatric injury. However, the House of Lords took the view that, in relation to psychiatric injury, rescuers must meet the same conditions as any other witnesses of injury to third parties. They must either objectively have exposed themselves to danger or have reasonably believed themselves to have done so. This had occurred in *Chadwick v British Railways Board* [1967] 1 WLR 912 where the plaintiff successfully recovered compensation when he sustained a form of psychiatric injury (what would now be termed PTSD) following spending the night attempting to rescue the victims of a major train crash which occurred near his home. *Chadwick* can probably be reconciled with *White* on the basis that, by putting himself into danger at the site of the train crash, the plaintiff was a primary rather than secondary victim.

D. Developments in Ireland

In *Mullally v Bus Éireann* [1992] ILRM 722, the plaintiff's husband and children were involved in a bus crash caused by the defendant's negligence. The plaintiff learned of the accident from a relative. She attended the hospitals where her husband and three children had been taken. There, she was met with horrific and distressing scenes of her badly injured family. One of her children subsequently died from his injuries. Denham J found that the plaintiff had suffered psychological harm and had symptoms consistent with post-traumatic stress disorder. The plaintiff's condition had been caused by the accident and its aftermath, not grief. In applying the "ordinary criteria of reasonable foreseeability" she found that it was readily foreseeable that a mother exposed to the experience that this plaintiff had been exposed to, would break down and suffer illness. Denham J made it clear that the duty of care of the defendants extended to injuries which were reasonably foreseeable. Therefore, "the defendants had a duty of care to this plaintiff and that was no bar in law, or under the Constitution, to this determination".

The Supreme Court addressed the issue of psychiatric injury again in *Kelly v Hennessy* [1995] 3 IR 253. In that case, the plaintiff was at home when she was informed by telephone that her husband and daughters had been seriously injured in a road traffic accident. She was brought to the hospital by neighbours and was faced with horrific and distressing scenes of her badly injured family. Following the accident, the plaintiff "led a traumatised existence". Her husband was hospitalised for over three months. He suffered permanent brain damage. One of the plaintiff's daughters was hospitalised for over a year. She also suffered brain damage. The plaintiff's other daughter made a full recovery.

Delivering the leading judgment for the Supreme Court, Hamilton CJ (with whom Egan J agreed; Denham J dissenting only on the question of quantum) considered that, in order to recover damages for nervous shock a plaintiff must establish:

(i)   that he or she actually suffered a recognisable psychiatric illness;
(ii) that such illness was shock-induced;
(iii) that the nervous shock was caused by the defendant's act or omission;
(iv) that the nervous shock sustained was by reason of actual or apprehended physical injury to the plaintiff or to a person other than the plaintiff; and
(v)   that the defendant owed him or her a duty of care not to cause him or her a reasonably foreseeable injury in the form of nervous shock as opposed to personal injury in general.

Having set out these five matters to be established, Hamilton CJ went on to state that the law permitted the recovery of damages for nervous shock and psychiatric illness induced where a plaintiff came upon the immediate aftermath of an accident—either at the scene or in hospital—involving a person with whom the plaintiff had a close relationship. The Chief Justice relied on and approved the decision of the High Court of Australia in *Jaensch v Coffey* (1984) 115 CLR 549. He noted that the plaintiff in that case had not been at the scene of an accident in which her husband was injured but saw him in his injured condition at the hospital. He was also guided by the decision of the House of Lords in *McLoughlin v O'Brian* [1983] 1 AC 410 in which Lord Wilberforce had said:

> "While damages cannot, at common law, be awarded for grief and sorrow, a claim for damages for nervous shock caused by negligence can be made without the necessity of showing direct impact or fear of immediate personal injuries for oneself."

Hamilton CJ pointed out that, in both *Jaensch* and *McLoughlin*, the plaintiffs were able to recover damages for nervous shock which they suffered as a result of injuries to members of their respective families which were not inflicted in their sight or hearing. He went on to say that it was sufficient that the psychiatric illness which the plaintiffs suffered were as a result of what they had seen or heard in the aftermath of the accident, at the scene, or even at the hospital where the injured relatives were taken following the accidents.

In a concurring judgment on this point, Denham J considered that the neighbour principle in *Donoghue v Stevenson* [1932] AC 562 was applicable. She said:

> "I am satisfied that a person with a close proximate relationship to an injured person, such as the plaintiff, who, while not a participant in an accident, hears of it very soon after and who visits the injured person as soon as practicable, and who is exposed to serious injuries of the primary victims in such a way as to cause a psychiatric illness, then she becomes a secondary victim to the accident."

Since it was foreseeable that a person in the plaintiff's position would suffer nervous shock as a result of the injuries sustained by her family arising from the driver's negligence, the driver was held to owe a duty of care to her. Because the plaintiff had, in the Court's view, suffered nervous shock as a result of what she had seen and been told, the driver was held to be in breach of that duty of care.

In *Curran v Cadbury Ireland Ltd* [2000] 2 ILRM 343, the plaintiff was working at a conveyor belt in the defendant's factory. The machine was turned off. Unknown to the plaintiff, there was a fitter inside the machine repairing it. The plaintiff turned on the machine and immediately became aware of a commotion and screams close to her. The plaintiff thought she had killed or seriously injured her fellow employee. She suffered psychiatric injury. The Court found that the plaintiff was a "primary victim" to whom a duty of care was owed by her employer not to cause her non-physical injury. The defendant had failed to take reasonable care for the safety of the plaintiff by failing to put in place an appropriate warning system that the machine was being repaired or to devise a system which would ensure that the machine could not be turned on while it was being repaired. The plaintiff succeeded in her claim as she had complied with the five conditions laid down by Hamilton CJ in *Kelly v Hennessy*.

In *Cuddy v Mays and Ors* [2003] IEHC 103, five young people were killed in a particularly horrific road traffic accident. The plaintiff was the porter at the hospital where the dead and injured were taken. He knew most of the victims of the accident personally. His own brother was among the dead and his sister was admitted with serious, life-threatening injuries. The Court applied Hamilton CJ's five criteria in *Kelly*.

The defendant had argued that no duty was owed to the plaintiff as it was not reasonably foreseeable that a brother of two of the victims would be the porter at the hospital that evening. This assertion was rejected by the Court. The plaintiff's employment

> "had nothing to do with the onset of nervous shock...Had he not been present on the night in question...he would almost certainly have come to the hospital...on hearing the news that his brother and sister had been involved in this...accident and would, as a matter of probability been exposed to most, if not all, of what he did actually see and experience."

The Court was satisfied that the plaintiff was in a "close proximate relationship" with the victims as required by Denham J in *Kelly*.

In *Devlin v National Maternity Hospital* [2008] 2 IR 222, the plaintiff claimed that she suffered nervous shock and post-traumatic stress disorder after learning that her daughter's organs has been unlawfully withheld by the defendant hospital after a post-mortem. Denham J confirmed that the common law had been stated by Hamilton CJ in *Kelly v Hennessy* [1995] 3 IR 253 with five conditions (see above), subsequently endorsed by Keane CJ in *Fletcher v Commissioners of Public Works* [2003] 1 IR 465. Denham J ruled that the plaintiff was not entitled to succeed because the fourth condition was not met.

E. Psychiatric Injury in the Workplace

An important and developing area of the law of negligence is the extent to which a duty of care is owed by employers to take adequate steps not to expose their employees to the risk of occupational stress and to take appropriate measures if employees suffer such stress. The English and Irish courts have addressed these matters in a number of cases.

Walker v Northumberland County Council [1995] 1 All ER 737 was the first successful claim in England by an employee for psychiatric injury resulting in a cumulative process of work-induced stress. In that case, a social services manager suffered a nervous breakdown due to his heavy workload. After some time off for recovery, he returned to work and his employer knowingly failed to reduce his workload. He suffered a second breakdown and had to cease working completely. His employer was held to be in breach of its common law duty of care owed to the plaintiff. There was no reason that psychiatric injury should not be within the scope of the employer's duty: the plaintiff's second breakdown was foreseeable and causation had been established.

In *Hatton v Sutherland* [2002] EWCA Civ 276 the English Court of Appeal set out guidelines to be applied in approaching future such claims. The approach adopted by the Court in this case was heavily relied on by the Irish High Court in *McGrath v Trintech Technologies Ltd & Anor* [2005] 4 IR 382 (below). *Hatton* was a combined claim by a number of teachers who suffered from psychological harm brought about by work-induced stress. The key points identified by the Court are:

- no jobs are inherently stressful;
- stress is a subjective concept;
- what is "reasonably foreseeable" must be determined in relation to the individual worker, rather than in a general sense;
- issues to be considered in relation to foreseeability include the nature of the work, the workload and any indications from the employee;
- unless there is evidence to the contrary, the employer is entitled to assume that the employee can cope with the normal stresses of the job;
- the precautions to be expected from the employer depend on the size of the operation, his resources, whether it is the public or private sector and the interests of other employees.

The House of Lords implicitly approved the *Hatton* guidelines in *Barber v Somerset County Council* [2004] 1 WLR 1089, while emphasising that there were, in effect, elaborations on what was fundamentally required for the "reasonable and prudent employer". In *Hartman v South Essex Mental Health NHS Trust* [2005] EWCA Civ 6 the first of the *Hatton* guidelines was confirmed in denying liability to a nurse who worked with children with learning disabilities.

In *Melville v Home Office* [2005] ICR 782, the Court held that there had been a breach of duty when a prison health care worker had not been offered support and counselling following distressing involvement in suicides, but *Daw v Intel* [2007]

EWCA Civ 70 confirmed that merely offering an employee counselling services would not be sufficient to discharge a duty of care in all cases.

In *McGrath v Trintech Technologies Ltd & Anor*, the High Court considered a claim for compensation for psychiatric or psychological damage alleged to have been negligently caused by workplace stress. The defendant employers were involved in the information technology sector and operated on a worldwide basis. The plaintiff was employed by them. He was sent to work abroad for a five-month period in 2003. During that time he claimed he was subjected to serious work-related stress which resulted in psychological injury. The Court held that the principles governing an employer's liability at common law for physical injury should be applied equally to liability for psychiatric injury where an employee claimed that the psychiatric injury had resulted from the stress and pressures of working conditions and workload. The appropriate test in relation to psychiatric injury claims was, firstly whether the employee suffered an injury to health, as distinct from occupational stress and secondly whether, as a matter of probability, it was attributable, in part at least, to stress at work as distinct from other factors. The Court followed *Walker v Northumberland County Council, Hatton v Sutherland* and *Barber v Somerset County Council* (see above) in so holding.

F. Future Development

The English Law Commission reported in 1998 on the state of the law relating to psychiatric injury within the law of negligence. Broadly, it recommended that the development of the law in respect of primary victims could be left the courts. However, in respect of secondary victims, other than rescuers or "involuntary participants", legislation should be considered which would bring about the following changes:

- remove the requirement for sudden shock, thereby opening up possible liability to plaintiffs whose condition has developed over time;
- the second and third of the *Alcock* criteria would no longer be required, so that plaintiffs might be successful even if they were not near to an event or its immediate aftermath and perceiving it with their own unaided senses; and
- the first of the *Alcock* criteria, that of the requirement for close ties of love and affection with the direct victim, would be maintained as a condition of liability, but the category of those relationships in which these ties would be presumed would be expanded; the group should include spouses, parents, children, siblings and cohabitees of at least two years. See: *Liability for Psychiatric Illness* (Law Com 249, 1999).

BREACH OF DUTY: THE STANDARD OF CARE

Learning Outcomes

Upon completion of this chapter, the reader should be able to:

- Explain the nature of the objective standard in determining the standard of care;
- Understand characteristics of the "reasonable person";
- Outline the factors pertaining to the defendant in determining the standard of care;
- Outline the factors extraneous to the defendant in determining the standard of care;
- Understand the distinctive approach adopted in determining the standard of care in professional cases;
- Discuss the legal tests applicable for standard of care in medical negligence cases.

A. Overview

As we have seen in chapter 2, the tort of negligence involves the existence of a duty of care, breach of that duty, damage and causation. These are the four key ingredients of the tort. In the absence of any one of them, the plaintiff cannot maintain an action in negligence. Thus, whilst the defendant may owe a duty of care to the plaintiff, if the defendant does not breach that duty, the plaintiff cannot succeed in his or her claim.

Figure 5.1

Duty of care + Breach of duty + Damage + Causation in fact and law = Action in negligence

Breach of duty in the negligence equation

Whether or not the defendant has breached his duty of care towards the plaintiff is a mixed one of law and fact. Having said that, the standard of care required of the defendant is essentially a legal construct, determined by the courts, as we will see below, as being that of a hypothetical reasonable person. To put it another way, if the defendant does something that causes loss and injury to the plaintiff, he may be able to avoid liability if he can show that he acted in the way in which a reasonable person would have acted. Accordingly, whether or not the defendant has breached his duty towards the plaintiff is largely determined by the standard of care the defendant is required to reach. If the defendant falls below the required standard, he will be considered to have breached his duty towards the plaintiff. But what is that standard and how is it set? In approaching this question, the courts consider the range of factors relevant to establishing the required standard. Within these parameters there will, on the one hand, be factors which pertain to the defendant himself and, on the other hand, contextual, or extraneous, factors which relate to the particular circumstances in which the act was done.

B. Factors Relevant to Establishing the Required Standard

Figure 5.2

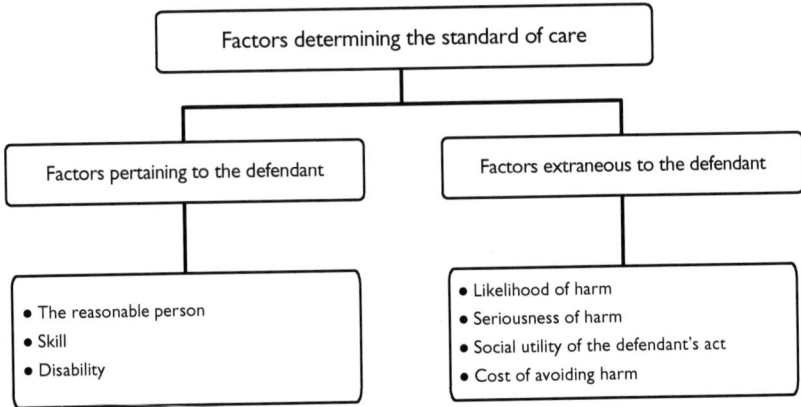

Factors determining the standard of care

Factors pertaining to the defendant

Factors extraneous to the defendant

- The reasonable person
- Skill
- Disability

- Likelihood of harm
- Seriousness of harm
- Social utility of the defendant's act
- Cost of avoiding harm

Factors Pertaining to the Defendant
The Reasonable Person

In *Blyth v Birmingham Waterworks Co* (1856) 11 Ex Ch 781, 156 ER 1047, the Court stated:

> "Negligence is the omission to do something which a reasonable person, guided upon those considerations which ordinarily regulate the conduct of human affairs, would do or doing something which a prudent and reasonable person would not do."

We can see from this definition that the standard of care is not the standard of the defendant himself, but of a reasonable person, one of ordinary prudence, a person using ordinary care and skill. The "reasonable person" is not real, but rather a hypothetical person. The standard of this hypothetical person was visualised by Lord Bowen as "the man on the Clapham omnibus" (see *McQuire v Western Morning News Co Ltd* [1903] 2 KB 100 per Collins MR). Gavan Duffy J in *Kirby v Burke* [1944] IR 207 represented the reasonable person in this way:

> "... the foundation of liability at common law for tort is blameworthiness as defined by the existing average standards of the community; a man fails at his peril to conform to these standards. Therefore, while loss from accident generally lies where it falls, a defendant cannot plead accident if, treated as a man of ordinary intelligence and foresight, he ought to have foreseen the danger which caused injury to his plaintiff."

In *Glasgow Corporation v Muir* [1943] AC 448 Lord Macmillan said:

> "Legal liability is limited to those consequences of acts which a reasonable man of ordinary intelligence and experience so acting would have in contemplation... The standard of foresight of the reasonable man is, in one sense, an impersonal test. It eliminates the personal equation and is independent of the idiosyncrasies of the particular person whose conduct is in question. Some persons are by nature unduly timorous and imagine every path beset by lions. Others, of more robust temperament, fail to foresee or nonchalantly disregard even the most obvious dangers. The reasonable man is presumed to be free both from over apprehension and from overconfidence, but there is a sense in which the standard of care of the reasonable man involves in its application a subjective element. It is still left to the judge to decide what, in the circumstances of the particular case, the reasonable man would have had in contemplation, and what, accordingly, the parties sought to be made liable ought to have foreseen."

The standard of care, therefore, is objectively determined. However, that is not to say that no reference is made to the particular defendant. When a person holds himself or herself out as being capable of attaining standards of skill in relation to the public generally, for example, by driving a car, he or she is required to display the skill normally possessed by persons doing that task. It is immaterial if the defendant does not in fact have that skill: if he or she engages in conduct usually associated with persons having the skill, the standard demanded is that of those who actually do possess the skill.

We can see the application of the objective standard in *Nettleship v Weston* [1971] 2 QB 691. In that case, the defendant asked the plaintiff, a friend, to teach her to drive. He agreed only after ensuring that he was covered under the defendant's comprehensive car insurance policy. During the course of a lesson and when the defendant was driving, she failed to straighten the car after having turned a corner with the result that it mounted the pavement and hit a lamppost. The plaintiff broke his kneecap as a result of the collision and sued for negligence. Lord Denning MR said that the civil law does not permit a driver to say: "I was a learner driver under instruction. I was doing my best and could not help it". He pointed out that a learner driver may be doing his best, but

> "his incompetent best is not good enough. He must drive in as good a manner as a driver of skill, experience and care, who is sound in mind and limb, who makes no errors of judgment, has good eyesight and hearing, and is free from any infirmity."

In other words, the defendant owed a duty of care to the plaintiff and that duty had been breached. The standard of care is measured objectively and it is the standard of care to be expected of an experienced, skilled and careful driver. No allowances can be made for the incompetence of the driver. The duty owed to other road users remained that of a careful qualified driver. To do otherwise would be to deny other road users protection from drivers who do not reach the required standard of competence. In *Nettleship*, the Court found for the plaintiff but reduced his damages by 50% for contributory negligence.

Skill

As mentioned above, where a person undertakes to do a particular thing, that person is required to display the skill and competence normally possessed by a person doing that thing. For example, a doctor making a clinical error cannot excuse himself by showing that he acted to the best of his skill if a reasonable doctor would not have made that error. Nor can a young hospital doctor avoid liability by arguing that he is inexperienced or overworked. He is obliged to attain the level of competence expected of a person holding his "post" and entrusted with his responsibilities. In relation to persons with special skill, however, it is important to realise that where such a person conforms to practices accepted as proper by only some responsible members of his profession, he will not be held liable in negligence merely because other members of his profession would have done things differently. This situation may arise in medical negligence cases in particular where there will often be a difference in opinion as to how a particular medical problem should be treated.

Phillips v William Whiteley Ltd [1938] 1 All ER 566 was a case where the plaintiff had her ears pierced by a jeweller and subsequently contracted a disease that might have been avoided had the work been done with normal medical skill. The Court held that the jeweller was required only to show the skill of a jeweller doing such work, not that of a doctor. Similarly, in *Wells v Cooper* [1958] 2 QB 265, a householder fitted a new door handle in his house insecurely. When the plaintiff used it, he lost his balance and suffered injury. The defendant householder was only required to show the standard of care of a normal DIY enthusiast, not that of a qualified carpenter.

It is important to bear in mind that skill, just like every other aspect of the standard of care test, has to be assessed in the context of all the circumstances surrounding the alleged breach of duty, and the extent to which the defendant represents that he or she holds a particular skill is only one of those several considerations. Interestingly, in *Woolridge v Sumner* [1962] 2 All ER 978, the Court considered that where someone has not held himself out as having special skill, he will not be liable when he shows merely average skill when carrying out the task, even though he does in fact have that special skill. In that case, a show jumper was concentrating his attention and focusing his skill to complete his round of the show jumping circuit when his horse, on a tight bend, plunged through the perimeter and injured the plaintiff. The Court took the view that the rider had made an error of judgment and was not negligent.

However, in *Condon v Basi* [1985] 2 All ER 453, a footballer suffered a broken leg as a result of a tackle by the defendant which was found by the referee to be serious foul play. The English Court of Appeal held that a clear breach of the rules of the game would be a relevant, but not conclusive, consideration in deciding whether there had been a breach of duty. In this case, the plaintiff succeeded in his claim. The same Court, in *Caldwell v Maguire* [2002] PIQR P 6, subsequently confirmed that the test is whether the defendant's disregard for the plaintiff's safety can be characterised as deliberate or reckless — bearing in mind the level of competency to be expected from players of the defendant's class — in which case the defendant will be held to be in breach.

Disability

Clearly, the relentless application of an objective standard will place persons under a disability at a disadvantage. Therefore, the courts will take into account the disposition of such persons in setting the standard of care in cases where they are defendants. The law does not require persons under a disability to achieve "the impossible by conforming to physical standards which [they] cannot meet" (Prosser and Keeton on Torts, West Publishing Co, 5th Ed, 1 Jan 1999). That is not to say, however, that a person with a physical disability can conduct himself without regard to his disability. Thus, a visually impaired motorist, who collides with another car because he fails to see it, will not be allowed to plead his lack of sight as an excuse. In this example, the defendant will have caused injury to the plaintiff, and will be considered negligent, not because of want of care at the time of the accident, but because, being aware of his lack of sight, he was careless enough to drive in the first place.

In *Mansfield v Weetabix Ltd* [1980] 1 All ER 7, a lorry driver was involved in a collision when he partially lost consciousness as a result of a hypoglycaemic state which was induced by a malignant condition of which he was totally unaware. The English Court of Appeal held that, where a disability or infirmity prevented the defendant from meeting the objective standard of care, and the defendant was not, and could not reasonably have been, aware of his condition, that condition must be taken into account in determining whether or not the defendant was negligent. A similar approach was taken by the Irish courts in *Counihan v Bus Átha Cliath* [2005] 2 IR 436. In that case, two pedestrians were injured when a bus, driven by the defendant's driver, veered off the road, mounted the footpath, and struck them. The driver had suffered from a condition that led, without forewarning, to a blackout. The Court dismissed the plaintiffs' claim, observing that a driver remains under a duty of care, after the onset of symptoms, to do his best to control the difficult situation in which he finds himself. There was no evidence of any failure on the part of the driver in this particular case to so act.

Factors Extraneous to the Defendant

An attempt to provide a systematic approach to the factors relevant in assessing the defendant's negligence was provided by the American judge Learned Hand J in *United States v Carroll Towing Co* (1947) 159 F 2d 169. He held that a decision as to whether particular conduct was negligent required consideration of three factors:

- the probability that the event would happen ("P");
- the gravity of the injury that would be caused if the event occurred ("L"); and
- the cost of preventing the event ("B").

This became known as the "Learned Hand formula" and held that there was a breach where $B < PL$, i.e. where the cost of preventing the injury was less than the cost of the injury discounted by the probability of it happening. This formula has been characterised by scholars as an example of the "economic analysis of law". In other words, liability would be imposed where it was economically efficient to do so (see Posner, "A Theory of Negligence" (1972) 1 J Leg Stud 29).

We have seen that the standard which the law requires a person to attain must be objectively determined. A person will be regarded as negligent if he or she fails to act according to that standard, even if it is more difficult for him or her as an individual to do so than for others. The reason for this is that we are all entitled to expect a certain level of protection from the acts of others. So the concept of the "reasonable person" does two things: it judges whether the defendant was careless and attempts to find the level of safety the plaintiff is entitled to expect.

Whilst the standard of the reasonable person gives some substance to the concept of negligence, a number of more specific indicators have been identified in an attempt to elaborate more specifically what is or is not reasonable in the particular circumstances. Four factors in particular have been discussed in the decisions and the commentaries on negligence. These are:

(a) the likelihood of harm;
(b) the seriousness of harm;

(c)   the social utility of the defendant's act; and

(d)   the relative cost of avoiding the harm.

Before considering each of these factors, it is important to bear in mind that none of them contains any particular predetermined "weight" relative to any of the others. Ultimately, the determination of what constitutes unreasonable conduct involves a value judgement. These four factors highlight the factual considerations on which that value judgment is to be based, but they do not of themselves contain the resolution of the negligence issue.

The Likelihood of Harm

The general principle is: the more likely the risk is to manifest itself, the greater the need for precaution to be taken. Lord Wright in *Northwestern Utilities Ltd v London Guarantee and Accident Co Ltd* [1936] AC 108 said:

> "The degree of care which that duty involves must be proportioned to the degree of risk involved if the duty of care should not be fulfilled."

Therefore, the likelihood of harm occurring is primarily a question of fact to be determined according to the particular circumstances of the case. The leading case of *Bolton v Stone* [1951] AC 850 provides a useful example. There, Mrs Stone was hit by a cricket ball in Cheetham Hill, Manchester. The ball had been struck from a cricket ground surrounded by a fence 17 feet above the level of the square. The batsman was 80 yards away. The ball was only the sixth in about thirty years to be hit out of the ground. The House of Lords held that there had been no breach of duty by the club in allowing cricket to be played without taking further precautions. The Court emphasised two points: first, the fact that the ball had to clear the fence which itself was a remote possibility and, second, that, having cleared the fence the ball would then have to strike a passer-by — an even more remote possibility. Lord Oaksey observed:

> "an ordinarily careful man does not take precautions against every foreseeable risk ... life would be almost impossible if he were to attempt to take precautions against every risk."

In essence, the Court in *Bolton v Stone* considered that the chance of harm occurring was so small that a reasonable person in the position of the cricket club could not be expected to take additional precautions against such a remote possibility. By contrast, in *Hilder v Associated Portland Cement Manufacturers Ltd* [1961] 1 WLR 1434, where the risk of injury to a road user from a football being kicked from a patch of open ground was much greater, the defendant responsible for the land was held to be in breach of a duty of care. Similarly, in *Miller v Jackson*

[1977] QB 966 the breach of duty occurred where cricket balls were struck out of the ground about eight or nine times every season.

In *Sullivan v Creed* [1904] 2 IR 317, liability was imposed on the defendant in leaving a loaded gun where his son was likely to find it and use it without due care. In meddling with the gun, the defendant's son pointed and fired it at the plaintiff, who lost an eye. Fitzgibbon LJ said

> "To suggest that a man who left a loaded gun on full cock against the fence of the pathway to his house in full view of every passer-by, is not guilty of negligence, is contrary to my estimate of the judgment of ordinary men."

In *Healy v Bray UDC* [1962-1963] Ir Jur 9, the plaintiff was injured by a loose rock which became dislodged and rolled down Bray Head and through a gap in a surrounding wall before hitting her. Liability in negligence was not imposed on the defendant Council. Kingsmill Moore J stated: "the combination of all these unlikely events seem to me to reduce the risk to such minute proportions that the Council cannot be held negligent".

Similarly, in *O'Gorman v Ritz (Clonmel) Ltd* [1947] Ir Jur Rep 35, the plaintiff, a patron at the defendant's cinema, stretched out her legs under the seat in front of her, in which another person was sitting. When that person stood up, his seat's mechanism caught the plaintiff's leg, causing a severe cut. The injury became septic and the plaintiff required medical treatment for some two months. Evidence adduced to the Court disclosed that, in the previous seven years, approximately 1,000,000 people had used the parterre seats in the defendant's cinema. During that time, no complaint had been received regarding the seats. The plaintiff's action was dismissed. The Court took the view that to guard against such a remote eventuality as that which led to the plaintiff's injuries would have required precautions of such a nature as could not reasonably be expected in the construction or management of a theatre.

The *Ritz* decision was invoked in *Walsh v Dublin Corporation* (23 July 1998). There, a visitor to a flat suffered injury when a door from the hallway to the kitchen slammed shut, injuring her thumb. She sued the landlord, the local authority. It appears that there was a "wind tunnel effect" when this particular door and the doors at the front and back of the flat were open at the same time. The plaintiff contended that a mechanism restraining the door should have been in place. Dismissing the plaintiff's claim, the Court held that the apartment in question was "small and compact" and space was "at a premium". The accident, the Court considered, was one that could befall any person at any time, whether in their own home or elsewhere.

The Seriousness of Harm

As we have seen, the likelihood of harm affects the standard of care demanded — so too does the seriousness of that harm. In *Paris v Stepney Borough Council* [1950] 1 KB 320, the House of Lords held that the gravity of the consequences of an accident befalling an already disabled man had to be taken into account in fixing the level of care required of the defendant. In that case, the plaintiff was employed as a fitter in a garage owned by the defendant Council. The Council knew that the plaintiff had the use of only one eye. While he was using a hammer to remove a bolt on a vehicle, a chip of metal flew off and entered his good eye. It was so seriously injured that he lost the sight in that eye, becoming totally blind. The defendant did not provide him with goggles to wear, and there was evidence that it was not the ordinary practice for employers to supply goggles to men employed in garages on the maintenance and repair of vehicles. This case was decided in favour of the plaintiff on a 3-2 majority of the House of Lords. The minority thought that there was no breach of duty on the facts of the case. This dissent was premised on the proposition that the risk to the plaintiff was not materially greater than that to the other workers engaged in the same task: such an accident would be serious in its consequences to any worker whether he had one eye or two eyes — and it was a risk which could reasonably be run. The majority, however, reflected in their judgments the broader view that the content of the defendant's duty of care must be tailored to the known, or reasonably foreseeable, characteristics of the individual plaintiff. An issue such as this arises not only where the plaintiff is at risk of more serious injury than other potential victims of the tort, but also where the risk is more likely to occur.

Where the potential for injury is greater than normal, the creation of even a slight risk may amount to negligence. In *Hughes v Ballynahinch Gas Co* (1898) 33 ILTR 74, in imposing liability on a gas company for injuries sustained in a gas explosion, the Court noted that:

> "… escapes of gas are matters most dangerous to human life, and, therefore, the highest degree of reasonable care is that which is due by this company that makes its living by supplying gas to the public."

The Social Utility of the Defendant's Act

The courts will take into account any relevant social utility associated with the defendant's conduct. This involves determining the general public interest in respect of the activity which gives rise to the injury. *Daborn v Bath Tramways Motor Co Ltd* [1946] 2 All ER 333 is a good illustration of this. In that case, the question before the Court was whether, in wartime England, the driver of a left-hand drive ambulance had been negligent in turning into a lane on the offside of the road without giving a signal. Holding that the driver had not breached the relevant standard, Asquith LJ, in encapsulating the key principles that the courts consider in determining the level at which the standard of care in any particular set of circumstances should be fixed, said:

> "In determining whether a party is negligent, the standard of reasonable care is that which is reasonably to be demanded in the circumstances. A relevant circumstance to take into account may be the importance of the end to be served by behaving in this way or that. As has often been pointed out, if all the trains in this country were restricted to a speed of five miles an hour, there would be fewer accidents, but our national life would be intolerably slowed down. The purpose to be served, if sufficiently important, justified the assumption of abnormal risk. The relevance of this applied to the present case is this: during the war which was, at the material time, in progress, it was necessary for many highly important operations to be carried out by means of motor vehicles with left-hand drives, no others being available. So far as this was the case, it was impossible for the drivers of such cars to give the warning signals which could otherwise be properly demanded of them. Meanwhile, it was essential that the ambulance service should be maintained. It seems to me, in those circumstances, it would be demanding too high and an unreasonable standard of care from the drivers of such cars to say to them: 'Either you must give signals which the structure of your vehicle renders impossible or you must not drive at all'."

Echoing the realities given expression by Asquith LJ in *Daborn*, Kingsmill Moore J, in *Christie v Odeon (Ireland) Ltd* (1957) 91 ILTR 25 observed: "to make accidents impossible would often be to make work impossible".

This pragmatic approach was similarly adopted by the Court in *Whooley v Dublin Corporation* [1961] IR 60. There, the plaintiff sustained injuries when she put her foot into an open fire hydrant box when she was walking along the footpath of a Dublin Street. The lid of the box appeared to have been removed by a third party. The box was designed so as to be easily accessible by the Fire Brigade in the case of fire. Accordingly, it was capable of being removed without difficulty. The Court took the view that "no other type of hydrant which could be devised, consistent with its necessary purpose, would be safe from ... malicious interference". The plaintiff's claim was dismissed.

Socially desirable objectives, such as the provision of home-helps, can operate to determine the standard of care in particular cases. In *Mulcare v Southern Health Board* [1988] ILRM 689, the plaintiff worked as a home-help for an elderly woman as an employee of the defendant health board. She twisted her ankle on an uneven part of the elderly woman's floor. The Court addressed the issue as to whether the health board had failed in its duty of reasonable care to the plaintiff in not having inspected the premises to ensure that it was safe for the employment of home-helps. The Court held that whilst a duty might exist, "at most", to inspect the premises, there was no duty to bring it up to a modern standard. The Court also found, as a matter of fact, that the house was not dangerously unsafe and therefore liability was not imposed on the defendants.

Where a defendant is faced with an emergency situation, where, for example, there may be little time for reflective decision-making, he or she may fall below the standard of care normally expected of him or her. But it is equally the case, that where the defendant may act incautiously in such circumstances, if he or she is acting with a view to assisting others, the courts, it appears, will provide a good deal of latitude to such defendants. In *Watt v Hertfordshire County Council* [1954] 2 All ER 368, the fire service was called upon to save a woman who was trapped under an overturned lorry. In order to do so, it needed to use a heavy jack that stood on wheels. The vehicle needed to transport it was unavailable. It was tried instead to get the jack to the accident using a different, but less suitable, vehicle. While en route, the driver of the vehicle made an emergency stop. This caused the jack to shoot forwards whereupon it injured the plaintiff, one of the firemen. The Court held that, given the short amount of time the fire service had to act, and in view of the efforts it was making to save the woman, there was no breach of duty to the plaintiff.

Likewise, in *Hayes v Minister for Finance* [2007] IESC 8 the Court took into account the important social objectives of the Gardaí in tackling crime. In that case, members of the Gardaí in a patrol car pursued a motorcycle which failed to stop at a speed trap. The motorcycle eventually crashed injuring the plaintiff, the pillion passenger. In seeking to determine the standard of care owed to the plaintiff in that particular set of circumstances, Kearns J said:

> "... it is obvious that the Gardaí may owe different standards of care in a pursuit situation depending on the particular circumstances. For example, if there are good grounds for believing the perpetrator of a recent bank robbery is attempting to escape, the standard of 'the duty owed to such a person may obviously be less than in the case of a trivial offender, particularly if the surrounding circumstances create particular risks in continuing the pursuit.'"

It should be remembered, that an emergency does not exonerate the defendant from displaying any level of care at all: all it does is reduce the standard demanded of the defendant. Therefore, if an emergency response vehicle is driven recklessly through a red light en route to an accident, there may still be a breach of duty: see *Ward v London County Council* [1938] 2 All ER 341 and *King v Sussex Ambulance NHS Trust* [2002] ICR 1413, where Buxton LJ expressed some disquiet about the approach adopted in *Watt v Hertfordshire County Council*, which, he thought, placed workers in the public sector, in particular those in the emergency services, at something of a disadvantage compared to those in the private sector.

The importance of socially utilitarian objectives was also considered in *Tomlinson v Congleton Borough Council* [2004] 1 AC 46. In that case, the plaintiff suffered catastrophic injuries when he waded into a lake at the defendant Council's country park, threw himself forward in a dive and hit his head on the sandy bottom. The lake was a popular local amenity, used for various water sports and by families for picnicking and sunbathing. The Council prohibited swimming because it was considered dangerous. It displayed warning notices, distributed warning leaflets and employed rangers to enforce the no-swimming policy. Despite these efforts, many visitors continued to swim in the lake. In response to this, the Council decided to make it impossible for people to swim in the lake. They covered the beaches with soil and established reed beds in their place, thereby effectively destroying the amenity for the community. The plaintiff took an action against the Council under the English Occupiers' Liability Act 1957 and 1984. He succeeded in the Court of Appeal but lost in the House of Lords. The House of Lords criticised the approach of the Council and emphasised the cost to society of "compensation culture" as being not simply pecuniary, because here the community had lost a valuable amenity: and the approach adopted by the Court of Appeal undermined personal autonomy and individual liberty (i.e. the right of individuals to expose themselves to risk of injury). This case brought into sharp focus the relevance of social utility in the determination of whether or not the defendant has exercised due care.

The Relative Cost of Avoiding the Harm

In determining the standard of care, the courts also take into account how extensive and costly it would be to eliminate the risk. In effect, there is a balancing of costs as between averting a danger measured against the cost of the danger transpiring. The issue of unreasonable costs of prevention was considered in *Latimer v AEC Ltd* [1952] 2 QB 701. In that case, the defendants owned a factory in the floor of which there was a channel through which there flowed an oily cooling agent. One day the factory flooded. When the flood had subsided the floor was covered with a thin film of the oily mixture. The defendants put sawdust down on most, but not all, of the floor. The plaintiff slipped and fell on a part of the floor without sawdust. The plaintiff claimed that the defendants should have closed the factory. The English Court of Appeal held that the defendants were not liable as they had acted as a reasonable employer would have acted. In other words, the defendant was not obliged to eliminate the risk completely, only to take reasonable steps to do so.

In *Sutherland v Supervalu* (11 March 1999) CC, a six-year-old girl's arm became trapped in a conveyor belt when she was helping her mother place goods on the conveyor belt at a checkout in a supermarket. The shopkeeper was held not to have been negligent. The Court found that it would impose an unreasonable duty of care on shopkeepers to require them to continuously police children helping their mothers putting goods on conveyor belts at supermarket checkouts.

Many proprietors of licensed premises find themselves subject to "slipping claims" where patrons slip on floors which have become wet through spillages of drinks. In *McSweeney v An Garda Síochána Boat Club* (5 June 1991), the defendant had allowed patrons to bring glasses of drink into an area where dancing took place. Inevitably, drinks were spilled from time to time. The plaintiff slipped on the dance floor and sustained injury. Liability was not imposed. The Court accepted the defendant's evidence as to their system of cleaning up after the spillages, concluding that any spillage could have been there only for a very short length of time and that it would be a "counsel of perfection" to expect such spills to be cleaned up immediately. Similarly, in *O'Connell v Breanagh Catering Limited t/a Copper Face Jacks* [2013] IEHC, the plaintiff had her claim against a nightclub dismissed. The Court considered that the important question was, not whether the floor was wet, but whether it was slippery. The Court found that whilst the floor may have been wet, it was not slippery. The plaintiff's claim was dismissed. However, in *Moore v Westwood Club Ltd* [2014] IEHC 44 the Court found in favour of the plaintiff despite noting a regulated system of maintenance in operation on the night of the accident. The plaintiff fell and injured her finger. The Court found that the cleaning and maintenance system so carefully set up by the defendants failed to operate effectively on the night of the accident. The plaintiff was awarded €56,000 in damages.

In *Barclay v An Post* [1999] 2 ILRM 385 the plaintiff suffered back injury which, he claimed, was a consequence of having to deliver letters to premises with letterboxes at the base of the door. The defendant employer had sought from the Department of the Environment the introduction of regulations to remedy this situation. In addition, the employer had provided a training course in manual handling for its employees. The Court held that the defendant had done all that it reasonably could have done to protect its employees. Liability was not imposed.

In *Connaughton v Minister for Justice, Equality and Law Reform* [2012] IEHC 203, the plaintiff, a prison officer, was injured in a prison when tea spilled from a floor above causing him to slip and fall. It appeared that a prisoner on an upper landing had accidentally spilled the tea. The plaintiff's claim in negligence was dismissed. The Court found that there had been in place an orderly system for the dispatch of tea which reduced the risk of congestion. The employer had not breached its duty of care towards the plaintiff.

As we have seen, the courts examine the extent to which the defendant has acted reasonably in seeking to discharge its duty of care to the plaintiff in deciding whether or not to impose liability. Two cases with similar facts, but which were decided differently, illustrate the courts' approach. In *Corkery v Bus Eireann* (6 May 2003) SC, a bus driver in Cork suffered injury when he was attacked by a robber. Evidence was given of previous incidents involving injuries to bus drivers in Cork. The Court said that the danger to drivers was reasonably foreseeable and could, and should, have been reduced or obviated by the practical solution of installing protective screens, particularly as the cost was minimal as compared with the time lost and distress caused by avoidable injury to drivers. Liability was imposed on the defendant employer for negligence and breach of statutory duty for its failure to provide drivers with adequate protection from the risk of being attacked when driving the bus.

In *Rogers v Bus Átha Cliath* (17 January 2000) CC, a similar attack on a bus driver in Dublin in 1995 had occurred. Liability was not imposed on the defendant employer in failing to provide a screen for the driver because it had taken reasonable steps to protect its drivers. It had spent considerable amounts of money in trying to design an acceptable screen and had continuously discussed the proposed solutions with the employees and unions. Initially the models for screens had proved too claustrophobic or had caused a glare from the Perspex surround: a later model had been found not to be sufficiently secure. Eventually, in the middle of 1995, an agreed model had been adopted and all new buses were fitted with it. In the Court's view, the steps were sufficient to discharge the duty of care.

C. Professional Negligence

Overview
There is no distinction in principle between the guidelines determining the standard of care for professionals from those applicable to other persons. Whether the defendant is an electrician or doctor, the primary question is whether in all the circumstances the defendant acted with the skill and competence to be expected from a person undertaking his particular activity and professing his specific skill.

However, professionals can be distinguished from other categories of person in a number of ways. Perhaps most importantly, there may not be full agreement within a particular profession as to what constitutes proper practice. This means that an approach adopted by a minority of members of a given profession may not be negligent just because a significant number of their fellow professionals would have done things differently. This approach is exemplified in *Maynard v West Midlands Regional Health Authority* [1984] 1 WLR 634 where the House of Lords held that a doctor's exercise of clinical judgment in a manner thought appropriate by a body of competent medical opinion could not be regarded as negligent simply because the trial judge "preferred" an alternative body of medical opinion. Also, the consequences of professional negligence are potentially more serious and far-reaching than for other categories of negligence. For instance, if a carpenter makes an error installing a new door, a person standing nearby may suffer personal injury if the door falls from its frame. However, if an architect makes an error in the plans for a skyscraper, the consequences for the occupants of the building could be catastrophic and the financial cost could be enormous. In addition, the high cost of professional negligence claims has led, in particular in the medical and legal fields, to significant increases in insurance premiums for those sectors. Doctors face particular difficulties in respect of professional negligence claims in that the difficult working conditions in public hospitals has resulted in doctors becoming overworked and stressed, thereby potentially affecting their ability to achieve the highest standards of care. Moreover, since professional defendants are more likely to have professional indemnity insurance cover, they are likely to be "worth suing". The other side of this particular coin is that insurance companies that provide such insurance are more likely to vigorously defend actions taken against the professionals they have insured.

Duty of Care and Breach of Duty

Professional relationships, such as doctor-patient relationships and solicitor-client relationships, give rise, in most cases, to relationships in contract also. The question as to whether a contractual relationship precludes the plaintiff taking an action in tort was addressed in *Finlay v Murtagh* [1979] IR 249. In that case, the plaintiff claimed damages from his solicitor, the defendant, in the tort of negligence. The plaintiff alleged that his solicitor was negligent in failing to institute an action on his behalf against a third party within the limitation period. The question for the court was whether there was a cause of action in tort, or whether the plaintiff was confined to taking the action in contract. The Court found for the plaintiff, holding that it was permissible to take an action in tort.

The matter was put to rest in England by the House of Lords in *Henderson v Merrett Syndicates Ltd* [1995] 2 AC 145. There, their Lordships ruled in favour of concurrent liability, provided that imposing a duty in tort does not conflict with the contractual terms agreed between the parties. When duties of care in contract and tort do arise concurrently, the question of whether there has been a breach of duty would generally be determined on exactly the same principles, whether the action is framed in tort or contract. It is important to bear in mind that it is possible for a contract to impose duties beyond those covered by the duty of care in tort.

The case of *Thake v Maurice* [1986] QB 644 before the English Court of Appeal illustrates this point. A surgeon failed to warn a private patient of the risk that a vasectomy could reverse. The patient's wife conceived. The patient argued that the surgeon contracted to render him sterile and that he was therefore liable for that breach of contract regardless of whether he was negligent. The Court of Appeal held, by a majority, that no reasonable man would infer from his contract with the doctor that the doctor guaranteed success. But the Court of Appeal unanimously held the surgeon liable in negligence. The failure to warn was held to be negligent. This case illustrates the separate roles of tort and contract where the plaintiff seeks to establish liability independent of the tort of negligence.

Medical Negligence

The general parameters of medical negligence were set out in *O'Donovan v Cork County Council* [1967] IR 173:

> "A medical practitioner cannot be held negligent if he follows general and approved practice in the situation with which he is faced. That proposition is not, however, without qualification. If there is a common practice which has inherent defects, which ought to be obvious to any person giving the matter due consideration, the fact that it is shown to have been widely and generally adopted over a period of time does not make the practice any the less negligent. Neglect of duty does not cease by repetition to be neglect of duty."

Whether or not a particular practice is a general and approved practice is a matter of fact to be determined by the court. If some medical witnesses say that a particular practice is a general and approved practice and other medical witnesses say that it is not, then it is an issue of fact, like any other issue of fact, to be determined by the court.

In *Roach v Peilow* [1986] ILRM 189, the Court stated:

> "The professional man is...not to be judged with the benefit of hindsight, but if it can be said that, if at the time, and giving the matter due consideration, he would have realised that the impugned practice was in the circumstances incompatible with

this client's interest, and if an alternative and safer course of conduct was reasonably open to him, he will be held to have been negligent."

The Supreme Court in *Dunne v National Maternity Hospital* [1989] IR 91 established the authoritative statement as to the standard of care expected of medical practitioners in Ireland and as to what constitutes a "general and approved practice". The *Dunne* test seeks to achieve a balance between ensuring that medical practitioners can practice without the constant fear of litigation on the one hand, and, on the other hand, that the rights of patients to an appropriate standard of care in diagnosis and treatment are protected.

1. "The true test for establishing negligence in diagnosis or treatment on the part of a medical practitioner is whether he has been proved to be guilty of such failure as no medical practitioner of equal specialist or general status and skill would be guilty of if acting with ordinary care;

2. If the allegation of negligence against a medical practitioner is based on proof that he deviated from a general and approved practice, that will not establish negligence unless it is also proved that the course he did take was one which no medical practitioner of like specialisation and skill would have followed had he been taking the ordinary care required from a person of his qualifications;

3. If a medical practitioner charged with negligence defends his conduct by establishing that he followed a practice which was general, and which was approved of by his colleagues of similar specialisation and skill, he cannot escape liability if in reply the plaintiff establishes that such practice has inherent defects which ought to be obvious to any person giving the matter due consideration;

4. An honest difference of opinion between doctors as to which is the better of two ways of treating a patient does not provide any ground for leaving a question to the jury as to whether a person who has followed one course rather than the other has been negligent;

5. It is not for a jury (or for a judge) to decide which of two alternative courses of treatment is in their (or his) opinion preferable, but their (or his) function is merely to decide whether the course of treatment followed, on the evidence, complied with the careful conduct of a medical practitioner of like specialisation and skill to that professed by the defendant;

6. If there is an issue of fact, the determination of which is necessary for the decision as to whether a particular medical practice is or is not general and approved within the meaning of these principles, that issue must in a trial held with a jury be left to the determination of the jury."

The Court further held that for a practice to be "general and approved" it need not be universal but must be approved of and adhered to by a substantial number of reputable practitioners holding the relevant specialist or general qualifications. Where certain statements of principle have referred to "treatment" only, those principles must apply in identical fashion to questions of diagnosis.

In propositions 1 and 2, the Court makes reference to "no medical practitioner" of equal specialisation and skill. This does not mean that if the defendant can find one single medical practitioner who would have done as he had done, liability could not be imposed — subject, of course, to the "inherent defects" qualification. Even if that were so, that single medical practitioner would have to pass the test of ordinary care also.

The reference in proposition 2 to an "honest" difference of opinion between doctors as to how best to treat a patient does not provide an exemption from liability where the belief is honest but unreasonable.

The Courts Act 1988 abolished juries for personal injuries litigation. This would appear to render proposition 4 otiose. However, it may still have relevance in that the trial judge may dismiss a claim at the conclusion of the plaintiff's evidence.

In *Dunne*, the plaintiff alleged negligence in the management of his mother's labour and of his birth, resulting in his sustaining brain damage. At trial, the jury awarded the plaintiff £1,039,334 in damages. The Supreme Court held that the trial judge had erred in his direction to the jury in failing to make it clear that deviation from general and approved practice would constitute negligence only if no other hospital medical administrator or consultant obstetrician would have so deviated if he were taking the appropriate ordinary care, and that adherence to such a practice would not involve negligence unless it was one which had inherent defects which should have been obvious on due consideration to a hospital administrator or consultant obstetrician. A retrial was ordered, which took place after the enactment of the Courts Act 1988 before a judge only. The matter was settled for £400,000 plus costs payable by the hospital. The claim against the consultant was dismissed without admission of liability.

The *Dunne* test was recently applied in *Kearney v McQuillan* [2012] IESC 43. In that case, the plaintiff was subjected to a symphysiotomy procedure by a Dr Connolly at Our Lady of Lourdes Hospital, Drogheda on 16 October 1969. She was 18 years old and had just given birth to her first child by Caesarean section. Applying the standards of the time, the Court found for the plaintiff and confirmed that the High Court had been correct in finding that there was no justification for the procedure carried out on the plaintiff. The Court concluded that no other practitioner of equal specialist knowledge or of equal status or skill would have carried out the procedure in the circumstances of the plaintiff's case; and the procedure carried out was deeply and fundamentally flawed in a way which should have been obvious to any doctor of similar skill or specialisation. The Supreme Court found that the evidence did not establish that the practice of symphysiotomy was sufficiently general by 1969, or generally approved by colleagues of a similar specialisation and skill to warrant this operation. In any case, none of the circumstances which might have justified a symphysiotomy procedure, even by the standards of the time, were present in the plaintiff's case. The plaintiff had already given birth to her child. Therefore, there was no rationale for carrying out this procedure. Indeed, evidence was given that standard medical textbooks of the time condemned the procedure outright.

In an uncompromising denunciation of what was done to the plaintiff, the Supreme Court stated:

> "The Constitution identifies rights which are to be protected and vindicated because they belong to each human person because of their very humanity. Among the values which have been recognised by the courts are human dignity, bodily integrity, and autonomy, that is the capacity to make informed decisions affecting one's own health. The duty to protect those rights is not confined to the courts. Each health professional is, and was always, under a similar duty. Although the finding of the court is founded in negligence, what happened here was a betrayal of trust; it was an invasion and violation of the rights just identified; it was the gravest kind of negligence."

Being Wise After the Event

The courts in both England and Ireland have consistently articulated the hazards of being wise after the event and the importance of making sufficient allowance for the complicated task facing the doctor, the wide range of possible diagnoses and treatments, the element of emergency that may be present, and the sometimes pressurised and demanding conditions in which decisions may have to be made. Once the court is satisfied that the doctor has conducted himself or herself in a manner that was reasonable to expect in the circumstances, it will be unwilling to impose liability.

For example, in *Daniels v Heskin* [1954] IR 73, a needle broke whilst a doctor was inserting stitches in a patient. He left the broken portion of needle in the patient's body after completing the procedure. He did not inform the patient or her husband at the time. The needle was subsequently removed some six weeks later by another doctor. The Supreme Court found no evidence to support a finding that the breaking of the needle was caused by negligence; that the defendant, in deciding to complete the stitching and to defer the operation for the removal of the broken portion of the needle, acted reasonably and without negligence. The Court also held that the non-disclosure to the patient or her husband of the fact that the broken portion of the needle remained in the patient's perineum did not cause damage, was reasonable in the circumstances, and did not amount to negligence. Kingsmill Moore J said:

> "There may be cases where the judgment of the physician has proved by subsequent events to have been wrong, but if it is honest and considered and if, in the circumstances known to him at the time, it can fairly be justified, he is not guilty of negligence."

In *Roe v Minister of Health* [1954] 2 QB 66, the English Court of Appeal had to consider whether the defendant's act, in the light of subsequent knowledge and events, could be held to be negligent. In that case, the plaintiffs underwent surgical procedures at the first defendant's hospital in 1947. In each case, the plaintiff was administered a spinal anaesthetic consisting of Nupercaine by the second defendant, Dr Graham, a specialist anaesthetist. The Nupercaine was contained in glass ampoules which were, prior to use, immersed in phenol solution. After the operations the plaintiffs developed a spastic paraplegia which resulted in permanent paralysis from the waist downwards. In an action for damages for personal injuries against the first and second defendants, the trial judge found that the injuries to the plaintiffs were caused by the Nupercaine becoming contaminated by the phenol which had percolated into the Nupercaine through molecular flaws or invisible cracks in the ampoules, and at the date of the operations the risk of percolation through molecular flaws in the glass was not appreciated by competent anaesthetists in general. The trial judge dismissed the plaintiffs' claims. They appealed to the Court of Appeal. Denning LJ said that the failure of the anaesthetists to foresee the possibility of contamination of the Nupercaine through invisible cracks was not negligent. Anaesthetists in 1947 did not know that there could be undetectable cracks in glass ampoules. Denning LJ said:

> "We must not look at the 1947 accident with 1954 spectacles... These two men [the plaintiffs] have suffered such terrible consequences that there is a natural feeling that they should be compensated. But we should be doing a disservice to the community at large if we were to impose liability on hospitals and doctors for everything that happens to go wrong. Doctors would be led to think more of their own safety than of the good of their patients. Initiative would be stifled and confidence shaken. A proper sense of proportion requires

us to have regard to the conditions in which hospitals and doctors have to work. We must insist on due care for the patient at every point, but we must not condemn as negligence that which is only a misadventure."

The plaintiffs' appeals were dismissed.

Diagnosis

The law does not require doctors to make a correct diagnosis; it requires them to make a reasonable diagnosis. That is, the diagnosis must be a reasonable one in the circumstances. Such circumstances will include the category of practice in question. Accordingly, a specialist will be expected to have the diagnostic skill of a reasonable specialist in the discipline in question. General practitioners will not be held to that standard, but they will be expected to be conscious of the need to refer a patient to a specialist in appropriate circumstances.

In *Coughlan v Whelton* (22 January 1993), the plaintiff attended the defendant consultant with severe pain in his chest and right arm after consuming small amounts of alcohol. The defendant subjected the plaintiff to an array of tests, none of which revealed the malady. It transpired that the plaintiff had Hodgkin's disease. The Court accepted evidence that "only two persons in the Irish population of 3.5 million would present with symptoms of Hodgkin's disease including a symptom of alcohol induced pain". Applying the *Dunne* principles and finding the doctor not guilty of negligence, the Court took the view that it was hard to see how a doctor could be guilty of negligence for failing to reach a diagnosis if he carried out all appropriate tests and all of those tests proved normal.

In *Goonan v Dooley* (23 March 1994), the plaintiff sued the hospital where she was born for failing to diagnose a dislocated hip. The Court had to decide whether in fact there had been a congenital condition capable of being identified at the time of the birth. The Court found that the relevant tests had been carried out on the plaintiff, and that it was improbable that the condition could have been diagnosed given that, in this case, three separate medical persons had examined the plaintiff on four occasions within two months of her birth and concluded that there was no abnormality. Liability was not imposed.

Error of Judgment

A doctor will not be liable for an error of judgment provided the error was not unreasonable. In *Whitehouse v Jordan* [1981] 1 All ER 267, the House of Lords said that an error of judgment may or may not be negligent; it depends on the nature of the error.

"If it is one that would not have been made by a reasonably competent professional man professing to have the standard and type of skill that the defendant held himself out as having, and acting with ordinary care, then it is negligent. If, on the other hand, it is an error that a man, acting with ordinary care, might have made, then it is not negligence" (Per Lord Fraser at 281).

Keeping Up-to-Date

Medical practitioners are obliged to keep up-to-date. This does not mean, however, that they are required to read every article in every medical journal which may have relevance to their practice. In *Crawford v Board of Governors of Charing Cross Hospital* (1953) *The Times*, 8 December, Lord Denning observed:

"… it would, I think, be putting too high a burden on a medical man to say that he has to read every article appearing in the current medical press; and it would be quite wrong to suggest that a medical man is negligent because he does not at once put into operation the suggestions which some contributor or other might make in a medical journal. The time may come in a particular case when a new recommendation may be so well proved and so well known and so well accepted that it should be adopted, but that was not so in this case."

Accordingly, a failure to remain up-to-date, which results in a medical practitioner delivering out of date or inappropriate treatment resulting in harm may well amount to negligence. There is no definitive modern decision setting out precisely what that obligation is. Given the profusion of up-to-date information relating to medical matters available to doctors on the Internet through online journals and specialist websites, it is not unreasonable to conclude that the courts would be less than indulgent towards doctors who do not keep up-to-date given the relative ease with which that can be done today. Courts would, of course, have to take into account time constraints upon doctors which, in both general and hospital practice, are, without question, severe.

Informed Consent

Generally, a doctor who performs treatment on a patient without consent will have committed a battery; a doctor who performs treatment on a patient without informed consent will be guilty of negligence. In the former case, the doctor will not have permission to touch the patient at all. In the latter case the doctor, by not obtaining informed consent, may have denied the patient the chance to forego the treatment, given the attendant risks. In *Walsh v Family Planning Services Ltd* [1992] 1 IR 496, the Supreme Court said, *obiter*, that negligence rather than trespass was the appropriate tort in cases where the patient's informed consent was not obtained. The Court said:

"If there had been such a failure to give a warning as to possible future risks that would not involve the artificial concept of assault, but, rather, a possible breach of a duty of care giving rise to a claim in negligence. The claim of assault should be confined to cases where there is no consent to the particular procedure and where it is feasible to look for a consent."

The Court cited the leading Canadian case of *Reibl v Hughes* (1980) DLR (3d) 1 at 10 where Laskin CJ said:

"I can appreciate the temptation to say that the genuineness of consent to medical treatment depends on proper disclosure of the risks which it entails, but in my view, unless there has been misrepresentation or fraud to secure consent to the treatment, a failure to disclose the attendant risks, however serious, should go to negligence rather than to battery. Although such a failure relates to an informed choice of submitting to or refusing recommended and appropriate treatment, it arises as the breach of an anterior duty of care, comparable in legal obligation to the duty of care in carrying out the particular treatment to which the patient has consented. It is not a test for the validity of the consent."

The approach in *Reibl v Hughes* has been characterised as a "patient centred" approach.

Duty to Disclose

When is a doctor under a duty to disclose the risks associated with a particular treatment? Three broad approaches have been developed by the courts.

First, there is the *Bolam* test, established in *Bolam v Friern Hospital Management Committee* [1957] 2 All ER 118. This test emphasises the fact that the decision of what to tell the patient has traditionally been regarded as primarily a matter of medical judgment and discretion.

Second, there is an approach which concentrates on the patient's right of self-determination in regard to what is to be done to his body. It requires full disclosure of all material risks pertaining to the proposed treatment, so that the patient, rather than the doctor, makes the real choice as to whether the treatment is to be undergone. In *Miller v Kennedy* (1975) 85 Wash 2d 151, 530 P 2d 334, the Court observed that:

"The patient has the right to chart his own destiny, and the doctor must supply the patient with the material facts the patient will need in order to intelligently chart that destiny with dignity."

The third approach, originating in *Sidaway v Governors of the Bethlem Royal Hospital* [1985] AC 871, lies between the previous two approaches. It applies *Bolam* save where disclosure of a particular risk "was so obviously necessary to an informed choice on the part of the patient that no reasonably prudent medical man would fail to make it".

The matter was addressed in Ireland in *Walsh v Family Planning Services*. In that case, the plaintiff had elected to have a vasectomy operation, and he and his wife had been duly counselled about the fact that, among other things, the plaintiff might suffer some discomfort in the immediate aftermath of the operation, and that in about one in forty cases a more severe swelling might occur which would result in time off work. The plaintiff underwent the procedure but subsequently developed orchialgia, an extremely rare and not fully understood consequence of vasectomy operations. The plaintiff also suffered impotence and constant low-level pain, which required surgical intervention.

The High Court held that there had been "a technical assault and battery", but that the plaintiff had not proved his case in negligence. All the evidence was that the operation had been performed with due care and skill. The first doctor, the Court considered, had given sufficient warning. The plaintiff was awarded £30,000 in damages for violation of his constitutional rights as well as special damages. The defendants appealed successfully to the Supreme Court.

The Supreme Court found that there had been no trespass: what the plaintiff had agreed to was the operation being carried out by a person or persons with the requisite skill and that it should be competently done. In relation to the appropriate test for determining the duty of disclosure, the five members of the Court approached the matter from different perspectives. Finlay CJ and McCarthy J were of the view that *Dunne* was the appropriate test to apply in disclosure of risk cases. Finlay CJ held that the issue as to whether there had been an adequate disclosure of risk to the plaintiff in the context of obtaining his consent to the vasectomy operation was to be determined by reference to the established law relating to medical negligence generally in Ireland, which has been characterised as the "doctor-centred" approach. By that standard, a medical practitioner would not be found guilty of failing to make adequate disclosure of a risk to a patient unless it could be said that no other medical practitioner of equal status or general status and skill would have been likely to have failed to disclose the risk in question. If, however, in failing to disclose a risk, the medical practitioner was following a general practice prevailing among medical practitioners, and approved of by his or her colleagues of similar specialisation and skill, he or she could still be found liable if the plaintiff could satisfy the court that such practice had inherent defects which ought to have been obvious to any person giving the matter due consideration. O'Flaherty J preferred a different approach and expressly rejected that taken by Finlay CJ regarding general and approved practice. O'Flaherty J thought that it should be a matter for the trial judge, in the first instance, to find whether there had been a breach of a duty of care owed by a medical practitioner to disclose foreseeable complications to a patient, which was an issue to be resolved on the established principles of negligence as had happened in *Reibl v Hughes* (i.e. a "patient-centred" approach).

However, all the judges in *Walsh* were agreed in their view that the elective nature of the surgery gave rise to a heightened duty to disclose. The majority position can be summarised thus:

(a) the requirement on a medical practitioner is to give a warning of any material risk which is a "known complication" of an operative procedure properly carried out;

(b) the test for materiality in elective surgery is to enquire only if there is any risk, however exceptional or remote, of grave consequences involving severe pain stretching for an appreciable time into the future, without qualification in respect of statistical frequency.

The decision in *Walsh* was applied by the Supreme Court in *Bolton v The Blackrock Clinic Limited* (20 December 1994) which again emphasised the obligation, in elective surgery, for the medical practitioner to inform the prospective patient "... of any possible harmful consequence arising from the operation".

The duty of disclosure was subsequently carefully considered by the High Court in *Geoghegan v Harris* [2000] 3 IR 536. In that case, the plaintiff had complained that a dental implant procedure, involving a bone graft taken from his chin, had been carried out negligently by the defendant leaving him with chronic neuropathic pain in his chin. He also claimed that the defendant had failed to disclose to him the risk that pain of this type might result from the procedure. The evidence in the case failed to disclose any previous instances of chronic neuropathic pain having arisen as a result of the procedure undergone by the plaintiff, but the procedure was of relatively recent origin. None of the medical experts called to give evidence from either side believed that a warning would have been necessary in respect of the likelihood of chronic neuropathic pain arising. Applying a doctor-centred approach, therefore, the defendant would not have been likely to have been found to owe a duty to disclose this risk to the plaintiff.

Applying the key elements of *Walsh* the Court posed two initial questions regarding the duty to disclose:

(a) Was chronic neuropathic pain a known or foreseeable consequence of the envisaged dental procedures? On the evidence, the Court held that nerve damage was a known complication of the procedure, and the fact that chronic neuropathic pain was a very remote or unusual particular manifestation of nerve damage was immaterial from a legal point of view;

(b) Once the answer to (a) was "yes", was the Court constrained by the decision in *Walsh* to hold that there was an obligation to warn, regardless of the remoteness of the risk and the views of the medical experts that a warning was not required? Having regard to the seriousness of the plaintiff's condition, the Court found the requirements of *Walsh* satisfied, and accordingly held that there had been a duty to warn which had been breached by the defendant.

However, the Court then went on to consider the issue as to whether the "reasonable patient" approach was a preferable option to the "doctor-centred" approach favoured by Finlay CJ in *Walsh*. The Court in *Geoghegan* considered that:

> "The application of the reasonable patient test seems more logical in respect of disclosure. This would establish the proposition that, as a general principle, the patient has the right to know and the practitioner a duty to advise of all material risks associated with the proposed form of treatment."

However, while defining "materiality" as applying to both the severity of the consequences and the statistical frequency of the risk, the Court stated:

> "The reasonable man, entitled as he must be to full information of material risks, does not have impossible expectations nor does he seek to impose impossible standards ... he must be taken as needing medical practitioners to deliver on their medical expertise without excessive restraint or gross limitation on their ability to do so ... at times a risk may become so remote, in relation at any rate to the less than most serious consequences, that a reasonable man may not regard it as material or significant ... an absolute requirement of disclosure in every case is unduly onerous, and perhaps in the end counter-productive if it needlessly deters patients from undergoing operations which are in their best interest to have."

In sum, the Court in *Geoghegan* held: First, that the defendant was obliged to give a warning to the plaintiff of any material risk which was a known or foreseeable complication of an operation. Despite the fact that the nature of the risk in this case was extremely remote, it was a known complication and a warning of the risk was required. Second, that the test to be adopted by the Court, as to what risks ought to be disclosed to a patient before an operation, was the test of the reasonable patient. By adopting that test it was the patient, thus informed, rather than the doctor, who made the real choice as to whether the treatment was to be carried out.

The question of disclosure was considered again in *Fitzpatrick v White* [2008] 3 IR 551. There, the plaintiff, who had a squint in his left eye, underwent surgery that, with no negligence on the part of the surgeon, resulted in double vision (known as diplopia), headaches and a poor cosmetic outcome. A rare complication involving loss or slippage of the medial rectus muscle had occurred. The surgeon had mentioned this risk before the operation. The plaintiff alleged that a proper warning of the risk had not been given. The Court found that, on the evidence, such a warning had in fact been given. On appeal, the plaintiff argued that the warning, which had been given at a time when he was already committed to the operation and was within 30 minutes of being taken to theatre, was simply too late to enable him to make an informed decision and give effective informed consent.

The Supreme Court, in dismissing the plaintiff's appeal, held as follows:

(1) if there were a material risk inherent in an operation which would affect the judgment of a reasonable patient, then in the normal course it was the responsibility of a doctor to inform the patient of that material risk;

(2) a risk was material if, in the circumstances of the particular case, a reasonable person in the patient's position, if warned of the risk, would be likely to attach significance to it.

Causation and Non-Disclosure

In negligence proceedings it is not enough for the plaintiff to show that the defendant has been guilty of negligence. The plaintiff must also establish that the negligence foreseeably caused injury to the plaintiff. Accordingly, in circumstances where a doctor has failed to make the necessary disclosure of risk, the court must determine if there is a causal link between that breach of duty and the injury to the plaintiff.

Where the plaintiff establishes that he or she would not in fact have undergone the proposed treatment if the doctor had made the appropriate disclosure, he or she will be able to recover damages. This is consistent with the general principles of causation (see chapters 6 and 7). However, this approach has been subject to criticism on the basis that patients will, with the benefit of hindsight, entirely understandably claim that they would never have undergone the treatment had they been informed of the risks.

The courts, therefore, have developed what is known as the "prudent patient" test, where liability will be imposed if a prudent patient, in the position of the plaintiff, would not have undergone the treatment if the appropriate disclosure had been made. In *Walsh v Family Planning Services*, the Court considered that it was necessary that the plaintiff prove that, had a proper warning been given, he would not have submitted to the original operation.

In *Geoghegan v Harris*, the Court noted that other common law jurisdictions, such as the United States and Canada favoured an objective "prudent patient" test, and other common law jurisdictions, such as Australia and England favoured a subjective plaintiff-centred test. The Court in *Geoghegan* opted for a hybrid test holding that, when deciding whether or not a warning would cause a patient to forego an operation, the Court was to first adopt an objective test. That test was to yield to a subjective test where there was clear evidence in existence from which a court could reliably infer what a particular patient would have decided.

At the objective stage the court should ask itself what a reasonable person, in the plaintiff's position, would have done if properly informed. Seeking to determine what a reasonable person would do would involve taking into account the views of medical practitioners as to the statistical likelihood of the risk occurring — taking account of the plaintiff's age, pre-existing health, and family and financial circumstances, as well as the nature of the surgery. In other words, anything that could be objectively assessed, though personal to the plaintiff. That objective test would sometimes have to yield to a subjective test, "but only when credible evidence, and not necessarily that of the plaintiff, in the particular case so demands" (*Geoghegan v Harris*, per Kearns J at 557). The Court explained that the purely subjective factors which could be taken into consideration would include, for example, the dialogue between the particular patient and the medical practitioner, information to be gleaned from contemporaneous notes or correspondence, admissions to third parties (particularly contemporaneous admissions), and, perhaps most importantly, evidence of the actual conduct of the patient prior to surgery, "given that actions generally speak louder than words" (*Geoghegan v Harris* [2000] 3 IR 536 per Kearns J at 557).

The issue of causation was also subjected to detailed consideration in *Fitzpatrick v White* [2008] 3 IR 551. It will be recalled that the plaintiff complained of the lateness of the warning, some 30 minutes before the operation took place, which he claimed, rendered it impossible for him to give informed consent. The Court found there was no evidence that this plaintiff could not assimilate or properly understand what he was being told on the day of the surgery. The Court held that, in general, in the absence of clear evidence that a plaintiff was actually disadvantaged in some material way by the lateness of a warning, a court would not declare or find a warning given to be invalid because it was given at a late stage. The plaintiff had not been in pain and had not been sedated prior to his operation. The Court cautioned, however, that "in other cases where a warning is given late in the day, particularly where the surgery is elective surgery, the outcome might well be different" (per Kearns J at 566).

The Court in *Fitzpatrick v White* was satisfied that the patient, anxious to achieve a cosmetic improvement to his eyes, would, having placed the benefits of the proposed surgery in balance with the statistically remote risk of muscle slippage causing diplopia, have nonetheless opted to proceed with the surgery. Thus, there could be no causal link between any breach of duty and the plaintiff's injury.

The hybrid test set down in *Geoghegan v Harris* was applied in *Buckley v O'Herlihy* [2010] IEHC 51. There, the plaintiff sustained a very rare injury to a blood vessel during an operation, which was carried out without any negligence on the part of the defendant doctor. Under both the objective and subjective stages of the test, the Court concluded that the plaintiff would have undergone the operation even if she had been appropriately informed of the risk. The court was satisfied that the plaintiff had not been deterred by the risks, which had been explained to her before the operation.

D. The Breach of Duty Must Result in Damage that is Actionable

As we have seen in chapter 2, when a plaintiff makes a claim in the tort of negligence it is not enough for the plaintiff to show that he or she was owed a duty of care by the defendant. Nor is it enough to show that a breach of that duty occurred. The plaintiff must show, not only that he has suffered a wrong, but also that he has suffered a *compensatable* wrong, damage, injury or consequential loss as a result of the breach of duty. This requirement is illustrated in the Northern Irish case of *A v A Health and Social Services Trust* [2011] NICA 28; [2012] NI 77. The appellants, who were twins, suing by their mother and next friend, brought proceedings in negligence against the Health and Social Services Trust. Those proceedings were instituted in October 2006 when they were eleven years of age. The twins were born to their mother following successful IVF treatment. They were healthy and perfectly normal children. Their complaint was that as a result of an error made by the treating Trust, the sperm used in the process came from a donor from a different ethnic background from that of the parents. Each parent was of white Caucasian background and they wanted and expected the children produced by the IVF process to have the same ethnic characteristics as their own. The children, however, were born with dark skin, and claimed to have been subjected to abusive and derogatory comments and hurtful name calling by other children causing them emotional upset. They also claimed emotional upset because of adverse comments made about the colour of their skin being different from the skin colour of their parents. They asserted that their quality of life had been adversely affected in consequence. Their claim failed in the High Court of Northern Ireland. They appealed to the Court of Appeal.

The Court emphasised that whether the defendant is liable in negligence involves a consideration of four requirements. Firstly, the question arises as to whether there existed a duty of care to the class of persons of whom the plaintiff is one. Secondly, a breach of the duty of care must have occurred. This necessitates proof of a failure to reach the standard set by law. Thirdly, there must be a causal connection between the defendant's conduct and resultant damage. Fourthly, the particular kind of damage must not be so unforeseeable as to be too remote in law.

The Court held that the appellants could not point to any damage or injury as a result of the error made by the Trust. They suffered no compensatable wrong, damage, injury or consequential loss as a result of the mistake made by the Trust. Girvan LJ (delivering the judgment of the Court) said:

> "Having a different skin colour from the majority of the surrounding population and their parents cannot sensibly be regarded as damage or disability just as the adoption of a child of a colour different from that of the adopting parents could not by any stretch of the imagination be described as subjecting the adopted children to some form of detriment, injury or damage. Furthermore ... a genetic inheritance carried from previous generations may manifest itself in a different skin colour in a child born to parents of an apparently different skin colour from that of the child. It would be perverse and objectionable to suggest that a child so born was in some way damaged, disabled or injured.

> The fact that the appellants have been subjected to abusive comments because of their skin colouring arises as a result of boorish and unacceptable behaviour of others. In the pluralistic, compassionate and tolerant society in which we aspire to live there should be no room for such behaviour which flows from the inability of some to accept and tolerate differences in others. In the imperfect world in which we do live there will inevitably be some who will make unpleasant

comments in relation to matters of differences in others whether it be in respect of skin colour, religion, the colour of an individual's hair, the clothes they wear and their family background. The fact that such intolerant and offensive remarks are made does not mean that the recipient of the comments is damaged, injured or disabled by the factors which led the intolerant to make the comments."

Their appeal was dismissed.

E. Establishing Breach: *Res Ipsa Loquitur*

What is *Res Ipsa Loquitur*?

The maxim *res ipsa loquitur*, meaning "the thing speaks for itself", or more loosely stated, "the accident tells its own story", allows the plaintiff to succeed in an action for negligence even where there is no evidence as to what caused the accident and, therefore, whether it was attributable to negligence on the part of the defendant. Generally speaking, in seeking to establish breach of duty in negligence cases, the burden is on the plaintiff to establish that there was a breach. The standard of proof is the civil standard: the balance of probabilities. In cases where *res ipsa loquitur* applies, however, the court will effectively give the plaintiff the benefit of the doubt by inferring negligence from what is known, in the absence of convincing evidence to the contrary.

Origins

The doctrine is thought to have originated from "an off-hand remark to counsel by Chief Baron Pollock during the course of argument" in *Byrne v Boadle* (1863) 2 H & C 722, 159 ER 299. In that case, the plaintiff had been injured by a barrel of flour which fell from a window above the defendant's shop. The defendant did not explain how the accident occurred. An assessor granted a non-suit. On appeal to the Court of Exchequer, counsel for the defendant argued that the plaintiff "was bound to give affirmative proof of negligence. But there was not a scintilla of evidence, unless the occurrence is of itself evidence of negligence". Pollock CB stated that "there are certain cases which it may be said *res ipsa loquitur* and this seems to be one of them…" Pollock CB stated in his judgment:

> "The learned Counsel was quite right in saying that there are many accidents from which no presumption of negligence can arise, but I think it would be wrong to lay down as a rule that in no case can presumption of negligence arise from the fact of an accident."

It was not long before the maxim of *res ipsa loquitur* was elevated to the status of a principle by later courts where it was held to apply where certain elements were in existence. These elements were set out by Erle CJ in *Scott v London & St*

Katharine's Docks Co (1865) 3 H & C 596 at 601, 159 ER 665 at 667. In that case, while near the door of the defendant's warehouse, the plaintiff was injured by some sugar bags falling on him. The judge directed the jury to find a verdict for the defendant on the grounds of lack of evidence of negligence by the defendant, who called no evidence. On appeal, a new trial was ordered. Erle CJ justified this decision by setting down the principles in which *res ipsa loquitur* would apply:

> "There must be reasonable evidence of negligence. But where the thing is shown to be under the management of the defendant or his servants, and the accident is such as in the ordinary circumstances does not happen if those who have the management use proper care, it affords reasonable evidence, in the absence of explanation by the defendants, that the accident arose from want of care."

Elements

We can see, therefore, that for *res ipsa* to apply, three elements must be present. They are:

1. The accident must be of a kind which does not normally happen in the absence of negligence;
2. The cause of the accident must have been under the defendant's control;
3. There must be no explanation of the cause of the accident.

In offering a more modern interpretation of *res ipsa loquitur* Megaw LJ in *Lloyde v West Midlands Gas Board* [1971] 2 All ER 1240 at 1246, said:

> "I doubt whether it is right to describe *res ipsa loquitur* as a 'doctrine'. I think that it is no more than an exotic, although convenient phrase, to describe what is in essence no more than a common-sense approach, not limited by technical rules, to the assessment of the effect of evidence in certain circumstances. It means that a plaintiff prima facie establishes negligence where (i) it is not possible for him to prove precisely what was the relevant act or omission which set in train the events leading to the accident, but (ii) on the evidence as it stands at the relevant time it is more likely than not that the effective cause of the accident was some act or omission of the defendant or of someone or for whom the defendant is responsible, which act or omission constitutes a failure to take proper care for the plaintiff's safety."

Application

Res ipsa loquitur is not relevant where there are sufficient facts known in order to prove negligence. Therefore, the principle will only apply where an explanation of what actually happened is not forthcoming. Accordingly, where an explanation is adduced before the court, and accepted by it, that case is no longer one to which the principle will apply. For example, in *Barkway v South Wales Transport Co Ltd* [1950] AC 185, the plaintiff was injured when a bus in which he was a passenger crashed. It was established that the cause of the crash was a burst tyre and that this would not have occurred had the defendant adopted a proper system of tyre inspection.

The courts have applied *res ipsa loquitur* to a wide range of situations from railway accidents and air crashes to things falling from buildings. According to the principle, "the thing" must be "under the control, management, of the defendant or his servants". The facts in *Byrne v Boadle*, where a barrel of flour fell from the defendant's shop over which only the defendant exercised control, would appear to satisfy this requirement. Things that have been held to be under the defendant's control have included the use of motor vehicles, aircraft, and firearms.

In *Corcoran v West* [1933] IR 210, the Court held that:

> "where a motor vehicle is so driven that it mounts on the footpath and injures a foot passenger thereon, the case falls within the principle *res ipsa loquitur*, and the onus is thrown on the owner of the vehicle of explaining the occurrence and showing that it took place without any negligence on his part."

There, a woman in her early 20s was knocked down and killed by a lorry when it mounted the footpath on King Street, Ballina, Co Mayo. Her parents sued. The Court (on appeal) applied *res ipsa loquitur* holding that the onus was on the defendant to show that the lorry got on the footpath and injured the woman without negligence on his part. He had not discharged that onus. Judgment was entered for the plaintiffs.

A modern example of the application of *res ipsa loquitur* to a road traffic accident is *Widdowson v Newgate Meat Corporation* [1998] PIQR P138. The plaintiff, who suffered from a mental disorder, was injured when struck by a car driven by one of the defendants whilst walking on the edge of the inside lane of a dual carriageway. The plaintiff was not competent to give evidence, and the driver chose not to, although in an earlier statement to police he could offer no explanation for the accident. There was also no evidence of why the plaintiff was on the road at the time or where he was going. Nonetheless, the English Court of Appeal allowed an appeal against the dismissal of the action, holding that there was no absolute rule against invoking *res ipsa loquitur* in road traffic cases. Here, there was evidence that the plaintiff had an awareness of road safety, it was a clear night, and the driver would have had a long clear view of the road ahead of him. This was sufficient to establish a *prima facie* case and, in the absence of evidence from either of the parties involved in the accident, the defendants could not rebut that inference. Ultimately, the plaintiff's damages were reduced by 50% for contributory negligence because he was not wearing brightly coloured clothing nor, it appeared, had he moved onto the grass verge as the car approached.

In *Gee v Metropolitan Railway Co* (1873) LR 8 QB 161 *res ipsa loquitur* was applied to an accident in which the door of a train flew open a few minutes after leaving the station causing the plaintiff to fall out. The train doors were presumed to have been the sole responsibility of the train company at the time. In contrast, in *Easson v London & North Eastern Railway Co* [1944] KB 421, a similar accident happened near the end of a journey from London to Edinburgh. In this instance, the court held that there would have been too many opportunities for others to tamper with the doors, so the "control" condition was not met.

The continued importance and application of the principle was confirmed by the Privy Council in *Ng Chun Pui v Lee Chuen Tat* [1988] RTR 298. There, a coach veered across the road colliding with a bus coming in the opposite direction on a dual carriageway in Hong Kong. The plaintiff called no evidence and the Privy Council held the facts *per se* raised an inference of negligence. But the defendants testified that an unidentified car cut across their coach causing the driver to brake suddenly and skid across the road. The defendants were found to have rebutted any inference of negligence since the driver's reaction to an emergency beyond his control did not constitute any breach of duty.

In *Ng Chun Pui v Lee Chuen Tat* the Privy Council explained that, in a case in which the plaintiff seeks to rely on *res ipsa loquitur*, he establishes a *prima facie* case by relying upon the fact of the accident. If the defendant adduces no evidence, there is nothing to rebut the inference of negligence and the plaintiff will have proved his case. But if the defendant does adduce evidence, that evidence must be evaluated to see if it is still reasonable to draw the inference of negligence from the mere fact of the accident. The Privy Council pointed out that, loosely speaking, this may be referred to as a burden on the defendant to show he was not negligent, but that only means that, faced with a *prima facie* case of negligence, the defendant will be found negligent unless he produces evidence that is capable of rebutting the *prima facie* case. The Privy Council considered that the burden of proof is a "poor way to decide cases": it is the duty of the judge to examine all the evidence at the end of the case and decide whether, on the facts, and on the inferences he or she is prepared to draw from those facts, he or she is satisfied that negligence has been established. Insofar as resort is had to the burden of proof, the Privy Council's view was that the burden remains at the end of the case where it was at the beginning, that is, upon the plaintiff to prove that his injury was caused by the negligence of the defendants.

The maxim was applied in respect of an air crash in *George v Eagle Air Services Ltd* [2009] 1 WLR 2133. The defendants' aeroplane crashed and the deceased, a passenger on the aircraft, was killed. In the subsequent action for damages for the benefit of the deceased's estate and dependents, it was alleged that the crash was caused by negligence on the part of the pilot, the defendants' employee. The defendants denied negligence, asserting that the aircraft had been serviced by the deceased, who was their mechanic, and was airworthy, but made no attempt to explain the crash. In those circumstances, the Privy Council found that *res ipsa loquitur* was applicable. The Privy Council quoted with approval the view of the US Federal Court of Appeals that

> "[l]ogic, experience and precedent compel us to reject the argument that aeroplane crashes ordinarily occur in the absence of default by someone connected with the design, manufacture, or operation of the craft" (*Higginbotham v Mobil Oil Corporation* (1977) 545 F 2d 422 at [19]).

Lord Mance further said:

> "Aircraft, even small aircraft, do not usually crash, and certainly should not do so. And, if they do, then, especially when the crash is on land as here, it is not unreasonable to suppose that their owner/operators will inform themselves of any unusual causes and not unreasonable to place on them the burden of producing an explanation which is at least consistent with the absence of fault on their part."

Since, on the facts, the defendants had provided no such explanation they had failed to displace the inference of negligence which resulted from the crash itself. It is important to note, that in this case, pilot negligence was not the only possible cause of the crash. It could have been caused by the deceased's own negligence in servicing the aircraft, or possibly a manufacturing defect. On the facts of this particular case, it was not so much the accident itself that gave rise to an inference that the pilot was to blame, but the defendants' failure to give any explanation of their own for the accident when they might reasonably have been expected to give one, or at least to explain why they could not.

In *Hanrahan v Merck Sharpe & Dohme (Ireland) Ltd* [1988] ILRM 629, at 635, Henchy J gave the following rationale for the maxim:

"The rationale behind the shifting of the onus of proof to the defendant in such cases would appear to lie in the fact that it would be palpably unfair to require a plaintiff to prove something which is beyond his reach and which is peculiarly within the range of the defendant's capacity of proof."

Keane J, in *O'Shea v Tilman Anhold and Horse Holiday Farm Ltd* (23 October 1996, Supreme Court) described this as a "restatement" of the maxim and commented that it may need to be reconsidered at some stage. He preferred to use the "classic formulation" of *res ipsa loquitur* in Erle CJ's judgment in *Scott v London & St Katharine's Docks Co.* In *O'Shea,* the plaintiff was injured when a horse jumped onto the roof of his car causing him to crash. He sued the defendants in negligence. The Supreme Court held that this was a case to which the principle of *res ipsa loquitur* clearly applied. However, this did not mean that the defendants were automatically liable and it did not require them to prove what actually happened. It simply required them to show that they had taken reasonable care. The Court found on the facts that the defendants had done so, and their appeal was allowed.

The authorities show that a former right to control the "thing" that causes the injury will not be sufficient to give rise to the application of *res ipsa loquitur* where the "thing" is no longer in the condition in which it was when control was exercised. This was the position and *Tracey v Hagan* (6 March 1973) where the Supreme Court held that *res ipsa loquitur* ought not to apply to the plaintiff who had been injured when he was servicing a machine used to make plastic bottles. The machine had been manufactured by the defendant and supplied to the plaintiff six months previously, the servicing of the machine being carried out by the plaintiff. *Res ipsa loquitur* was held not to be applicable on the ground that the machine, which was not under the control or management of the defendant, had not been proved to have been in the condition in which the defendant had provided it.

The Procedural Effect of *Res Ipsa Loquitur*

When the maxim is invoked before the court in an appropriate case, it appears that the onus will be on the defendant to show that he was not negligent. However, the burden of proving causation still lies with the plaintiff. The courts will treat separately the question of causation and the issue of the absence, or otherwise, of reasonable care. In medical negligence cases, where no evidence of the defendant's lack of care is adduced by the plaintiff then, before the principle of *res ipsa loquitur* becomes applicable, the onus is on the plaintiff to establish that the accident was such that, in the ordinary course of things, did not happen with the use of reasonable care.

In *Lindsay v Mid Western Health Board* [1993] 2 IR 147, the Supreme Court considered precisely what the defendant had to do in order to avoid liability in a case where *res ipsa loquitur* applies. In that case, a girl, when she was aged 8, had been admitted to the defendant's hospital with suspected appendicitis. She was operated on. Unfortunately, the girl lapsed into a deep coma and did not regain consciousness. The plaintiff's action for negligence against the hospital involved the invocation of *res ipsa loquitur*. Expert witnesses identified three possible causes for the plaintiff's condition. The High Court held in favour of the plaintiff, but the Supreme Court reversed that decision. O'Flaherty J thought that, in the instant case, the most that the defendant should be required to do was to show that it had exercised all reasonable care; it should not be required to take the further step of proving, on the balance of probabilities, *what* had caused the plaintiff's injury. The effect of this position is that a defendant can escape liability in a case where *res ipsa loquitur* applies even where the cause of the accident remains unknown. In other words, once the defendant has established that, whatever the cause of the injury, it cannot expressly be attributed his or her negligence, then the defendant has done enough to avoid liability.

No Need to Expressly Plead *Res Ipsa Loquitur*

Res ipsa loquitur does not have to be specifically pleaded before a plaintiff may rely on it if the facts pleaded and proved show that the doctrine is applicable to the case: see *Mullen v Quinnsworth Ltd t/a Crazy Prices (No 1)* [1990] 1 IR 59 at 63; *O'Reilly v Lavelle* [1990] 2 IR 372.

CAUSATION IN FACT

Learning Outcomes

Upon completion of this chapter, the reader should be able to:

- Understand the role of factual causation in determining liability in tort;
- Explain what is meant by the "but for" test;
- Appreciate the limits of the "but for" test;
- Explain how multiple and consecutive causes of injury are dealt with by the courts;
- Understand what is meant by "loss of a chance";
- Discuss why the courts developed the "material contribution" test;
- Explain how liability is apportioned under Part III of the Civil Liability Act 1961 in respect of concurrent wrongdoers.

A. Causation Generally

Causation is relevant in all torts. Problems arise right across tort law in relation to two particular issues:

- whether the defendant's wrongful conduct did in fact cause the plaintiff's loss; and
- whether the defendant ought to be held responsible for the full extent of that loss.

Causation, however, is probably most relevant to the tort of negligence. Many, but not all, of the more complex causation issues concern negligence. In addition negligence, unlike torts that are actionable *per se*, is a tort in which causation must be specifically proved before any liability can be imposed.

This chapter should be studied in conjunction with Chapter 7.

Figure 6.1:

Causation in Fact in the Negligence Equation

B. The "But For" Test

Winfield has described causation in fact as "primarily a matter of historical mechanics". Causation in fact (in Latin: *causa sine qua non*) involves establishing the facts about how something came about at a given time. The central question is whether the defendant can be said to have been a factual cause of the plaintiff's loss or harm. This question, in most cases, can be answered by applying what is known as the "but for" test. Under this test, the defendant can generally be said to have been a factual cause of the plaintiff's loss or harm if, "but for" the defendant's breach of duty, he or she would not have suffered in the way that he or she did.

The "But For" Test Applied

The "but for" test involves asking the question: "but for the defendant's breach of duty, would the plaintiff's damage still have occurred?" If the answer to this question is "yes", then the defendant's breach generally can be eliminated as a factual cause of the damage. The "but for" test was applied in *Barnett v Kensington & Chelsea Health Management Committee* [1968] 2 WLR 422. In that case, a night-watchman became ill after drinking tea. He went to the hospital but the doctor on duty did not examine him. The doctor told him to go home and that if he did not improve that he should contact his own doctor. During the night, the man died. The hospital admitted that the doctor was negligent in failing to carry out a proper examination of the patient. Had such an examination taken place it is possible that a correct diagnosis could have been made. It transpired that the patient had died from arsenical poisoning and that, on the balance of probabilities, the treatment which the doctor would have given him could not have saved him. The Court accepted that although there had been negligence in failing to examine the patient, even if the breach of duty had not taken place, the death would still occurred. Therefore the hospital's negligence was eliminated as a cause of the death of the patient.

The *Barnett* case concerned the failure of a medical practitioner to undertake diagnosis or treatment at all. However, the "but for" test has application in cases where a medical practitioner has been negligent in failing to adequately explain to the patient the risks of a possible course of treatment. In such cases, it is essential for the plaintiff, in order to succeed, to be able to establish that had those risks been explained he would not have given consent to the treatment and the adverse outcome would thereby have been avoided (see chapter 5).

In *Chester v Afshar* [2004] UKHL 41, a patient consulted a neurosurgeon about her back pain. She was advised to undergo surgery. The surgery carried a risk of 1-2% of serious nerve damage even if performed with due care and skill. The plaintiff was not informed by the surgeon of this risk. Following the operation she was found to have suffered the nerve damage. It was held that the "but for" test had not been satisfied. This was because even though, had she been properly informed, the plaintiff would not have agreed to the operation at that time, she might well have gone on to have the surgery in the future when the risk would still have existed. Notwithstanding this, a majority of the House of Lords ruled in favour of the plaintiff. Their decision was made on policy grounds: that of upholding patient autonomy which justified "a narrow and modest departure from traditional causation principles".

The "but for" test operated against the plaintiff in *Kenny v O'Rourke* [1972] IR 339. There, the plaintiff was a painter. He was injured when he fell from a defective ladder. The plaintiff gave evidence that he fell because he lent over too far. Accordingly, his employers were not liable because his fall was not caused by the defect in the ladder.

The application of the "but for" test can also be illustrated in *Collier v Earl of Mountcharles and Others* (19 December 1969) (SC). In that case, the plaintiff, a fee-paying visitor, was injured when a stone stairway collapsed in the defendant's castle. The plaintiff argued that the defendant should have engaged an architect to examine the stairs. The defendants produced professional evidence, which was accepted, that even if they had engaged an architect he would not have warned them that the stairway was dangerous. Since the collapse would have occurred anyway, that omission was not a factual cause of the accident. The Court, in any event, found no negligence on the part of the defendants as they had no reason to suspect any defect in the structure which had stood firmly for 180 years.

In the Canadian case of *Cook v Lewis* [1952] 1 DLR 1, the Court had to adapt the normal rules of causation to achieve a just result. There, two hunters negligently fired their guns in the direction of the plaintiff. One bullet hit him, but it was not established which gun had fired the bullet. In the absence of the necessary proof, it was held that the hunters would be jointly and severally liable.

In *McWilliams v Sir William Arrol & Co* [1962] 1 WLR 295, the deceased's employer had been negligent in failing to provide a safety harness for a steelworker. The worker fell to his death. It was established that had the defendant provided a safety harness, the worker would not have used it. But for the defendant's breach, the damage would still have occurred and so there was no liability on the part of the employer.

A similar determination was made by the Court in *Duffy v Rooney and Dunnes Stores (Dundalk) Ltd* [1997] IEHC 102. The infant plaintiff was burned when a coat she was wearing caught fire while standing too close to a sitting room fire. The Court found that the retailer had been negligent in not fixing a warning notice to the garment stating that it should be kept away from fire. However, the Court also found, given the particular circumstances of the case, that the plaintiff would have worn the coat anyway. Accordingly, the failure to attach a warning notice was not an operative cause of the plaintiff's injury.

When the "But For" Test is Insufficient

The application of the "but for" test becomes problematic in two particular sets of circumstances:

- when the answer to the question leads to an unjust or contradictory result; and
- when it is impossible to answer the "but for" question.

This difficulty can best be illustrated through a classic hypothetical example. Two people, A and B, simultaneously and negligently light a match in a gas-filled room which results in an explosion. If we ask the question: "But for the negligence of A would the explosion have occurred?" The answer would be "yes". If we then ask: "But for the negligence of B would the explosion have occurred?" Again, the answer would be "yes". If we then apply the "but for" test to this situation, we can see that neither A nor B would be regarded as a cause of the explosion and thus neither would be liable. This is because both A and B could legitimately say: "Even if I had not lit my match, the explosion would have occurred anyway, because the other person's match would have ignited the gas". Therefore, on a strict application of the "but for" test both A and B would be able to escape liability. That is why the test is insufficient where there are multiple causes of the injury.

C. Consecutive Causes

By consecutive causes we mean later unconnected events causing the same or greater harm as the first tort. Some cases involve two torts. In such circumstances, the second wrongdoer may find that his breach of duty caused no additional damage to a victim and that he is therefore not liable in respect of the tort that he committed. The courts have dealt with consecutive causes in a number of cases.

For example, in *Performance Cars v Abraham* [1962] 1 QB 33 (CA), a Rolls-Royce was damaged in a collision due to the fault of A. As a result, the bottom half of the car had to be re-sprayed. Two weeks later, before the damage could be repaired, B collided with the same car. The damage done required a re-spray of the bottom half of the car. But because B had created no additional damage, the total liability remained with A.

In *Baker v Willoughby* [1970] AC 467, the defendant negligently injured the plaintiff's left leg. The Court assessed damages, including past and future loss of earnings, at £1600. However, before the trial, and while the plaintiff was working at a new job he had taken up after his accident, he was the victim of an armed robbery in the course of which he suffered gunshot wounds to the same left leg. The injuries were of such severity that the leg had to be amputated. The defendant argued that his liability was limited to the loss suffered before the date of the robbery: all loss suffered thereafter was merged in and flowed from the robbery. Put simply, the defendant was arguing that the second event overtook, or wiped out, the effect of the damage done by the first event. This argument was rejected by the House of Lords because it would have been unfair to the plaintiff. Even if the robbers had been successfully sued to judgment, they would only have been liable to the plaintiff for depriving him of an already damaged leg and the plaintiff would therefore have been left uncompensated in the period after the robbery for the "difference" between a sound leg and a damaged one. The defendant's argument was said to contain a fallacy in its assertion that the injury to the leg was obliterated by the subsequent amputation because, as Lord Reid put it, a person:

"[i]s not compensated for the physical injury: he is compensated for the loss which he suffers as a result of the injury. His loss is not in having a stiff leg: it is his inability to lead a full life, his inability to enjoy these amenities which depend on freedom of movement and his inability to earn as much as he used to earn or could have earned if there had been no accident. In this case the second injury did not diminish any of these. So why should it be regarded as having obliterated or superseded them?"

In other words, the plaintiff's loss after the removal of the leg was regarded as having two concurrent causes, though it is clear that if the robbers had shot him dead the defendant's liability would not have extended beyond that point. It is worth noting, that in a purely factual sense, the plaintiff's first accident was a cause of the injury in the robbery since the plaintiff changed his job as a result of that accident. However, it could not be contended, as a matter law, that the defendant was liable for the shooting.

A slightly different approach was adopted in *Jobling v Associated Dairies Ltd* [1982] AC 794. In that case, the plaintiff suffered a back injury owing to the defendants' breach of duty. He was left with an ongoing disability. Three years later and before the trial the plaintiff was diagnosed as suffering from a condition (myelopathy), unrelated to the accident and arising after it, which of itself rendered him totally unfit for work. The defendants argued that the onset of the myelopathy terminated the period in respect of which they were liable for the effects of the back injury. The plaintiff argued that the case should be governed by *Baker v Willoughby*. The House of Lords found for the defendants. The myelopathy, they said, was one of the "vicissitudes of life" which had to be taken into account in full when it had actually occurred before the trial. The courts regularly made discounts in the assessment of damages for future loss of earnings by taking into account the chance of such "vicissitudes" arising during the course of a person's life. Lord Bridge said:

"When the supervening illness or injury which is the independent cause of the loss of earning capacity has manifested itself before trial, the event has demonstrated that, even if the plaintiff had never sustained the tortious injury, his earnings would now be reduced or extinguished. To hold the tortfeasor, in this situation, liable to pay damages for a notional continuing loss of earnings attributable to the tortious injury, is to put the plaintiff in a better position than he would be in if he had never suffered the tortious injury."

It will be recalled that in *Baker* the plaintiff's second injury was caused by a tort. In *Jobling*, the plaintiff's second injury was not caused by a tort. The second injury in *Baker*, arguably therefore, should not be treated as one of the "vicissitudes of life", thus making a distinction between tortious and non-tortious second injuries. This matter was addressed in the Irish courts in *R (L) v Minister for Health and Children* [2001] 1 IR 744. In that case, the applicant was a haemophiliac who suffered injury when he contracted Hepatitis C as a result of treatment he was given. He was entitled to compensation under statute. The Court had to assess future loss of earnings. The applicant argued that he was restricted in the kind of work he could do as a result of his injury thereby limiting his ability to earn a living. However, before trial, the applicant was involved in a road traffic accident. He suffered serious injury and had to give up work altogether. The Court took the view that the limitation introduced by *Jobling* should not apply to this case because the supervening event was tortious. In other words, a tortious event should not be considered to be one of the "vicissitudes of life". Accordingly, it should not, as a matter of principle, operate to relieve the respondent of liability just because the applicant was the victim of a second tortious event.

In summary, the two cases of *Baker* and *Jobling* should be distinguished as follows: *Baker* concerned two torts, whereas *Jobling* concerned one tort followed by a natural occurrence. In addition, the outcome in *Baker* was designed to avoid under-compensating the plaintiff. The two cases represent different approaches to different sets of facts.

D. Loss of a Chance

Loss of chance concerns the idea that the defendant's negligence increased the likelihood of a poor outcome for the plaintiff or deprived him of the possibility of avoiding such an outcome. This issue will often arise in clinical cases. In *Hotson v Berkshire Area Health Authority* [1987] AC 750, a schoolboy injured his hip when he fell from a tree. When taken to hospital the seriousness of his condition was not immediately recognised. Five days later, his condition was correctly diagnosed and appropriately treated. However, he developed a serious disability of the hip as an adult, which he claimed was caused by the delayed diagnosis. The hospital admitted negligence, but it denied liability on the grounds of lack of causation. According to the medical evidence, given proper treatment the boy would only have had a 25% chance of complete recovery. The plaintiff failed in his action because, on the balance of probabilities, the disability would have occurred even without the defendant's negligence.

The approach adopted in *Hotson* was also adopted in *Gregg v Scott* [2005] 2 AC 176. There, the plaintiff had complained to Dr Scott of a lump under his arm.

Dr Scott concluded that it was benign and did not order any further investigation or tests. A year later it was discovered that the lump was a symptom of cancer. The plaintiff was given a 25% chance of ten years' survival. That chance would have been as high as 42% at the time he visited the defendant. By a narrow majority, the House of Lords found in favour of the defendant. Their Lordships concluded that the plaintiff's loss had been described in terms of the potential for ten years' survival: he could not prove that he had a likelihood of survival higher than 50%, even at the time of his first medical consultation. Their Lordships also found that the relative diminution in his chances of survival was not a type of loss recognised in negligence claims, because, on the balance of probabilities, he had never had a chance of a positive outcome.

E. Alternative Approaches — "Material Contribution"

The English courts have developed a particular approach to difficult issues of causation in circumstances where there are multiple possible causes of the injury. It is described as "material contribution". This can arise in cases where the plaintiff is unable to establish which one of separate unconnected factors caused his injury or, alternatively, to what extent connected causes may have accumulated to bring about his injury. This approach has been used in cases in which the process giving rise to the injury has been cumulative and the resultant injury can be viewed as indivisible, that is, it cannot be broken down into different parts which can separately be attributed to different causes.

In *Bonnington Castings v Wardlaw* [1956] AC 613, the plaintiff developed an industrial lung disease after working in the defendant's workshop. His injury was caused by the cumulative inhaling of dust, some of which occurred as a result of the employer's negligence, but some of which was unavoidable. The plaintiff was unable to establish that "but for" the employer's negligence he would not have suffered the disease. Nevertheless, he recovered his full loss. This is because the House of Lords was satisfied that the employer's negligence had made a "material contribution" to the plaintiff's injury.

This approach was also adopted in *Bailey v Ministry of Defence* [2008] EWCA Civ 883. There, the plaintiff suffered brain damage whilst under the care of the defendant's hospital. She suffered a cardiac arrest due to the aspiration of vomit. It was claimed that this would not have happened had she not been in a weakened state due to the defendant's earlier failures in her post-operative care. The defendants did not dispute negligence. However, this case turned on a question of causation: had this breach caused the plaintiff's injury? The English Court of Appeal found in favour of the plaintiff. The Court found that her loss had cumulative causes: i.e. her physical vulnerability combined with the defendant's negligence. Although it was not possible to establish the proportion of causation to be attributed to the defendant, it was found that "but for" the inadequate care given to the plaintiff she would not have been so weak and so the defendant's breach had materially contributed to her injury.

A similar approach was adopted by the English Court of Appeal in *Dickens v O2 plc* [2008] EWCA Civ 1144 where the Court held that the plaintiff should be successful in her claim due to the fact that the defendant's negligence had made a material contribution to her psychiatric injury.

The "material contribution" approach can be applied in cases where there is no process of accumulation but rather only one, but unidentifiable, cause. This is described as causing "a material increase in risk". The leading case is *McGhee v National Coal Board* [1973] 1 WLR 1. There, a worker sustained a skin disease which was caused by contact with brick dust after many years of working in a brick kiln. His employer admitted negligence in failing to provide adequate washing facilities at the end of the working day. The plaintiff alleged, but was unable to prove, that it was this extended exposure at the end of the day which had caused his injury. The defendant argued, however, that because his job involved exposure to brick dust all day long, it was more likely than not that the plaintiff's injury had been caused by non-negligent rather than negligent exposure. The House of Lords found for the plaintiff. This was notwithstanding the fact that they recognised that there was an "evidential gap" on the basis that, when proof is impossible, justice is best served if the party at fault bore the loss which had been suffered. Lord Wilberforce said that the fault in this case consisted not in adding a material quantity to the accumulation of injurious particles, but by failing to take a step which had the effect of materially increasing the risk.

These cases can be distinguished on this basis: in *Bonnington* and *Bailey* different factors combined cumulatively, but in *McGhee* one single factor was involved in bringing about the plaintiff's injury. However, in *Wilsher v Essex Area Health Authority* [1988] AC 1074, there were five separate possible factors, only one of which actually caused the injury and there was no process of accumulation. The plaintiff, shortly after birth, had been given excess oxygen owing to the negligence of the hospital where he had been prematurely born. He was later found to be blind. One cause of blindness in premature babies is excess oxygen. But there are four other potential causes. All of these could have applied in this case. The plaintiff, at trial, was unable to prove on a balance of probabilities that the excess oxygen had been the cause of his blindness. The House of Lords distinguished the "material contribution" approach which had been adopted in *McGhee* holding that the defendant had merely added one additional possible cause to four other separate and distinct innocent causes. Without conclusive evidence that the hospital's negligence had been the operative cause, liability could not be imposed.

The House of Lords considered a complex causation issue which arose in a number of asbestos compensation claims in *Fairchild v Glenhaven Funeral Services* [2002] UKHL 22. The plaintiffs had contracted mesothelioma (a lung disease, normally fatal, caused by exposure to asbestos dust). It was not known scientifically whether the disease was initiated by one fibre of asbestos or by many, or exactly how the cumulative development of the disease had occurred. The issue of causation arose because the plaintiffs had been negligently exposed to asbestos while working for several different employers. Some of these employers had gone out of business and could not now be sued. Furthermore, it was impossible to establish which exposure had caused the injuries. Applying the "but for" test, the English Court of Appeal had rejected all three claims. On appeal, however, the House of Lords took a different approach. Following the decision in *McGhee*, each of the defendants was treated as having created a "material increase of risk" of damage to the plaintiffs. Their Lordships unanimously allowed the appeals and held all of the employers jointly and severally liable. This was a controversial departure from the normal "but for" legal principle. Its basis was in policy where the Court sought to ensure that genuinely injured plaintiffs received compensation.

The House of Lords adopted a slightly different approach in *Barker v Corus UK* [2006] UKHL 20. There, their Lordships characterised the damage caused by the defendants (an asbestos-related condition) as creating a material increase in the risk of contracting the disease. Departing from the decision in *Fairchild*, their Lordships held that the liability of each defendant would be apportioned. That is, each defendant would only be liable in proportion to the amount of risk they had created. The decision in *Barker* on apportionment was reversed by statute (s 3 of the Compensation Act 2006) restoring the *Fairchild* position on joint and several liability in cases of asbestos-related mesothelioma. This means that, in the UK, by virtue of the 2006 Act, any one negligent defendant could be ordered by the court to bear 100% of the liability, irrespective of the extent of his involvement with the plaintiff. Interestingly, the UK Supreme Court held in *Sienkiewicz v Grief* [2011] UKSC 10 that the "*Fairchild* exception" would apply even when the mesothelioma was attributable to only one negligent source, providing the plaintiff was able to satisfy the Court that the increase in risk caused was "material".

In *Quinn (a minor) v The Mid Western Health Board and Donal O'Sullivan* [2005] IESC 19 the Irish Supreme Court expressed a reluctance to depart from the "but for" principle. There, the plaintiff was born on 4 May 1990 at a gestation age of

39 weeks and 1 day. The defendants admitted negligence in failing to deliver the plaintiff before full term of 36 weeks. The plaintiff had sustained brain damage. The defendants contended that the brain damage was sustained, not as a result of the defendants' omissions, but as a result of an acute episode which occurred between the 28th and 30th weeks of pregnancy. Accordingly, the outcome, they claimed, would not have been different had she been delivered before 4 May. In applying the "but for" test, the Court found for the defendants. It should be noted, however, that this case did not involve multiple defendants or multiple causes, nor was it pleaded that the defendants' delay had "materially contributed" to the plaintiff's condition. The Court made it clear that special circumstances did not exist in this case to bring it within the more relaxed requirements for establishing causation which were found to exist in *McGhee v National Coal Board* and *Fairchild v Glenhaven Funeral Services*. The Court in *Quinn* stated that *Fairchild* turned on its own unique facts and it was expressly confined by the House of Lords to a particular set of circumstances where it would be patently unjust not to find for the plaintiff in circumstances where his condition must have been caused through the negligence of employer A or employer B, or both, but on application of the conventional "but for" test of causation it could not be held that the plaintiff had successfully made out a case against either. The Court in *Quinn* was therefore unwilling to countenance transferring the onus of proof to the defendant because such a step would be a major change in the law which would require a "full court", or "perhaps even legislation".

F. Concurrent Wrongdoers under Part III of the Civil Liability Act 1961

Part III of the Civil Liability Act 1961 deals with the liability of concurrent wrongdoers. This legislation seeks to ensure that the injured plaintiff can recover compensation for his injuries from as many sources as possible; that concurrent wrongdoers may recover fair contributions from each other in respect of damages they have to pay to the plaintiff, and that all matters concerning the plaintiff's injuries should, as far as possible, be litigated in one court action. This section highlights some important aspects of Part III.

Section 2 of the 1961 Act defines, for the purposes of the Act, a "wrongdoer" as "a person who commits or is otherwise responsible for a wrong"; and a "wrong" is defined as

> "a tort, breach of contract or breach of trust, whether the act is committed by the person to whom the wrong is attributed or by one for whose acts he is responsible, and whether or not the act is also a crime, and whether or not the wrong is intentional".

Section 11(1) provides that "two or more persons are concurrent wrongdoers when both or all are wrongdoers and are responsible to a third person for the same damage, whether or not judgment has been recovered against some or all of them." It will be noted that if the wrongdoers are not responsible for the "same damage", they will not be "concurrent wrongdoers" for the purposes of Part III. In other words, if it is possible to attribute specific items of loss or damage to specific wrongdoers, they will not be "concurrent wrongdoers" for the purposes of s 11.

Section 11(2)(a) provides that persons may become concurrent wrongdoers as a result of vicarious liability of one for another, breach of joint duty, conspiracy, concerted action to a common end or independent acts causing the same damage. Section 11(2)(b) provides that the wrong on the part of one or both may be a tort, breach of contract or breach of trust, or any combination of them: and s 11(2)(c) declares that it is immaterial whether the acts constituting concurrent wrongs are contemporaneous or successive.

Section 11(3) provides that where two or more persons are at fault and one or more of them is or are responsible for damage while the other or others is or are free from causal responsibility, but it is not possible to establish which is the case, such two or more persons shall be deemed to be concurrent wrongdoers in respect of the damage. This provision could deal with cases such as *Cook v Lewis* [1952] 1 DLR 1 (see above) where two wrongdoers fired guns in the direction of the plaintiff; one bullet hit the plaintiff, but it was not possible to say from which gun the bullet came. Section 11(3) could also operate, for example, in respect of multiple polluters in circumstances where it is difficult to establish which of the polluters caused the damage.

Section 12(1) of the 1961 Act provides that concurrent wrongdoers are each liable for the whole of the damage in respect of which they are concurrent wrongdoers. The court is empowered under s 12(2) to apportion liability between two or more persons who are not concurrent wrongdoers but whose conduct causes independent items of damage of the same kind to the injured party or to one of their number. The court can apportion liability in such manner as is justified by the probabilities of the case. Where the plaintiff is at fault the court may reduce his damages. If the proper proportions cannot be determined, the damages may be apportioned or divided equally. By virtue of s 12(3), where the independent acts of two persons combine to cause a nuisance, even though the independent acts would not create a nuisance on their own, both individuals may have their liability apportioned.

Under ss 13 and 14 the plaintiff may bring an action against all or any of the wrongdoers and judgment may be given against the defendants together or separately. Where judgment is given against concurrent wrongdoers who are sued together, the court may give judgment against the defendants together or against the defendants separately and, if the judgment is given against the defendants together, it shall take effect as if it were given against them separately.

Section 21(1) provides for contribution between concurrent wrongdoers where they are "liable in respect of the same damage". Where one concurrent wrongdoer settles a claim with the plaintiff, the effect of which is to bar the plaintiff's claim against the other concurrent wrongdoers, the concurrent wrongdoer who has entered into the settlement with the plaintiff is entitled to seek a contribution from the other concurrent wrongdoers provided the amount of the settlement is reasonable. In circumstances where a concurrent wrongdoer obtains a judgment for contribution, s 23 operates to prevent judgment being executed against the other concurrent wrongdoer before satisfaction has been made to the plaintiff.

CAUSATION IN LAW

Learning Outcomes

Upon completion of this chapter, the reader should be able to:

- Appreciate the distinction between causation in fact and causation in law;
- Understand the role of causation in law in limiting the defendant's liability in tort;
- Explain when an event may amount to a *novus actus interveniens*
- Demonstrate a clear understanding of test set down in *The Wagon Mound (No 1)*;
- Explain how the concept of "remoteness" operates to absolve the defendant of liability;
- Discuss the operation of the "eggshell skull" rule.

A. Causation in Law — Overview

A convenient way of explaining causation in negligence is as a chain of events. As we have seen in chapter 6, there will be a range of situations in which the defendant's act can be said to be a cause of the plaintiff's loss because it satisfies the "but for" test. However, the defendant's act can be followed by one or more events which contribute to the eventual damage suffered by the plaintiff in such a way that it could be said that the chain of causation is broken. This concept is referred to in Latin as *novus actus interveniens* — or "new intervening act". In addition, whilst the injury suffered by the plaintiff may be factually linked to the defendant's act, the court may consider that the plaintiff's injury is so far removed from that act that it would be unjust to impose liability on the defendant for that injury. This concept is referred to as "remoteness" of damage. Hence, it is convenient to consider causation in law, or "legal causation", under two broad headings:

- *novus actus interveniens* (a new intervening act);
- remoteness of damage ("remoteness").

Figure 7.1

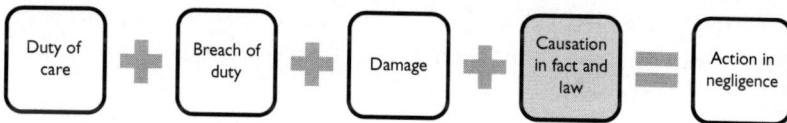

Causation in Law in the Negligence Equation

B. *Novus Actus Interveniens*

New intervening acts can usefully be divided into three categories:

(1) the plaintiff's conduct;
(2) acts by a third party;
(3) natural events.

The Plaintiff's Conduct

The plaintiff's own conduct can constitute a *novus actus interveniens*. In *Corr v IBC Vehicles Ltd* [2008] 2 WLR 499, Lord Bingham explained the position in this way:

> "[i]t is not fair to hold a tortfeasor liable, however gross his breach of duty may be, for damage caused to the plaintiff not by the tortfeasor's breach of duty but by some independent, supervening cause and [it] is not the less so where the independent, supervening cause is a voluntary, informed decision taken by the victim".

This principle can be see from the following cases. In *McKew v Holland & Hannens & Cubitts (Scotland) Ltd* [1969] 3 All ER 1621, the defendant's negligence caused injury to the plaintiff's leg. The plaintiff later broke his ankle attempting, while still suffering from the effects of the first injury, to descend a steep staircase unassisted. The plaintiff's unwise and unreasonable conduct constituted a fresh and separate cause of the second injury. Accordingly, the defendant was only liable for the initial injury. By contrast, in *Wieland v Cyril Lord Carpets* [1968] 3 All ER 1006, the plaintiff's conduct was held not to be unreasonable. In that case, as a result of the defendant's negligence the plaintiff had to wear a neck brace which restricted her ability to use her bifocal spectacles. This caused her to miss a step on a staircase and fall. She sustained further injuries. It was held that her conduct in walking down the steps had not been unreasonable on the particular facts of that case and therefore the defendant was liable for the additional injuries resulting from the plaintiff's fall.

In cases where the level of unreasonableness by the plaintiff is relatively low, the court may approach the matter in terms of the defence of contributory negligence rather than *novus actus interveniens*. In *Spencer v Wincanton* (2009) EWCA Civ 1404, for example, the facts were very similar to those of *McKew*. There, the English Court of Appeal stated that the level of unreasonableness which will break the chain of causation must be very high. There, the plaintiff's action in attempting to fill his car with petrol, despite the fact that he was physically disabled, had not reached this level. However, one-third contributory negligence was applied.

In *Reeves v Metropolitan Police Commissioner* [2000] 1 AC 360, the plaintiff's partner, who was a known suicide risk, had committed suicide in a police cell in circumstances where the police had breached their duty of care to supervise him. It was held that the suicide had not broken the chain of causation, because it was the precise risk against which the police had a duty to guard. Damages were reduced, however, on the grounds of contributory negligence. Lord Hoffmann said:

> "it would make nonsense of the existence of such a duty if the law were to hold that the occurrence of the very act that ought to have been prevented negatived the causal connection between the breach of duty and the loss".

Contributory negligence instead of *novus actus* was found to apply in *Doran v Dublin Plant Hire Ltd* [1990] 1 IR 488. In that case, the plaintiff was injured whilst repairing a machine at work. The defendant employer had failed to properly advise the plaintiff as to how the repairs should be carried out. As a result the plaintiff suffered an injury following an accident. The Court found that the plaintiff should have realised that the way in which he was carrying out the repairs was hazardous. Nevertheless, this did not break the chain of causation between the defendant's negligence and the injury to the plaintiff. It was not a *novus actus*. Instead, the Court found 25% contributory negligence on the part of the plaintiff. It was the negligence of the employer that created a dangerous situation within which the plaintiff was trying to work.

Acts by Third Parties

A third party is usually the last person to carry out an act before the damage occurs. It is therefore likely to be a person either responding to a situation created by the defendant's act (reacting to the danger or emergency, possibly as a rescuer) or he or she is a deliberate wrongdoer, in some cases committing a criminal act.

In respect of the first situation, as we have seen, rescuers are a category of plaintiff who are traditionally regarded favourably in the law of negligence, particularly in relation to the question of duty of care. However, it may be argued that a rescuer who negligently causes further damage has broken the chain of causation.

In *The Oropesa* [1943] 1 All ER 211, a collision at sea between two ships was partially due to the fault of the defendant. In the aftermath of the collision the captain of the damaged vessel ordered a lifeboat to be put to sea so that salvage arrangements could be made with the defendant. The lifeboat capsized and several crew members were lost, including the plaintiff's son. His death was caused by a combination of the defendant's initial negligence and the captain's subsequent order to board the lifeboat in rough seas. It was held that this order was reasonable in the circumstances. Here, the conduct of the third party was brought about by the initial negligence of the defendant.

However, it is still possible that a subsequent act will constitute a *novus actus* even where the defendant's initial negligence brought that about. In *Rahman v Arearose Ltd* [2001] QB 351, the plaintiff had been assaulted by two youths. The assault left him needing surgery. The surgery he received was negligently performed by the defendant. As result, the plaintiff was left blind in one eye. Partly in response to the blindness and partly as a consequence of the assault, the plaintiff suffered post-traumatic stress disorder (PTSD). The Court held that the blindness was exclusively attributable to the negligent surgery even though that surgery had been necessitated by the original torts of the two youths. On the other hand, the negligent surgery was only part of the cause of the psychiatric injury and the two youths remained partly responsible for that.

In a similar vein, in *Knightley v Johns* [1982] 1 All ER 851, we can see an example of behaviour sufficiently unreasonable to break the chain of causation. In that case, a road traffic accident occurred in a tunnel due to the negligence of the defendant. A police officer, who had arrived on the scene, ordered one of his motorcyclists to ride through the tunnel against the flow of traffic. This led to a second accident which injured the plaintiff. In holding that the police officer's order intervened in the chain of causation from the first accident, emphasis was placed by the Court on the following:

- the fact that his was a positive act rather than a mere omission;
- the second accident could not be seen as a "natural and probable consequence" of the negligence of the defendant;
- it was said to be a matter of "common sense" that the officer's negligence was a new cause disturbing the sequence of events.

The sequence of events was disturbed in *Conole v Red Oyster Bank Co* [1976] IR 191. There, Fairway Fabrics Ltd built a boat for the defendants. The boat was defective and unseaworthy. The defendants knew this. They ordered that the boat be tied up. In contravention of this order, the captain (their employee) brought the boat out with some 50 children on board. The boat capsized. The plaintiff's daughter, along with nine others, drowned. The Supreme Court held that the negligence of Fairway Fabrics in constructing an unseaworthy boat was not the operative cause of the accident. The Court held that:

> "[t]he direct and proximate cause of the accident was the decision of the defendants to put to sea with passengers when they had a clear warning that the boat was unfit for that task. The defendants were the sole initiators of the causative negligence..."

Accordingly, the negligent act of the defendants was a *novus actus* which broke the chain of causation between the negligence of the boat's manufacturers Fairway Fabrics and the plaintiff's loss.

The chain of causation was similarly broken in *Crowley v AIB and O'Flynn* [1988] ILRM 225. There, the plaintiff was injured when he fell from the flat roof of premises owned by the AIB. The second defendants were the architects. They had designed the roof without specifying the need for a railing around it. The Supreme Court held that the chain of causation between the plaintiff's injury and the architects' negligence was broken by the fact that the bank knew that boys regularly played on the unguarded roof and did nothing to prevent this from happening. The inactivity of the bank, therefore, constituted a *novus actus* which relieved the architects of liability.

In *Home Office v Dorset Yacht Co* [1970] AC 1004, the deliberate wrongful acts of Borstal trainees in colliding with the plaintiff's yacht could have broken the chain of causation from the guards' negligent supervision of them, but this was not accepted by the Court. An act which is "very likely to happen" will not break the chain of causation because it will be reasonably foreseeable. This was held to be the case in respect of the vandalism of the boys.

Issues of remoteness of damage and policy may also be considered in the context of *novus actus*. For example, in *Lamb v Camden London Borough Council* [1981] QB 625, the defendants carelessly broke a water main outside the plaintiff's house. The escaping water undermined the foundations. The house subsided and was rendered uninhabitable. The plaintiffs were forced to move out until repairs could be carried out. In the meantime, squatters moved in. By the time they had been evicted they had caused £30,000 worth of damage. It was held that, on policy grounds, the damage should be held to be too remote even though it was foreseeable. The Court took into account the following factors: (i) the plaintiff could have insured against the risk (ii) the plaintiff could have been more proactive in seeking to prevent the squatters entering his home, and (iii) the squatters were, in any case, wrongdoers and it would be wrong, on policy grounds, to make a public authority liable for damage they had caused. This was despite the fact that an Official Referee had made a finding that squatting was "foreseeable".

The intentional act of a third party was held not to break the chain of causation in *Stansbie v Troman* [1948] 2 KB 48. In that case, a householder left a decorator working alone in his house. The decorator had to leave the house to get some wallpaper. He did not have a key so he left the door unlocked. Whilst he was gone a thief entered the house and stole jewellery. The decorator was held liable for the loss. The Court took the view that the decorator was negligent in leaving the house unlocked and it was this breach of duty that resulted in the thief entering the house and stealing the goods. The act of the thief, although wrongful, did not break the chain of causation between the decorator's negligence and the plaintiff's loss.

In *Breslin v Corcoran* [2003] IR 203, the owner of a car left the keys in the ignition whilst he went into a shop. A thief took the car and drove it negligently injuring the plaintiff. The owner was sued by the plaintiff for negligence. The plaintiff's claim was dismissed in the High Court. The Supreme Court upheld that decision. Fennelly J said:

> "It is the negligent driving, not the taking of the car, which has caused the damage. It would have to be shown that the owner should have foreseen not merely the taking but also the negligent driving. There would have to be some basis in the evidence, such as that suggested by the learned trial judge, for a finding that the car, if stolen, was likely to be driven in such a way as to endanger

others. Cars may be stolen for reasons which do not carry such implications. Some of these, though criminal, do not necessarily imply dangerous driving. The line would, on any view, have to be drawn somewhere. If a car were stolen for resale, the owner would scarcely be responsible for the driving of the purchaser, whether that person were honest or not."

Fennelly J made these general observations:

"A person is not normally liable if he has committed an act of carelessness, where the damage has been directly caused by the intervening independent act of another person, for whom he is not otherwise vicariously responsible. Such liability may exist, where the damage caused by that other person was the very kind of thing which he was bound to expect and guard against and the resulting damage was likely to happen, if he did not."

In *Hayes v Minister for Finance* [2007] 3 IR 190, the plaintiff was a pillion passenger on a motorcycle driven by her boyfriend. The boyfriend failed to stop at a Garda checkpoint. The Gardaí pursued them. The motorcycle was driven recklessly for some distance and eventually crashed. The plaintiff was injured. She sued the Gardaí in respect of her injuries. The Court held that even if the Gardaí were negligent (which the Court found they were not), the chain of causation would have been broken by the criminal recklessness of the plaintiff's boyfriend. It was he who exposed his girlfriend to danger, not the Gardaí. In such cases, the courts will take into account the public responsibility of the Gardaí to uphold the law and to apprehend lawbreakers.

We can see from the case law that, generally, the act of a third party must be something very likely to happen if it is not to break the chain of causation. In other words, the more foreseeable the conduct of the third party, the less likely it is to be a *novus actus*: in many instances, the courts will require that the act of the third party be intentional or reckless.

Natural Events
An unanticipated intervention might come from wind, lightning, storms or even chemical reactions. In some cases, these are unlikely to be within the risk of the original negligence, but on the other hand, should they be held to break the chain of causation they would leave the injured party without any source of redress.

In *Carslogie Steamship Co Ltd v Royal Norwegian Government* [1952] AC 292, the defendant caused damage to the plaintiff's ship. The ship required repairs which would take approximately 10 days. Some temporary work had been done in England but then, whilst sailing to the United States, where further repairs were to be undertaken, the ship was caught in a storm at sea. This necessitated an extra 30 days' repair when it reached America. The plaintiff argued that the ship had been caught in the storm due to the defendant's negligence. Nevertheless, it was held that this event had broken the chain of causation. Accordingly, the defendant was only liable for the repair costs of the first collision and not for the loss of profits during the days in which it was being repaired for both the collision and the storm damage concurrently.

C. Remoteness

Remoteness — An Overview

The concept of remoteness concerns the extent of the defendant's duty. Even where there is a clear factual link between the defendant's act and the plaintiff's loss (causation in fact), the outcome may be either so removed from the original negligence, or of a type which is outside the risk created so that the law would regard it as unjust to make the defendant liable for it. Remoteness has been described by Winfield as a situation where a defendant should not be made responsible infinitely for all the consequences of his wrongful conduct so "the law must draw a line somewhere...for practical reasons". Accordingly, in negligence, and most other torts, certain consequences of the defendant's tortious conduct would be considered too remote from his wrongdoing to impose on him responsibility for those consequences.

Re Polemis

Historically, the common law has adopted two approaches to determining where that line should be drawn in respect of remoteness of damage. In *Re Polemis and Furness Withy & Co Ltd* [1921] 3 KB 560, an agent of the charterers of a ship, whilst unloading the vessel in Casablanca, negligently knocked a plank into the hold of the ship. The impact of the plank in the hold caused a spark which ignited petrol vapour which had accumulated in the hold. An explosion occurred. A fire engulfed the ship and it sank. The owners of the ship took an action against the charterers who alleged that the damage was too remote. The Court held that, if the charterers could reasonably foresee *some* damage, liability in negligence was established: and in such circumstances the charterers should be liable for *all* the direct consequences of their acts. Scrutton LJ said:

> "To determine whether an act is negligent, it is relevant to determine whether any reasonable person would foresee that the act would cause damage; if he would not, the act is not negligent. But if the act would or might probably cause damage, the fact that the damage it in fact causes is not the exact kind of damage one would expect is immaterial, so long as the damage is in fact directly traceable to the negligent act..."

In *Re Polemis*, it was clear that negligence in knocking the plank into the hold might cause damage of some sort, whether to workmen or cargo. That would establish liability. The charterers would then be liable for all the direct consequences — including the destruction of the ship. This would be so even if the destruction of the ship was not foreseeable. The approach set out by the Court distinguished between the initial issue of liability, where *foreseeability* was the test, and the issue of the extent of the liability where *directness* was the test.

The Wagon Mound (No 1)

Re Polemis was overruled in *Overseas Tankship (UK) Ltd v Morts Dock and Engineering Co Ltd (The Wagon Mound) (No 1)* [1961] AC 388 (PC). In that case, the defendants carelessly discharged oil from their ship into Sydney Harbour. The oil was carried by wind and tide to the plaintiffs' wharf, 200 yards away. After being advised that they could safely do so, the plaintiffs continued welding operations on their wharf. Later, molten metal from the welding operations, when fanned by the wind, set fire to some cotton waste or rag floating in the oil beneath the wharf. The burning cloth ignited the oil and fire severely damaged the wharf. The defendants neither knew nor ought to have known that the oil was capable of being set alight when spread on water. The Judicial Committee of the Privy Council held that the defendants were not liable in negligence because they could not reasonably have foreseen that the plaintiffs wharf would be damaged by fire when they carelessly discharged the oil into the harbour. In other words, the harm was of an unforeseeable kind.

The Wagon Mound (No 1) established the principle that harm suffered must be of a kind, type, or class that was reasonably foreseeable as a result of the defendant's negligence.

The principle was applied in *Bradford v Robinson Rentals Ltd* [1967] 1 All ER 267. There, the defendants carelessly exposed their employee van driver, the plaintiff, to extreme cold in the course of his work. As a consequence, the plaintiff suffered frostbite. The Court held that the defendants had exposed the plaintiff to severe cold and fatigue likely to cause a common cold, pneumonia, or chilblains. It further held that since frostbite was of the same type and kind as these forms of harm, the defendants could be held liable.

It should be noted that *Re Polemis* and *The Wagon Mound (No 1)* are primarily concerned with unintentional damage. Damage, of course, may be intentional. If so, the defendant will be liable for the damage he intends to cause. This will be so even if the intended damage was a highly unlikely outcome.

Foreseeable Type of Harm

Prior to *The Wagon Mound (No 1)* the Irish courts' lack of enthusiasm for the approach in *Re Polemis* was evident in *O'Mahony v Ford* [1962] IR 146. There, the plaintiff was employed as a riveter by the defendant company. The electric drill and riveter the plaintiff used was operated resting against his chest. Both tools vibrated constantly whilst being used. In 1956 he noticed a small swelling, which was diagnosed as scirrhus carcinoma. The plaintiff sued. The Supreme Court entered judgment for the defendants. The Court thought that although the defendants could foresee physical injury, for example bruising, no such injury had in fact occurred. The damage that had occurred, scirrhus carcinoma, was not reasonably foreseeable. The Court insisted that for the defendant to be liable, the foreseeable damage must be of the same "kind" as the damage which actually occurred. In other words, not only must the defendant foresee some damage but he must foresee the *type* of damage which occurred before he should be liable for it.

In *Burke v John Paul & Co Ltd* [1967] IR 277, the plaintiff used a steel cutter in the course of his employment. The blades on the cutter were blunt. Consequently, the plaintiff was obliged to exert much greater pressure than he would have needed to had the blades been properly maintained. As a result, he suffered a hernia. The defendants argued that they could not reasonably have anticipated that the plaintiff would suffer a hernia because of the pressure he was required to apply. They might have anticipated tearing or straining muscles, but not a hernia, which was due to a congenital precondition of the plaintiff. The "eggshell skull" rule was applied in this case (see below). The Court found for the plaintiff, stating:

> "[T]he test is not whether the defendants could reasonably have foreseen that a straining or tearing of the muscles would cause a hernia in this particular man, but the question is rather whether they could have reasonably foreseen the type of injury he did suffer, namely, the tearing or straining of the muscles which resulted in the hernia... [I]t is immaterial that the defendants could not anticipate the full extent of the damage."

However, in *Tremain v Pike* [1969] 3 All ER 1303, the plaintiff's injury was found to be too remote. The plaintiff was a herdsman working for the defendants. He contracted a rare condition called Weil's disease. This disease is caused by coming into contact with rats' urine. Weil's disease, *per se*, was not foreseeable, even though other diseases associated with rats were foreseeable. The defendants were held not liable. The Court took the view that Weil's disease "was entirely different in kind from the effect of a rat bite, or food poisoning by the consumption of food or drink contaminated by rats... [The court does not] accept that all illness or infection arising from an infestation of rats should be regarded as of the same kind".

Means by Which the Harm Was Caused

Since the decision in *The Wagon Mound (No 1)* the courts have broadly taken the view that the defendant may be liable even though he or she could not envisage the precise set of circumstances which caused the harm of the foreseeable kind. *Hughes v Lord Advocate* [1963] AC 837 is an important early case in which the *The Wagon Mound (No 1)* test of "reasonable foreseeability" was applied. There, workmen left an open manhole, guarded by paraffin lamps. Some children began playing with the lamps and dropped one of them into the manhole which caused an explosion. This resulted in one of the children being knocked into the manhole and being badly burned. The defendant argued that this outcome was not reasonably foreseeable. The House of Lords did not agree. Leaving paraffin lamps in this way created a risk of reasonably foreseeable injury due to burns. The fact that the plaintiff's burns came about in an unlikely way did not prevent liability. In other words, the plaintiff was injured as a result of the type or kind of accident or occurrence that could reasonably have been foreseen, even though the workmen could not have foreseen the exact way in which the plaintiff would play with the alluring objects that had been left lying around, or the exact way in which, in so doing, the plaintiff might suffer injury. The workmen's conduct created a risk of the relevant kind of harm i.e. personal injury from burning, and this is in fact what happened.

Glasgow Corporation v Muir [1943] AC 448 is also instructive. There, the Corporation owned a building in which tearooms managed by Mrs Alexander were located. A picnic party came in. Two of the party, with Mrs Alexander's permission, carried a heavy tea urn into the tea room from another room. One of them dropped his side of the urn and six children were scalded by hot tea. The plaintiffs alleged that the manageress was negligent in allowing the urn to be carried into the tearooms. The House of Lords held that the manageress was not negligent. She had no reason to anticipate such an event could happen as a consequence of granting permission for the tea urn to be carried. She was entitled to assume that the two people carrying it would do so safely and use ordinary care.

The "Eggshell Skull" Rule

It was well established at common law, before *The Wagon Mound (No 1)* was decided, that, in relation to personal injury, the defendant had to "take the plaintiff as he found him". This meant that the victim could claim damages for all of the harm to his person, even though, due to some special physical vulnerability, that harm was greater than would have been suffered by an ordinary individual. Accordingly, if the defendant could foresee a particular type of physical or psychological injury to the plaintiff then he will be liable for all of the physical or psychological injury that follows on account of the plaintiff's particular vulnerable pre-accident condition even if the injury to the plaintiff turns out to be far more serious than might otherwise have been expected.

For example, in *Smith v Leech Brain & Co Ltd* [1962] 2 QB 405, the plaintiff suffered a burn on his lip which had been negligently inflicted. This resulted in him dying of cancer. The tissues in his lip in which the cancer developed were in a premalignant condition at the time the burn occurred. The defendants were held liable for the damage resulting from the death.

The "eggshell skull" rule was also applied in *Burke v John Paul & Co Ltd* [1967] IR 277 (see above) and in *Robinson v Post Office* [1974] 2 All ER 735. In the latter case, the defendants carelessly lacerated the plaintiff's leg. A doctor subsequently gave the plaintiff an anti-tetanus injection which caused encephalitis because the plaintiff was allergic to the injected serum. The defendants were held liable for all of the plaintiff's injuries. This case is also an interesting example of the application of the "but for" test in factual causation. The plaintiff also sued the doctor. When the plaintiff went to the doctor he was given a test to see if there would be an adverse reaction to the serum. The doctor was supposed to wait half an hour to see if there was a reaction. He did not. He only waited half a minute. The doctor was, therefore, clearly negligent. However, he was not held liable because the reaction, in this case, did not become apparent for nine days. Accordingly, the test, even if performed properly, would have made no difference to the plaintiff.

A similar approach in respect of psychiatric harm was adopted in *McCarthy v Murphy* [1998] IEHC 23. In that case, the plaintiff suffered foreseeable soft-tissue injury in a minor road traffic accident which was caused by the defendant's negligence. The plaintiff subsequently developed a depressive reaction which was attributable in part to an underlying depressive condition. The Court recognised that the defendant could not have anticipated that the plaintiff was a person with a predisposition to depression, but he could have reasonably foreseen a soft-tissue injury and, that being so, the defendant was liable for the damage which flowed from that injury. He had to take the plaintiff as he found her.

The House of Lords has made it clear that, in general, there was no justification for treating physical and psychiatric injury as different "kinds" of injury. Once it is established that the defendant is under a duty of care to avoid causing personal injury to the plaintiff, it does not matter whether the injury in fact sustained is physical, psychiatric or both. In *Page v Smith* [1996] 1 AC 155, the House of Lords, by a majority, held that where a defendant negligently risks causing personal physical injury to the plaintiff, and the plaintiff sustains an unforeseeable psychiatric injury, liability should be imposed for that injury.

The English courts have ruled that the "eggshell skull" rule can apply to property damage in tort. In *Parsons v Uttley Ingham* [1978] QB 791, the defendants negligently failed to install proper ventilation in a device used in the feeding of the plaintiff's pigs. The nuts fed to the pigs went mouldy as a result. The pigs died of a rare disease. It might have been foreseen that they would suffer mild "food poisoning", but death was not anticipated. The Court of Appeal held, in effect, that the defendants had to "take the pigs as they found them". Full compensation was awarded for the loss of the pigs. Although this case was pleaded as a breach of contract the Court of Appeal made the decision on the basis that the rules of remoteness in contract and tort were the same. However, this approach has been questioned. In contract, remoteness turns on what is foreseeable to both the contracting parties, as opposed to what is foreseeable to the reasonable person: see *Jackson v Royal Bank of Scotland* [2005] UKHL 3. Notwithstanding this, the foreseeability of illness caused to the pigs by mouldy nuts would, in any event, be foreseeable by both contracting parties *and* the hypothetical reasonable person for the purposes of tort law.

The courts in both England and Ireland have considered the application of the "eggshell skull" rule in cases where the defendant could foresee damage of a pecuniary nature to the plaintiff and where that damage was exacerbated by the plaintiff's impecuniosity. In other words, the plaintiff, in mitigating his loss, might have to incur extra expenditure solely because of his poor financial situation. In an early English decision, the courts there were distinctly unenthusiastic about applying the "eggshell skull" rule in such circumstances. In *Liesbosch Dredger v Edison SS* [1933] AC 448, the House of Lords refused to award damages in respect of the additional element caused by the plaintiff's impecuniosity.

A different approach was adopted with *Lagden v O'Connor* [2003] 1 AC 1067. In that case, the House of Lords decided that losses attributable to a plaintiff's impecuniosity should be treated no differently from any physical weakness with which the plaintiff may be afflicted. Accordingly, the impecunious plaintiff in that case, whose car the defendant had damaged, and was only able to obtain a replacement at 30% above the standard rate for car hire, was nonetheless able to recover the full cost of hire. This illustrated what could be described as the "financial eggshell skull rule". Their Lordships stated that the test for remoteness was whether the:

"… loss was reasonably foreseeable. The wrongdoer must take his victim as he finds him… This rule applies to the economic state of the victim in the same way as it applies to his physical and mental vulnerability. It requires the wrongdoer to bear the consequences if it was reasonably foreseeable that the injured party would have to borrow money or incur some other kind of expenditure to mitigate his damages."

The "financial eggshell skull rule" has been considered in a number of Irish cases. In *Riordan's Travel Ltd v Acres and Co Ltd (No 2)* [1979] ILRM, the defendants, in demolishing a building, damaged the plaintiffs' business premises. The Court took the view that the plaintiffs were entitled to recover from the defendants costs they reasonably incurred in mitigating their loss by paying interest on borrowings. In *Rabbette v Mayo County Council* [1984] ILRM 156, the plaintiff took court action to prevent the defendant carrying out blasting operations near his property. The plaintiff was allowed to recover certain losses suffered which would not have arisen but for his impecuniosity. Also, in *Doran & Doran v Delaney & Others* [1999] 1 IR 303, the plaintiffs sued solicitors and the vendors of a site for a dwelling house for breach of contract and misrepresentation. In order to retrieve their situation, the plaintiffs "acted perfectly reasonably" in incurring certain costs as a result of their inability to raise alternative funds. The plaintiffs were entitled to recover all losses that were reasonably foreseeable.

Employers' Liability and Vicarious Liability

Learning Outcomes

Upon completion of this chapter, the reader should be able to:

- Explain the obligations employers have towards their employees at common law;
- Understand the approach of the courts in respect of dangerous work environments;
- Discuss the law concerning psychological injury caused by employers' negligence towards employees;
- Explain the role of *volenti non fit injuria* in Irish law;
- Outline the scope of vicarious liability;
- Explain how, and in what circumstances, vicarious liability will apply.

A. Overview

Employers' liability concerns the breach of an employer's duty to its employees. The risk of personal injury suffered in an accident at work, or by contracting an industrial disease, is greater in certain types of employment than others. Legislative provisions have been introduced to prevent such injuries from occurring, for example, the Safety, Health and Welfare at Work Act 2005. Such provisions have reduced the importance of the common law, but have by no means eliminated it. The general liability of employers under the common law remains liability in negligence alone. Although much of the discussion around employers' responsibilities towards their employees uses the language of duty, in reality, the vast majority of cases on employers' liability concern the standard of care. The central issue, therefore, in considering employers' liability, is the question of what kinds of safeguards employers must put in place to discharge their duty of care in tort for the health and safety of their workers. It should be noted that older cases refer to employees as "servants" and employers as "masters".

B. Non-Delegable Duty

An employer's duty is a non-delegable, personal one, of a general nature. In other words, an employer cannot avoid his duty towards his employees by simply delegating it to somebody else. This position has been recognised since *Wilsons & Clyde Coal Co Ltd v English* [1938] AC 57. There is another form of tortious duty, known as vicarious liability, under which an employer is held liable not for breach of his own personal duty, but for the tort of his employee.

Employers' duties towards their employees fall into four broad categories:

(1) the provision of competent staff;
(2) the provision of a safe place of work;
(3) the provision of proper equipment; and
(4) the provision of a safe system of work.

The non-delegable character of the employer's duty towards his or her employees can be brought into sharp focus in cases where an employee is allocated by his or her general employer to work for a temporary employer. An example is *McDermid v Nash Dredging and Reclamation Co Ltd* [1987] AC 906. In that case, the plaintiff was employed by the defendants as a deckhand. He was sent to work on a rig owned by a Dutch company. The plaintiff had no idea that he was not continuing to work on one of the defendant's boats under one of the defendant's captains. The plaintiff suffered serious injury as a result of the Dutch captain's carelessness. The defendants denied responsibility on the basis that they were not vicariously liable for the conduct of someone else's employee. The House of Lords held that the defendants were liable on very straightforward grounds. The evidence showed that the plaintiff was injured because no safe system of work was in place. The duty incumbent on his employers to devise and ensure the operation of such a system had not been fulfilled. In that case, the House of Lords said that the essential characteristic of the employer's non-delegable duty

> "… is that, if it is not performed, it is no defence for the employer to show that he delegated its performance to a person, whether his servant or not a servant, whom he reasonably believed to be competent to perform it. Despite such delegation the employer is liable for the non-performance of the duty."

It is important to remember that even though the employer's duty is personal, and cannot be discharged by simply delegating it to another, fault must still be proved for liability in negligence to be imposed.

In *Connolly v Dundalk Urban District Council and Mahon & McPhillips* [1990] 2 IR 1, an employee of the first defendants, the Council, was injured by faulty pipework at the first defendant's waterworks. The waterworks had been designed, built and maintained for the first defendants by the second defendants. The first defendants had sought unsuccessfully to avoid liability on the basis that the responsibility for any failure of the pipework or any failure to implement safety measures should be laid at the door of the second defendants, who were responsible for its design, installation, service, and maintenance. The Court rejected this proposition. O'Hanlon J said that it was

> "well-established… that an employer owes a duty to his employee to provide a safe place of work, and cannot escape liability for breach of such duty by employing an independent contractor – no matter how expert – to perform the duty for him."

In *Armstrong v William J Dwan & Sons Ltd* [1999] IEHC 215, the plaintiff, a lorry driver, was employed by the first defendants. He was injured by faulty crash bars on his vehicle. The second defendants, Westpark Motor Company, had repaired the vehicle negligently. The Court held that the employer had not been guilty of any negligence. The second defendants were the main Ford truck dealers in the area, were a reputable company, upon whom the first defendants were entitled to rely. The Court was of the view that it would be unreasonable to expect the first defendants to inspect the work of the second defendants prior to putting the truck back into service. The first defendants were entitled to assume that the second defendants had carried out their work satisfactorily.

It seems that an employer's non-delegable duty may not extend to the purchase of equipment from a supplier on a once-off basis with no customised specifications: see *Keenan v Bergin* [1971] IR 192. In addition, *Armstrong v William J Dwan & Sons Ltd* would appear to suggest that a non-delegable duty may not operate where the supplier of equipment, or one who services or repairs equipment, used by employees is in an ongoing commercial relationship with the employer.

The Provision of Competent Staff

Employers are under a duty to use due care to select proper competent fellow employees: see *Skerritt v Scallon* (1877) IR 11 CL. At one time, the defence of "common employment" would absolve the employer from vicarious liability resulting from the torts of his employees. That is no longer the case. The defence of "common employment" was abolished by the Law Reform (Personal Injuries) Act 1958, s 1. Now, if an employer fails to take reasonable care in the selection of competent staff and an accident results, then the employer will be liable. However, in circumstances where employees injure fellow employees, or members of the public, an employer is more likely to be sued on the basis of vicarious liability i.e., where the employer is liable not because he or she was negligent but because he or she exercises "control" over the negligent employee.

Before the employer will be liable for having failed to provide competent staff, it must be shown that the employer had reason to be aware of the employee's incompetence. In circumstances where an employer employs someone, and then subsequently discovers that they are incompetent, and they continue to employ that person in the knowledge that they are incompetent, the employer will do so at his or her peril. For example, in *Hudson v Ridge Manufacturing Co Ltd* [1957] 2 QB 348, knowingly to employ a workman continually indulging in horseplay was held to violate the duty to provide competent staff.

In *Hough v Irish Base Metals Ltd* (unreported, 8 December 1967, the Supreme Court), the plaintiff suffered serious burns when a workmate, when "larking", placed a gas fire under his legs. The plaintiff sued in negligence. The High Court found that the employers had failed to meet the standard of a reasonable and prudent employer in that supervision was inadequate and found the defendants liable on that basis. On appeal, the Supreme Court considered whether the defendant employers had fallen below the standard of care required. That Court held that the employer had not fallen below the standard of a reasonable and prudent employer and allowed the appeal. It had been submitted on behalf of the plaintiff that the employers, although not having actual knowledge of this dangerous larking, ought to have known about it and prevented it, and could have known of it by a proper system of supervision.

The Court in *Hough* said that the supervision required in a situation such as this was supervision which was appropriate to the ordinary work of a repair shop. The Court observed that what occurred in this case could be characterised as "a bit of fun" or "devilment" which would be over in an instant. The nature of this type of larking was, therefore, such as to not make it easily detectable: and, in any event, it could not reasonably be said that an employer who did not detect it had failed in his duty to provide a safe system of supervision as the larking in question was of such recent origin and was not of such frequency as must necessarily have been detected in any system of reasonable supervision.

The Provision of a Safe Place of Work

The employer is under a duty to supply a safe place of work in order to avoid any accidents that could reasonably be foreseen by the employer. It is not sufficient for the employer to show that the employee was aware of the danger on the premises (see *Vaughan v Cork & Youghal Railway Co* (1860) 12 ICLR 297 stating the former approach). The obligation on the employer to protect employees from injury on the employer's premises is clear. In those circumstances, the employer exercises control over those premises. However, the position is less clear where the employee works on premises over which the employer has little or no control. In *Wilson v Tyneside Window Cleaning Co* [1958] 2 QB 110, the Court articulated the limits of the employer's duty in this respect:

> "if a master sends his plumber to mend a leak in a respectable private house, no one could hold him negligent for not visiting the house himself to see if the carpet in the hall creates a trap."

In *Mulcare v Southern Health Board* [1988] ILRM 689, this issue was considered. In that case, for about seven years, the plaintiff worked as a home-help for an elderly woman as an employee of the Southern Health Board. On one visit, she twisted her ankle on the floor of the house. The Court held that whilst a duty might exist, "at most", to inspect the premises, there was no duty to bring it up to a modern standard. The Court noted that the plaintiff had not fallen there in the previous seven years of work and, therefore, the house appeared not to be so unsafe as to require the defendant to oblige the elderly woman to carry out improvements or lose the services of the home-help. No liability was imposed on the defendants.

An unsafe place of work was considered in *Barclay v An Post* [1988] ILRM 385. A postman injured his back in June 1993 while delivering post to houses with letterboxes at the bottom of the doors. He was off work for some time and returned in October 1993. He undertook some overtime which involved delivering letters to letterboxes at the bottom of doors. He sued his employer, An Post, in respect of his injuries. The Court held that the employer was not liable for the first injury suffered, given the steps An Post had taken in response to the dangers posed by such letterboxes. However, the Court found that An Post had fallen below the standard of a "reasonable and prudent" employer in allowing the plaintiff to undertake the overtime in question which resulted in the injury.

In *McMahon v Irish Biscuits Ltd and Power Supermarkets T/A Quinnsworth* (unreported, 28 January 2002), the plaintiff, a sales representative, was injured while checking stock in a Quinnsworth supermarket on behalf of his employer, Irish Biscuits Ltd. The plaintiff, Mr McMahon, engaged in stocktaking activity every Monday for the purpose of placing orders for Quinnsworth with his employer. The only means of accessing all shelving was to climb onto the shelves in question, in the course of which, Mr McMahon fell from the shelves. It was accepted in evidence that while his employers, Irish Biscuits, were aware of the circumstances in which Mr McMahon undertook the stocktaking, management of Quinnsworth was not. The Court held that Irish Biscuits owed a duty to ensure that the facilities their employees visited were free from danger. They had not only failed in that duty but also failed to take steps, after having become aware of the danger on the premises of Quinnsworth, to eliminate that danger. Fault was apportioned as follows: Irish Biscuits Ltd 60%; Powers Supermarkets 30%; and the plaintiff 10% contributory negligence. The Court also found that the defendants' negligence constituted a "breach of their statutory obligations under the relevant provisions of the Factories Acts and Regulations made thereunder".

The role of employees in keeping the workplace safe may also be considered by the Court. In *Aherne v Showerlux (Cork) Ltd* DPIJ: *Hilary* and *Easter* terms 1992, 73 (HC), the plaintiff fell over a pallet that had been left down by a colleague in breach of the employer's safety regulations. The Court reduced the plaintiff's damages by 50% on account of his contributory negligence. It was the responsibility of the plaintiff and his colleagues to see that this area was properly maintained and that every worker was to have regard for his own safety.

The Provision of Proper Equipment

An employer is under a duty to take reasonable care to ensure that proper equipment is provided and maintained in a proper condition so as not to subject those employed to unnecessary risk: see *Smith v Baker & Sons* [1891] AC 325 and *Burke & John Paul & Co Ltd* [1967] IR 277. In considering what steps are reasonable, the court will take into account standards in the industry as a whole. Each case, however, will be decided on its own facts and on the basis of what is reasonable in the particular circumstances of the case.

In *Burke & John Paul & Co Ltd* liability was imposed on an employer who supplied a "guillotine" machine for cutting steel bars which, though quite safe for the purpose of cutting steel, had blunt blades, which required its operator to apply increased physical pressure, resulting in injury to himself. In *Garry v John Sisk & (Dublin) Ltd* (29 January 1973), the Supreme Court imposed liability on an employer who ignored his employee's complaints about the erratic operation of a cement mixer. The employee was subsequently injured by the machine.

In *Bradley v Córas Iompair Éireann* [1976] IR 217, the plaintiff was employed by the defendants as a signalman on the railway. He had replaced a damaged signal light. While he was descending by way of a ladder, he fell and was injured. In the High Court, evidence was submitted that had a steel cage surrounded the ladder the accident could have been prevented. Liability was imposed on the defendants for failing to provide a safe place of work. On appeal to the Supreme Court, the issue to be decided was whether the defendants had fallen below the standard of a reasonable and prudent employer in failing to have installed the safety cage. The Court decided that the issue was to be decided taking into account the following matters: whether the cage in question was one commonly used in the industry; if not, whether it was something that was obviously wanting in the interests of health and safety; and finally, if it was so wanting, whether it was reasonable (taking into account issues such as risk and cost) to impose such a requirement on the defendants. After having taken these considerations into account, the Court held that the defendants were not liable in not having installed safety cages.

Evidence was adduced before the Court that no railway company in Ireland, the United Kingdom or Holland (and possibly other European countries) fitted safety cages of the kind suggested to ladders of the kind from which the plaintiff fell. In addition, the Court heard that for the 10 years prior to this accident, evidence showed that, despite the fact that over 1000 of these uncaged ladders were in operation on the defendants' railway system, not one accident related to their use was reported.

In *Rogers v Bus Átha Cliath* (January 2000), a bus driver had been assaulted on two separate occasions in 1995. The problem of drivers being assaulted was recognised by the employer and steps were taken to put in place safety screens. The Court held that the employer had acted reasonably in all the circumstances: they recognised the existence of the problem, they took steps to address it seriously, they spent significant sums of money in trying to design an acceptable frame, they continuously discussed the proposed solutions with the workers and the unions and when, finally, an acceptable solution was devised they began to implement that solution in a reasonable manner. Liability was not imposed on the employer.

The Provision of a Safe System of Work

An employer is under an obligation to provide a method of working which is as safe as far as is reasonably possible. The fact that an employee is experienced and aware of the risks is not sufficient to absolve the employer of all liability but, it is a factor the courts will take into account.

In *Speed v Thomas Swift & Co Ltd* [1943] KB 557, Lord Greene MR approved the following description of "system of work":

> "What is system and what falls short of system may be difficult to define... but, broadly stated, the distinction is between the general and the particular, between the practice and method adopted in carrying on the master's business of which the master is presumed to be aware and the insufficiency of which he can guard against, and isolated or day-to-day acts of the servant of which the master is not presumed to be aware and which he cannot guard against; in short, it is the distinction between what is permanent or continuous on the one hand, and what is merely casual and emerges in the day's work on the other hand."

In *Caulfield v Bell* [1958] IR 326, Murnaghan J said:

> "The expression, 'a safe system of work' ... has to be considered in every case, to which it is appropriate, in relation to the particular circumstances of the job in hand. In the expression the word, 'safe', means no more than 'as safe as is reasonably possible in the circumstances.' The degree of safety would depend on the particular job, and would vary between wide limits."

In *O'Reilly v Iarnród Éireann* (8 May 2002), the Supreme Court held to be unsafe a system of long-standing tradition among train guards to descend from trains still in motion as they came into stations. In this case, the plaintiff was a guard on a train. He received serious injuries when he stepped off the train which was travelling at between 5 and 15 mph. The Court found the practice to be "patently an unsafe system of work".

In *McSweeney v McCarthy* (Supreme Court, 1986/9039), the plaintiff, an experienced painter, fell from an unsecured ladder when carrying out some painting work for the defendants at the factory of a client. On appeal, the Supreme Court considered whether, given the experience of the plaintiff, it was reasonable to impose liability on the employer for the unsafe system of work which left the ladder unsecured and therefore dangerous. The Court held that, while the experience of the employee was not a complete defence, it was a factor to be considered when deciding what steps should reasonably have been taken. The test for liability should be decided on the basis of control. Ordinarily, it will be the employer who is in control, but in some cases the employee could also be said to exercise control over how the work is done. The Court held that a system did not exist in this case and that, as the injury was foreseeable, the defendants were liable. Liability was apportioned between both parties on the basis of the employee's unreasonable behaviour.

A significant issue in the workplace, which can often give rise to injury, is that of the requirement to lift weights. If an employee is required to lift excessive weights in the course of his or her work, that system of work could be deemed unsafe. The whole area of lifting weights in the course of employment is dealt with primarily through statutory provisions and regulations (see generally the Safety, Health and Welfare at Work (General Application) Regulations 2007 (SI No 299 of 2007), Pt 2, Ch 4). The statutory regime operates alongside the common law. Employers are under an obligation to ensure that employees receive appropriate training in the proper way to lift weights that they are likely to encounter in the course of their work. If an employee suffers injury lifting a weight which is not in itself excessive, that employee can still succeed in an action if it can be shown that the employee had not received the appropriate training in how to lift the weight safely.

In *Kirby v South Eastern Health Board* DPIJ: *Trinity* and *Michaelmas* Terms 1993, 234 (HC), 1993, the plaintiff, a nurse, suffered a back injury lifting and turning a patient. The Court found that the procedure used for turning patients constituted an unsafe system of work. The Court rejected an allegation of contributory negligence on the part of the plaintiff on the basis that the plaintiff "could not reasonably have been aware of the danger present in using this method of lifting without instruction from the defendants".

In *Allen v Ó Suilleabháin and Mid-Western Health Board* (unreported, 28 July 1995, High Court), the plaintiff was a student seeking qualification as a midwife. The second defendant employed the plaintiff, and the first defendant, Mr Ó Suilleabháin, was the senior obstetrician. The plaintiff was working in the delivery ward in the second defendant's hospital. A patient was pregnant with twins. The first was delivered with no complications, but there were difficulties with the second. Mr Ó Suilleabháin, in attempting to deliver the second twin, declined to use the stirrups that were available. Instead, he required the plaintiff and a doctor to hold the legs of the patient. In doing so, the plaintiff suffered a back injury. The issue before the Court was whether the first defendant owed the plaintiff a duty of care. It was held that he did owe her a duty of care and that she was entitled to damages for her injuries. Furthermore, the Court found that the system of work operated by the defendants was unsafe and the plaintiff was acquitted of any contributory negligence. The Court considered that it would be unfair to expect a student midwife to interrupt the obstetrician or the other fully trained midwives in the particular circumstances of this case; Kinlen J said that the plaintiff did "the best she could and could not be faulted for that".

C. Dangerous Work Environments

The courts have addressed, in a number of instances, cases where employees work in dangerous environments. Broadly, there are two such categories of employee: (i) members of the defence forces; and (ii) employees of security firms.

The Defence Forces

Members of the defence forces may, in the course of their work, be placed in situations which expose them to the risk of death or injury. In *Ryan v Ireland* [1989] IR 177, the plaintiff was a member of the defence forces serving voluntarily with the United Nations International Force in Lebanon. He was on guard duty in a guard post. The post was a likely target for mortar attack by militants. The plaintiff was injured when such an attack took place. He sued the State for negligence, claiming that the guard tent should have been better protected with sandbags which would have afforded him greater protection from the effects of the attack. The Supreme Court did not accept the defence of immunity from liability and considered that the State had a duty of care to soldiers even in times of war or armed conflict. Precisely how that duty was to be discharged would necessarily be a matter to be determined on the precise facts and circumstances in which the injury occurred. Plainly, combat situations demanding immediate decision-making ought to be assessed in a manner that takes account of the urgency of such battlefield conditions. Likewise, where soldiers are engaged in passive tasks, such as being on guard duty, there will be greater opportunity for precautions to be taken to minimise exposure to risk.

Employees of Security Firms

In *Walsh v Securicor (Ireland) Ltd* [1993] 2 IR 507, the plaintiff, an employee of the defendant security company, collected a large amount of money, with a colleague, from a bank in order to deliver it to smaller banks and a post office. Their security van was ambushed. Shots were fired at the van. The plaintiff was struck on the head with what was probably the butt end of a rifle. The robbers escaped with most of the money. The plaintiff successfully sued the defendant for negligence. The Supreme Court, in imposing liability, took into account the fact that the time of the delivery had been the same every week for a period of seven years leading up to this robbery; this was a high-risk route, and the delivery times should have been varied periodically. Every precaution, the Court thought, should have been taken in order to minimise risk to the employees.

In *McCann and Cummins v Brinks Allied Ltd and Ulster Bank Ltd* (12 May 1995), the plaintiffs were security men employed by the first defendant. They were injured delivering cash to a bank. They were assaulted by raiders and the first plaintiff received a gunshot wound to the leg. The plaintiffs sued in negligence. They argued that the location and position of the bank relative to the main road and a nearby shopping centre car park made it an attractive target for robbers. The bank had been raided on three previous occasions, two of which involved intercepting the security guards in the process of making deliveries to the bank. The nearest the security van could be driven to the door of the bank was 47 feet. All these factors, the Court found, meant that the employees were exposed to unnecessary risk. The Court concluded that a raid was entirely foreseeable and considered that it was "a self-evident fact that the shorter the distance the money is exposed to potential raiders than the safer the delivery would be". The plaintiffs' employer, Brinks, was held liable in negligence for its failure to provide the plaintiffs with a safe system of work and to take all proper and reasonable precautions for their safety.

D. Liability for Psychological Injury

Employers are responsible for the protection of both the mental and physical health of their employees through ensuring that they provide a safe working environment. This is part of their common law duty of care towards their employees. Employees can suffer psychological injury due to a variety of factors, including, for example, "fear of disease" (see *Fletcher v Commissioners of Public Works* [2003] 1 IR 465), or stress-related injury — which can be the result of being given an unmanageable workload. In *McGrath v Trintech Technologies Ltd & Anor* [2005] 4 IR 382, the Court accepted the proposition that employers can be liable at common law for psychological injury caused to employees as a result of the stress and pressures of the employee's working conditions and workload.

Employers are also under a duty to ensure that their employees do not suffer workplace bullying. Relatively few bullying cases make it to the courts as negligence claims as they are more likely to be dealt with before the Employment Appeals Tribunal as constructive dismissal cases. "Workplace Bullying" is defined in paragraph 5 of the Industrial Relations Act 1990 (Code of Practice Detailing Procedures for Addressing Bullying in the Workplace) (Declaration) Order 2002 (SI No 17 of 2002) as follows:

> "Workplace Bullying is repeated inappropriate behaviour, direct or indirect, whether verbal, physical or otherwise, conducted by one or more persons against another or others, at the place of work and/ or in the course of employment, which could reasonably be regarded as undermining the individual's right to dignity at work. An isolated

incident of the behaviour described in this definition may be an affront to dignity at work but, as a once off incident, is not considered to be bullying."

In *Quigley v Complex Tooling & Moulding Ltd* [2009] 1 IR at 349, it was held by the Supreme Court that for conduct to amount to bullying it had to be repeated, inappropriate, and undermining of the dignity of the employee at work. In his judgment, Fennelly J said:

"The plaintiff cannot succeed in his claim unless he also proves that he suffered damage amounting to personal injury as a result of his employer's breach of duty. Where the personal injury is not of a direct physical kind, it must amount to an identifiable psychiatric injury."

Examples of behaviour that may constitute bullying are as follows (HSA):

- Purposely undermining someone;
- Targeting someone for special negative treatment;
- Manipulation of an individual's reputation;
- Social exclusion or isolation;
- Intimidation;
- Aggressive or obscene language;
- Jokes that are obviously offensive to one individual by spoken word or email;
- Intrusion by pestering, spying and stalking;
- Unreasonable assignments to duties which are obviously unfavourable to one individual;
- Repeated requests with impossible deadlines or impossible tasks.

E. Voluntary Assumption of Risk (*Volenti Non Fit Injuria*)

In earlier times, the defence of voluntary assumption of risk operated to absolve employers of liability in cases where their employees suffered injury in the course of their employment. The defence can still operate under the Civil Liability Act 1961, s 34(1)(b), but is quite restrictive. Only a communicated waiver of a right of action will constitute a voluntary assumption of risk: an uncommunicated determination to waive a right of action will not be enough. Under the 1961 Act the defendant must establish that the plaintiff agreed to waive his legal rights in respect of the defendant's act and that such agreement was made before the act. In *O'Hanlon v Electricity Supply Board* [1969] IR 75, the Supreme Court held that an uncommunicated decision to undergo a risk was insufficient to allow the defendant to rely on the defence.

F. Vicarious Liability

What is Vicarious Liability?

Vicarious liability is where the law holds one person liable for a wrong committed by another even though the person held liable is not at fault. The most important example of vicarious liability is that of the liability of an employer for the torts of an employee. There is, however, a distinction to be made between the personal liability of the employer for the acts of the employee and the vicarious liability of the employer for the torts of the employee. If an injured person complains that the employer authorised the employee to commit the action complained of, or that the employer was at fault, in selecting or supervising the employee, for example, he or she is alleging that the employer is personally liable. In a case such as this, the claim is made against the employer directly, not against the employer through the employee. This is not vicarious liability.

An example of an employer being liable for injury caused to a third party is *Dowling v Moore* (1897) 31 ILT 367 & Sol J (CC). The defendant's employee was in charge of a pony and van for the purpose of making deliveries. He left the van unattended to deliver some parcels. The unattended pony injured the plaintiff's horse. The Court held that the defendant was liable because he had imposed on the driver two incompatible duties: tending the pony and delivering parcels. He could not realistically do both. The defendant employer was liable because the system of work put in place was defective. Another example is *Curley v Mannion* [1965] IR 543. The defendant's daughter, whilst closing the back door of the defendant's parked vehicle, struck and injured a cyclist. The Supreme Court held that the defendant, as owner and driver of the vehicle, owed a duty to other persons using the highway not merely not to use or drive the car negligently but to take reasonable precautions to ensure that the car, while under his control and supervision, was not used in a negligent fashion. This was a personal duty under which the owner might be liable, even if the girl in question, because of her age, was not negligent.

Employers' Liability for the Torts of Employees

As mentioned, vicarious liability is where the law imposes liability on the employer for the torts of the employee if they are committed within the scope of his employment. Vicarious liability may be justified on the following bases:

- that the employer is taken to have control over his or her employee; he or she determines who they employ, what work is done and how, and is thus assumed to be the best able to ensure that care is taken;
- it is seen as a means of loss spreading: owing to the fact that employers will generally be insured, and the fact that they may defray costs by charging

higher prices, the employer will have the "deepest pocket" when it comes to compensation;

- because the employer stands to profit from the enterprise, it is fair that he or she should also bear the risks;
- identifiability: for example, for a wrong occurring in a hospital setting, an injured patient need not identify the precise medical profession responsible but may claim against the hospital or the HSE.

The Three Ingredients of Vicarious Liability

Vicarious liability makes the employer liable for:

(a) a tort;

(b) committed by his employee;

(c) in the scope of employment.

A Tort

This will most commonly be a common law tort, such as negligence or battery, but will include statutory torts. Costello P in *Health Board v BC* (19 January 1994), at 10 stated:

> "In the absence of express statutory provision … in relation to the liability of an employer for the tortious acts (including statutory torts) of his employee… an employer is vicariously liable where the act is committed by his employee within the scope of his employment."

Committed by His/Her Employee

Who, for the purposes of vicarious liability, is an employee? The general rule is that vicarious liability applies only to employees, not independent contractors. Since not all workers are employees, it is important to understand the distinction between employees and independent contractors. The term "employee" has been held to include those doing work of a casual nature and on a voluntary basis.

It must be established that the wrongdoer was actually an employee (as mentioned, the older cases refer to employees as "servants" and employers as "masters"). For the purposes of establishing vicarious liability, an important feature is the "control" that the employer exercises over the worker. But this "control test" is not decisive. Other factors may be taken into account, for example: the method of pay (whether the worker is paid a salary or fee); whether the worker provides his or her own equipment or not; whether the contract is a "contract of service" or a "contract for services"; whether there is a right to sub-contract, the extent to which the person doing the work is integrated into the business. For instance, a private chauffeur would be an employee, whereas a taxi driver would be an independent contractor. The law takes the full range of circumstances into account in determining whether a person is an employee or not and essentially relies on the reality of the relationship, rather than the terms of the contract or what is the understanding between the parties.

The Supreme Court examined the issue of control in *Henry Denny & Sons (Ireland) Ltd v Minister for Social Welfare* [1998] 1 IR 34. The appellants employed a Ms Mahon as a shop demonstrator, i.e. a person in a supermarket who offered free samples of the appellants' products to shoppers. They argued that she was employed under a "contract for services" (an independent contractor) and therefore they were not required to make any social insurance contributions on her behalf. The Department of Social Welfare disagreed and required that the insurance contributions be made. Although a statement of terms and conditions from the appellants expressly stated that Ms Mahon was to be an independent contractor and that she was to be responsible for her own tax affairs, the Court found that there was sufficient control exercised by the appellants over the work of Ms Mahon such that she was quite properly classified as an employee rather than an independent contractor.

In the leading case of *Mersey Docks and Harbour Board v Coggins & Griffiths* [1947] AC 1, the issue of borrowed, or "hired out", employees fell to be considered. There, the Board employed the tortfeasor as crane driver and lent both him and his crane to a firm of stevedores, C & G. The contract between the Board and C & G provided that the crane driver should be the employee of C & G. The driver continued to be paid by the Board, which also had the power to dismiss him. When a third party was injured as a result of the crane driver's negligence, the question arose as to who was to be treated as his employer for the purposes of vicarious liability. The House of Lords held that, despite the terms of the contract, the Board had failed to rebut the presumption that it remained the employer for the purposes of vicarious liability. The fact that the crane was lent at the same time strengthened the presumption.

In *Lynch v Palgrave Murphy Ltd* [1964] IR 150 the "control test" was given consideration. There, Palgrave Murphy Ltd were stevedores, who hired out from Crosbie a forklift operator (Byrne) at the rate of £1 an hour. While operating the forklift, Byrne injured the plaintiff, a casual dock labourer employed by Palgrave Murphy Ltd. The plaintiff sued Palgrave Murphy Ltd claiming that it was vicariously liable for the tort of the forklift operator. Byrne was employed, paid, and subject to dismissal by Crosbie, but was subject to the general directions of Palgrave Murphy Ltd. For example Palgrave would determine what load to take, where to put it, etc. The Supreme Court had to decide whether or not the forklift operator was an employee or an independent contractor. It held the matter should be determined by the degree of control the defendants were entitled to exercise in relation to the act which was performed negligently. The mere fact that they could assign the task to be done by the forklift operator was not sufficient control to make them liable. For this to happen, it would have to be shown that Palgrave had the power to control the method by which the negligent act of the operation was done. In this case, the Court approved the tests applied by the Court in the *Mersey Docks Case* and held that the plaintiff had failed to show that the required degree of control had passed to the temporary employers, the defendants.

In *JGE v The Trustees of the Portsmouth Roman Catholic Diocesan Trust* [2012] EWCA Civ 938, the English Court of Appeal confirmed that vicarious liability could be imposed on a Roman Catholic bishop who had appointed a parish priest who then went on to sexually abuse children living in a children's home administered by his diocese. Despite the absence of a contract of employment, direct control and payment of wages, the Court held that the relationship was "sufficiently akin to employment" to found vicarious liability in the case of this "complex social ill".

Control was brought into sharp focus in *Phelan v Coilte Teoranta* [1993] 1 IR 18. A Mr Carswood, a welder/fitter, was engaged almost full-time by Coilte Teoranta. He travelled extensively tending to forestry machinery needing repair and servicing. Coilte paid him an hourly rate which was negotiated annually and a mileage allowance in respect of his own car. He supplied his own tools and equipment. He received no holiday pay or pension entitlements. Coilte made no deductions for PAYE tax or PRSI contributions. Occasionally he was given some instruction by a Coilte employee. In this particular case, the plaintiff, a Coilte employee, was directed to assist him. The plaintiff was injured through Mr Carswood's negligence. The Court was of the view that the element of control was the overriding consideration, even though the operative was an independent contractor. Coilte was held vicariously liable.

The English courts have more recently established that dual vicarious liability may be possible in cases where the negligent employee was working under the supervision and control of employees of two different companies. This occurred in *Viasystems (Tyneside) Ltd v Thermal Transfer (Northern) Ltd* [2006] QB 510. In that case, the plaintiff engaged the first defendant to install air conditioning in its factory. The first defendant subcontracted the ducting involved to the second defendant. The second defendant contracted with the third defendant to provide fitters and fitters' mates on a "labour only" basis. The fitters and their mates in this instance, Megson and Strang, were installing ductwork under the supervision or instruction of Mr Horsley who was a self-employed fitter contracted to the second defendant. Strang, one of the mates, was sent to get some fittings by Megson and while he was away Mr Horsley was assisting Megson. When he was returning, the fitter's mate, Strang, set off a fire protection sprinkler system, which caused flooding resulting in loss to the plaintiff. Strang had, without question, been negligent. The English Court of Appeal held that in the circumstances, both the second and third defendants could be vicariously liable for Strang's negligence. Whether dual vicarious liability arises depends on the facts of each case, but in particular, on the circumstances relating to the level of control which the defendant exercises on each occasion.

This approach was later approved by the UK Supreme Court in *Various Claimants v Catholic Child Welfare Society* [2012] 3 WLR 1319. There, dual vicarious liability was imposed upon a religious order of brothers and the manager of a residential school where some of the brothers had sexually abused pupils. The Court ruled that dual vicarious liability could be imposed

> "where the employee in question, at any rate for relevant purposes, is so much a part of the work, business or organisation of both employers that it is just to make both employers answer for his negligence".

Whether or not the Irish courts adopt a similar approach remains to be seen.

In the past, "hospital cases" gave rise to some uncertainty on the basis that it could not be said that employers controlled the way in which surgeons, anaesthetists, or nurses carried out their respective tasks. However, it is well accepted now that the medical staff in the full-time service of hospitals are employees for the purposes of vicarious liability. For example, in *O'Donovan v Cork County Council* [1967] IR 173, in an action against the defendant Council for the alleged negligence of a surgeon and an anaesthetist, the defendant did not even contest the proposition that it would be vicariously liable if negligence were proved on the part of the surgeon or the anaesthetist. However, in *Bolton v Blackrock Clinic Ltd* (20 December 1994), the plaintiff unsuccessfully sued a cardiothoracic surgeon and a consultant thoracic physician for negligence in her treatment. She also sued the hospital on the basis of vicarious liability. The plaintiff's claim was dismissed against the specialists: but the Court observed that "as the plaintiff was a private patient of the doctors in a private hospital, the question of vicarious liability may not arise".

In *Byrne v Ryan* [2009] 4 IR 542, the Court found a hospital to be vicariously liable in respect of the plaintiff, a public patient, who had been referred to the hospital and not to an individual consultant. The Court cited the important English decisions of *Cassidy v Minister of Health* [1951] 2 KB 343 and *Roe v Minister of Health* [1954] 2 QB 66.

We can see from these cases that the key factor the courts take into account in determining whether or not liability can be imposed vicariously is the degree of control the principal exercises over the wrongdoer. Although most vicarious liability cases will concern employer/employee relationships, the principle operates in situations of *de facto* service too. In *Moynihan v Moynihan* [1975] IR 192, for example, the plaintiff, aged 2, was injured when visiting her grandmother's house, when she accidentally pulled a teapot containing hot tea over herself causing serious injury. The tea had been prepared by the defendant's daughter, Marie, and left unattended and within reach of the unsupervised plaintiff. She sued the defendant in the High Court for negligence and vicarious liability. The case was withdrawn from the jury on the basis that no reasonable grounds for liability existed. The Supreme Court reversed, holding that the defendant's daughter had been negligent and the defendant, as the householder and as the person in control of the hospitality being provided by her in her own house, would be vicariously liable for damage resulting from the negligence of her daughter.

It is also important to note that, although the general rule is that a person is not vicariously liable for the torts of his or her independent contractors, such liability can arise in limited circumstances. This might occur where an employer has been personally negligent, for example in selecting incompetent contractors. In addition, in torts such as nuisance, *Rylands v Fletcher*, and breach of statutory duty, liability may be imposed irrespective of fault on the defendant's part: the defendant may be responsible even where the acts complained of are committed by his independent contractors: see *Rivers v Cutting* [1982] 1 WLR 1146; *Rylands v Fletcher* (1868) LR 3 HL 330.

In the Scope of Employment

The rationale for vicarious liability requires that it be restricted to torts committed in the scope of employment, rather than, say, where the employee is engaged in private activities. Whether an employee is acting in the scope of his employment may involve an examination of temporal and spatial considerations. Temporal considerations would involve examining acts that took place outside normal working hours, and spatial considerations would involve examining acts that took place away from the place of work.

In *Boyle v Ferguson* [1911] 2 IR 489, for example, a car salesman who, in the company of two women, went out for "a spin" at 7 pm on a Saturday evening was held to be acting within the scope of his employment. The Court took into account the fact that the employer was paying for the petrol at the time, and the fact that the salesman had been given significant latitude in his hours and methods of work. On the other hand, in *Kiely v McCrea & Sons Ltd* [1940] Ir Jur Rep 1, the High Court held that a commercial traveller, whose terms of employment provided that he should "use his best endeavours to effect the sale of the goods of the company" but was expressly prohibited from using the company's motor car for private purposes, was found to be acting outside the scope of his employment when he negligently drove his car so as to cause an accident while coming home from a dance. Although some employees of firms with which he dealt were passengers in the car at the time of the accident, this was held to be not sufficient on this particular occasion to render his employer liable.

In general, we can see that where the employee is doing what he is supposed to do, even if he is doing it badly, the employer is liable for the employee's torts. On the other hand, if the employee is doing something that he is not employed to do, the employer will not be liable. The courts' approach in determining the employer's liability nowadays is to examine whether the act in question was within the scope of the employee's duties, not whether the act was permitted by the employer.

In *Farry v Great Northern Railway Co* [1898] 2 IR 352 (QB), a station employee detained the plaintiff in order to examine his ticket. The plaintiff sued the company for false imprisonment. The Court held the company vicariously liable. Palles CB said:

> "… two separate things are to be considered: first, the act done; secondly, the purpose for which it is done… If the act is outside the scope of the servant's employment, the master is not responsible, and in such a case it is unnecessary to consider the purpose… But, when the act… is one within the ordinary scope of the servant's employment then arises the question whether the act complained of was done for the employer; as, if the act, although of a class within the scope of the employment, was done by the servant, for his own purposes, such, for instance, as wreaking his own vengeance or spite upon a particular person, the act, although capable of being done within the scope of employment, is not in fact done within such scope; it is not done for the employer."

In *Rose v Plenty and Co-Operative Retail Services Ltd* [1976] 1 All ER 97, a 13-year-old boy was injured while riding with a milkman on his float to help him deliver milk. Such giving of lifts on the float was expressly prohibited by the employer. Nonetheless, it was held to be within the scope of employment because it was an improper way of doing exactly what the milkman was employed to do, and thereby further the employer's business. On the other hand, in *Twine v Beans Express* [1946] 1 All ER 202, a driver giving a lift in his delivery van to someone, contrary to instructions, was held to be outside the scope of employment. The passenger was a trespasser and was in no way contributing to the purpose of the employment. In *Murphy v Ross* [1920] 2 IR 199, the Court held that when a boy, who was asked by a foreman to point out a route to a new driver, was injured by the negligence of the driver, there was sufficient evidence that the foreman was acting within the scope of his employment for the matter to go to a jury.

We can see, therefore, that an employer's prohibition forbidding the employee from acting in a particular way does not automatically exonerate the employer from liability. Such prohibition is just one of the many factors to be taken into account by the court.

The State was held vicariously liable for the actions of two members of An Garda Síochána in *McIntyre v Lewis* [1991] 1 IR 121. There, the plaintiff had been beaten up by two Garda officers and then arrested and charged with assaulting one of the officers in question. The State was held vicariously liable in assault, false imprisonment and malicious prosecution.

In some cases, injuries occur in the workplace through horseplay or "larking". In such circumstances, it could be said that if the horseplay is merely an amusing or dangerous way of doing something that the employee is engaged to do, then the employer should be held vicariously liable. In *Harrison v Michelin Tyre Co Ltd* [1985] 1 All ER 118, for example, where an employee was employed to push a truck along a passageway and, for fun, diverted the truck against a fellow employee, the employer was held vicariously liable. On the other hand, in *Aldred v Nacanco* [1987] IRLR 292, an employee pushed a wash basin, known to be unsteady, against another employee in order to frighten her. It was held that this was a deliberate act which had nothing to do with anything the employee was employed to do. Accordingly it was entirely outside the scope of her employment. The employers were not vicariously liable.

Employees who engage in detours or "frolics" may be doing something so unconnected with their employment that vicarious liability will not be imposed on their employers. In *O'Connell v Bateman* [1932] LJ Ir 160, the employee borrowed his employer's lorry to visit his parents. The lorry was involved in an accident, but the employer was held not liable. By contrast, in *Jameson v Byrne and Maguire* (1926) 60 ILTR 11, the employee completed a petrol delivery and made a detour on his journey for a reason unconnected with his employment and was involved in an accident. The High Court held that there was evidence from which a jury might infer that the employee was acting within the scope of his employment. Accordingly, it seems that slight deviations will not relieve the employer of liability, whereas major deviations ("frolics"), might.

As we have seen, if the employee acts outside the scope of his employment, the employer will not be vicariously liable. But if the employee is doing the kind of thing he or she is employed to do, the employer will remain liable even if the employee does it improperly. However, it is also possible for the employer not to be liable if the employee is doing something different in kind from that which he or she is employed to do. In *Irving & Irving v Post Office* [1987] IRLR 289, a post office worker wrote an offensive racist remark on a letter addressed to a couple of Jamaican origin. The Post Office was held not to be vicariously liable because the substance and purpose of what the employee had written was unconnected with the performance of his duties.

The liability of the State in respect of the wrongs of teachers has been examined in a number of cases. In *Delahunty v South Eastern Health Board & Others* [2003] IEHC 132, a visiting boy to St Joseph's Industrial School was sexually assaulted by a house parent in the school. The plaintiff took an action against the South Eastern Health Board, St Joseph's Industrial School and the Minister. The Minister was not held vicariously liable as the State was considered not to have had sufficient control or managerial functions in the running of the school to attract vicarious liability for the tort of the house parent.

Similarly, in *O'Keefe v Hickey & the Minister for Education and Science, Ireland and The Attorney General* [2008] IESC 72, the State was not held vicariously liable where the plaintiff, as a child, was subjected to a number of sexual assaults by a schoolteacher in the early 1970s. The Supreme Court took the view that the State defendants could not be liable for the teacher's tortious and criminal acts on the ordinary and established principles of vicarious liability. This was on the basis that the perpetrator was not the Minister's employee: the Minister did not employ or direct him. The Minister merely laid down rules for national schools but they were general in nature and did not allow him to govern the detailed activities of any individual teacher. Although the Minister inspected the schools for academic performance, it went no further than that. The Supreme Court also stated that the Minister was deprived of the direct control of the schools because "there was interposed between the State and the child the manager or the committee or board of management". All these factors distanced the Minister and the State authorities from the management of the school and the control of the teacher in question. These factors were the direct consequences of the long established system of education, mandated in the Constitution, whereby the Minister pays and, to a certain extent, regulates: but the schools and teachers are controlled by their clerical managers and patrons. The Court also said that it was not its concern either to endorse or to criticise that system but merely to register its existence and the obvious fact that it deprives the Minister and the State of direct control of schools, teachers, and pupils.

The plaintiff in this case, Louise O'Keefe, subsequently brought her case to the European Court of Human Rights (*O'Keeffe v Ireland* [GC], No 35810/09, ECHR 2014). Its judgment was handed down in January 2014. It ruled that Ireland had violated Article 3 of the European Convention on Human Rights which states: "No one shall be subjected to torture or to inhuman or degrading treatment or punishment." Ireland was found, in this particular case, to have failed to have in place proper systems to prevent or punish sexual abuse. The State was also found by the Court to have failed in its positive obligations towards Louise O'Keeffe to prevent and punish the torture, inhuman and degrading treatment that she suffered. The Court also ruled that Ireland had violated Article 13 of the Convention, which obliges the State to provide an effective remedy in respect of complaints of rights violations.

In *Poland v John Parr and Sons* [1927] 1 KB 236, a carter in the employment of the defendants, while on his way home in the middle of the day, was following close behind a wagon laden with sugar in bags and being driven by one of his employers. He saw the plaintiff, a boy, walking beside the wagon with his hand on one of the bags. Honestly and reasonably thinking that the plaintiff was stealing sugar from the bag, he gave him a blow with his hand on the back of his neck. The plaintiff fell and the wheel of the wagon injured his foot. It was held that in the circumstances the carter had implied authority to make reasonable efforts to protect and preserve the defendants' property: that the violence exerted was not so excessive so as to take his act outside the scope of the authority, and that the defendants were liable.

Poland was cited in *Reilly v Ryan* [1991] 2 IR 247. There, the plaintiff sued the defendant for injury suffered while he was on the defendant's licensed premises. The incident occurred when a robber, wearing a balaclava and wielding a knife, sought to steal money from the till. The manager of the bar grabbed the plaintiff and, while using him as a human shield, the plaintiff was stabbed. The plaintiff sued the defendant on the basis that he was vicariously liable for the acts of his employee. The action was dismissed by the Circuit Court, but was appealed to the High Court. There, the Court considered whether the defendant was vicariously liable for the acts of the bar manager, and, in particular, whether the bar manager had been acting in the scope of his employment when he held the plaintiff and used him as a human shield. The Court ruled that the bar manager had exceeded his authority when he used the customer in that way and was therefore acting outside the scope of his employment. The Court accepted as correct the statements of the law set out in *Salmond on Torts* (10th ed) p 89 and (18th Ed) p 437 which was approved by the Court of Appeal in England in *Poland* at p 240:

> "A master is not responsible for a wrongful act done by his servant unless it is done in the course of his employment. It is deemed to be so done if it is either (a) a wrongful act authorised by the master, or (b) a wrongful and unauthorised mode of doing some act authorised by the master."

LIABILITY FOR DEFECTIVE PRODUCTS

Learning Outcomes

Upon completion of this chapter, the reader should be able to:

- Explain the relationship between the common law rules and the strict liability regime under statute;
- Appreciate how actions may be taken under both the common law and statute;
- Trace the development of common law remedies for injury caused by defective products;
- Identify and explain the key features of the Liability for Defective Products Act 1991;
- Understand how key concepts are defined in the 1991 Act;
- Outline the defences available to producers under the 1991 Act.

A. Overview

At common law, where a person was injured by a defective product, they were restricted to suing only those with whom they had a contractual relationship. The doctrine of privity of contract meant that manufacturers would not be liable to the end-users of their products unless those end-users had a contract with them. All that changed with *Donoghue v Stevenson* [1932] AC 562. There, the House of Lords recognised the plaintiff's right to sue the manufacturer even though the parties were not in a contractual relationship with each other. Liability under *Donoghue v Stevenson* was in the tort of negligence. Therefore, it was fault-based. The plaintiff had to prove that the manufacturer was at fault, or negligent. This placed a significant burden upon injured plaintiffs. In response to this, the European Union has sought to make manufacturers of products strictly liable for injury caused as a result of defects in their products. This was done through Council Directive No 85/374/EEC of 25 July 1985 (the "product liability Directive"). This Directive was transposed into Irish law by the Liability for Defective Products Act 1991.

Figure 9.1

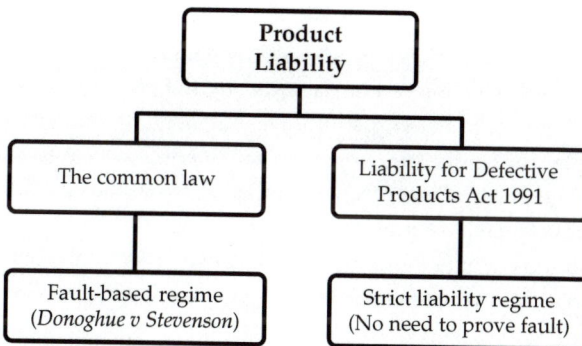

B. The Common Law

Historical Context

Historically, as mentioned above, the courts were reluctant to recognise the right of persons injured by products to recover damages in negligence against those with whom there was no privity of contract. In *Winterbottom v Wright* (1842) 10 M & W 109, 152 ER 402, the plaintiff, a coach driver of the mail coach from Hertford to Holyhead, was seriously injured when the coach he was driving broke down on account of a latent defect. The plaintiff's employer was under a contractual obligation to supply coachmen to the Postmaster General to convey the mail. The defendant was under a contractual obligation with the Postmaster

General to keep the coach in a proper state of repair. The plaintiff's claim was dismissed because it disclosed no cause of action.

Over time, the courts relaxed their approach. In the United States, in *McPherson v Buick Motor Co* (1916) 217 NYS 382, 111 NE 1050, the Court held that the category of "inherently dangerous things" should include "anything which would be dangerous if negligently made". In the Canadian decision of *Buckley v Mott* (1920) 50 DLR 408 general liability for negligent manufacture was imposed. That step was taken in the UK in *Donoghue v Stevenson* in 1932 (see chapter 2).

In Ireland, in *Power v Bedford Motor Co* [1959] IR 391 the Supreme Court approved *Donoghue v Stevenson* as a settled principle in Irish law. Lavery J said:

> "It is clear in principle that the obligation is not confined to manufacturers of goods but extends to persons undertaking repairs to articles which will be dangerous to users who should be in contemplation if there is a want of reasonable care in the work. It must also apply to persons doing work on an article which they foresee would be used by others without examination."

This meant that manufacturers of products owed a duty of care towards those who may foreseeably be injured or damaged by the product. This also applied to repairers of goods. In *Power*, liability was imposed on the defendant garage for the negligent repair of a car, which left the steering mechanism dangerously unsafe after the repairs had been completed. Even those who install and assemble products have been held liable. In *Brown v Cotterill* (1934) 51 TLR 21, liability was imposed on a monumental mason where a tombstone that he had erected fell on a child who was placing flowers on her grandmother's grave.

Liability of Suppliers, Retailers and Repairers

Suppliers of products can also be held liable at common law. In *Keegan v Owens* [1953] IR 267, the Supreme Court held that a supplier for reward of swing-boats for a charity carnival owed a duty to protect a worker employed by the carnival committee from injury in operating the swing-boats.

Retailers may also owe a duty of care in tort to those who may foreseeably be injured by the products they sell. Retailers will, of course, already have contractual relationships with those who purchase goods in their shops. Tortious liability will run in parallel to these wide-ranging contractual obligations: see *Duffy v Rooney and Dunnes Stores (Dundalk) Ltd* (23 June 1997) affirmed (23 April 1998) (Supreme Court), see chapter 2.

What about cases where a manufacturer manufacturers a product which contains a defective component manufactured by someone else? This question was considered by the Supreme Court in *Fleming v Henry Denny & Sons Ltd* (29 July 1955). There, the defendants were manufacturers of black puddings. They were supplied with the following ingredients: meal, rusk meal and spices. The Court held that the manufacturers were entitled to rely on the firms that supplied them with these ingredients to take care that they were free from hidden dangers, such as a piece of steel. The Court was of the view that, in general, a manufacturer whose duty is to take reasonable care not to send out food containing any harmful substance may, in so far as the ingredients of that food are concerned, discharge his duty by obtaining the ingredients from firms of high repute who have a like responsibility to see that the ingredients are free from any dangers. The Court made it clear, however, that this will not be so in every case. The defect may be so obvious that it is a failure of reasonable care not to observe it.

It is clear from the case law that a duty will be owed to any person, not just consumers, who would foreseeably come into proximity with the dangerous product. In *Power v Bedford Motor Co*, the Court observed that all users of the highway, not just the driver of the vehicle in question, are persons to whom the repairer owed a duty. In *Barnett v H & J Packer & Co Ltd* [1940] 3 All ER 557, a confectioner was injured by a sweet which he was placing in a display tray. The sweet contained a piece of wire or steel which pricked the plaintiff's hand and gave him serious blood-poisoning. He was permitted to sue, even though the goods in question had not reached the "ultimate consumer".

Duty to Warn

Manufactures, retailers and suppliers may be under a duty to warn users of products about dangers attached to their use. In *O'Meara v O'Brien and B Braun Medical Ltd* (30 June 1999), the Court imposed liability on the supplier of a machine used for sterilising instruments in a hospital. The plaintiff, a nurse, suffered burns using the machine. The defendant supplier was aware of the danger but failed to mention it in the technical data. In *Bolands Ltd v Trouw Ireland Ltd* (1 May 1978) (HC) the Court stated that a person in control of a dangerous substance, whether a supplier, manufacturer or vendor, is under a duty to take reasonable care that any person acquiring it from him, whether by sale or otherwise, does not suffer injury or loss.

Manufacturers and retailers are under a duty to ensure that appropriate warning labels are attached to garments that are flammable. In *O'Byrne v Gloucester* (3 November 1988), the Supreme Court upheld a finding of negligence against the makers of a brushed cotton skirt for their failure to attach to it a warning that the skirt was highly flammable. The plaintiff, who was aged 15 at the time, had been severely burned after the hem of her skirt had touched a gas heater in her living room. The Court observed that this was a danger that the defendants should have foreseen. The injury to the plaintiff could have been avoided by taking the simple precaution of attaching a warning that the garment was dangerous if exposed to a naked flame and would burn rapidly. This was a precaution, the Court said, that a reasonably careful manufacturer and vendor of this type of clothing should have taken.

A warning label was attached to a garment in *Browne v Primark t/a Penneys* (10 December 1990). In that case, the plaintiff was a boy aged about five years. He was playing with matches and his pyjamas caught fire as result of which he was badly burned. He sued the manufacturer and retailer in negligence. The warning label clearly stated "Keep away from fire", which satisfied the relevant standards at the time. The Court granted a non-suit, concluding that the manufacturer and retailer had exercised reasonable care.

A rather different issue arose in *Duffy v Rooney and Dunnes Stores (Dundalk) Ltd* [1997] IEHC 102. A girl aged two years and 10 months was badly burned when a coat she was wearing on a visit to her grandparents' home came in contact with an open fire in the sitting room. No warning label was attached to the coat. The Court was of the view that a reasonably prudent manufacturer or retailer, if it had properly addressed the issue, would have fixed a label on the coat warning that it should be kept away from fire. However, the plaintiff's claim against the retailer was dismissed on the basis that even if the label had been attached to the coat, the child would still have worn it. This case demonstrates that, in such cases, the plaintiff must not only prove that a breach of duty occurred by failing to warn, but also that the breach resulted in the injury (see chapter 6: Causation in Fact).

In *Cassells v Marks & Spencer plc* [2002] 1 IR 179, a five-year-old girl was burned when her cotton day dress was brought too a close to a fire. The Court in this case made a distinction between day dresses and nightdresses, taking the view that nightdresses presented a greater risk of injury caused by fire than daywear. The Court also considered that the defendant was entitled to take into account that the official independent bodies in Britain and Ireland, which regulated the market, had not deemed it necessary in the interests of public safety to impose any flammability test or fire warning for children's day dresses.

If a product is given by one person to another as a gift the law traditionally required that the donor of the gift give a warning of any danger known to him or her. It appears this would also apply where a person gratuitously lends a product to another. In *Campbell v O'Donnell* [1967] IR 2 226 the Court stated that there was

> "ample authority for the proposition that, independently of any contractual relationship between the parties, the donor owes at least the duty to give warnings of any dangers actually known to him."

Non-Dangerous Defects

Dangerous defects will usually result in physical injury to person or property. Non-dangerous defects will usually result in economic loss. There is a serious question as to whether economic loss is recoverable in negligence in Irish law at all outside of negligent misstatement and the particular circumstances in *Siney v Corporation of Dublin* [1980] IR 400 and *Ward v McMaster* [1988] IR 337. In *Glencar Explorations plc v Mayo County Council (No 2)* [2002] 1 IR 84, Keane CJ said that he would

> "expressly reserve for another occasion the question as to whether economic loss is recoverable in actions for negligence other than actions for negligent misstatement and those falling within the categories identified in *Siney* [...] and *Ward* [...] and whether the decision of the House of Lords in *Junior Books Ltd v Veitchi Co Ltd* [1983] 1 AC 520 should be followed in this jurisdiction."

C. The Liability for Defective Products Act 1991

The Liability for Defective Products Act 1991 provides a strict liability regime for liability for defective products. Its source is Council Directive No 85/374/EEC of 25 July 1985, a European Directive, which Ireland was obliged under its EU Treaty obligations to transpose into Irish law. The 1991 Act achieves this. The essence of the Act is set out in s 2(1), which states:

> "The producer shall be liable in damages in tort for damage caused wholly or partly by a defect in his product."

This provision makes it clear that liability is based on proof of the existence of a defect in the product which has caused damage to the plaintiff, rather than wrongful conduct. This distinguishes it from negligence which requires proof of wrongful conduct, or fault. The words "in tort" clarify that matters such as contributory negligence, concurrent wrongs, and damages will be relevant. Also, the words "or partly" reflects the objective of Article 8(1) of the Directive which provides that the liability of the producer "shall not be reduced when the damage is caused both by a defect in the product and by the act or omission of a third party."

What is a "Product"?

Section 1(1) defines a "product" as including all movables except "primary agricultural products", even where the movables are incorporated into other movables or into immovables. This provision has since been amended by the European Communities (Liability for Defective Products) Regulations 2000 (SI No 401 of 2000) which means that primary agricultural products are now subject to the same strict regime has other products. This amendment was introduced following the CJD scare in the 1990s. Electricity is a "product" for the purposes of the Act where "damage is caused as a result of a failure in the process of generation of electricity". In England, blood has been held to be a "product": see *A v National Blood Authority* [2001] 3 All ER 289.

The Act only applies to "movables". Immovables are generally land, such as buildings. The Act may apply, however, to defective products "incorporated into" buildings which result in damage. For example, if a defective girder incorporated into a house causes the house to collapse, the Act may apply. It would be important to distinguish between a defective movable which has been incorporated and a movable which has been defectively incorporated. The latter situation would probably not be covered by the Act, assuming the movable itself is not defective.

Who is a "Producer"?

Section 2(2) defines "producer". It states:

"In this Act, 'producer' means—

(a) the manufacturer or producer of a finished product, or

(b) the manufacturer or producer of any raw material or the manufacturer or producer of a component part of a product, or

(c) in the case of the products of the soil, of stock-farming and of fisheries and game, which have undergone initial processing, the person who carried out such processing, or

(d) any person who, by putting his name, trade mark or other distinguishing feature on the product or using his name or any such mark or feature in relation to the product, has held himself out to be the producer of the product, or

(e) any person who has imported the product into a Member State from a place outside the European Communities in order, in the course of any business of his, to supply it to another, or

(f)   any person who is liable as producer of the product pursuant to subsection (3) of this section."

It will be noted that under para (e), a who person imports into the EU a product for sale, hire, leasing or any form of distribution in the course of his business is deemed to be a producer within the meaning of the Act.

Section 2(3) of the Act provides a useful device for injured persons experiencing difficulty in identifying the producer of a defective product. It provides that where the producer of the product cannot be identified by taking reasonable steps, each supplier of the product is treated as its producer unless the supplier informs the injured person "within a reasonable time" of the identity of the producer, or of the person who supplied him or her with the product. By virtue of s 2(3)(b) and (c), the requirement as to "reasonable time" applies not merely to the supplier after he or she has received the request for information, but also to the injured person in making the request. The request must be made "within a reasonable time after the damage occurs and at a time when it is not reasonably practicable for the injured person to identify" the producer.

It should be noted that only a person who imports the product into the EU, in order, in the course of his or her business, to supply it to another will be treated as a producer. This means that the Act will not apply where holidaymakers import items on a non-commercial basis into the EU from outside. The effect of this provision is that EU consumers should not have to go abroad to litigate in non-EU jurisdictions in circumstances where they suffer injury as a consequence of a defect in a product commercially imported from outside the EU.

What is Meant by "Defective Product"?
Section 5 of the 1991 Act sets out the circumstances in which a product is deemed to be defective. Section 5 states:

"(1)   For the purposes of this Act a product is defective if it fails to provide the safety which a person is entitled to expect, taking all circumstances into account, including—

(a)   the presentation of the product,
(b)   the use to which it could reasonably be expected that the product would be put, and
(c)   the time when the product was put into circulation.

(2)   A product shall not be considered defective for the sole reason that a better product is subsequently put into circulation."

This definition appears to confine "defectiveness" to products that are unsafe. Therefore, products that are safe but shoddy do not fall within the Act. The use of the word "safety" is important. A product is defective when it does not "provide the safety which a person is entitled to expect, taking all the circumstances into account". Section 5(1) refers to three such circumstances. The first is "the presentation of the product". If a product, for example, is represented through advertising as being of a particular quality then a consumer who is injured or suffers damage as a result of the product's dangerousness may have a claim under the Act. So, if a seesaw purchased for a child is represented as being capable of taking the weight of an adult, and it is not, an injured user who relies on this representation may be able to claim under the Act because the product has not provided the safety he or she was entitled to expect.

The second circumstance referred to in s 5 is "the use to which it could reasonably be expected that the product would be put". Most products are manufactured for specific purposes. If a competent adult departs significantly from the user's instructions of a particular product, they may have no right to complain if they suffer injury as a result of their failure to comply with the manufacturer's instructions. If, for example, a consumer attempts to use a chainsaw designed for cutting wood to cut fabricated steel, and suffers injury as a result, it could hardly be said that this was a use to which it could reasonably be expected that the chainsaw would be put. It is possible for culpable misuse of products to constitute contributory negligence which is specifically allowed for under s 9(2) of the Act.

The third circumstance mentioned in s 5 is "the time when the product was put into circulation". This covers situations where products, when used over a long period of time, may develop malfunctions due to wear and tear, rather than due to any defect in the product's manufacture. Motor vehicles and electrical products would be examples. This provision may also operate in respect of safety standards which may change over time. What might have been thought of as an acceptable risk for a product ten years ago may not be acceptable today.

In addition, s 5(2) states that the product is not to be considered defective "for the sole reason that a better product is subsequently put into circulation". This acknowledges the fact that technology and production techniques are subject to constant scientific and industrial advancement. To deem a product as "defective" simply because a better one has been produced would be unfair and unduly disruptive.

What is Meant by "Damage"?

"Damage", for the purposes of s 2(1), is defined in s 1(1) as meaning:

"(a) death or personal injury, or

(b) loss of, damage to, or destruction of, any item of property other than the defective product itself:

Provided that the item of property—

(i) is of a type ordinarily intended for private use or consumption, and

(ii) was used by the injured person mainly for his own private use or consumption."

It will be noted that the Act covers only damage to items of property "other than the defective product itself". Accordingly, a defective toaster which self-destructs through an electrical fault within the product itself, causing no other damage, will not be recoverable under the Act. Section 1(1) also requires that the item of property damaged by the defective product be of a type "ordinarily intended for private use or consumption and that it had been used by the injured person mainly for his own private use or consumption". This provision would appear to exclude damage to property used in the course of a trade, business or profession.

Proof of Damage and Defect

Section 4 states:

"The onus shall be on the injured person concerned to prove the damage, the defect and the causal relationship between the defect and damage."

The three elements: proof of damage; the defect; and the causal relationship between the defect and the damage, must be proved by the injured person. There is no need to establish breach of duty, which would be necessary in a negligence action at common law.

The injured person must prove, not that they were injured by a defective product, but that the defect in the product injured them. It will be recalled that s 2(1) states that the producer shall be liable in damages in tort for damage caused wholly or partly by a defect in his product. The injured person, therefore, is required to prove the causal link between the defect in the product and the injury they have sustained.

Defences

Section 6 of the 1991 Act provides six defences to claims under the Act. Accordingly, the producer will not be liable if he proves:

(a) that he did not put the product into circulation; or

(b) that, having regard to the circumstances, it is probable that the defect which caused the damage did not exist at the time when the product was put into circulation by him or that that defect came into being afterwards; or

(c) that the product was neither manufactured by him for sale or any form of distribution for an economic purpose nor manufactured or distributed by him in the course of his business; or

(d) that the defect concerned is due to compliance by the product with any requirement imposed by or under any enactment or any requirement of the law of the European Communities; or

(e) that the state of scientific and technical knowledge at the time when he put the product into circulation was not such as to enable the existence of the defect to be discovered; or

(f) in the case of the manufacturer of a component or the producer of a raw material, that the defect is attributable entirely to the design of the product in which the component has been fitted or the raw material has been incorporated or to the instructions given by the manufacturer of the product.

In relation to defence (a), the producer will not be strictly liable if he did not release the product into circulation. Thus, if a product is released onto the market through theft, the producer will not be liable. It would, in theory, be possible for liability under negligence to arise if the theft was foreseeable. Defence (b) seeks to protect the producer from liability for defects coming into being some time after the product was put into circulation by him.

Defence (c) protects non-commercial producers, for example a grandparent making a swing or slide for a grandchild. Defence (d) seeks to ensure that a commercial producer will not be subject to liability where he complies with mandatory regulations and at the same time runs the risk of being liable under the 1991 Act. An example might be safety regulations or standards which themselves cause harm.

Defence (e) means the producer will be relieved of liability that would otherwise attach if he can prove that the state of scientific and technical knowledge at the time when he put the product into circulation was not such as to enable the existence of the defect to be discovered. That is, if the product was as safe as the "state of the art" would allow at the time the product was manufactured, later improvements in safety in the production process may not be relied upon by an injured person as setting the relevant safety standard.

Defence (f) allows the manufacturer of a component part to escape liability where, in effect, the responsibility lies with the manufacturer of the product in which the component is fitted (the final product). The responsibility of the manufacturer of the final product can arise where the defect is attributable: (i) to the design of the product in which the component is fitted; or (ii) to the instructions given by the manufacturer of the final product. This defence would also appear to place the producer of a raw material in the same position as the manufacturer of a component so far as its integration into a final product is concerned.

Limitation of Actions

Section 7 deals with limitation periods and the extinction of liability. Section 7(1) provides that a limitation period of three years is to apply to proceedings for recovery of damages. This limitation period begins to run from the date on which the action accrued or the date (if later) on which the plaintiff became aware, or should reasonably have become aware, of the damage, the defect and the identity of the producer. No distinction is made here between personal injury and property damage.

Although s 7 of the Civil Liability and Courts Act 2004 reduced the limitation period for personal injuries cases from three to two years, the three-year limitation period in s 7(1) of the Liability for Defective Products Act 1991 has not been affected: see *O Haonghusa v DCC Plc* [2011] IEHC 300. Any purported amendment to that effect would, in any event, be contrary to EU law as the three-year limitation period is contained in an EU Directive. Domestic laws regulating the suspension or interruption of limitation periods are not affected by the Directive (Article 10).

Section 7(2)(a) of the 1991 Act provides that rights conferred on the injured person pursuant to the Act are to be extinguished on the expiry of a period of ten years from the date on which the producer put into circulation the actual product which caused the damage, unless the injured person has in the meantime instituted proceedings against the producer. It should be noted that the effect of s 7(2)(a) in extinguishing the injured person's right after the expiry of ten years from the date the producer put the product into circulation, is to render inoperative the law of Member States regulating suspension or interruption of the limitation period on the basis of minority or mental incapacity, for example. Although, as mentioned above, Article 10 of the Directive provides that such laws "shall not be affected by this Directive"; Article 11 relates to the extinction of rights, not limitation periods. Accordingly, s 7(2)(b) operates to give clear priority to Article 11 over Article 10. The purpose of this ten-year cut-off point appears to be that it is in the producer's interests that he or she should be able to close his or her books on a product after it has been in circulation for a fixed period. It allows producers to assess the risk relating to such products and facilitates insurance and amortisation, thereby keeping insurance premiums down. It would also have the effect of relieving the producer of the burden of having to prove that a product which has caused an accident was not defective when he put it into circulation. This burden would become increasingly difficult to discharge as the years pass. On the other hand, it could be said that some products, aircraft, for example, are expected to (and indeed do) last much longer than ten years, and, for such products, ten years would appear to be a relatively short time span in relation to their operational lives.

Joint and Several Liability

Section 8 of the 1991 Act provides for the liability of concurrent wrongdoers in relation to injury caused by a defect in a product. It provides that:

> "Where two or more persons are liable by virtue of this Act for the same damage, they shall be liable jointly and severally as concurrent wrongdoers within the meaning of Part III of the Civil Liability Act, 1961."

Contributory Negligence

Section 9(2) brings contributory negligence into operation in the Act. It states:

> "Where any damage is caused partly by a defect in a product and partly by the fault of the injured person or of any person for whom the injured person is responsible, the provisions of the Civil Liability Act, 1961, concerning contributory negligence, shall have effect as if the defect were due to the fault of every person liable by virtue of this Act for the damage caused by the defect."

The effect of this provision is that contributory negligence is permitted to operate in largely the same way as it does at present in a negligence action at common law. Section 9(2) appears to allow for reduction or disallowance of the claim by virtue of a consideration of "all the circumstances" where the damage is caused by both a defect in the product and the fault of the plaintiff.

Prohibition on Exclusion from Liability

Section 10 of the 1991 Act prohibits "contracting out". This means that the liability of the producer may not, in relation to the injured person, be limited or excluded by a provision limiting his liability or exempting him from liability. Section 10 provides:

> "The liability of a producer arising by virtue of this Act to an injured person shall not be limited or excluded by any term of contract, by any notice or by any other provision."

TRESPASS TO LAND

Learning Outcomes

Upon completion of this chapter, the reader should be able to:

- Explain the nature and characteristics of the tort of trespass to land;
- Appreciate role of the Constitution in recognising the inviolability of the dwelling;
- Discuss, and give examples of, acts that may amount to trespass to land;
- Understand the courts' approach to trespasses to airspace and below ground;
- Identify who may sue in trespass to land actions;
- Outline the defences available to defendants in actions for trespass to land.

A. Trespass to Land: Characteristics

Trespass to land was defined in *Royal Dublin Society v Yates* (31 July 1997) as:

> "...any unjustifiable intrusion by one person upon land in the possession of another. The intrusion may be intentional or it may be negligent: in either case, it is actionable in the absence of lawful justification."

This tort protects the interest of the plaintiff of having his or her land free from the unjustified physical intrusion of another. Trespass to land is actionable *per se*. That is, it is not necessary for the plaintiff to prove actual damage. An actionable trespass will arise even where the incursion is very limited. Accordingly, the slightest crossing of the boundary onto the plaintiff's land will constitute a trespass. Indeed, crossing the boundary may not be necessary: physical contact with the land may suffice. Placing things (including animals) on land, causing any object or substance directly to cross the boundary of another's land, or even to reach the boundary, will constitute a trespass. For example, in *Whelan v Madigan* [1978] ILRM 136 the defendant was found to have committed an act of trespass against the plaintiff when he damaged his door by striking it even though the defendant did not cross the boundary.

The interference with land must be direct rather than consequential. The distinction between "direct" and "indirect" incursions is not always easy to make. In *Gregory v Piper* (1829) 9 B & C 591, it was held to be a trespass where rubbish that was placed near the plaintiff's land, when it dried out, rolled onto the plaintiff's land due to natural forces. In contrast, in *Lemmon v Webb* [1894] 3 Ch 1, the encroachment of roots and branches of trees was not a trespass, but a nuisance. The courts have consistently regarded the spread of tree branches and roots as consequential rather than direct. This is so even where an occupier consciously allows this to happen over time. Other intrusions onto another's property, because of their lack of directness, such as noise or smell, are also generally treated as nuisances rather than trespasses.

The defendant's interference with another's land must be voluntary. If it is not voluntary, no liability will be incurred. Therefore, if a person is carried against his will, or sleepwalks onto another's property, a trespass will not have been committed. Where the plaintiff establishes an act which physically constitutes a trespass, the onus is on defendant to show that he was neither negligent nor intentional. However, where a person mistakes his neighbour's house for his own, he will be guilty of trespass — unless the mistake was brought about by the neighbour's conduct. In *Basely v Clarkson* (1683) 3 Lev 37; 83 ER 565 the plaintiff owned land adjacent to the defendant's. The defendant involuntarily and by mistake mowed grass on the plaintiff's land when he was mowing his own grass. Judgment in trespass was given for the plaintiff. The point here is that the defendant did not mean to cut the plaintiff's grass, but rather he made a mistake about where the boundary was. He was held liable in trespass because he intentionally did the act of cutting the grass (albeit under a misapprehension) which, as a matter of fact, was an invasion of the plaintiff's land.

Figure 10.1

The elements of trespass to land:

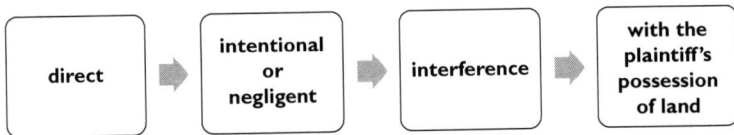

direct		intentional or negligent		interference		with the plaintiff's possession of land

B. The Constitutional Dimension

Article 40.5 the Constitution provides that "[t]he dwelling of every citizen is inviolable and shall not be forcibly entered save in accordance with law". The reference to "law" in this provision refers to both common law and statute. The Supreme Court in *The People (Attorney General) v O'Brien* [1965] IR 142 has made it clear that this does not mean that a person's dwelling cannot be forcibly entered. A forcible entry may occur provided it is permitted by law. That case concerned admissibility of evidence obtained during a search of a person's home rather than a trespass action. The Court considered that such evidence should not be admissible in court if it is obtained by the State as a result of a

> "deliberate and conscious violation of the constitutional rights of the accused person where no extraordinary excusing circumstances exist, such as the imminent destruction of vital evidence or the need to rescue a victim in peril".

The Court also considered that evidence obtained by a search incidental to and contemporaneous with a lawful arrest would be admissible even if made without a valid search warrant.

At common law, search warrants may be obtained from a District Justice or a Peace Commissioner. Information must be sworn before him or her alleging a suspicion that goods have been stolen and are in the house which is to be the subject of the search warrant. In addition, s 48(2) of the Criminal Justice (Theft and Fraud) Offences Act 2001 provides for the issuing of search warrants by a judge of the District Court to search places and persons thereon where there are reasonable grounds for suspecting that an offence under the Act has been committed.

The Supreme Court in *DPP v Forbes* [1994] 2 IR 542 stated that the Gardaí have implied (though rebuttable) authority to come onto the forecourt of a householder's dwelling (though not to enter the dwelling itself) to see to the enforcement of the law or prevent a breach thereof. Section 39(2) of the Road Traffic Act 1994 authorises the Gardaí for the purposes of arresting a person under s 49(8) or s 50(10) of the Road Traffic Act 1961 to enter without a warrant (using reasonable force if necessary) any place (including the curtilage of a dwelling but not the dwelling itself) where a person is or where the member of the Gardaí reasonably suspects him to be. Section 6 of the Criminal Law Act 1997 now sets out the powers of the Gardaí to enter and search premises to effect an arrest. The Gardaí also have powers under the Criminal Damage Act 1991 to enter any place to arrest a person in respect of offences committed under that Act. The Gardaí have similar powers in respect of arrest without warrant under the Domestic Violence Act 1996.

C. Abuse of Right of Entry

A person can be considered to have abused his right of entry if he enters land for a purpose other than that for which he has permission. In *DPP v McMahon* [1987] ILRM 87, two Gardaí entered licensed premises in the course of investigating suspected offences under the Gaming and Lotteries Act 1956. They needed a search warrant in order to do so. Since they did not have one they were found by the Court to be "in law trespassers". They would have had the right, by way of implied invitation, to enter the premises for the purposes of consuming food or drink, but since that was not their purpose for entering the premises, they could not rely on that implied invitation.

It is possible to trespass on the public highway. The public have a right to use the highway for the purpose of passing and re-passing and for other purposes for which it is reasonable and usual to use the highway. If the highway is used by a person for some other purpose, that person may be a trespasser against the owner of the subsoil (who is rebuttably presumed to be the owner of the adjoining land). In *Iveagh (Earl) v Martin* [1961] 1 QB 232 the Court stated the common law position in this way:

> "On the highway I may stand still for a reasonably short time, but I must not put my bed upon the highway and permanently occupy a portion of it. I may stoop to tie my shoelaces, but I may not occupy a

pitch and invite people to come upon it and have their hair cut. I may let my van stand still long enough to deliver and load goods but I must not turn my van into a permanent stall."

Accordingly, misusing the highway for the purposes of intimidating a householder by standing on the public roadway and staring in at them in their home can amount to a trespass: see *L v Ireland* [2008] IEHC 241. An interesting example of trespass on the highway is *Hickman v Maisey* [1900] 1 QB 752. There, the plaintiff possessed land which was crossed by a highway. A racehorse trainer had agreed with the plaintiff to use of some of his land for the training and trial of race-horses. The defendant spent about an hour and a half on the roadway observing the trials and taking notes. The plaintiff brought an action of trespass against him in respect of his user of the highway. The Court held that the "defendant had exceeded the ordinary and reasonable user of a highway as such to which the public are entitled, and he therefore was guilty of a trespass on the plaintiff's land".

At common law, picketing on the public highway was historically a trespass. The position was changed with the Trade Disputes Act 1906, s 2(1), which made it lawful to hold a picket "at or near" a house or place where a person resides or works or carries on business, if those attending there are acting in contemplation or furtherance of a trade dispute and are there merely for the purpose of peacefully obtaining or communicating information, or of peacefully persuading any person to work or abstain from working. The current law is to be found in s 11 of the Industrial Relations Act 1990. Pickets not protected by statutory authority will be a trespass.

D. Trespass by Remaining on Land

If a person remains on land after his permission to be there has ended, he will become a trespasser. Therefore, a failure or refusal to leave the land after the request to do so will amount to a trespass. The occupier of the land may use reasonable force to eject the person if he has allowed a reasonable time for the trespasser to leave.

Where a person enters land under lawful authority rather than by private invitation, and they subsequently abuse or exceed that authority, they are deemed to have become a trespasser *ab initio*. That is, they will be a trespasser from the time they entered the premises. A person can only become a trespasser *ab initio* by an act of positive misfeasance, as opposed to mere nonfeasance. The principle was established in *The Six Carpenters' Case* (1610) 8 Co Rep 146a, 77 ER 695. There, the defendants, six carpenters, declined an invitation to pay for bread and wine which they had consumed in a tavern. Because this was an act of nonfeasance as opposed to misfeasance, they were held not to be trespassers *ab initio*.

Where an abuse takes place after entry, the entry does not become a trespass *ab initio* if there remains an independent ground for the entry which is unaffected by the abuse. For example, in *Elias v Pasmore* [1934] 2 KB 164, police officers lawfully entered premises to arrest a man but wrongfully seized documents whilst there. It was held that they were trespassers only as to the goods and were not trespassers *ab initio*. As mentioned, the doctrine of trespass *ab initio* has been limited to cases of entry by authority of law rather than private invitation or licence. However, in *Webb v Ireland* [1988] ILRM 565, two people who entered private land with the implied licence of the owners to visit an ancient church and tomb, but who dug into the ground to remove valuable chalices (the Derrynaflan Hoard), were characterised as trespassers *ab initio* by the Supreme Court.

E. Trespass Above and Below the Surface of Land

A direct infringement over the airspace of a person's land may constitute a trespass. In *Baron Bernstein of Leigh v Skyviews & General Ltd* [1978] QB 479, the defendants flew above Lord Bernstein's country house and took a photograph of it. They then offered to sell it to him. The plaintiff claimed damages for trespass by invasion of his airspace. It was held that the defendants were not liable. The plaintiff relied on the old Latin maxim, *cujus est solum ejus est usque ad coelum et ad inferos*, first coined by the Accursius in Bologna in the 13th century, meaning "who owns the land owns it up to the sky and down to the depths". The Court, however, could find no support in authority for the proposition that a landowner's rights in the airspace above his property extends to an unlimited height. The balance was best struck by restricting the rights of an owner in the airspace above his land to such height as is necessary for the ordinary use and enjoyment of his land and the structures upon it, and that, above that height he has no greater rights in the airspace than any other member of the public.

In *Anchor Brewhouse Developments Ltd v Berkely House Ltd* [1987] 2 EGLR 172, the defendants were using a tower crane in construction work at a building site. The jib of the tower crane swung over the plaintiff's property. This was held to be a trespass of the plaintiff's airspace. In this case, the Court had to consider whether the plaintiffs were limited to a remedy in damages or whether they could obtain an injunction, and, if so, whether that injunction could be suspended temporarily to allow the defendants to complete the building work. It was held that since it was a trespass to the airspace, an injunction was granted. In acknowledging the difficulties with regard to injunctions in cases such as this, the Court accepted that the effect of granting the injunction would be to strengthen the bargaining position of the plaintiff who may be tempted to charge an exorbitant sum for permission to use the airspace.

By virtue of the Air Navigation and Transport Act 1936, s 55, as amended by the Air Navigation and Transport Act 1988, s 47(1), no action lies in respect of trespass or nuisance by reason only of the flight of aircraft over any property at a height above the ground, which, having regard to the wind, weather and all the circumstances of the case, is reasonable. Furthermore, liability will not attach for the "ordinary incidents of the flight", provided that the provisions of any order made under Part II of the Air Navigation and Transport Act 1946, to give effect to, or to supplement, the Chicago Convention 1944 have been duly complied with. The Chicago Convention established certain principles and arrangements so international civil aviation can develop in a safe and orderly manner, and that international air transport services be established on the basis of equality of opportunity and be operated soundly and economically.

Entry beneath the surface of land, however deep, is actionable as trespass. Therefore, it may be a trespass to tunnel beneath the surface of another's land, to mine there, to use a cave beneath it, or to drive building foundations through the soil, however small that incursion might be. Where there is no specific provision to the contrary, the owner of the surface is presumed to own that which is underground. This common law position was affirmed by the UK Supreme Court in *Bocardo SA v Star Energy UK Onshore Ltd* [2010] UKSC 35. In that case, the defendant had been granted a licence under statute to search for, bore for, and extract petroleum. In order to extract the maximum amount of petroleum from the underground reservoir, the defendant drilled diagonally from an external entry point with pipes that ran under the plaintiff's land. The defendant's operations took place at a depth of no less than 800 feet under the plaintiff's land. However, the defendant sought no permission for this and the plaintiff claimed damages for trespass. The UK Supreme Court considered whether the maxim *cujus est solum ejus est usque ad coelum et ad inferos* applied. It held that this did indeed represent the law, so far as it was sensible to apply it, though doubted its continued application to airspace. It has been observed that there will be a point below the earth's crust where pressure and heat would make any human activity impossible: see Sprankling (2008) 55 UCLA LR 979. In Ireland, under statute and Article 10 of the Constitution, the State has the right to most mineral resources in the ground: see the Minerals Development Acts 1940, 1960, and 1979.

F. Continuing Trespass

If a person places an object on the land of another, he or she will have committed a continuing trespass if he or she fails to remove it. However, if a person wrongfully does something which damages the plaintiff's land, he or she will not have committed a continuing trespass. For example, if a person goes on to another person's land, cuts down a tree and removes it, he or she will have committed a trespass, but not a continuing one, even though the tree is permanently gone. The conceptual distinction lies in the fact that the tree can never be replaced but the thing placed on land can be removed. This distinction is important in relation to remedies. Further actions in trespass are possible in respect of continuing trespasses, but only one action in trespass lies in respect of damage to land: see *Clarke v MGW Railway Co* [1895] 2 IR 294.

G. Who May Sue?

Generally, it is said that it is possession of the land that entitles a plaintiff to sue in trespass. The tort of trespass is essentially an interference with possession. Therefore, the tort generally cannot be availed of by persons not in possession at the time of the interference. Accordingly, mere use of land without exclusive possession will not be sufficient to support an action in trespass. In *Hill v Tupper* (1863) 2 H & C 121, X leased certain land to the plaintiff, which adjoined X's canal. The plaintiffs were also given "the sole and exclusive rights" to rent out pleasure boats for use on the canal. Subsequently, the defendant set up a rival enterprise. The plaintiff then sued the defendant in trespass. The plaintiff conceded that X could sue the defendant in trespass, but at the same time the plaintiff argued that he could sue also. Since the plaintiff's concession was tantamount to an admission that he did not have exclusive occupation, the Court dismissed the action.

It is less straightforward where two persons assert occupation of land. In *Jones v Chapman* (1847) 2 Exch 803, it was observed by the Court that:

> "... if there are two persons in [a] field, each asserting that the field is his, and each doing some act in the assertion of the right of possession, and if the question is, which of those two is in actual possession, I answer, the person who has the title is in actual possession, and the other is a trespasser."

This approach was approved in *Lows v Telford* (1876) 1 App Cas 414. Both *Jones v Chapman* and *Lows v Telford* were approved in the Irish case of *Hegan v Carolan* [1916] 2 IR 27.

A person holding a legal or equitable interest in land in the nature of an easement or a *profit à prendre* may sue in trespass for direct interference with that interest: see *Cronin v Connor* [1913] 2 IR 119.

It is generally no defence to a trespasser that the plaintiff's possession of the land is unlawful and rests with a third party (*jus tertii*): see *Graham v Peat* (1801) 1 East 244.

H. Defences to Trespass to Land

Figure 10.2

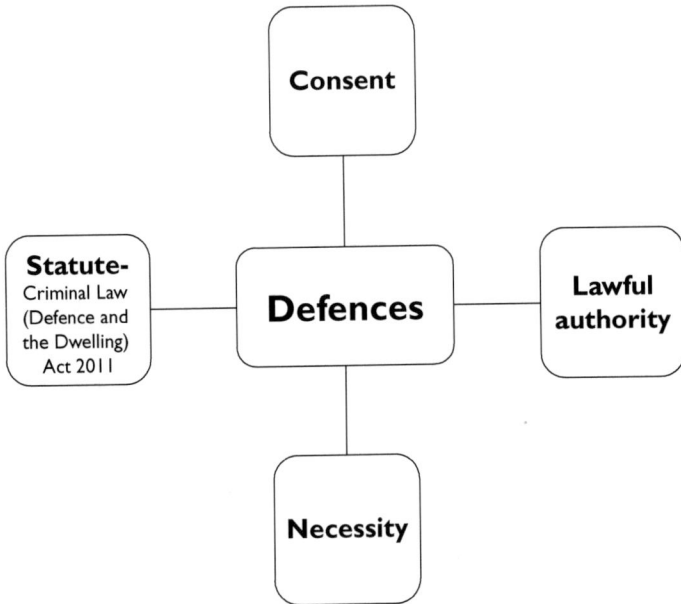

Consent

The defendant may raise the defence of consent; that is, that the plaintiff landowner has granted him permission, whether express or implied, to enter his land. If the entrant exceeds the permission conferred by the permission he will become a trespasser. For example, if an entrant is granted permission to enter the owner's land for the purposes of photographing wildlife, he may not fish in the landowner's lake without becoming a trespasser. Similarly, if the landowner revokes the permission, the entrant may not remain on the land. This is so irrespective of whether the permission was granted gratuitously or under a contract.

Lawful Authority

A person will not be a trespasser where he enters another's property with lawful authority. If the entrant exceeds or abuses his or her authority, he or she will become a trespasser *ab initio*.

Necessity

Necessity may operate as a defence to an action in trespass in cases of emergency. Such emergencies might arise from a state of war or armed rebellion, major accident, acute emergencies caused by fire, natural disasters, or other circumstances necessitating emergency services entering a person's property in order to deal with that situation: see *Dellway Investments v NAMA* [2011] IESC 14.

In *Southwark London Borough Council v Williams* [1971] Ch 734, the English Court of Appeal rejected the defence of necessity relied upon by squatters. Lord Denning said: "[i]f drunkenness were once admitted as a defence to trespass, no one's house would be safe". Similarly, the defence of necessity failed in *Dublin City Council v Gavin* [2008] IESC 444. In that case, a Traveller family trespassed on the plaintiff's land. They claimed they had nowhere else to go and were subject to violence and violent threats at the last site they occupied. The Court rejected the defence of necessity. Peart J said:

> "The defence of necessity... was never, and never could be, intended to permit an uncontrolled and uncontrollable regime whereby persons... could simply enter upon the lands of others and claim an entitlement to be there until such time as the local authority for the area provides them with accommodation...".

Statute: Criminal Law (Defence and the Dwelling) Act 2011

The Criminal Law (Defence and the Dwelling) Act 2011 offers some protection to householders who use reasonable force against trespassers, which they honestly believe to be justified, to protect their dwellings.

Section 2(1) of the Act states:

> "2.— (1) Notwithstanding the generality of any other enactment or rule of law and subject to subsections (2) and (3), it shall not be an offence for a person who is in his or her dwelling, or for a person who is a lawful occupant in a dwelling, to use force against another person or the property of another person where—
>
> (a) he or she believes the other person has entered or is entering the dwelling as a trespasser for the purpose of committing a criminal act, and
>
> (b) the force used is only such as is reasonable in the circumstances as he or she believes them to be—

    (i)   to protect himself or herself or another person present in the dwelling from injury, assault, detention or death caused by a criminal act,

    (ii)   to protect his or her property or the property of another person from appropriation, destruction or damage caused by a criminal act, or

    (iii)   to prevent the commission of a crime or to effect, or assist in effecting, a lawful arrest."

This provision does not apply when the force is used against a member of the Gardaí acting in the course of his or her duty, or a person assisting the Gardaí, or a person lawfully performing a statutory function. Nor does it apply where the householder brings the situation about in which the force is used (s 2(2)). The person using the force is protected if he or she honestly believes that the circumstances justify the force, even if, objectively, no such justification exists (s 2(4)). The common law required a person invoking the defence of self-defence in these circumstances to retreat of possible. That is no longer the case (s 2(5), s 3).

INTENTIONAL INTERFERENCE WITH THE PERSON

Learning Outcomes

Upon completion of this chapter, the reader should be able to:

- Discuss the range of torts coming under the heading of Intentional Interference with the Person;
- Explain the relationship between trespass to the person and negligence;
- Discuss the internal rules of each tort comprising trespass to the person;
- Appreciate the role of the tort in *Wilkinson v Downton* in Irish and English law;
- Outline the defences available in respect of trespass to the person.

A. Overview

Intentional interference with the person is a category of civil wrongs which includes trespass to the person and the tort in *Wilkinson v Downton*. Trespass generally is an ancient set of torts which mainly deals with the direct, and usually intentional, invasion of a plaintiff's interest in his or her person, his or her land, or his and her chattels (goods). Trespass to the person is made up of three separate torts: battery, assault and false imprisonment. Since these are among the most ancient of the nominate torts, their main features are well-settled within the law.

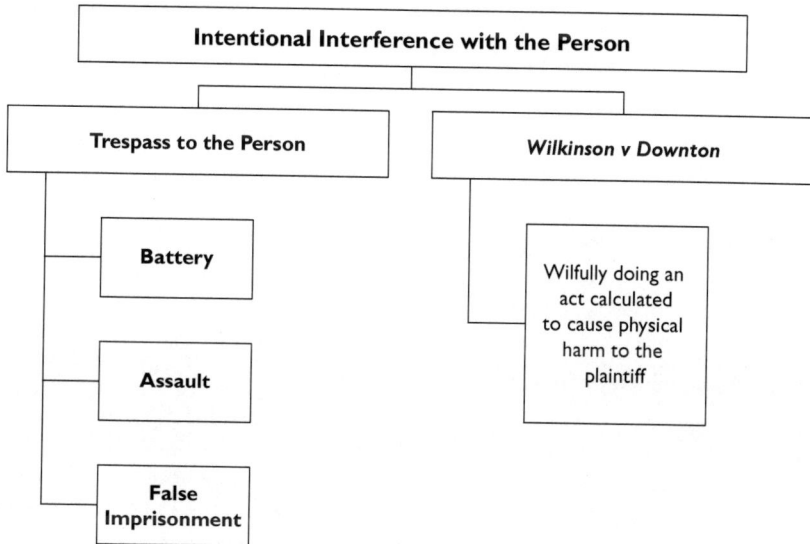

Battery is any act of the defendant that directly and intentionally (or negligently), causes some physical contact with the plaintiff's person without his consent. Assault is any act of the defendant that directly and intentionally (or negligently) causes the plaintiff reasonably to apprehend the imminent infliction of a battery. False imprisonment is an act of the defendant that directly and intentionally (possibly negligently) causes the plaintiff's confinement within an area delimited by the defendant. The tort in *Wilkinson v Downton* concerns the intentional infliction of physical or emotional harm. Each of these torts will be dealt with separately below.

B. Trespass and Negligence

Historically, the requirement for bringing the writ of trespass *vi et armis* was directness. This requirement was, theoretically at least, capable of being satisfied by either intentional or unintentional conduct. By the time these forms of action were abolished in the 1870s it was generally accepted that unintentional wrongs causing direct harm (i.e. what we would now call negligence) were actionable in case. Accordingly, the substantive, as opposed to procedural, distinction between trespass and negligence was that trespass required an intentional wrong whereas negligence required an unintentional wrong.

This important distinction between trespass and negligence was considered in *Fowler v Lanning* [1959] 1 QB 426. There, the plaintiff merely alleged in his statement of claim that the defendant had shot him. Neither intention nor negligence was alleged. The plaintiff, however, argued that the statement of claim did allege a good cause of action on the grounds that in trespass the burden of disproving negligence was on the defendant. Rejecting that argument, Diplock J held that

> "trespass to the person does not lie if the injury to the plaintiff, although the direct consequence of the act of the defendant, was caused unintentionally and without negligence on the defendant's part"

and that the onus of proving negligence was on the plaintiff. Diplock J thought that trespass could still be committed negligently, but that in such cases the plaintiff would have to prove both the negligence alleged, and that there was resulting harm. Therefore, the plaintiff would gain no practical advantage from framing his action in trespass rather than negligence.

The English Court of Appeal gave this question detailed consideration in *Letang v Cooper* [1965] 1 QB 232. In that case, Doreen Letang was sunbathing in the grounds of a hotel in Cornwall. The defendant negligently drove over her legs with his Jaguar. The writ was issued more than three years later. Under the then limitation period, a writ should have been issued within three years of the accident if it related to personal injuries and the claim was for "negligence, nuisance or breach of duty". The plaintiff admitted that an action in negligence was out of time, but claimed that she could sue for trespass (for which the general limitation period was six years) on the basis that this did not come within the phrase "breach of duty". She succeeded in the High Court but the defendant's appeal was allowed. The Court of Appeal held that the action was time-barred and the defendant was not liable. Lord Denning MR explained the position in this way:

> "Instead of dividing actions for personal injuries into trespass (direct damage) or case (consequential damage), we divide the causes of action now according as the defendant did the injury intentionally or unintentionally. If one man intentionally applies force directly to another, the plaintiff has a cause of action in assault and battery, or, if you so choose to describe it, in trespass to the person… If he does not inflict injury intentionally, but only unintentionally, the plaintiff has no cause of action today in trespass. His only cause of action is in

negligence, and then only on proof of want of reasonable care. If the plaintiff cannot prove want of reasonable care, he may have no cause of action at all. Thus, it is not enough nowadays for the plaintiff to plead that 'the defendant shot the plaintiff'. He must also allege that he did it intentionally or negligently. If intentional, it is the tort of assault and battery. If negligent and causing damage, it is the tort of negligence."

In *Wilson v Pringle* [1987] QB 237, Croom-Johnson LJ said that "[i]t has long been the law that claims arising out of an unintentional trespass must be made in negligence". In England, therefore, it can be said that trespass deals with direct intentional acts, and negligence with careless or indirect acts. Following the decision in *Letang v Cooper*, it would appear that actions for negligent trespass had effectively disappeared from English law. Negligent trespass remains a feature of Irish law although, in practice, most plaintiffs will sue for negligence rather than trespass, even where the injury has been directly caused. Nevertheless, there are clear advantages to suing in trespass. First, trespass is actionable *per se*, so, unlike in negligence, there is no need to prove damage. Second, the remoteness requirements in negligence can be problematic. In negligence the defendant is only responsible for injuries or harm of a kind that are reasonably foreseeable, whereas in trespass all the damage actually ensuing from the defendant's unlawful act is generally recoverable. Third, in trespass, the onus shifts to the defendant to show that he or she acted neither intentionally nor negligently.

C. Battery

Battery consists of the following:
- Intentional (or negligent);
- Direct;
- Application of force to another;
- Without his or her consent.

Intentional or Negligent
The requirement for "intention" means that the act which caused the harm must be intentional, or voluntary. It is not necessary that the outcome, or harm, be intended.

In *Breslin v McKevitt* [2011] NICA 33, the Northern Ireland Court of Appeal held in a case against a number of individuals allegedly involved in the Omagh bombing in 1998 that recklessness can satisfy the intention requirement for battery.

In the context of battery, the meaning of "intentional act" has two broad possibilities. First, we could say that the defendant intended only to act in the way that he or she did. Second, we could say that the defendant intended both to act in the way that he or she did *and* that the resulting contact with the plaintiff take place. For example, if A throws a punch at B and succeeds in striking him, A's act (the thrown punch) and the outcome of that act (for example, B's broken nose) are effectively part of the same transaction. But, there may be instances where A may do something without intending the outcome. If A aims a gun at B, and then pulls the trigger, there is little doubt that he intended to shoot B. But if A aims a gun at a pheasant on a hunting trip and accidentally shoots B, there is little doubt that A intended the act (firing the gun) but not necessarily the outcome (B's injury). In those circumstances, it is unlikely A will be held liable in battery.

However, if A aims his gun at B, and then pulls the trigger missing B but shooting C standing next to B, would the tort of battery operate to hold A liable? If this were a criminal case, the courts would be in a position to apply the doctrine of "transferred intent". But in a civil case it is not clear that this would be so. The doctrine of transferred intent is certainly part of American law (*American Restatement, Torts* (2d), § 32). In the American case of *Talmage v Smith* (1894) 101 Mich 370, the defendant threw a stick towards a group of boys. There was evidence it was thrown towards a particular boy, whom it missed, but struck the plaintiff. He sued successfully in trespass. The Supreme Court of Michigan said:

> "The right of the plaintiff was made to depend upon the intention on the part of the defendant to hit somebody, and to inflict an unwarranted injury upon someone. Under the circumstances, the fact that the injury resulted to another than was intended does not relieve the defendant from responsibility…"

This doctrine of transferred intent appears to have been applied in *James v Campbell* (1832) 5 C & P 372. There, the defendant was held liable for hitting the plaintiff, even though he intended to hit a third person and did not know that he had struck the plaintiff. In relation to the application of transferred intent in battery cases generally, both the English and Irish judiciary have, thus far, not expressed great enthusiasm for this approach. The question, therefore, remains to be definitively settled.

In most cases, contact with the plaintiff will not be problematic. It is settled law that the defendant need not have intended the plaintiff any harm. Since battery is actionable *per se*, it is sufficient that the defendant understood that his conduct was beyond the bounds of physical contact "generally acceptable in the ordinary conduct of everyday life" (see *Collins v Wilcock* [1984] 3 All ER 374). In *Wilson v Pringle* [1987] QB 237, the Court said that the plaintiff must show that the defendant's touching of the plaintiff was a "hostile" touching. But it is clear from this case that the term "hostile" should not be equated with ill-will or malevolence.

It really means that the defendant is doing something to which the plaintiff may object. That is, something which the plaintiff may regard as an unlawful intrusion to his bodily integrity. In *Wilson v Pringle*, the mere allegation that one 13-year-old boy jumped on another during horseplay in a school corridor was not sufficient in and of itself to establish a battery.

The term "hostile" was considered by the Court in *F v West Berkshire Health Authority* [1989] 2 AC 1 to be unhelpful in describing the necessary state of mind in a battery case. A surgeon carrying out an operation on a patient will be motivated by his judgment as to the patient's best interests, rather than hostility towards the patient. But it is clear that if the patient is competent to do so, and has refused to consent to a particular course of treatment, the surgeon commits a battery.

Direct

The direct application of physical contact upon the person is required. It is insufficient that the act "causes" contact. Contact must follow immediately from the act of the defendant (see *Leame v Bray* (1803) 3 East 593); or at least be a continuation of his act (see *Stevens v Myers* (1830) 4 C & P 349). Such contact can occur in a wide range of circumstances. Typically it will occur through physical attacks by one person upon another. The tort can be committed by spitting in a person's face (*R v Cotsworth* (1704) 6 Mod Rep 172, 87 ER 928), cutting another's hair against his will (*Forde v Skinner* (1830) 4 C & P 239), or overturning a chair on which another is sitting (*Hooper v Reeve* (1870) 7 Taunt 698). In *Scott v Shepherd* (1773) 2 Wm Bl 892, sufficient directness was held to exist where the defendant threw a lighted squib into a crowded marketplace that was tossed from one trader to another before it eventually exploded injuring the plaintiff.

In *Cole v Turner* (1704) 87 ER 907 Holt CJ said that the "least touching of another in anger is a battery". This, however, is considered to be too narrow because an unwanted kiss will be just as actionable as a blow delivered in anger. We can see, therefore, that the act must be a positive one for it to amount to a battery. A mere omission or passive conduct, for example, obstructing the entrance to a room by standing in a person's way, is not enough. In *Innes v Wylie* (1844) 1 Car & Kir 257; 174 ER 800, the plaintiff was a member of a society which attempted to expel him. Under orders from the defendant, a policeman stopped the plaintiff entering the room in which the society was dining. But because the policeman took active measures to prevent the plaintiff from entering the room the Court found for the plaintiff. He was awarded damages of 40 shillings.

In *Fagan v Metropolitan Police Commissioner* [1969] 1 QB 439, the issue of a mere omission was considered in the context of a criminal case. Vincent Fagan unwittingly parked his car on a policeman's foot. The policeman asked him to move the car. Fagan responded with verbal abuse and turned off the car's engine before eventually complying with the policeman's request. The majority of the Court of Appeal Criminal Division held that Fagan was guilty of criminal assault (which included battery) as his act was a continuing one. Accordingly, the offence was complete once he had knowledge of the car's position. Interestingly, Bridge J dissented. He considered that:

> "the car rested on the foot by its own weight and remained stationary by its own inertia. The appellant's fault was that he omitted to manipulate the controls to set it in motion again."

This, he thought, was simply a failure to act, and was not sufficient to constitute the offence.

A broad meaning was given to the term "directly" in *Haystead v CC Derbyshire* [2000] 2 Cr App R 339. There, the defendant punched a woman in the face, with the result that the baby she was holding fell to the floor. He was convicted of assault (which in this context included battery) on the baby. The Court said:

> "[T]he movement of the woman whereby she lost hold of the child was entirely and immediately the result of the [defendant's] action in punching her. There is no difference in logic or good sense between the facts of this case and one where the defendant might have used a weapon to fell the child to the floor, save only that this is a case of reckless and not intentional battery."

In *DPP v K* [1990] 1 WLR 1067, the defendant, a schoolboy, put a dangerous acid into a hand dryer. Another schoolboy suffered injury when he was sprayed with the acid when he used the dryer. The defendant was held to have inflicted force directly upon the other schoolboy.

Application of Force

Some physical contact with the plaintiff (or his or her clothes) is required. In *Humphries v Connor* (1864) 17 ICLR 1, the Court held that the removal by a policeman of an orange lily from the coat of a woman could constitute a battery. This was so even though no force was applied to her person. It is clear, therefore, that neither force nor physical injury need occur to satisfy the requirements of battery. In *Kaye v Robertson* [1991] FSR 62, the Court considered that it might be a battery if a bright light is shone into a person's eye causing injury to his sight or damages him in some other way. It has been pointed out that this appears to ignore the fact that damage is irrelevant to liability in trespass. If the harm to sight is intended it would be actionable as intentionally inflicted harm: if it ought to have been foreseen, it would be negligence (*Winfield*).

Without Consent

Where there is consent to the contact there is no battery. Consent can be express or implied. There is presumed to be consent in relation to ordinary social touching, such as brushing against people in a crowd, or tapping another on the shoulder to get his or her attention. The generally accepted standard is derived from *Collins v Wilcock*, which is that touching will not be treated as a battery if it is "contact acceptable in the ordinary conduct of everyday life".

Even where the touching is outside the boundaries of ordinary everyday life, consent can negative battery. This will usually arise in medical cases where, subject to the issues relating to capacity, explicit or even presumed consent will justify contact. In *F v West Berkshire Health Authority* the House of Lords gave detailed consideration to the tort of battery in a case of a medically-imposed sterilisation on a patient with an intellectual disability. The contact in question (the surgical intervention) could not be described as "hostile", but in the absence of meaningful consent it would constitute a battery, unless a different source of authority could be found for that contact. The Court gave a declaration that the procedure was necessary and in the best interests of the patient.

An adult of full capacity has the right to choose whether or not to consent to medical treatment, even if the treatment is necessary to save his or her life. Similarly, an adult of full capacity has the right to choose whether to eat or not, even if the refusal of food is likely to result in the person's death: see *St George's Healthcare NHS Trust v S* [1999] Fam 26; *Re-a Ward of Court* [1995] 2 ILRM 401. The practice of forcible feeding, which was a feature of the prison system in earlier times, would now be considered to be a battery, assuming the person is of full understanding: see *Leigh v Gladstone* (1909) 26 TLR 139.

D. Assault

An assault is committed when the defendant has caused another to:

* reasonably apprehend
* imminent infliction of a battery.

"Reasonable apprehension" is determined objectively. If A points an unloaded gun at B in such a way that B reasonably apprehends that he or she is about to be shot, A will have committed an assault, even though no shot could have been fired: see *R v St George* (1840) 9 C & P 483. If C brandishes a stick at D in such a manner that D reasonably apprehends that he or she is about to be struck, C will have committed an assault. The gist of the tort is an act which would cause a reasonable person to apprehend an imminent battery. Therefore, if the plaintiff suffers from paranoia and perceives the innocuous waving of the defendant's hand in the air during conversation as a threat, there is no assault.

Where there is no apprehension of the battery before it takes place, for example, in the case where a person is struck from behind or struck whilst asleep, that person may not sue for assault, as the tort consists of "a touching of the mind, not the body": see *Kline v Kline* (1902) 64 NE 9. Furthermore, apprehension, not fear, is the test.

An unfounded apprehension will not found an action in assault. In *Thomas v National Union of Mineworkers* [1986] Ch 20, working miners had threats yelled at them by picketers as they were transported past picket lines on buses. It was held that this did not constitute assault as it would have been impossible for the threats to have been carried out because the picketing miners were held behind police lines. In *Stephens v Myers* (1830) 4 C & P 349, 172 ER 735, the plaintiff was acting as chairman at a parish meeting. He sat at the head of the table at which the defendant also sat. There were about six or seven persons between him and the plaintiff. The defendant became very angry and vociferous during the meeting. A motion was passed that he be turned out. The defendant then advanced towards the chairman as if to strike him but someone intervened and prevented him from doing so. Here, an assault was committed as it had been reasonable for the plaintiff to anticipate being struck. The plaintiff received damages of one shilling.

Mere words may or may not amount to an assault. It depends on the circumstances and context. In *Dullaghan v Hillen* [1957] Ir Jur Rep 10 "a filthy and insulting remark" was directed at a customs officer who responded by striking the person who made the remark. The Court held that the remark could not be regarded as an assault observing that

> "mere words, no matter how harsh, lying, insulting and provocative
> they may be, can never amount in law to assault."

This premise was based on earlier authority, in particular an observation by Holroyd J to a jury that "no words or singing are equivalent to an assault" (see *Meade's and Belt's Case* (1823) 1 Lew CC 184, 168 ER 1006).

It is now acknowledged that it is possible that words by themselves can induce fear. In *R v Ireland* [1996] 3 WLR 650 the Court accepted that words, even if not accompanied by any actions, could cause apprehension of immediate contact. In that case, the defendant made "silent" phone calls to a woman. The Court observed that

"A thing said is also a thing done. There is no reason why something said should be incapable of causing an apprehension of immediate personal violence."

Ireland ended any doubt over whether mere words could amount to an assault.

It has long been the law that words accompanied by actions could amount to an assault. This was so even if the words amounted to a conditional threat which did not expose the plaintiff to immediate danger. For example, in *Read v Coker* (1853) 13 CB 850, 138 ER 1437, the plaintiff was told to leave premises where he conducted his business. He refused. The defendant then collected together some of his workmen who stood near the plaintiff with their sleeves rolled up. They told the plaintiff that they would break his neck if he did not leave. He did leave. He then brought an action for assault in which he succeeded. The Court was of the view that:

"If anything short of actual striking will in law constitute an assault, the facts here clearly showed that the defendant was guilty of an assault. There was a threat of violence exhibiting an intention to assault, and a present ability to carry the threat into execution."

Not every conditional assault will, however, be actionable. In *Turberville v Savage* (1669) 1 Mod 3, 86 ER 684 the defendant put his hand on his sword and said to the plaintiff: "If it were not assize time I would not take such language from you". It was held that this amounted to a clear statement that the plaintiff would not be assaulted because the judges were in town. Accordingly, there could be no assault.

E. False Imprisonment

The tort of false imprisonment has been classically defined by Blackstone, vol III, "Of Private Wrongs", ch 8, II thus:

"To constitute the injury of false imprisonment there are two points requisite: 1. The detention of the person; and, 2. The unlawfulness of such detention. Every confinement of the person is an imprisonment, whether it be in a common prison, or in a private house, or in the stocks, or even by forcibly detaining one in the public streets. Unlawful, or false, imprisonment consists in such confinement or detention without sufficient authority..."

The tort of false imprisonment has been defined in the Irish courts by Fawsitt J in *Dullaghan v Hillen* [1957] Ir Jur Rep 10, 15 thus:

> "False imprisonment is the unlawful and total restraint of the
> personal liberty of another whether by constraining him or
> compelling him to go to a particular place or confining him in a
> prison or police station or private place or by detaining him against
> his will in a public place. The essential element of the offence is the
> unlawful detention of the person, or the unlawful restraint on his
> liberty. The fact that a person is not actually aware that he is being
> imprisoned does not amount to evidence that he is not imprisoned,
> it being possible for a person to be imprisoned in law, without his
> being conscious of the fact and appreciating the position in which
> he is placed, laying hands upon the person of the party imprisoned
> not being essential. There may be an effectual imprisonment without
> walls of any kind. The detainer must be such as to limit the party's
> freedom of motion in all directions. In effect, imprisonment is a total
> restraint of the liberty of the person. The offence is committed by
> mere detention without violence."

Like other forms of trespass to the person, this tort is actionable *per se*. It is clear
from the case law, however, that the courts insist upon total, as opposed to partial,
restraint of the person. A good example is *Bird v Jones* (1845) 7 QB 742. In August
1843, the Hammersmith Bridge Company cordoned off part of their bridge. They
placed seats on it and charged spectators for viewing a regatta. The plaintiff
objected to this. He forced his way into the enclosure, where he was stopped by
two police officers. He was prevented from proceeding across the bridge, but he
was allowed to go back the way he came. He refused and was arrested. The
plaintiff sued for wrongful arrest. The Court held that this was not an
"imprisonment" and the defendant was not liable for the subsequent arrest.
Coleridge J said:

> "Some confusion seems… to arise from confounding imprisonment
> of the body with mere loss of freedom…Imprisonment… includes
> the notion of restraint within some limits defined by a will or power
> exterior to our own."

The significance of this case is that the tort of false imprisonment only protects a
person against restraint and does not give a right to absolute choice in one's
freedom of movement. Thus, the tort will be committed only where a person is
confined within fixed bounds. Where a person's way is merely blocked so that
they have to return the way they came or make a diversion, this will not constitute
false imprisonment. It is clear, however, that a person is not expected to risk
injuring himself (by climbing out a window on an upper floor) or embarrassing
himself (by walking down the street naked) in seeking to escape from his
confinement.

The defendant must intend to do an act which is at least substantially certain to effect the confinement. Normally, therefore, there must be intention. There is no need to show malice. Even where the defendant acts in good faith, he may be held liable under the tort. In *R v Governor of Brockhill Prison*, ex parte *Evans (No 2)* [2001] 2 AC 19, a prison governor who calculated the plaintiff's day of release in accordance with the law as understood at the time of her conviction was held liable when a subsequent change in the law meant that the prisoner should have been released 59 days earlier. It is clear that an honest mistake as to the right to continue detention "does not excuse a trespass to the person" (see also *Hepburn v CC of Thames Valley Police* [2002] EWCA Civ 1841).

Imprisonment may be physical or psychological. Physical imprisonment means the plaintiff is unable to physically escape. A psychological imprisonment may mean that the plaintiff obeys the defendant in doing something they do not want to do for fear that force will be used against them. This will be imprisonment "without walls of any kind" (see *Dullaghan v Hillen*). In *Phillips v Great Northern Railway Co Ltd* (1903) 4 NIJR 154 a woman was suspected by railway staff of travelling on a train without a ticket. When she arrived at the station in Dublin, while ordering a cab, she was told by the ticket collector not to move. After she had been waiting for some time, the stationmaster came along. Following a further conversation, the plaintiff got into the cab and drove off. The plaintiff sued for false imprisonment. She succeeded before a jury but lost before the King's Bench Division. That Court was of the view that, whilst the plaintiff had been subjected to some delay, there was no evidence that she had been so dominated by the actions of the railway staff that "she lost her liberty". The Court also considered that she could have left the station at any time and there was not "a total restraint of the liberty of the person".

There is no requirement that the plaintiff alleging false imprisonment be aware of the relevant restraint to his freedom at the time of the confinement. This was not always the case. In *Herring v Boyle* (1834) 1 Cr M & R 377, a mother went to fetch her 10-year-old son from school on 24 December 1833 to take him home for the Christmas holidays. The headmaster refused to allow her to take him home because she had not paid the last term's fees. He kept the boy at the school over the holidays. His mother took an action for false imprisonment. It failed. The fact that the boy appeared to have been unaware that he was being detained seems to have influenced the judge. However, in *Meering v Grahame-White Aviation Co* (1919) 122 LT 44 a man was persuaded by works police to remain in an office. He was unaware that had he tried to leave he would have been prevented from doing so. Notwithstanding this, his action for false imprisonment was successful. This judgment was endorsed by the House of Lords in *Murray v Ministry of Defence*

[1988] 2 All ER 521 where their Lordships made it clear that knowledge of detention is not a necessary element of false imprisonment. Proof of a total restraint should suffice. However, in such circumstances, no more than nominal damages would be recoverable.

It appears that vulnerable persons may be prevented from leaving psychiatric facilities in circumstances where they cannot look after themselves outside the facility. In *McN v HSE* [2009] IEHC 236, the applicants had been detained involuntarily at the respondent's hospital. The orders detaining them had subsequently been revoked on the basis that they were no longer suffering from the psychiatric disorders under which they were originally detained. Despite this, they were prevented from leaving the facility on the basis that they could not care for themselves outside. The Court took the view that they were not "detained" because they were free to leave at any time provided they were with someone who could look after them.

In *Herd v Weardale Steel, Coal and Coke Co* [1915] AC 67, the plaintiff was one of a number of miners who entered Thornley Colliery, owned by the defendants, at 9:30 am on 30 May 1911. Their shift should have ended at 4 pm. During the morning they believed that the work they were being asked to do was unsafe and in breach of an agreement with the employers. They asked to be taken to the surface at 11 am. The employers refused. They were not brought up until 1:30 pm. The employers successfully sued the miners for breach of contract. The plaintiff replied with an action for false imprisonment. He lost. The employers were not liable. The House of Lords stated that the plaintiff had chosen to go into the mine under the particular conditions in question. The plaintiff had no right to call upon the employers to make use of special machinery and incur cost in bringing him to the surface "just when he pleased". This approach was adopted by the Irish courts in *Burns v Johnston* [1916] 2 IR 444; [1917] 2 IR 137 where factory workers were detained until 6:30 pm under new arrangements whereas previously their finishing time was 6 pm. The plaintiffs sued unsuccessfully for false imprisonment. The Court held that the plaintiffs were bound by their conditions of employment to remain at work until 6:30 pm.

F. The Intentional Infliction of Physical or Emotional Harm

This tort can be committed where a person intentionally or recklessly inflicts physical or emotional harm on another. The leading case is *Wilkinson v Downton* [1897] 2 QB 57. There, Thomas Wilkinson, landlord of the Albion public house in Limehouse, went by train to the races at Harlow, leaving his wife Lavinia behind the bar. Downton was a customer who decided to play a practical joke on Mrs Wilkinson. He went into the Albion and told her that her husband had decided to return in a horse-drawn vehicle which had been involved in an accident in which he had been seriously injured and that his legs were broken. The story was completely false. Mr Wilkinson returned safely by train later that evening. But the effect on Mrs Wilkinson was dramatic. Her hair turned white. She became so ill that for some time her life was thought to be in danger. She sued and a jury awarded her £100 for nervous shock. The difficulty for the judge, Wright J, was the decision of the Privy Council in *Victorian Railways Commissioners v Coultas* (1888) 13 App Cas 222 which prohibited recovery for nervous shock induced by negligence. *Coultas* was distinguished on the ground that Downton was not merely negligent but had *intended* to cause injury. However, it is clear on the facts that Downton did not intend to cause any kind of injury but merely wanted to give Mrs Wilkinson a fright. Wright J said, however, that as what the defendant had said could not fail to produce grave effects "upon any but an exceptionally indifferent person", an intention to cause such effects should be "imputed" to him. In holding the defendant liable to the plaintiff, Wright J said that:

> "[T]he defendant has... wilfully done an act calculated to cause physical harm to the plaintiff – that is to say, to infringe her legal right to safety, and has in fact thereby caused physical harm to her. That proposition without more appears to state a good cause of action, there being no justification alleged for the act."

The outcome of *Wilkinson v Downton* was approved in *Janvier v Sweeney* [1919] 2 KB 316. During World War I, Mlle Janvier lived as a paid companion in a house in Mayfair, London. She corresponded with her German lover who was interned as an enemy alien on the Isle of Man. Sweeney was a private detective who wanted secretly to obtain some of her employer's documents. He sent his assistant to induce her to co-operate by pretending to be from Scotland Yard and saying that the authorities wanted her because she was corresponding with a German spy. Mlle Janvier suffered severe nervous shock from which she took a long time to recover. She was awarded £250 by a jury. Interestingly, the Court in this case, unlike in *Wilkinson*, was not troubled by the decision in *Victorian Railways Commissioners v Coultas*.

The tort in *Wilkinson v Downton* has been considered across the common law world, for example Canada, Australia, New Zealand, Singapore, and Hong Kong. In the United States it is committed by the defendant where his "extreme and outrageous" conduct intentionally or recklessly causes severe emotional distress to another.

In England, in *Wainwright v Home Office* [2004] 2 AC 406 a mother and son with learning difficulties were strip-searched before being admitted to a prison as visitors. Although no physical contact was made with the mother, she complained of the humiliating and improper way in which the search was conducted. She claimed that the prison staff had wilfully forced her to do something which infringed her legal right to privacy and exacerbated her existing depression. The House of Lords held that the plaintiffs could not rely on *Wilkinson* because the tort did not provide a remedy for distress which does not amount to recognised psychiatric injury. In any case, the necessary intention was not established.

In *Wong v Parkside Health NHS Trust* [2003] 3 All ER 932, the English Court of Appeal rejected the proposition that *Wilkinson* could generate liability where the wrongful conduct resulted, even foreseeably, in harm or distress falling short of physical harm or a recognised psychiatric illness.

In Ireland, in *Cronin v Kostal Ireland* (1 December 2005) (CC) the Court recognised the principle underlying *Wilkinson v Downton* holding that the test for the wrongful conduct in question is that it be "gratuitous or reprehensible". Mere negligence would not be sufficient. The defendant would have to intend to humiliate or embarrass the victim or unjustifiably run the risk of such an outcome. The tort was also considered in *Sullivan v Boylan (No 2)* [2013] IEHC 104. There, the plaintiff was aggressively harassed by a debt collector. The Court considered that the essential elements of the tort were that the words are spoken falsely and calculated to cause physical harm. In that particular case, the debt collector believed that what he was saying was true i.e. that the money was actually due. Accordingly, it was not a false statement capable of bringing the act within *Wilkinson*. In any event, the plaintiff had suffered acute distress, not physical injury.

The question arises: what is the role of *Wilkinson v Downton* nowadays? It is clear that the facts of *Wilkinson* could comfortably come within the compass of negligence today. Indeed, Lord Hoffmann in *Wainwright v Home Office* thought that *Wilkinson* had no role as far as claims for psychiatric injury were concerned because liability in negligence would provide a satisfactory remedy. But that is not to say that there are no cases in which *Wilkinson* may provide an important cause of action. Notwithstanding the narrow construction placed upon it in *Wainwright*, the rule was promulgated in terms wide enough to encompass distress falling short of recognised psychiatric injury, and there are many intentional or reckless acts besides the spoken word that can indirectly cause harm. The indirect nature of such acts would bring them outside the ambit of trespass. Thus, without the rule in *Wilkinson*, it is uncertain whether there would be a cause of action available in such cases at all, bearing in mind that recourse to negligence might be precluded if the loss is regarded as too remote for that particular tort.

As mentioned above, we could say that the facts in *Wilkinson* suggest that its real home now is that of negligence rather than trespass. Indeed, that is arguably what has happened in Australia. In *Carrier v Bonham* [2001] QCA 234 McPherson J observed that the expression "calculated" used by Wright J in *Wilkinson* is capable of meaning either "subjectively contemplated and intended" or "objectively likely to happen". He thought that the word was used in the latter sense, not the former. If that is so, McPherson J was effectively recasting *Wilkinson* as a negligence case. Thus far, that approach has not been adopted in England or in Ireland where it remains a distinct tort from negligence and from trespass to the person. Plainly, *Wilkinson v Downton* is a little used tort in this part of the world but, despite that, the judiciary in both England and Ireland have shown a marked reluctance to abandon it.

G. Defences to Trespass to the Person

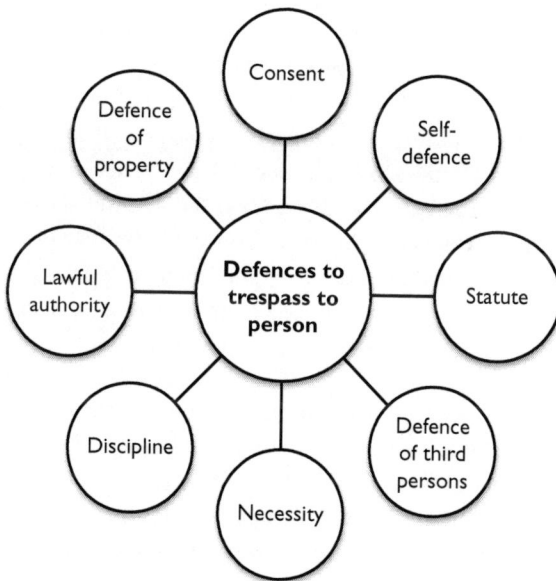

Consent

Physical contact which would otherwise constitute a trespass to the person will be rendered lawful by consent. Consent may be express or implied. What the courts take into account is external acts manifesting consent. Accordingly, even if a victim does not subjectively consent, the defendant will not be liable if the victim's external conduct indicates consent. For example, in *O'Brien v Cunard SS Co* (1891) 154 Mass 272, 28 NE 266, the plaintiff was a passenger on board one of the defendant's ships. The plaintiff had presented herself to the defendant's surgeon in the quarantine area and did not object when he indicated his intention to vaccinate her. Nevertheless, she sued for assault and negligence. The Court found for the defendant on the basis that the plaintiff had consented. The Court took the view that the totality of the circumstances must be considered, but only overt acts and outward manifestations may demonstrate consent or lack thereof.

Employees may consent to physical contact as part of their terms of employment. In *Corcoran v W & R Jacob & Co* [1945] IR 446, employees of the defendant employer had agreed as part of their terms of employment to be liable to be searched by security personnel as they were leaving the factory. On one occasion, whilst such a search was being carried out, security personnel had carried out an exceptionally aggressive search on the plaintiff. He sued. The Supreme Court held that the consent given in the terms of employment did not justify such aggressive searching. In other words, the defendant had exceeded the terms of the consent.

Consent must be genuine and freely given. Therefore, fraud, duress, or illegality will vitiate consent. The courts have held that consent obtained by fraud going to the quality of the conduct will be invalid but that fraud which is merely collateral will not vitiate the consent. The issue arose in *Hegarty v Shine* (1878) 4 LR Ir 288. In that case, a woman consented to sexual intercourse with the defendant (with whom she was in a relationship). He infected her with a sexually transmitted disease. He had concealed the fact that he had the disease. She sued for battery. The Court of Appeal dismissed her action on the basis that her consent to the sexual intercourse was real and had not been vitiated by fraud. The Court also considered that the action arose *ex turpi* ("from a base cause or matter an action does not arise").

It is a general principle of law that individuals of full capacity have autonomous entitlement to accept or reject medical treatment. In *Re a Ward of Court (No 2)* [1996] IR 79, the Supreme Court made it clear that if medical treatment is given without consent it may be a trespass against the person and a breach of the individual's constitutional rights. However, there may be circumstances in which consent may not be required; for example, cases of contagious disease or medical emergency where the patient cannot communicate. Though in the latter category, implied consent may operate as a defence (see *Holmes v Heatley* below).

Where a minor is incapable of providing consent to medical treatment, the practice is for medical practitioners to obtain the consent of the parents or guardian. Indeed, this occurs even in cases where the minor is capable of giving consent. In *Holmes v Heatley* [1937] Ir Jur Rep 74, the parents of a 16-year-old boy gave their consent for an operation to be carried out on him. They had been informed that only a local anaesthetic would be necessary. During the operation, the boy became distressed so a general anaesthetic was administered. The boy died on the operating table. There appeared to have been no negligence in the administration of the anaesthetic. The plaintiffs' action was dismissed. The Court stated that there was

> "no evidence which would entitle a jury to hold that there was an assault...The surgeon was bound to act as he did in the emergency with which he was faced...[administering the] anaesthetic was the only course open to him."

Under s 23 of the Non-Fatal Offences against the Person Act 1997, a minor who has reached the age of 16 may lawfully consent to medical treatment without the need to obtain consent for the treatment from his or her parents or guardian. The legislation, however, is silent in respect of minors under the age of 16. Regarding the provision of contraception to a child under the age of 16, it would appear to be open to a court to conclude on the evidence of a particular case that the child in question has sufficient maturity to make that decision themselves. In Britain, the House of Lords, by a majority, in *Gillick v West Norfolk & Wisbech Area Health Authority* [1986] 1 AC 112 authorised the provision of contraception by health professionals to minors with sufficient maturity under the age of 16.

In Ireland, the constitutional dimension may operate in respect of parents' duty and corresponding entitlement to control their children's conduct in the exercise of their constitutional and statutory role as guardians. In *North Western Health Board v HW* [2001] 3 IR 63, the Supreme Court gave significant latitude to parents in respect of decision-making which may negatively impact on a child's right to life, bodily integrity or health. However, in *Temple Street v D* [2011] IEHC 1, the Court made an order that an infant, whose parents objected to a blood transfusion on religious grounds, should have the transfusion.

Self-Defence

The Court in *Dullaghan v Hillen* [1957] Ir Jur Rep 10 made it clear that "it is lawful to repel force by force, provided that no unnecessary violence is used". Accordingly, reasonable force may be applied to defend oneself. What amounts to reasonable force will depend on the circumstances and will be a question of fact in every case. The importance of such force being proportionate to the threat faced was emphasised by the Court in the earlier decision of *Gregan v Sullivan* [1937] Ir Jur Rep 64. That case was an action in the Circuit Court for damages for assault. The defendant, a man under the age of 40, had used a pitchfork to inflict 13 puncture wounds on the arms of the 65-year-old plaintiff, as well as breaking one of his arms, in response to being struck on the lip by the plaintiff. The jury found for the defendant on the ground of self-defence. On appeal, the High Court found that the jury's decision was perverse and set it aside. Judgment was entered for the plaintiff.

Statute — Criminal Law (Defence and the Dwelling) Act 2011

The Criminal Law (Defence and the Dwelling) Act 2011 places on a statutory footing the degree of force permitted to repel trespassers from entering one's dwelling. The Act relieves from both criminal and civil liability the use of force by a person who is in his or her dwelling, or by a person who is a lawful occupant in a dwelling, against another person (or that of a person's property) where the person using the force honestly believes that the other person has entered or is entering the dwelling as a trespasser for the purpose of committing a criminal act. This defence is available only where the force used is such as is reasonable in the circumstances as the person using the force honestly believes them to be:

(i) to protect himself or herself or another person present in the dwelling from injury, assault, detention or death caused by a criminal act;

(ii) to protect his or her property or the property of another person from appropriation, destruction or damage caused by a criminal act; or

(iii) to prevent the commission of a crime or to effect, or assist in effecting, a lawful arrest.

Defence of Third Persons

The present law on the defence of third persons appears to be that "everyone has the right of defending any person by reasonable force against unlawful force, even if he has made a genuine mistake about the perilous position of that other" (21st ed, *Salmond & Heuston on The Law of Torts*, Sweet and Maxwell, London, 1996). The Court of Criminal Appeal approved this approach in *People (AG) v Keatley* [1954] IR 12.

Necessity

It appears to be possible for a defendant to seek to justify a trespass to the person on the ground of necessity. However, it is not clear that the courts would accept this defence. Minor trespasses may be tolerated (for example a paramedic pushing through a crowd to get to an injured person), but serious ones may not. The criminal authorities suggest that the defence of necessity will not operate in relation to killing another. In *R v Dudley and Stephens* (1884) 14 QBD 273, the crew of a ship were stranded in a lifeboat after their ship sank. They killed and ate a cabin boy to sustain themselves. On their return to England, they were prosecuted for murder. Their defence of necessity was not accepted: see also *US v Holmes* (1842) 1 Wall Jr 1.

Discipline

Parents may use physical force or confinement in order to discipline their children, provided it is not excessive. It is referred to as the power of "reasonable chastisement of children". It is a common law power which received statutory recognition in s 37 of the Children Act 1908. Children, of course, are perfectly entitled to sue their parents for battery or false imprisonment where chastisement goes beyond what is reasonable.

The concept of "reasonable chastisement" was considered in *A v United Kingdom* [1998] 2 FLR 959 (ECHR). That case concerned the stepfather of a 9-year-old boy who had struck the boy on a number of occasions with a garden cane causing bruising on several parts of his body. The stepfather was charged with causing actual bodily harm but was acquitted by a jury. His defence was that the boy was difficult and had not responded to parental or school discipline. The child argued that English law had failed to protect him from ill-treatment by his stepfather. The European Court of Human Rights found that the child's Article 3 rights had been breached. Article 3 prohibits torture or inhuman or degrading treatment or punishment. The Court concluded that English law had not provided adequate protection to the child against treatment or punishment contrary to Article 3.

In the past, schoolteachers, by virtue of being in *loco parentis*, had broad discretion to use corporal punishment on schoolchildren in their charge. The criminal immunity of schoolteachers to use such force was independent of the immunity of parents. The use of "reasonable and moderate force" in schools was not open to a charge of assault, irrespective of the wishes of the parents. Claims against schoolteachers generally met with little success. In *McCann v Mannion* (1932) 66 ILTR 161 the Court stated that

> "A teacher is justified in inflicting proper corporal punishment when it is necessary... It would require proof of malice or of something approaching to malice to induce [the court] to interfere with [the teacher's] discretion."

Rule 130 of the *Rules for National Schools* (1965), which provided for corporal punishment in schools in certain circumstances, was amended by Circulars 9/82 and 7/88. The 1982 circular purported to abolish corporal punishment in National Schools. The change in practice was announced in the Dáil by the Minister for Education in March 1982. As we have seen, at common law, it was permissible for a parent and those in *loco parentis* (such as teachers) to administer reasonable corporal punishment to a child. The administrative circulars, being mere circulars and not instruments of hard law, could not effect the abolition of corporal punishment in schools; only legislation could do that. That legislation was eventually enacted as the Non-Fatal Offences Against the Person Act 1997. Section 24 provides that "[t]he rule of law under which teachers are immune from criminal liability in respect of physical chastisement of pupils is hereby abolished". Although s 24 refers only to criminal liability, immunity in the civil law has almost certainly been abolished too.

Lawful Authority

Conduct which would otherwise constitute a trespass to the person, where its purpose is to prevent, control, or respond to suspected criminal activity, will be permitted by law. Accordingly, members of An Garda Síochána have broad powers of arrest under warrant and, in some cases, without a warrant. Civilians also have a limited power of arrest where they reasonably believe that an offence has been committed or where they reasonably suspect that a person is in the act of committing an offence. This power is subject to strict limitations set down in s 4 of the Criminal Law Act 1997.

The Gardaí may do acts that would otherwise constitute a trespass where their object is to prevent a breach of the peace. The person against whom the act is done need not have been the one likely to breach the peace. This occurred in *Humphries v Connor* (1864) 17 ICLR 1 (QB). There, a police constable removed an orange lily from a woman who was walking on a street in the town of Swanlinbar. It was held to be a good defence that the act was done to preserve the public peace, in that the woman, although being followed by a threatening crowd, refused to remove the lily.

In *O'Kelly v Harvey* (1883) 14 LR Ir 105, a public meeting was organised by the Land League at Brookeborough. An inflammatory poster had been published calling on opponents of the Land League to assemble in large numbers "and give Parnell and his associates a warm reception". A magistrate forcibly dispersed the meeting in order to avoid a breach of the peace.

Defence of Property

At common law, the position traditionally has been that where a person enters another's land or premises, that other may thereupon evict the intruder, using no more force than is necessary to do so. Where no violence or force is used in the intrusion, the trespasser should be requested to leave before physical measures are resorted to: see *Greene v Goddard* (1798) 2 Salk 641, 91 ER 540.

The issue of reasonable force was considered by the Circuit Court in *MacKnight v Xtravision* (5 July 1991). There, the defendants were tenants of a lock-up shop in a shopping centre. The plaintiff was a security man at the shopping centre. Following a dispute with the landlord, the plaintiff sought to prevent the defendants re-entering their lock-up shop by anchoring himself to the doors. In doing so, he was trespassing. The defendants forcibly removed the plaintiff from the doors, in the course of which the plaintiff received a "roughing up" which involved receiving several punches sufficient, according to Carroll J, to support a charge against the defendants of assault causing actual bodily harm. Carroll J said that reasonable force in this particular case meant that the defendants were undoubtedly entitled to lay hands lightly upon the plaintiff to move him aside: but when that failed, they should have desisted. The defendants were not entitled to assault the plaintiff so as to inflict the type of injuries he sustained. The defendants should have gone to the courts and secured an injunction against the plaintiff and his employers. This would, the judge acknowledged, have involved delay and may have harmed their commercial interests, but in a civilised State, that would have been the correct course of action. The judge added that if the parties were to resort to private violence in cases such as this, there would be "an end to all law or order". Liability was imposed on the defendants, but the plaintiff's damages were reduced by half on account of his contributory negligence.

TRESPASS TO GOODS

Learning Outcomes

Upon completion of this chapter, the reader should be able to:

- Identify the ingredients of the tort of trespass to goods
- Provide examples of acts which may amount to a trespass to goods
- Explain what is meant by "possession" the purposes of the tort
- Discuss the relevance of the defendant's state of mind in actions for trespass to goods
- Outline the circumstances in which lawful authority may apply

A. Overview

The gist of the tort of trespass to goods is the wrongful physical interference with the possession of chattels. Chattels (or "chattels personal") are movable, tangible articles of property. This tort can take many forms, such as scratching the panel of a vehicle, removing a tyre from a vehicle, or otherwise causing intentional damage to personal property.

B. Examples of Trespass to Goods

- Taking a chattel out of the possession of another — *Brewer v Dew* (1843) 11 M & W 625, 152 ER 955;
- Asportation (moving a chattel from one place to another) — *Kirk v Gregory* (1876) 1 Ex D 55;
- Damaging a chattel with one's person — *Fouldes v Willoughby* (1841) 8 M & W 540, 151 ER 1153;
- Damaging a chattel with one's property — *M'Cormick v Ballantine* (1859) 10 ICLR 305;
- Beating an animal — *Slater v Swann* (1730) 2 Stra 872;
- Killing an animal — *Sheldrick v Abery* (1793) 1 Esp 55.

C. Elements of the Tort of Trespass to Goods

The ingredients of the tort of trespass to goods were identified in *Farrell v Minister for Agriculture and Food* (11 October 1995) HC as the wrongful and direct interference with the possession of chattels (per Carroll J). In that case, it was held that there had been a direct interference with the plaintiff's right to possession of his cattle where the Minister constrained the plaintiff to have his herd taken for slaughter on the purported authority of *ultra vires* regulations.

The interference with the plaintiff's goods must be direct. If the interference is indirect, there can be no trespass: *Covell v Laming* (1808) 1 Camp 497. Accordingly, if a room in which the plaintiff's goods are kept is locked by the defendant, there will be no trespass to them: *Hartley v Moxham* (1842) 3 QB 701. If a vehicle is wheel-clamped unlawfully, there will be a trespass: *Vine v Waltham Forest LBC* [2000] 1 WLR 2383. In *Kirk v Gregory*, a woman who moved rings belonging to a man who had just died from one room in his house to another was held liable.

The requirement that the interference be direct was brought into sharp focus in *McDonagh v West of Ireland Fisheries Ltd* [1986] IEHC 55. There, the defendant was held not liable in respect of trespass to a boat where it had temporarily removed the boat from its moorings in a harbour. The boat was later damaged in circumstances which could not be ascertained, but most likely due to her settling on some obstruction on the seabed. Since the damage to the boat was not direct, no action in trespass lay.

As with trespass to the person, it is not easy to determine where directness ends and indirectness begins. Mixing a drug with the feed of a racehorse will be a trespass to the feed, but will not be a trespass to the racehorse when it is later given the feed: *Hutchens v Maughan* [1947] VLR 131. Chasing animals seems to be a borderline case: on the one hand, there is no physical contact; on the other hand, chasing humans has always been accepted as assault, which is a variety of trespass. Winfield suggests that the better view is that chasing animals probably is trespass, a proposition which gains some support from *Farmer v Hunt* (1610) 1 Brownl 220 and *Durant v Childe* (1611) 1 Brownl 221.

D. Actionable *Per Se*?

The tort of trespass to goods appears to be actionable *per se*. Trespass generally is actionable *per se* and there is no reason to suppose that trespass to goods should be any different. There are good reasons for this. If the mere touching of objects such as exhibits in a gallery or museum, or waxworks, were not trespass, the possessor of those goods would be left without a remedy.

E. The Plaintiff Must Be In Possession

Since trespass to goods is an interference with possession, it follows that if the plaintiff were not in possession at the time of the interference, he cannot sue for trespass. In other words, the plaintiff must be exercising physical control with the intention to exercise such control on his own behalf over the goods at the time of the interference. Whether the plaintiff owns the goods at the relevant time is immaterial.

In *Keenan Bros Ltd v CIE* [1963] 97 ILTR 54, the plaintiffs carried on business as agricultural and structural engineers. They ordered a consignment of steel which was delivered by train to Bagenalstown railway station. Due to an industrial dispute between the defendant and some of its employees, the plaintiffs' goods could not be delivered because the defendants' employees would not handle them. The plaintiffs sought an interlocutory mandatory injunction compelling the defendants to deliver the goods or to permit the plaintiffs' employees to remove the goods from the wagons in which they were languishing. The Court declined to grant the injunction. The Court observed that it would be an act of trespass at common law for any person to open the defendants' wagons and remove the goods from them unless by virtue of the defendants' permission or by virtue of some legal right. The fact that the goods belonged to the plaintiffs did not alter that position and entitle them to commit an act of trespass to recover their goods.

F. The Defendant's State of Mind

There is no liability in trespass to goods in respect of an act that is neither intentional nor negligent. Hence, in order to be actionable, a trespass must be either wilful or negligent. This was confirmed in *ESB v Hastings & Co Ltd* [1965] Ir Jur 51. In that case, the defendants, in resurfacing a road, opened a trench and allowed a mechanical shovel to damage a high-tension cable in the possession of the plaintiffs. The defendants had been made aware by the plaintiffs of the presence of the cable. The Court held that this put the defendants "on notice sufficiently to render them liable for trespass". The approach adopted by the courts in England in *National Coal Board v Evans (JE) & Co (Cardiff) Ltd* [1951] 2 KB 861 and *Fowler v Lanning* [1959] 1 QB 426 was approved.

G. Lawful Authority

There will be circumstances in which an act done by a person that would otherwise constitute a trespass to goods will be rendered innocent because that person has lawful authority to do the act. This may arise where members of An Garda Síochána, in the course of effecting a valid arrest, seize, without a search warrant, property in the possession or custody of the person arrested when they believe it necessary to do so to avoid the abstraction or destruction of that property if it is believed to be evidentially relevant or reasonably believed to be stolen or unlawfully in the possession of that person: see *Jennings v Quinn* [1968] IR 305. There are also a number of statutory provisions which authorise the Gardaí and others to seize goods in certain circumstances.

NUISANCE

Learning Outcomes

Upon completion of this chapter, the reader should be able to:

- Explain the ingredients of the tort of nuisance;
- Discuss the relationship between nuisance and other torts;
- Explain the central characteristics of the tort of private nuisance;
- Outline the defences available to defendants in nuisance cases;
- Identify ineffectual defences in nuisance;
- Appreciate and explain the role of the tort of public nuisance in protecting the public's rights.

A. Nuisance in Context

Overview

There are two separate torts falling under the rubric of nuisance: private nuisance and public nuisance. Private nuisance turns on the infringement of private rights. Public nuisance, on the other hand, is primarily a common law crime, but also turns on the infringement of public rights. Both private and public nuisance are actionable under the civil law. Since public nuisance is essentially a common law criminal offence, its internal rules are quite unlike those of private nuisance. O'Higgins CJ in *Connolly v South of Ireland Asphalt Co* [1977] IR 99 provided a useful definition of the two torts:

> "It has been said that actionable nuisance is incapable of exact definition. The term nuisance contemplates an act or omission which amounts to an unreasonable interference with, disturbance of, or annoyance to another person in the exercise of his rights. If the rights so interfered with belong to the person as a member of the public, the act or omission is a public nuisance. If these rights relate to the ownership or occupation of land, or of some easement, profit, or other right enjoyed in connection with land, then the acts or omissions amount to a private nuisance."

Nuisance and Other Torts

The law of nuisance should not be viewed in isolation to other torts. Whilst nuisance overlaps with negligence, it differs in important respects from trespass. In *Goldman v Hargrave* [1967] 1 AC 645, Lord Wilberforce observed that a nuisance "may comprise a wide variety of situations, in some of which negligence plays no part, in others of which it is decisive". It is clear, therefore, that concurrent liability in both nuisance and negligence can arise out of a single set of facts. For example, if a land owner lights a fire near his neighbour's fence and then leaves it unattended, he might be held liable in either negligence or nuisance if the fire were to spread to the neighbour's property. Whilst the interrelationship between nuisance and negligence is clear, the tort of trespass can be easily distinguished from nuisance. Trespass to land concerns direct rather than consequential harm. Therefore, the encroachment of roots and branches from one property to another will be a nuisance rather than trespass because interference such as this lacks the directness and voluntariness normally required in trespass actions. Moreover, trespass is actionable *per se*, whereas nuisance requires the plaintiff to prove damage. Thus, in *Kelsen v Imperial Tobacco Co (of Great Britain and Ireland) Ltd* [1957] 2 QB 334, where a sign erected by the defendants projected into the space above the plaintiff's shop, it was held that the erection of the sign constituted a trespass but not a nuisance.

The Court stated that "the presence of the sign... caused no inconvenience and no interference with the [plaintiff's] use of his air". On the other hand, where damage occurs as a result of a trespass it appears to make little difference to the result whether the action is framed in trespass or in nuisance: see *Home Brewery Co v William Davies & Co (Loughborough) Ltd* [1987] QB 339.

Nuisance and Environmental Protection

Nuisance law has historically played an important role in the protection of the environment. But nowadays it is fair to say that nuisance law, whether public or private, plays a relatively limited role in environmental protection. There has been a steady increase in concern for the protection of the environment in recent years. This has resulted in the enactment of a range of statutes (many of which are European in origin) imposing a system of regulation that renders the common law very much a secondary means of protection. Many of the sorts of conduct that would formerly have sounded in nuisance alone are now dealt with by statutes such as the Air Pollution Act 1987 and the Environmental Protection Agency Act 1992. The enactment of such legislation has meant that it is easier and more effective to pursue a grievance via the public bodies that can prosecute environmental offences, rather than suing in nuisance where the costs for private litigants may be prohibitive.

Furthermore, the effect of planning legislation has, to some extent, displaced the law of nuisance in relation to protecting residents from interferences with their use and enjoyment of their land. Generally, planning permission must be obtained prior to a change of use of existing premises or the construction of new ones. This has meant that some potential nuisances can be avoided prospectively. Thus, where a person is denied planning permission to turn his house into a small factory, the obvious potential for disturbance to a neighbour due to vibrations or noise, for example, is avoided in advance. In such cases, nuisance law, which operates retrospectively, i.e. in response to an existing interference, is denied any role. However, it would be wrong to assume that the tort of nuisance is in any way redundant in the environmental context. On the contrary. It retains the potential to perform a number of important and useful functions. For example, it can operate as an enforcement mechanism additional to those contained in statute. Also, whenever such a case is decided in favour of the plaintiff, the effect of the judgment may be to establish standards in relation to, say, pollution control, which are additional to those set down in statute.

Since the torts of private nuisance and public nuisance differ significantly, it is appropriate to consider them separately.

Figure 13.1

```
                          ┌─────────────────────┐
                          │      Nuisance       │
                          └─────────────────────┘
                    ┌───────────────┴───────────────┐
        ┌─────────────────────┐         ┌─────────────────────┐
        │   Private Nuisance  │         │   Public Nuisance   │
        └─────────────────────┘         └─────────────────────┘
                    │                               │
┌───────────────────────────────┐   ┌───────────────────────────────┐
│ Continuous, unlawful and      │   │ An act which materially affects│
│ indirect interference with    │   │ the reasonable comfort and     │
│ use or enjoyment of land      │   │ convenience of a class of      │
│                               │   │ members of the public          │
└───────────────────────────────┘   └───────────────────────────────┘
```

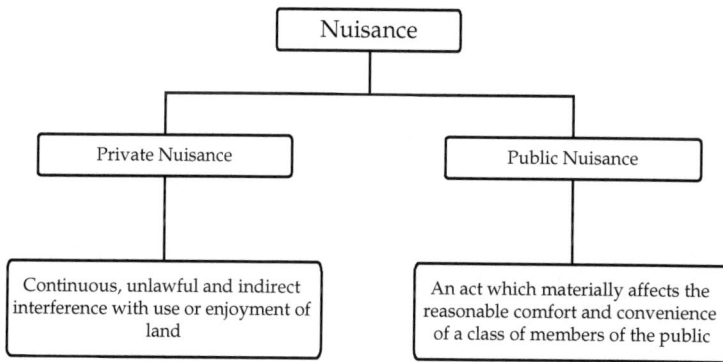

B. Private Nuisance

General

Private nuisance defies exact definition. In *Brand v Hammersmith and City Railway Co* (1867) LR 2 QB 223, Erle CJ observed that the law of nuisance is "immersed in undefined uncertainty". Professor Newark has stated that "the boundaries of the tort of nuisance are blurred" (1949) 65 LQR 480. It is clear, therefore, that a wide range of interferences can amount to an actionable nuisance. In *Royal Dublin Society v Yates* (31 July 1997) HC, the Court stated that private nuisance consists of any interference without lawful justification of a person's use and enjoyment of his property. In *Hanrahan v Merck Sharp & Dohme (Ireland) Ltd* [1988] ILRM 69 the Supreme Court held that, in the context of the law of nuisance,

> "what an occupier of land is entitled to as against his neighbour, is
> the comfortable and healthy enjoyment of the land to the degree that
> would be expected by an ordinary person whose requirements are
> objectively reasonable in all the particular circumstances."

Accordingly, it is possible to say that there are three distinct kinds of interests to which the law of nuisance provides protection: the protection of land *per se*; the protection of the use of land; the protection of the enjoyment of land.

Not all interferences will amount to an actionable nuisance. The law requires tolerance and reasonableness between neighbours in respect of the uses to which each puts his land. As Lord Goff said in *Cambridge Water Company v Eastern Counties Leather plc* [1994] 2 AC 264, 299, liability for nuisance is "kept under control by the principle of reasonable user…". It is inevitable that neighbours will, from time to time, annoy each other as they use their land. The law, however, does not entertain actions in nuisance for every minor irritation that one neighbour may cause to another. In *Bamford v Turnley* (1862) 3 B & S 66; 122 ER 27, Bramwell B characterised nuisance as "A rule of give and take, live and let live". In *Hughes v Riley* [2006] 1 P & CR 29, Chadwick LJ described nuisance as a principle of "good neighbourliness… [which] involves reciprocity".

We can see from this notion of "give-and-take", or reciprocity, a recognition that the interests of neighbours may compete. For example, one resident may complain that the volume of his neighbour's music is so loud that it amounts to an interference with his use and enjoyment of his home. However, his neighbour may argue that it is he who is suffering the wrong, because he has the right to play his music in the privacy of his own home without complaint or interference. In these situations it is the role of the court to apply the law in order to decide which of these competing interests should receive legal protection under the tort of nuisance.

In relation to the degree of interference required, the Court observed in *Benjamin v Storr* (1874) LR 9 CP 400 that the injury must be of "a substantial character, not fleeting or evanescent". In *Mullin v Hynes* (13 November 1972, SC) it was stated that the courts would be unwilling "to grant relief where the damage claimed is in respect of trivial, fanciful or exaggerated inconvenience". Accordingly, minor, temporary, or "one-off" interferences will not normally be considered to be sufficiently substantial to maintain a nuisance action. So, for an interference to amount to an actionable nuisance it must be both substantial and unreasonable.

The courts, therefore, tend to regard nuisance as a continuing wrong rather than an interference of a fleeting nature which is unlikely to recur. Accordingly, it could be characterised as a wrongful state of affairs for which the defendant is responsible. This does not mean, however, that a nuisance cannot arise where damage results from a single act: this might occur, for example, in the case of a single escape of a substance, such as gas: see *Midwood & Co Ltd v Manchester Corporation* [1905] 2 KB 597. The essence of nuisance, then, is not so much an isolated act, but rather the continuous or permanent management by the defendant of his affairs on his property in such a way that it results in injury to the plaintiff.

In *St Helen's Smelting Co v Tipping* (1865) 11 HL Cas 642 the Court set out a distinction between activities of a neighbour which cause "material injury to property" and those which cause "sensible personal discomfort". Lord Westbury said that the locality in which the activity is pursued is not relevant in cases of material injury to property. This is because material damage to property can never arise from a reasonable use of land. Locality is, however, relevant in circumstances where the alleged nuisance causes loss of amenity. In such cases, a landowner is expected to put up with inconveniences resulting from activities which would be perfectly normal and reasonable in a particular neighbourhood.

In private nuisance cases, damage may consist of:

(a) substantial interference with use or enjoyment of land;
(b) physical damage to land; or
(c) an interference with servitudes.

Private nuisance, as mentioned above, is not generally actionable *per se*. Actual damage, of one (or more) of the three above categories, must be proved. Plaintiffs in nuisance actions can seek a range of remedies. The continuing nature of most nuisances means that the plaintiff's primary concern is to bring the nuisance to an end, or reduce it, by means of an injunction. Damages can be awarded along with, or instead of, an injunction. In a limited number of cases the "self-help" remedy of abatement might be appropriate. This is where the injured party takes appropriate steps to stop the nuisance. However, a person who wrongly exercises abatement may be criminally liable. For example, in *Burton v Winters* [1993] 1 WLR 1077 the plaintiff took a nuisance action against her neighbour in relation to a garage on the defendant's property which encroached onto the plaintiff's property. The plaintiff attempted to abate the nuisance herself by demolishing part of the offending structure. The defendant secured an injunction against the plaintiff. She breached the terms of injunction, was arrested by the police for criminal damage and eventually committed to prison for two years.

Since interferences with servitudes represents a form of damage rarely litigated in nuisance actions, and is, in any case, more appropriately dealt with in a text on real property, it will not be considered here.

Figure 13.2

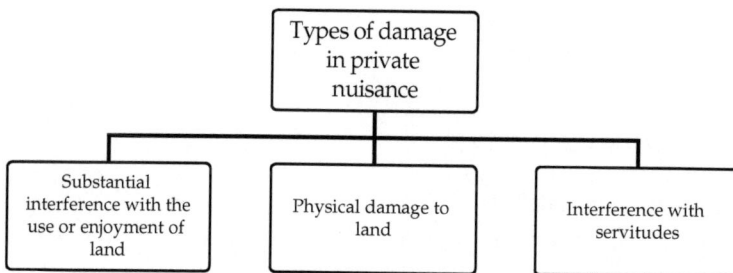

Substantial Interference with the Use or Enjoyment of Land

Where interference with the use or enjoyment of land (otherwise known as "amenity nuisance") is concerned, give-and-take on the part of neighbouring landowners is something which, as we have seen, the law requires. The general principle was stated by Lord Wright in *Sedleigh-Denfield v O'Callaghan* [1940] AC 880. He said:

"[a] balance has to be maintained between the right of the occupier to do what he likes with his own [land] and the right of his neighbour not to be interfered with".

In *St Helen's* Lord Westbury characterised this type of harm as

"... personal inconvenience and interference with one's enjoyment, one's quiet, one's personal freedom, anything that discomposes or injuriously affects the senses or the nerves...".

In deciding whether loss of amenity has occurred, the courts will be required to determine if the interference with the enjoyment of land is unreasonable. There are two possible dimensions to unreasonableness in this context:

- the nature of the interference with the plaintiff's land; and
- the conduct of the defendant.

The courts tend to focus on the nature of the interference rather than the defendant's conduct, but this does not mean that they ignore the latter. This is because the unreasonableness of the defendant's user will often be a relevant factor in how the court characterises the nature of the interference. For example, if I make noise on my land in the pursuit of an entirely legitimate objective, it may not be an actionable nuisance. However, if I make the same noise for the sole purpose of disturbing my neighbours, that will be an actionable nuisance. In determining whether the interference is unreasonable, the courts typically take into account a range of factors. These include:

(i) the sensitivity of the plaintiff;
(ii) the nature of the locality;
(iii) the utility of the defendant's conduct;
(iv) the defendant's motive;
(v) the impact of planning permission.

Each is considered below.

The Sensitivity of the Plaintiff

A plaintiff may feel that his neighbour is committing a nuisance, but this may be as a result of his own unreasonably high standards or particular requirements. Henchy J, in *Hanrahan v Merck Sharp & Dohme (Ireland) Ltd* [1988] ILRM 69, stated that the position in Irish law is that the plaintiff "is not entitled to insist that his personal nicety of taste or fastidiousness of requirements should be treated as inviolable". Therefore, an extra-sensitive plaintiff may not succeed in a nuisance action if that same conduct by the defendant would not give rise to an interference in respect of a "reasonable" plaintiff. An example of a particular sensitivity can be seen in *Robinson v Kilvert* (1889) 41 Ch D 88. In that case, the defendant landlord let premises to the plaintiff but the defendant remained in occupation of the cellar. Due to the nature of the defendant's business it was necessary to keep the cellar dry and hot. The heat from the cellar passed through the ceiling to the floor above, which was used by the plaintiff as a paper warehouse. It damaged the plaintiff's stock of brown paper. He sought an injunction to restrain the defendant from keeping his cellar so hot. The Court refused the injunction. It held that it was only the fact that the plaintiff was engaged in an "exceptionally delicate trade" that caused him to suffer loss. In contrast, in *McKinnon Industries v Walker* [1951] 3 DLR 577 the plaintiff suffered damage to orchids. In this case, it was held that the plaintiff's use of his land was not especially sensitive because any ordinary plants would have been similarly affected by the defendant's activity.

Interestingly, the Court of Appeal in England has recently questioned, though not expressly ruled on, the existence of the concept of "sensitive user". In *Network Rail Infrastructure Ltd v CJ Morris* [2004] EWCA Civ 172, electromagnetic fields from the defendant's signalling system interfered with the sound of electric guitars in the plaintiff's nearby recording studio. The Court had to determine whether this was a nuisance. One of the defendant's arguments was that the plaintiff's use of his land was "extra-sensitive". Doubt was cast on the existence of a separate limitation on liability for extra-sensitive uses of land. Buxton LJ thought that the rule was subsumed under the general requirement of the reasonableness of the defendant's use of land. The Court divided on the question of whether the plaintiff's use of his land was in fact extra-sensitive but ultimately held for the defendant on the broad notion of what was reasonable as between neighbours. They held that the interference as a result of the defendant's conduct was not reasonably foreseeable; it could not, therefore, amount to an unreasonable use of land.

Locality

Localities might be characterised as: rural; semi-rural; urban; suburban; commercial; industrial; residential. Lord Westbury in *St Helen's Smelting Co v Tipping* explained the importance of locality:

> "[A]nything that discomposes or injuriously affects the senses or the nerves, whether that may or may not be denominated a nuisance, must undoubtedly depend greatly on the circumstances of the place where the thing complained of actually occurs. If a man lives in a town, it is necessary that he should subject himself to the consequences of those operations of trade which may be carried on in his immediate locality, which are actually necessary for trade and commerce, and also for the enjoyment of property, and for the benefit of the inhabitants of

the town and of the public at large. If a man lives in a street where there are numerous shops, and a shop is opened next door to him, which is carried on in a fair and reasonable way, he has no ground for complaint, because to himself individually there may arise much discomfort from the trade carried on in that shop".

In *Sturges v Bridgman* (1879) 11 Ch D 852 the issue of locality was central to the Court's decision. For more than 20 years a doctor had a property which adjoined a confectionery works. He then built a new consulting room at the end of his garden. His consultations in that room were disturbed by noise and vibration from the confectionery works. It was held to be an actionable nuisance. Thesiger LJ, holding that the Court should take account of the fact that the area consisted largely of medical specialists' consulting rooms, said:

"Whether anything is a nuisance or not is a question to be determined, not merely by an abstract consideration of the thing itself, but in reference to its circumstances; what would be a nuisance in Belgrave Square would not necessarily be so in Bermondsey; and where a locality is devoted to a particular trade... [the courts] would be justified in finding, and may be trusted to find, that the trade... is not an actionable wrong."

The significance of this statement lies in the fact that in Victorian London, Belgravia was a fashionable residential district whilst Bermondsey was the home of the notoriously smelly leather industry. The law required the residents of Bermondsey to be rather more tolerant, by virtue where they lived, than those of Belgravia. We can also see this approach in *Adams v Ursell* [1913] 1 Ch 269 and *Baxter v Camden London Borough Council (No 2)* [2001] 1 AC 1. In *Adams* a smelly fish and chip shop established in a fashionable street was held to be a nuisance. In *Baxter* the plaintiff complained of noise created by her upstairs neighbours. The neighbour and the plaintiff lived in a converted house and were tenants of the defendant local authority. The plaintiff's action failed because the noise was part of the "ordinary use" of such premises. Tuckey LJ, in the Court of Appeal said: "[o]ccupiers of low-cost, high density housing must be expected to tolerate higher levels of noise from their neighbours than others in more substantial and spacious premises".

The character of the neighbourhood was considered in *Dewar v City & Suburban Racecourse Co* [1899] 1 IR 345. In that case, the defendants organised race meetings on Sundays on lands at Drumcondra, a residential area of Dublin. The practice of holding races there had commenced at a time when houses in the area were "few in number and scattered". Over time, the area became more and more built up. It became what the Court described as essentially a "residentiary district for the middle classes". The residents in that area then complained of noise and other disturbances caused by the races. These included interruptions to religious services. The Court granted an injunction against the defendants prohibiting the holding of race meetings on Sundays. The Court recognised that the character of the locality had changed and that what once was not a nuisance could be so now.

In *O'Kane v Campbell* [1985] IR 115 HC, a shop was located on the corner of North Circular Road and Glengarriff Parade. The North Circular Road was described as a "wide busy street both by day and by night" and Glengarriff Parade as an "old established residential street... just removed from the bustle of other more busy places in the area". The shop began to trade on a 24-hour basis. This significantly increased the level of noise emanating from the shop during the night. The noise disturbed the plaintiff who lived opposite the shop on Glengarriff Parade. The Court was satisfied that had the shop been on Glengarriff Parade there would have been a clear nuisance and, if the shop was on North Circular Road, there would have been no actionable nuisance at all. However, the shop was at the junction of the two streets. Consequently, the position was less clear-cut. The Court took the view that the 24-hour trading had "drastically altered the amenity of Glengarriff Parade as a residential street". An injunction was granted which prohibited trading between the hours of midnight and 6 am.

In *Molumby v Kearns* (19 January 1999) HC, the plaintiffs were occupants of a house on a residential street in Dublin. They sued in nuisance when the gate into an adjoining industrial estate was widened, allowing larger, louder and more polluting trucks to access the estate. The plaintiffs claimed that there was a dramatic increase in the number, size and hours of traffic. O'Sullivan J noted that the locality was zoned residential in the local authority's development plan so that the policy of the planning authority was to preserve the amenity of the residents. Against this he recognised that the locality consisted of residences which adjoined a busy road and that the industrial estate, authorised by appropriate planning permission, was "in its midst". O'Sullivan J accepted that the plaintiffs were not afforded "the comfortable and healthy enjoyment" of their property on the basis set out by Henchy J in *Hanrahan*. He did not think it would be reasonable to close the estate down, but equally, he did not think that the noise, fumes and general activity and traffic movement on the estate should be such as to cause an undue impact on the amenities of the nearby residences. He granted an injunction restricting access to the industrial estate by commercial vehicles to 8.15 am to 6.15 pm Monday to Friday and 9 am to 1 pm on Saturday and requiring that forklift and pallet trucks be electric or battery operated units with rubber wheels. This compromise provided for the continuing commercial viability of the industrial estate and mitigated the more serious effects of the estate's activities on the amenity of the residents.

A further important question arises in relation to locality: what if the character of a locality changes because of the activities of the defendant? Can the defendant then argue that because the character of the locality has changed, albeit due to his or her own activity, what might have been a nuisance before the change in character is not a nuisance now? The general principle appears to be that a defendant cannot rely upon his own wrongdoing to change the nature of a locality. If, for example, a factory owner makes noise over a protracted period of time and then claims that, as a result of that noise, the locality has changed to one of industrial character rather than residential; can that amount to a defence to an action in nuisance? It appears not. Whilst a noisy activity or set of activities may be relevant to the character of the locality, this principle does not go so far as to justify noises so loud as to amount to a nuisance; for the latter, the plaintiff can still sue: see *Coventry v Lawrence* [2014] UKSC 13.

The Utility of the Defendant's Conduct

The relevance of public utility of the defendant's conduct was considered as early as 1628 in *Jones v Powell* (1628) Hut 135, Palm 536. In that case, the Court of King's Bench considered whether fumes from a brewhouse which caused inconvenience and damage to a neighbour's property (some papers) was actionable. Whitelock J said: "… it is better that they [the plaintiff's papers] should be spoiled than the commonwealth stand in need of good liquor". The issue of the availability of brewed beverages was important because they were safer to drink than ordinary water.

The issue a public benefit was also considered by the Court of Exchequer Chamber in *Bamford v Turnley* (1862) 3 B & S 66; 122 ER 27. The plaintiff complained that the defendant's use of his land (burning bricks) resulted in smoke and smell which affected the plaintiff in the enjoyment of his land. Bramwell B took the view that an activity is for the public benefit only if it is profitable after paying compensation to those injured by it. Therefore, if the social benefit after the activity is undertaken is greater than before it, the activity is economically desirable and should be undertaken.

We can see, therefore, the mere fact that the defendant's activity provides some public benefit, for example employment or an amenity, will not mean that it cannot still be held to be a nuisance. In *Adams v Ursell* (see above) a smelly — but popular — local fish and chip shop was held to be a nuisance. Also, in *Bellew v Cement Ltd* [1948] IR 61, the plaintiff sought an injunction to restrain the defendants from continuing to carry on blasting operations at their quarry. The defendants argued that to restrain them from doing so would have a serious effect on building operations throughout the country — which would be contrary to the public good.

The Court held that it was not entitled to take the public convenience into consideration when dealing with the rights of private parties. Murnaghan J said: "I do not think that we are entitled to deprive [the plaintiff] of his legal rights on some idea of public convenience". This decision is, however, somewhat inconsistent with later decisions.

Generally, any public or social utility provided by the maker of a nuisance may affect the remedy which the court prescribes. *Clifford v Drug Treatment Centre Board* (7 November 1997) HC concerned a drug treatment centre that operated in the Pearse Street area of Dublin under statutory authority. The plaintiffs were the proprietors of local businesses. They claimed that the addicts attending the centre were harming their trade by antisocial activities. The Court declined to grant an interlocutory injunction reducing the numbers of drug addicts eligible to attend the facility. McCracken J said that the immediate result of granting such an injunction would be that fewer "drug addicts would be treated, which is clearly against the public interest, besides depriving possibly hundreds of individuals of badly needed treatment". The Court did, however, grant an injunction restraining the expansion of the centre.

Similarly, in *Gleeson v Syntex Ireland Ltd* (7 September 1982) HC, the plaintiff complained of a "sickly sweet smell" emanating from a nearby factory. The Court took the view that the intensity of the smell was insufficient to justify the grant of an injunction which would have had the effect of closing down the factory which employed 300 people. The Court awarded damages instead. However, in *Lynch v Brown & Polson* (29 October 1953) HC, where noise emanating from a factory in a residential area of Dublin seriously disrupted the sleep of local residents, the Court granted an injunction restraining the defendants from committing a nuisance by noise. The Court stated that the defendants were "not entitled to expect or require adjoining residents to tolerate the noise from their factory in the hope that they might get used to it and cease to regard it as a nuisance".

A number of cases have come before the English courts in which the European Convention on Human Rights has been argued in nuisance cases following the (limited) incorporation of the Convention into UK law by the Human Rights Act 1998. For example, in *Dennis v Ministry of Defence* [2003] EWHC 793, a large private land owner took an action in nuisance in respect of noise caused by low-flying military aircraft training flights. The plaintiff succeeded both in private nuisance and in establishing a breach of Article 8 (right to private and family life) and Article 1 of Protocol 1 (peaceful enjoyment of possessions). The Court, however, recognised the public interest in the continuation of the training flights. Accordingly, damages were awarded in lieu of an injunction.

Planning Permission

Modern planning legislation dates back to the Local Government (Planning and Development) Act 1963. Decisions made by local planning authorities reflect an attempt by the authorities to balance the likely benefits of a proposed development against any potential adverse consequences. The law of private nuisance fulfils the function of protecting the interests of property owners. However, planning legislation exists to protect and promote the public interest, whereas nuisance law protects the rights of particular individuals. Planning decisions, therefore, may require individuals to bear burdens for the benefit of others, the local community or the public as a whole.

In some cases, a grant of planning permission may change the character of a locality. This may have implications in nuisance litigation. If a plaintiff complains of conduct that has been authorised by a planning permission, the court may be required to determine whether the character of the locality has changed as result of that planning consent. In *Hunter v Canary Wharf Ltd* [1997] AC 655 the House of Lords held that interference with television reception caused by the erection of a large tower block (the Canary Wharf Tower) did not amount to an actionable nuisance. In his speech, Lord Hoffmann said that the planning system was a far more appropriate form of control in respect of developments which were likely to have an adverse impact upon many people over a large area than the law of nuisance. This appeared to suggest that very large "strategic" planning decisions can bring about a change in the character of a neighbourhood thereby rendering certain activities innocent which, prior to the change, would have been an actionable nuisance.

The Court in *Kelly v Simpson* [2008] IEHC 374 recognised that the effect of a planning permission can be that, what might have been a nuisance prior to the planning consent may, after the consent, "be changed into something which those living in the area will simply have to tolerate". Also, in *Lanigan v Barry* [2008] IEHC 39 Charleton J emphasised the importance of the planning process in setting local standards of amenity. He observed that the standard of amenity that is reasonably to be expected by people living in an area can change as that area is lawfully developed through the planning process. In the course of his judgment, Charleton J cited with approval a passage by Buckley J in the English High Court in *Gillingham Borough Council v Medway (Chatham) Dock Co Ltd* [1993] QB 343 in which he referred to the key role the planning process plays in determining the character of a neighbourhood. In that case, planning permission had been granted for the redevelopment of an old naval dockyard into a commercial dock. It was held that the area around it could no longer be regarded as residential, but industrial. Similarly, in *Lawrence v Fen Tigers Ltd* [2012] 1 WLR 2127 the Court stated that the implementation of planning permission may so alter the character of the locality as to shift the standard of reasonable user which governs the question of nuisance or no nuisance. Here, planning permission had been granted which allowed for various types of car and motorcycle racing in a previously semi-rural area. These permissions were held to change the character of the neighbourhood.

By contrast, in *Wheeler v Saunders* [1996] Ch 19, permission to extend a pig breeding operation did not alter the nature of the locality. Also, in *Watson v Croft-Promo-Sport Ltd* [2009] 3 All ER 249, the "essentially rural" character of the locality was not changed by a series of planning permissions allowing motor racing in that area. Likewise, a regulatory consent granted by the UK Environment Agency in respect of a waste disposal facility in *Barr v Biffa Waste Services Ltd* [2012] 3 WLR 795 was held not to have changed the character of the neighbourhood. Carnwath LJ stated that statutory authority to carry out a particular activity does not in and of itself limit private rights. He said:

> "The common law of nuisance has co-existed with statutory controls, albeit less sophisticated, since the 19th century. There is no principle that the common law should 'march with' a statutory scheme covering similar subject-matter. Short of express or implied statutory authority to commit a nuisance … there is no basis, in principle or authority, for using such a statutory scheme to cut down private law rights."

In *Gillingham* Buckley J accepted that "planning permission is not a licence to commit a nuisance", but went on to say that "a planning authority can, through its development plans and decisions, alter the character of a neighbourhood". More recently, in *Coventry v Lawrence* [2014] UKSC 13, Lord Neuberger observed that:

> "…the mere fact that the activity which is said to give rise to the nuisance has the benefit of a planning permission is normally of no assistance to the defendant in a claim brought by a neighbour who contends that the activity causes a nuisance to her land in the form of noise or other loss of amenity".

In Ireland, the Court in *Cork County Council v Slattery Precast Concrete Ltd* [2008] IEHC 291 also took the view that the mere fact that a party operates in accordance with a valid planning permission does not give that party the right to commit a civil wrong to neighbouring properties. Clarke J said:

> "…the fact that a defendant might operate in accordance with a valid planning permission does not, of itself, preclude the possibility that there might nonetheless be a nuisance actionable at the suit of neighbouring property owners".

So, can a planning permission ever authorise a nuisance? The case law — in England at any rate – seems to point in different directions. But as we have seen, the UK Supreme Court has recently considered this question in *Coventry v Lawrence*. Permissions for small scale developments (e.g. an extended pig farm in *Wheeler* or motor racing in *Watson*) have been held not to authorise a nuisance, whereas large infrastructure projects (*Canary Wharf* or *Gillingham*) could authorise a nuisance. In *Coventry v Lawrence*, the UK Supreme Court thought that this was illogical. The Court questioned the rationality of something causing a nuisance to a large number of people being more readily justified than something causing a nuisance to a few. Accordingly, the Court reversed decisions suggesting that a planning permission could authorise a nuisance. That is not to say that a court might not be assisted by the evidence before a local planning authority or planning inspector, but it appears that this will be no more than evidence which the court can take into account.

In Ireland in recent years there have been a number of planning applications for large-scale wind turbine developments. Wind turbines can cause a range of disturbances to neighbours such as noise and "shadow flicker", not to mention the impact on visual amenity. Whilst most challenges to such developments in the UK have centred on procedural matters concerning the planning process, an important question in relation to nuisance arises: is planning permission for large developments such as wind farms a defence to nuisance? As we have seen, the traditional answer appears to be "no", at least not in itself. The ordinary common law principles still apply. Objective unreasonable interference with the comfort of a neighbouring landowner constitutes a nuisance, despite planning permission. However, the character of the area must also be considered. Therefore, a wind turbine in a noisy industrial area might not detract from an already noisy and built-up area. Furthermore, wind turbines may already have penetrated a locality to such an extent that the original unspoilt and uncluttered character of the area has already been irretrievably changed. Nuisance actions relating to such developments will inevitably be considered by the courts on a case-by-case basis, with judicial discretion and public policy playing an important role.

The Defendant's Motive
If the activity in question is done deliberately or with malice then this may convert what would otherwise be lawful into a nuisance. In *Christie v Davey* [1893] 1 Ch 316, the plaintiff's family occupied one half of a semi-detached property. They used the house for playing, practising and teaching music. This annoyed the defendant, their next door neighbour. He wrote a letter to the plaintiff complaining about the noise. The plaintiff ignored the letter. The defendant then commenced

making noises in his own house whenever the playing of music was going on in the plaintiffs' house. The defendant started knocking on the party wall, beating on trays, whistling, shrieking and imitating what was being played next door. The plaintiffs sought an injunction against the defendant in respect of this conduct. The defendant counterclaimed for an injunction against the plaintiffs. The Court rejected the counterclaim but granted the plaintiffs their injunction. North J said:

> "… the noises which were made in the defendant's house were not of a legitimate kind… I am satisfied that they were made deliberately and maliciously for the purpose of annoying the plaintiffs… I am persuaded that what was done by the defendant was done only for the purpose of… vexing and annoying his neighbours."

Similarly, in *Hollywood Silver Fox Farm Ltd v Emmett* [1936] 2 KB 468 the defendant repeatedly fired a gun in order to disrupt the breeding season of silver foxes on the plaintiff's neighbouring fox farm. A dispute had arisen between the plaintiff and defendant when the defendant objected to a noticeboard on the plaintiff's property. He thought the sign was detrimental to his attempt to sell off some land as plots for bungalows. When the plaintiff refused to take down the sign, the defendant threatened to shoot on his own property as near as he could to the breeding pens. The defendant said: "[y]ou will not raise a single cub". The defendant carried out his threat. As a result, one of the plaintiff's vixens would not breed and another ate her cubs. Liability was imposed on the basis that the defendant was motivated by malice.

However, not all malicious uses of property will affect the legality of its use. In *Bradford Corporation v Pickles* [1895] AC 587 (HL) the defendant owned land which contained a spring that supplied water to one of the plaintiff's dams. The defendant proposed to carry out some drainage work on his land. This would have resulted in the water which supplied the spring being diverted. This in turn would have rendered the plaintiff's dam useless. The plaintiff sued. The defendant alleged that his purpose in draining the land was only to quarry stone – a legitimate use. The trial judge, however, found that his true purpose was to force the plaintiff to buy his land in order to protect its dam. Lord Halsbury LC held (at 594):

> "If it was a lawful act, however ill the motive might be, he had a right to do it. If it was an unlawful act, however good his motive might be, he would have no right to do it. Motives and intentions in such a question as is now before your Lordships seems to me to be absolutely irrelevant."

Figure 13.3

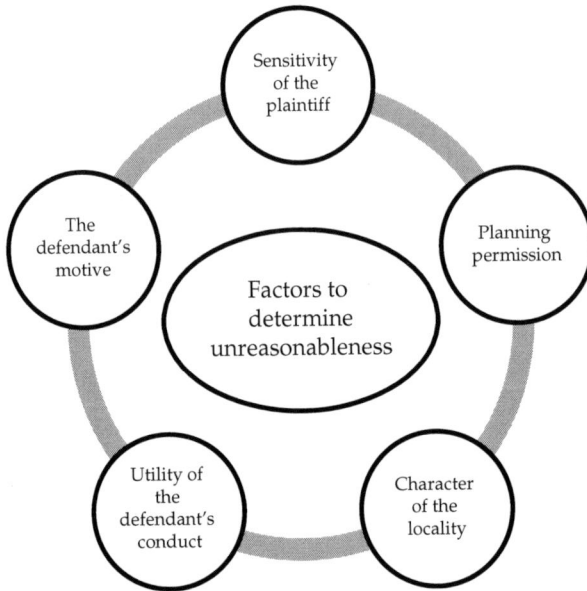

Physical Injury to Land

This type of nuisance includes damage to land caused by such things as: the encroachment of roots and branches; drenching or flooding; damage to vegetation caused by the emission of noxious fumes; vibration damage; collapses of the defendant's property on to the plaintiff's land. The courts' approach in cases involving physical injury is not the same as in cases involving amenity nuisance.

In the first instance, where physical injury to land has occurred, the character of the neighbourhood is not a material factor. The rationale for this, as mentioned above, appears to be that physical injury to property can never arise from a reasonable use of property. In other words, whilst it may be possible to justify interfering with a person's enjoyment of his property, it is difficult to justify physically damaging it. This general position was set out in the *St Helen's* case where the plaintiff's shrubs and been damaged by the emission of noxious fumes from the defendant's copper smelting plant. Lord Westbury said:

> "It is a very desirable thing to mark the difference between an action brought for a nuisance upon the ground that the alleged nuisance produces material injury to the property, and an action... on the grounds that the thing alleged... is productive of personal discomfort. With regard to the latter... a nuisance must undoubtedly depend greatly on the circumstances of the place where the thing complained of actually occurs. But where [physical damage is caused]... there unquestionably arises a very different consideration."

In reality, of course, where physical damage to land occurs, an interference with amenity will normally occur simultaneously. For example, if vibrations from quarry blasting causes plaster to break off a neighbour's walls, those same vibrations will almost certainly adversely affect the comfort and enjoyment of the neighbour's home. Establishing material damage to land will normally be straightforward but the courts have made some attempt to clarify what is meant by "material damage" for the purposes of nuisance. In *Gaunt v Fynney* (1872) 8 Ch App 8 Lord Selbourne suggested that it was sufficient if science could trace a "deleterious physical change" in the property. This will be clear-cut in most cases, but there is authority to suggest that even where physical damage is clearly established it will have to be substantial in nature. Hence, in *Darley Main Colliery Co v Mitchell* (1886) 11 App Cas 127 the Court held that minor subsidence, although real, which caused the plaintiff no appreciable harm, was not an actionable nuisance.

In certain circumstances the effect of nature on the defendant's land may give rise to a nuisance if he fails to take action to correct it. In *Goldman v Hargrave* [1967] 1 AC 645, a tree on the defendant's land was struck by lightning and it went on fire. He failed to take adequate steps to put it out. The fire spread to the plaintiff's land causing damage. The defendant was held liable for the damage in nuisance. Also, in *Leaky v National Trust* [1980] QB 485 a large natural mound was situated on the defendant's property. The mound eventually toppled onto the plaintiff's property causing damage. Liability was imposed in nuisance on the basis that the defendant had failed to take preventative action despite receiving appropriate warnings. Liability was not, however, imposed in *Holbeck Hall Hotel Ltd v Scarborough Borough Council* [2000] 2 All ER 705. In that case, the plaintiff was the proprietor of a cliff-top hotel. The land beneath the hotel was owned by the defendant local authority. The hotel collapsed due to loss of support from the land. Although the defendant had generally been aware of the potential for landslips, the one that caused the damage could only have been predicted following an extensive geological survey. The Court accepted that it would not have been reasonable to expect the defendant to undertake such a survey on the basis of cost. The defendant was therefore not liable in nuisance for failing to take steps to avert the damage because the landslip in question was not reasonably foreseeable.

The encroachment of roots and branches from one property to another causing damage will amount to an actionable nuisance. In such cases, plaintiffs may seek damages and an injunction. They may also seek a *quia timet* injunction (an injunction restraining wrongful conduct that has not yet been committed). An example is *Masters v Brent London Borough Council* [1978] QB 841. In that case, the plaintiff owned a house on a residential street in London. The defendants planted a lime tree immediately adjacent to the plaintiff's premises. The roots of the tree encroached on plaintiff's property and undermined the foundations of his house. They also extracted moisture from the sub-soil causing loss and damage to the plaintiff. The Court held that an actionable nuisance had occurred and that the plaintiff could recover the total cost of the necessary works of remedying the damage caused by the roots of the tree. Similarly, in *Delaware Mansions Ltd v Westminster City Council* [2001] 3 WLR 1007 the defendant was held liable for damage caused by encroaching tree roots because he "knew or ought to have known" that they constituted a continuing nuisance.

Liability in nuisance can also arise in circumstances where users of the public highway suffer loss and damage due to an occupier's use of his premises. In *Caminer v Northern & London Investment Trust* [1951] AC 88 a 130-year-old elm tree in a residential area of London fell from the defendant's property across an adjoining street. It struck a motor car in which the plaintiffs were travelling. The House of Lords accepted that the tree was apparently sound and healthy and that the evidence did not establish that inspection by an expert would have revealed that it was dangerous. In the circumstances it was held that the occupiers were not liable in either negligence or nuisance. However, their Lordships did suggest that it might be appropriate to take into account the location of the premises in cases such as this where occupiers in urban areas might be expected to exercise greater care than those in rural areas where the risk of a falling tree causing injury would be rather lower.

In *Gillen v Fair* (1956) 90 ILTR 119 (HC) a branch of an ash tree growing on the defendant's land beside a public road in County Mayo broke off in stormy weather. It fell on a passing car. The driver was killed and the plaintiff, a passenger, was injured. The Court found that "the tree was rotten in some respects, but the defects being high up were not apparent to a casual glance, and the defendant was not aware of their existence". The Court held that the defendant was not liable to the plaintiff in either nuisance or negligence as he could not reasonably have foreseen or guarded against the accident. Similarly, in *Lynch v Heatherton* [1990] ILRM 857 an ash tree fell on the plaintiff's car while he was driving along a country road. The Court found that the tree was rotten on the inside. The defendant could not have known this. He had previously inspected all his trees and could see no evidence that this particular tree posed a danger to road users. The Court held that the defendant occupier was not under an obligation to employ an expert. Even if he had done so, it is unlikely the danger would have been detected. Liability was not imposed.

By contrast, liability was imposed in *Lynch v Dawson* [1946] IR 504 (HC). In that case, the plaintiff suffered injury when a branch of a tree which projected onto the highway became entangled in the creels of a turf lorry. The Court took the view that the defendant ought to have been aware of the danger and, in particular, ought to have been conscious of the changing use of the road over time where lorries with creels had become relatively common. The risk of such an event should therefore have been obvious.

Who May Sue?

The traditional approach was set out in *Malone v Laskey* [1907] 2 KB 141. Here, the Court of Appeal held that only a person with a possessory or proprietary interest in the land in question could sue in nuisance. Therefore, an occupier of land could sue in respect of an interference with the use and enjoyment of that land, as can a tenant in possession, even where the tenancy is only a weekly tenancy or a tenancy at will. The Irish courts have, however, adopted a more flexible approach. In *Hanrahan v Merck, Sharp & Dohme (Ireland) Ltd* [1988] ILRM 629, the Supreme Court accepted that the son and daughter-in-law of the registered owner of the premises were as entitled as she was to claim damages in nuisance.

The more restrictive approach of the English courts can be seen in such cases as *Hunter v Canary Wharf Ltd* [1997] 655. There, the House of Lords limited the right to sue to those who have "a right to the land affected", such as freeholders, tenants in possession or licensees with exclusive possession. This approach has not been followed in Ireland. In *Molumby v Kearns* (19 January 1999) HC, the Court held that a plaintiff would have sufficient *locus standi* to sue in nuisance if he is the "occupier of the land", with no necessity to establish a legal interest over and above that.

A landlord who retains a reversionary interest in the land but is not in occupation at the time of the interference complained of may sue in respect of a nuisance provided he can prove that his reversionary interest has been affected. If the damage is of a temporary nature, then he has no basis upon which to sue. This will be so even if the reversioner can show that it is likely that a similar, temporary interference will take place in the future: see *Simpson v Savage* (1856) 1 CBNS 347 (where the nuisance complained of comprised merely of temporary annoyance caused by the emission of smoke from a fire). If physical damage is caused to the reversioner's buildings, he will have a cause of action: see *Meux's Brewery Co v City of London Electric Lighting Co* [1895] 1 Ch 287.

Who Can Be Sued?

Broadly speaking, the following categories of person can be sued in the law of nuisance:

(a) creators;
(b) occupiers;
(c) landlords.

Creators

The creator of the nuisance will be liable, irrespective of whether he is an occupier of the premises from which the nuisance emanates. In general, a person may be liable if he created the nuisance with the authority of the occupier of the premises. This is so even if he was not in occupation or control of the premises from which the nuisance emanated, either at the time of the proceedings, or at the time when he created the nuisance. Liability may be imposed even if he does not have the right to enter on to the premises in order to abate the nuisance: see *Thompson v Gibson* (1841) 7 M & W 456. In *Hussain v Lancaster City Council* [1999] 4 All ER 125, the plaintiff, a local shopkeeper, complained of racial harassment by tenants of the defendant local authority. It was held that since there was no direct connection between the behaviour of the tenants and their use of the premises they rented from the defendant, liability in nuisance could not be imposed on the defendant. The defendant could only be held liable in respect of uses of the tenants' council houses that they had authorised and that had caused a nuisance. Since no such use of the council houses had occurred, the defendant could not be liable.

Occupiers

As we have seen, an occupier of premises will be liable in respect of nuisances that he himself has created. But he may also be liable where he has "adopted" or "continued" a nuisance emanating from land which he occupies where he has failed to take reasonable steps to bring it to an end. An example is *Sedleigh-Denfield v O'Callaghan* [1939] 1 All ER 725. There, a drainage pipe had been made by a trespasser. The defendant occupiers initially had no knowledge that this had been done. The defendants discovered the existence of the pipe later. They began to use it themselves to drain excess water from their land. The pipe became blocked because of a misplaced grating. A servant of the defendant was responsible for maintaining the drainage system. He ought to have noticed that a risk of flooding existed but he did not. The blocked pipe subsequently caused water to overflow onto the plaintiff's property. The House of Lords held the defendant liable. Their Lordships made it clear, however, that an occupier is not *prima facie* responsible for a nuisance created without his knowledge and consent; but where he has the knowledge or means of knowledge, or that he knew or should have known, of the nuisance in time to correct it, he will be liable.

In *Vitalograph (Ireland) Ltd v Ennis Urban District Council and Clare County Council* (23 April 1997) HC, the plaintiffs complained of a nuisance created by Travellers who occupied land owned by the defendants. The defendants denied responsibility on the basis that the Travellers had entered and remained on their land without authorisation. The Court was satisfied that the defendants had adopted the nuisance by failing to take appropriate steps within a reasonable period to bring it to an end.

Landlords

A landlord, in some cases, will be liable if his land is the source of a nuisance. We have already seen that a landlord who authorises his tenant to commit a nuisance is treated, as a matter of law, as the creator of the nuisance. In such circumstances, he himself will be liable for that nuisance. In *Lippiatt v South Gloucestershire County Council* [1999] 4 All ER 149, the defendant local authority was held liable for the antisocial activities of Travellers where it had allowed them to occupy a site, and it had not taken action to evict them. In *Goldfarb v Williams & Co* [1945] IR 433 (HC), liability was imposed on the lessors of premises let to a social and athletic club. The club operated dances and other social activities. This caused a nuisance by noise to the plaintiffs. The construction of the premises allowed the easy transmission of noise to floors above and below the one occupied by the club. Liability was imposed on the basis that the nuisance, given the construction of the premises, was the inevitable consequence of the intended use of the premises. Similarly, in *Tetley v Chitty* [1986] 1 All ER 663, where land was let for the purpose of holding go-kart racing, the landlord was held liable for the resulting noise because such noise was the natural consequence of the letting.

A landlord may also be liable in nuisance for dangerous conditions that may arise from want of repair during the currency of the tenancy, provided he has covenanted to perform such repairs, reserves the right to enter and repair, or has an implied right to enter and repair: see *Payne v Rogers* (1794) 2 Hy Bl 350; *Mint v Good* [1951] 1 KB 517.

C. Defences

Prescription

If the defendant's activity has been causing a nuisance for 20 years or more, then he has acquired a legal right which operates as a defence to a nuisance claim. The defendant's activity must be overt, undisturbed and continuous. For example, it may be possible to acquire the right to discharge effluent into a stream, but not if done secretly: see *Liverpool Corporation v H Coghill & Son* [1918] 1 Ch 307. The 20 year period begins to run from the time the nuisance was created, not from the time the activity began. In *Sturges v Bridgman* (1879) 11 Ch D 892, the plaintiff's neighbour had a long-standing confectionery business. The noise and vibrations emanating from the business did not amount to a nuisance until the plaintiff moved his consulting room to the end of his garden. The defence of prescription could not be used: although the machinery had been in operation for more than 20 years, it had not constituted a nuisance to the plaintiff until he had built his consulting room.

It is not possible to acquire a prescriptive right to every nuisance. For example, the encroachment of branches or roots of a tree on to a neighbour's property is not one to which the defence can apply: see *Lemmon v Webb* [1895] AC 1. Prescription is not a defence for public nuisance.

Statutory Authority

The defence of statutory authority must be distinguished from the effect of planning permission. The latter relates to altering the character of a locality, whereas the former relates to authorisation for the creation of a nuisance.

This defence may be relied upon where activities which interfere with the enjoyment of land are carried out by public or private enterprises under statutory authority. A nuisance action can, therefore, be defeated where the activity complained of is explicitly authorised by statute. Whether or not the statute does authorise the nuisance is a matter of statutory interpretation. The defence of statutory authority was explained by Viscount Dunedin in *Manchester Corporation v Farnworth* [1930] AC 171:

> "When Parliament has authorised a certain thing to be made or done in a certain place, there can be no action for nuisance caused by the making or doing of that thing if the nuisance is the inevitable result of the making or doing so authorised. The onus of proving that the result is inevitable is on those who wish to escape liability for nuisance, but the criterion of inevitability is not what is theoretically possible but what is possible according to the state of scientific knowledge at the time, having also in view a certain common sense of appreciation, which cannot be rigidly defined, of practical feasibility in view of the situation and of expense".

This case concerned an action by a farmer against the defendant, Manchester Corporation, for an injunction and damages on the ground of nuisance by the emission of poisonous fumes from the chimneys of an electrical generating station erected by the defendant in the neighbourhood of his farm. The defendant pleaded that the acts the farmer complained of were done in pursuance of the powers conferred by an Act of Parliament. The House of Lords affirmed the decision of the Court of Appeal that the farmer be awarded an injunction and damages on the basis that the defendant had failed to prove that it had taken all reasonable precautions to prevent the nuisance. Here, the House of Lords recognised that the immunity from action in nuisance conferred by statute is premised on the defendant proving that it has carried out the authorised works and conducted the authorised operations with all reasonable regard and care for the interests of others. The reference to "a common sense of appreciation… of practical feasibility in view of the situation and of expense" in Viscount Dunedin's speech appears to suggest that the defendant is expected to implement current best practice in carrying out the authorised works, and that expense was a factor to be taken into account in determining what was reasonable for the defendant to do.

In *Allen v Gulf Oil Refining Ltd* [1981] AC 1001, statute authorised the construction and operation of an oil refinery and subsidiary works. The refinery produced noxious odours, vibrations and offensive noise levels. Local residents brought an action for nuisance. The House of Lords decided, after careful consideration of the statute in question, that it had effectively authorised the nuisance.

An example of statutory authority to commit a nuisance in Irish law can be seen in s 47 of the Air Navigation and Transport Act 1988. This provides that an action will not lie in trespass or nuisance by reason only of the flight of an aircraft over any property, subject to compliance with certain statutory requirements.

In *Kelly v Dublin County Council* (21 February 1986) HC, the defendants were authorised by statute to carry out road works in the course of which it was permitted to cause a nuisance. It used a site close to the plaintiffs' home as a storage depot for vehicles and materials. The plaintiffs complained of noise, dust and fumes emanating from the depot. The Court found that the defendant had committed an actionable nuisance. The statutory authority to create a nuisance extended only to the defendants' functions of maintenance and construction of roads, not to the setting up of, and operating, the depot.

In *Superquinn Ltd v Bray Urban District Council* (18 February 1998) HC the plaintiff's premises were flooded when a river burst its banks during "Hurricane Charlie" in 1987. The defendant was under a statutory duty to drain the area. The plaintiff claimed that the defendant had failed to do this adequately. The Court held the defendant not liable in tort unless it was negligent in the exercise of that statutory duty.

In *Smyth v Railway Procurement Agency* [2010] IEHC 290, a couple complained of noise from the operation of Luas trams behind their Dublin home. The Court held that the plaintiffs had not established nuisance at common law because the operators of the Luas line had complied with the relevant statutory provisions authorising the construction and operation of the line and that the line was being operated both within the noise levels predicted in the Environmental Impact Statement and without negligence. Therefore, the defendant was operating the tramline

> "without infringing the comfortable and healthy enjoyment of [the plaintiff's home] that would be expected by an ordinary person whose requirements were objectively reasonable in the particular circumstances [of the case]."

D. Ineffectual Defences

Coming to the Nuisance

The plaintiff coming to the nuisance is no defence. In other words, it is not open to the defendant to argue that the plaintiff is barred from complaining about a situation of which he should have been aware. In *Bliss v Hall* (1838) 4 Bing NC 183, 132 ER 785, the defendant operated a candle-making business which emitted offensive smells and vapours onto the plaintiff's property for three years before the plaintiff arrived. The Court held that this afforded no defence to the defendant. The plaintiff had come to the "house with all rights which the common law affords, and one of them is a right to wholesome air". Also, Lord Halsbury LC in *London, Brighton and South Coast Railway Co v Truman* (1885) LR 11 App Cas 45, 52 said that the idea that coming to the nuisance was a defence was an "old notion ... long since exploded". He also observed in *Fleming v Hislop* (1886) LR 11 App Cas 686, 697 that "whether the man went to the nuisance or the nuisance came to the man, the rights are the same".

As Lord Neuberger pointed out in *Coventry v Lawrence* [2014] UKSC 13, the notion that coming to the nuisance is no defence is consistent with the fact that nuisance is a property-based tort, so that the right to allege a nuisance should, as it were, run with the land. It would seem odd if a defendant was no longer liable for nuisance owing to the fact that the identity of his neighbour had changed, even though the use of his neighbour's property remained unchanged. The implication here, however, is that a plaintiff who builds on, or changes the use of, his property, after the defendant has started the activity alleged to cause a nuisance by noise, or any other emission offensive to the senses, should not have the same rights to complain about that activity as he would have had if his building work or change of use had occurred before the defendant's activity had started. That raises a rather different point from the issue of coming to the nuisance, namely whether an alteration in the plaintiff's property after the activity in question has started can give rise to a claim in nuisance if the activity would not have been a nuisance had the alteration not occurred.

On this basis, Lord Neuberger suggested, where a plaintiff builds on, or changes the use of, his land, it may well be wrong to hold that a defendant's pre-existing activity gives rise to a nuisance provided that: (i) it can only be said to be a nuisance because it affects the senses of those on the plaintiff's land; (ii) it was not a nuisance before the building or change of use of the plaintiff's land; (iii) it is and has been, a reasonable and otherwise lawful use of the defendant's land; (iv) it is carried out in a reasonable way; and (v) it causes no greater nuisance than when the plaintiff first carried out the building or changed the use. This, Lord Neuberger made clear, is not intended to imply that in any case where one or more of these requirements is not satisfied, a claim in nuisance would be bound to succeed.

Something akin to this approach can be seen in *Miller v Jackson* [1977] 1 QB 966. In that case, the plaintiff built his house adjacent to a cricket ground. He then found himself subject to a nuisance in the form of cricket balls landing in his garden. The majority of the Court of Appeal held that the defence of coming to the nuisance was well-established, accepting, albeit reluctantly, that it was not for the Court of Appeal "to alter a rule which has stood for so long", namely

> "that it is no answer to a claim in nuisance for the defendant to show that the plaintiff brought the trouble on his own head by building or coming to live in a house so close to the defendant's premises that he would inevitably be affected by the defendant's activities, where no one had been affected previously".

Accordingly, the plaintiff could succeed in nuisance. Interestingly, Lord Denning MR, in the minority, considered that the proper approach was for the Court to "balance the right of the cricket club to continue playing cricket on their cricket ground", as they had done for 70 years, "as against the right of the householder", whom he described as "a newcomer" who had built "a house on the edge of the cricket ground which, four years ago, was a field where cattle grazed". He thought that there was no nuisance given that the cricket club had "spent money, labour and love in the making of [the pitch]: and they have the right to play upon it as they have done for 70 years". Notwithstanding Lord Denning's strong dissent, the principle in *Bliss v Hall* remains. However, Lord Denning's position in *Miller* is perhaps logical given that that case was not concerned with damage to the senses, but with physical encroachment on, and potential physical damage to, the plaintiffs and their property. It could, therefore, be distinguished from "amenity" cases.

Combined Acts

Where the defendant's activity is not by itself a nuisance, but, combined with the activity of another, it is, it will be no defence for the defendant to argue that his activity does not in and of itself amount to a nuisance. In *Lambton v Mellish* [1894] 3 Ch 163, two rival merry-go-round operators carried on business near the plaintiff's home. The noise produced by the operators individually was insufficient to give rise to a nuisance but taken together the noise did amount to a nuisance. An injunction was granted against both of them. The Court stated the rule as follows:

> "The acts of two or more persons may, taken together, constitute such a nuisance that the Court will restrain all from doing the acts constituting the nuisance although the annoyance occasioned by the act of any one of them if taken alone would not amount to a nuisance."

E. Public Nuisance

The Basis of Liability

A public nuisance is a crime as well as a tort. Like private nuisance, its scope is difficult to define. It is said to cover a "multitude of sins, great and small" (*Southport Corporation v Esso Petroleum Co Ltd* (1954) 2 QB 182). Where the public, or some section of it, is injured by the nuisance, only the Attorney General can take civil proceedings. This prevents a multiplicity of actions being taken against a single wrongdoer. Furthermore, it is only where a person has suffered "particular" or "special" damage over and above that suffered by other members of the public, that he or she, as a private person, may take civil proceedings. Unlike private nuisance, it is not necessary for the plaintiff to have any interest in land in order to succeed in a public nuisance action. This is not so for the defendant. In *Convery v Dublin County Council* [1996] 3 IR 153, the Supreme Court held that liability in public nuisance is contingent on the defendant's ownership or occupation of premises in the area or the fact that the defendant has caused some activity on land in the area.

What is "Particular" or "Special" Damage?

Particular or special damage may arise where a member of the public suffers injury greater than other members of the public as a result of the public nuisance. Such damage can comprise pecuniary losses, inconvenience, or personal injury. In *Boyd v Great Northern Railway* [1895] 2 IR 555 (Ex Div), the plaintiff, a doctor, was delayed at a level crossing for 20 minutes due to the default of the defendant's servants. The Court found that he was "in a very large practice", "whose time was of pecuniary value". The Court held that he had suffered "some appreciable damage peculiar to himself beyond that suffered by other members of the public ordinarily using the highway". He was awarded 10 shillings in damages.

In *Smith v Wilson* [1903] 2 IR 45 (King's Bench Division) the plaintiff, an elderly small farmer, used to regularly walk to the market in Ballymena on the public highway. The defendant obstructed the road by removing a bridge and erecting a fence. This meant that the plaintiff was required "to take a longer and more circuitous route" to the market. Sometimes he had to pay for a car to do so. The Court held that there was evidence that the "plaintiff had sustained peculiar, direct and substantial damage in farm business, and expenses". The Court also made it clear that "everyone who individually sustains particular injury may apply for damages or an injunction".

Public Nuisance and the Public Highway

Many public nuisances will occur on the public highway. For example, in *Cunningham v McGrath Bros* [1964] IR 209 (SC), the Court stated that, generally, any obstruction of the public highway will be a public nuisance. It is clear, however, that not every obstruction of the roadway creates a cause of action. In *Herring v Metropolitan Board of Works* 19 CBNS 510, the Court made clear that normal use of the highway, for example vehicles stopping at doors of shops and warehouses for the purpose of loading and unloading goods, and the erection of hoardings for the purposes of building, rebuilding, and repairing houses, will not amount to a public nuisance on the basis that such activity benefits the community.

Unreasonable interferences with the highway will, however, amount to a public nuisance. Such interferences might be digging a trench in the highway or leaving a vehicle on the highway for an unreasonable time. In *Wall v Morrissey* [1969] IR 10 (SC) Fitzgerald J stated that "A stationary, or even an unlighted, vehicle on a highway may not amount to a nuisance unless the owner permits it to remain for longer than a reasonable time". It is also clear that anything which makes the use of the highway unsafe or dangerous to the public can amount to a public nuisance: see *Hassett v O'Loughlin* (1943) 78 ILTR 47.

In *Convery v Dublin County Council*, the plaintiff sued the local authority in relation to large volumes of traffic using the road in front of her house as a "shortcut". This was due to planning consents granted by the local authority in respect of large-scale residential developments which resulted in a huge increase in traffic levels in the area in which the plaintiff lived. The plaintiff complained that the local authority had failed to undertake appropriate remedial action to ensure that disturbance due to these traffic levels was lessened. The Supreme Court held that the local authority should not be held to be the legal author of the public nuisance as this would be contrary to principle and was unsupported by authority.

In *Connolly v South of Ireland Asphalt Co Ltd* [1977] IR 99 (SC), the death of a road user was held to constitute "particular damage" so far as the road user's widow was concerned. In that case, damage caused to the road surface by the defendant's use of it resulted in an accident which led to the road user's death. In England, however, the courts have demonstrated greater reluctance in relation to awarding remedies to those suffering personal injuries due to a public nuisance, preferring that such claims be taken in the law of negligence: see *Hunter v Canary Wharf Ltd* [1997] AC 655 and *Transco plc v Stockport MBC* [2004] 2 AC 1.

THE RULE IN *RYLANDS v FLETCHER*

Learning Outcomes

Upon completion of this chapter, the reader should be able to:

- Trace the historical development of the rule in *Rylands v Fletcher*;
- Identify the key elements of the tort;
- Distinguish between "natural" and "non-natural" use of land;
- Discuss the role of *Rylands v Fletcher* in the tort system;
- Differentiate between *Rylands v Fletcher* and the torts of nuisance and negligence;
- Explain who may sue and be sued in the tort;
- Identify the relevant defences to an action in *Rylands v Fletcher*.

A. Overview

The Rule in *Rylands v Fletcher* is a strict liability tort. This means that the plaintiff, in order to establish liability, does not have to prove fault on the part of the defendant. This area of strict liability was recognised by the House of Lords in *Rylands v Fletcher* (1866) LR 1 Ex 265; (1868) LR 3 HL 330. The facts of the case are as follows. A reservoir was being built on the defendant's land by his independent contractor. His contractor did not properly seal up shafts on the land. Unknown to the defendant, those shafts were connected to the plaintiff's mine shafts on adjacent land. When the reservoir was filled, the plaintiff's mine was flooded. The defendants had no means of knowing the risk: they were not themselves negligent; nor were they vicariously liable for the negligence of the independent contractors. Nonetheless, they were held liable by both the Court of Exchequer Chamber and, on appeal, the House of Lords. The case established the principle that someone who, for his own purposes, brings onto his land and keeps there anything "non-natural" that is likely to cause harm if it escapes is liable for all of the harm that it causes when it does escape.

Blackburn J delivered the judgment of the Court of Exchequer Chamber. He said:

> "We think that the true rule of law is that the person who for his own purposes brings on his lands and collects and keeps there anything likely to do mischief if it escapes, must keep it in at his peril, and if he does not do so, is *prima facie* answerable for all the damage which is the natural consequence of its escape." (1866) LR 1 Exch 265, at 279-80.

Lord Cairns in the House of Lords broadly agreed with Blackburn J's judgment, but he restricted the scope of the rule to circumstances where the defendant had engaged in a "non-natural use" of the land. The significance of this addition to Blackburn J's formulation was not recognised at the time, but it subsequently gave rise to considerable debate as to what was meant by "non-natural use". We now consider that a new strict liability tort was created in *Rylands v Fletcher*, but it is clear that Blackburn J himself did not consider that he was making new law at the time. This can be seen from the following section of his judgment:

> "The general rule, as above stated, seems on general principle just. The person whose grass or corn is eaten down by the escaping cattle of his neighbour, or whose mine is flooded by the water from his neighbour's reservoir, or whose cellar is invaded by the filth of his neighbour's privy, or whose habitation is made unhealthy by the fumes and noisome vapours of his neighbour's alkali works, is damnified without any fault of his own; and it seems but reasonable and just that the neighbour, who has brought something on his own property which was not naturally there, harmless to others so long as it is confined to his own property, but which he knows to be

mischievous if it gets on his neighbour's, should be obliged to make good the damage which ensues if he does not succeed in confining it to his own property."

It was thought, following this judgment, that *Rylands v Fletcher* might have created a general theory of strict liability for ultra-hazardous activities. However, the scope of *Rylands v Fletcher* was somewhat limited by the decision of the House of Lords in *Read v J Lyons & Co Ltd* [1947] AC 156. In that case, the appellant was working in the respondent's factory. She was injured by an explosion there and sued the respondent in respect of her injuries. She made no allegation of negligence against the respondents. The basis of her claim was that they carried on the manufacture of high explosive shells, knowing that they were dangerous things. The House of Lords found in favour of the respondents holding that the rule in *Rylands v Fletcher* does not apply unless there has been an *escape* from a place where the defendant has occupation or control over land to a place outside his control. Since the appellant was injured on the respondent's land, no action in *Rylands v Fletcher* lay. It was clear, therefore, that there could only be liability under *Rylands v Fletcher* where all the individual preconditions (or "ingredients") of that tort are satisfied.

Figure 14.1

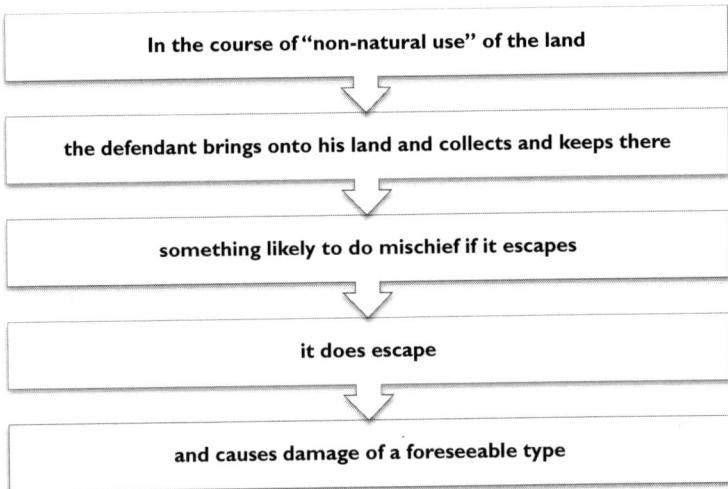

In the course of "non-natural use" of the land

the defendant brings onto his land and collects and keeps there

something likely to do mischief if it escapes

it does escape

and causes damage of a foreseeable type

The elements of the tort are as follows:

(1) Non-natural use of land;
(2) Accumulation on the land;
(3) Things likely to do mischief if they escape;

(4) Escape;

(5) Damage of a foreseeable kind.

B. The Elements of the Tort

Non-Natural Use

"Non-natural use" in the rule in *Rylands v Fletcher* was defined by Lord Moulton in *Rickards v Lothian* [1913] AC 263 as:

> "Some special use bringing with it increased danger to others and [which] must not merely be the ordinary use of the land or such a use as is proper for the general benefit of the community."

In *Read v J Lyons & Co Ltd*, Viscount Simon thought Lord Moulton's statement to be "of the first importance". In the same case, Lord Porter said:

> "each seems to be a question of fact subject to a ruling of the judge as to whether... the particular use can be non-natural, and in deciding this question I think that all the circumstances of the time and place and practice of mankind must be taken into consideration so that what might be regarded as... non-natural may vary according to those circumstances."

Therefore, the definition of "non-natural" in this context is necessarily subjective and will vary over time in line with societal and technological change. The meaning of "non-natural use" was most recently considered in *Transco plc v Stockport Metropolitan Borough Council* [2004] 2 AC 1. In that case, the defendants' owned an 11 storey tower block near Stockport, England. The tower block was provided with a high-pressure water main which supplied large tanks in the basement. The water was then pumped to the flats. The pipe fractured and a significant quantity of water escaped before the break was discovered and repaired. The water had run into an old landfill and from there along an old railway formation. Transco had laid a gas main under the old railway line. Where the formation had become an embankment, the water washed away the formation leaving the gas pipe suspended. Transco had to carry out urgent repairs costing £93,681. They pursued the defendants under the rule in *Rylands v Fletcher*. In considering what was meant by "non-natural user", Lord Bingham said:

> "I think it is clear that ordinary user is a preferable test to natural user, making it clear that the rule in *Rylands v Fletcher* is engaged only where the defendant's use is shown to be extraordinary and unusual. This is not a test to be inflexibly applied: a use may be extraordinary and unusual at one time or in one place but not so at another time or in another place... The question is whether the defendant has done

something out of the ordinary in the place and at the time when he does it. In answering that question, I respectfully think that little help is gained (and unnecessary confusion perhaps caused) by considering whether the use is proper for the general benefit of the community."

There has been a further restriction on the ambit of the rule as a result of the decision in *Cambridge Water Co v Eastern Counties Leather plc* [1994] 2 WLR 53. In that case, chemical solvents which had been used by the defendants in their tannery over many years were frequently spilt on to the floor of the defendant's factory. From there, they seeped into a natural groundwater aquifer which was drawn upon by the plaintiff in order to fulfil its statutory duty to supply drinking water to the city of Cambridge. This seepage caused the water to become contaminated to the extent that it was not fit for human consumption under EU standards. No one thought that such contamination could take place. It was thought that the solvents were too volatile to mix with water and, in any case, it was believed they had simply evaporated from the defendant's factory floor. The House of Lords held the defendants not liable on the basis of the unforeseeably of the harm caused to the plaintiff's water supply.

In *Hanrahan v Merck Sharp & Dohme (Ireland) Ltd* [1988] ILRM 629, Henchy J stated that "dangerous chemical substances" brought into a factory for processing would be considered to be "things which were likely to do mischief if they escaped". The issue of "non-natural" use was not addressed in that case.

Examples of Non-Natural and Natural Use of Land

Non-Natural use	Natural use
Northwestern Utilities Ltd v London Guarantee and Accident Co Ltd [1936] AC 108: the storage of water, gas, and electricity in abnormal or excessive quantities.	*Rickards v Lothian* [1913] AC 263: water pipe installations in buildings.
Balfour v Barty-King [1956] 2 All ER 555: using a blow lamp to thaw pipes in a loft.	*Noble v Harrison* [1926] 2 KB 332: growing trees, even though planted by the defendant, so long as they are not poisonous.
Mason v Levy Autoparts [1967] 2 QB 430: the storage of large quantities of inflammable auto-parts.	*Read v J Lyons & Co Ltd* [1947] AC 156: operating a munitions factory in wartime.
E Hobbs (Farms) Ltd v Baxenden Chemical Co Ltd [1992] 1 Lloyd's Rep 54: the storage of ignitable material in a barn.	*Sochaski v Sas* [1947] 1 All ER 344: lighting a fire in the fireplace of a house.
Cambridge Water Company v Eastern Counties Leather plc [1994] 2 WLR 53: storing large quantities of industrial chemicals.	*British Gas plc v Stockport MBC* [2001] Env LR 44: supplying gas to flats in a tower block.

Accumulation

An accumulation must be artificial, as distinct from something naturally present on the land. Accordingly, in *Giles v Walker* (1890) 62 LT 933, it was held that there was no accumulation owing to a failure to cut thistles naturally growing on the defendant's land. Similarly, in *Healy v Bray* UDC [1962 – 1963] Ir Jur 9 (SC), liability was not imposed where the plaintiff was injured by a rock which became dislodged from the top of a hill and rolled down the side of the hill injuring the plaintiff. Kingsmill Moore J said:

> "The defendants did not bring the rocks or outcrop on to [their] land for their own purpose (or at all). They are there as the result of natural forces operating in geological time, as indeed is the land. They are, in short, the land itself and not things naturally brought onto it."

Things Likely to do Mischief if they Escape

The thing in question need not be inherently dangerous. It must, however, be capable of causing mischief, or harm, if it does escape. In *Rylands v Fletcher* itself the accumulation was a large quantity of water in an artificial reservoir on the defendant's land. The water was clearly capable of causing mischief if it escaped, as indeed it did. Water, of course, is not "dangerous" in and of itself, but it can be if it escapes onto neighbouring land in sufficient quantity.

Things which have been held to be capable of giving rise to liability in Rylands v Fletcher:

Case	Thing
National Telephone Co v Baker [1893] 2 Ch 186	Electricity
Batchellor v Tunbridge Wells Gas Co (1901) 84 LT 765	Gas likely to pollute water supplies
Rainham Chemical Works Ltd v Belvedere Fish Guano Co [1921] 2 AC 465	Explosives
Rigby v Chief Constable of Northamptonshire [1985] 1 WLR 1242	CS gas canisters
LMS International Ltd v Styrene Packaging & Insulation Ltd [2006] TCLR 6	Fire

Escape

In *Read v Lyons & Co*, the explosion which injured the plaintiff occurred within the factory. It was, therefore, held to fall outside the rule in *Rylands v Fletcher* because there was no "escape from the place where the defendant [had] occupation of, or control over, land to a place which [was] outside his occupation or control". In *Ponting v Noakes* [1894] 2 QB 281, a horse was poisoned by eating the leaves of a yew tree by reaching its head over on to the land of the defendant. No liability was imposed because there was no "escape" of the "dangerous" leaves.

The defendant need not have any proprietary interest in the land from which the escape occurs. This is clear from authorities such as *Midwood & Co Ltd v Manchester Corporation* [1905] 2 KB 597. In that case, an explosion occurred in a cable which belonged to, and was laid by, the defendant in the public highway. This caused inflammable gas to escape into the plaintiff's house which was nearby, setting fire to its contents. There was held to be a sufficient escape to fall within the rule in *Rylands v Fletcher*. Moreover, in *Rigby v Chief Constable of Northamptonshire* [1985] 1 WLR 1242 , Taylor J said that he could see "no difference in principle between allowing a man-eating tiger to escape from your land into that of another and allowing it to escape from the back of your wagon parked on the highway". That case involved the deliberate release of CS gas ("tear-gas"), but the rule in *Rylands v Fletcher* was thought not to be applicable because the release was voluntary. It was suggested that the tort of trespass would be the appropriate cause of action.

The requirement for an "escape" has been the subject of some criticism. As we have seen, this means escape from a place where the defendant has occupation of, or control over, to a place which is outside his occupation or control. In *Read v Lyons* this meant that if the plaintiff had been injured by the explosion when just outside the factory gates, she might have been able to recover. As it was, she was denied a remedy because she was injured inside the factory gates. Lord Porter in *Read v Lyons* justified this limitation on the basis that liability under *Rylands v Fletcher* was an exception to the general rule of fault-based liability and hence should be restricted. This view was accepted by Lord Scott in *Transco*.

Damage of a Foreseeable Kind

The English courts have limited the type of damage recoverable under *Rylands* to damage to land or to property on land. Recovery for personal injuries can only occur, if at all, under the tort of negligence. Whilst it is true that earlier cases such as *Read v Lyons* (see above) and *Perry v Kendricks Transport Ltd* [1956] 1 WLR 85 (see below) appeared to assume that damages for personal injury could be recovered under *Rylands*, more recent cases such as *Cambridge Water* and *Transco* clarified the close relation between *Rylands* and nuisance and, as such, allowed recovery only in respect of land-based damage. This is consistent with the decision of the House of Lords in *Hunter v Canary Wharf Ltd* [1997] AC 655 which restricted claims in nuisance to those with proprietary interests. The Irish courts, for their part, have not closed off the possibility of recovery for personal injuries under *Rylands*, although if *Cambridge Water* and *Transco* were to be expressly followed in that respect, that would probably be the result.

Cambridge Water makes clear that all the ingredients of the tort are satisfied only when the relevant damage is of a *reasonably foreseeable* type. Lord Goff stated that "foreseeability of damage of the relevant type should be regarded as a prerequisite of liability in damages under the rule". The law was further clarified by Lord Bingham in *Transco* when he said:

> "It must be shown that the defendant has done something which he recognised, or judged by the standards appropriate at the relevant place and time, he ought reasonably to have recognised, as giving rise to an exceptionally high risk of danger or mischief if there should be an escape, however unlikely an escape may have been thought to be."

Accordingly, the key question to be asked by the court is: given the escape, would this type of damage have been reasonably foreseeable? If it is not, liability in *Rylands* will not be imposed.

C. Defences to *Rylands v Fletcher*

Consent of the Plaintiff or Common Benefit

The rule in *Rylands v Fletcher* does not apply to the escape of things brought by the defendant onto the defendant's premises with the consent of the plaintiff where there has been no negligence on the part of the defendant. So, if the plaintiff permits the defendant to accumulate the thing the escape of which he or she complains of, then he or she cannot sue if it does escape. Implied consent will suffice for the purposes of this defence. A typical application would be where an escape of water occurs from an upper storey premises in the occupation of several tenants. It should be noted, however, that if such water is collected for domestic purposes it is likely that, in any case, such an accumulation would not amount to a non-natural use of land. It would, therefore, fall outside the rule.

The defence of consent also applies in cases of "common benefit". In *Carstairs v Taylor* (1871) LR 6 Exch 217, rainwater was collected and stored on the roof of a block of flats. A rat gnawed through the container which resulted in flooding. No liability under *Rylands* was imposed because the collection and storage of the water had been for the benefit of all the inhabitants.

Contributory Negligence

The default of the plaintiff will operate as a defence in actions under *Rylands*. In *Dunn v Birmingham Canal* (1872) LR 7 QB 244, a mineworker worked his mine under the defendant's canal in the knowledge of the danger above and brought the water from the canal down upon himself. Cockburn CJ described the matter in this way: "the plaintiff saw the danger and may be said to have courted it". Accordingly, the plaintiff could not invoke the rule.

In *Eastern and Southern African Telegraph Co Ltd v Cape Town Tramways Co Ltd* [1902] AC 381, the plaintiff complained that the tramways of the defendant caused electrical interference with the receipt of messages through his submarine cable. His action failed because no damage to the cable itself was caused. The plaintiff suffered loss only because he relied on the cable for the transmission of messages. The Court stated that "a man cannot increase the liabilities of his neighbour by applying his own property to special uses, whether for business or pleasure".

Act of a Stranger

If the escape is caused by the deliberate act of a third party, then a defence may be available, as was the case in *Rickards v Lothian*. In that case, an unknown third party maliciously turned on a water tap in the defendant's premises and blocked up the waste pipe of the lavatory basin. This resulted in flooding to the plaintiff's premises. The defendant was held not liable. Similarly, in *Box v Jubb* (1879) 4 Ex D 76, the defendant's reservoir overflowed when a third party, carrying out operations higher up the stream supplying it, discharged an unusually large volume of water downstream without giving any warning. No liability was imposed.

In *Perry v Kendricks Transport Ltd* [1956] 1 WLR 85 the plaintiff, a 10-year-old boy, was injured when the petrol tank of a disused coach parked on the defendant's land exploded. The petrol tank had been drained and the cap secured. As the plaintiff approached the coach he saw two other small boys near the coach. As he drew alongside the vehicle these boys jumped away and there was an explosion. The trial judge found that the cap of the tank had been removed that day by persons unknown and that one of the two boys had thrown a lighted match into the tank causing an explosion when the fumes ignited. The trial judge dismissed a claim in negligence. The plaintiff appealed arguing a cause of action under *Rylands*. The Court of Appeal, holding that the act of the boys was the act of a stranger, said that a stranger was someone over whom the occupier had no control. However, it was accepted that the act of a trespasser child might not amount to a defence

> "if it was a reasonable and probable consequence of their [the occupiers'] action, which they ought to have foreseen, that children might meddle with the dangerous thing and cause it to escape".

In such a case the escape would be brought about by the defendant's negligence in dealing with the dangerous thing, and once that point was reached the claim would become one of negligence rather than *Rylands*. The plaintiff could then rely on the defendant's negligence.

In such cases, two questions must be addressed by the court: First, is the person responsible for the escape a stranger? Second, if so, could the act of the stranger be anticipated and steps taken to prevent it? A trespasser will be a stranger, but a guest of the occupier may not be, unless the act of the guest is entirely alien to the invitation (*Winfield & Jolowicz*, para. 15.15). If, on the facts, it is found that the act was that of the stranger, liability, if any, will be in negligence in that the defendant may have failed to take reasonable steps to control the risk.

Act of God (Vis Major)

This defence will arise where an escape is caused through natural causes and without any human intervention. An Act of God was described by Lord Westbury in *Tennent v Earl of Glasgow* (1864) 2 M 22 as "circumstances which no human foresight can provide against, and of which human prudence is not bound to recognise the possibility". The defence succeeded in *Nichols v Marsland* (1876) 2 Ex D 1. In that case, the defendant had formed some artificial ornamental lakes on his land by damming up a stream. Due to an unusually violent storm, the embankments broke down and the rush of escaping floodwater carried away some of the plaintiff's bridges. The storm was described at the time as the heaviest in living memory. Liability was not imposed on the defendant as the jury found the defendant could not reasonably have anticipated the events in question. However, in *Greenock Corporation v Caledonian Railway Co* [1917] AC 556, extraordinary and unprecedented rainfall was held not to be an Act of God. There, the House of Lords explained the decision in the earlier case of *Nichols v Marsland* as being one where the jury found that no reasonable person could have anticipated the storm and the Court was unwilling to disturb that finding of fact.

In *Dockery v Manor Park Homebuilders Ltd* (10 April 1995) HC the Court held that the defence of Act of God had not been made out where flooding occurred as a result of rainfall that would occur once every 20 years. The defence was also applied in *Superquinn Ltd v Bray UDC* [1998] 3 IR 542. In that case, extensive flooding caused damage to the plaintiff's property following "Hurricane Charlie" in 1987. Laffoy J, in finding for the fourth defendant, Coillte Teoranta, stated:

> "... I consider that the test [in respect of the defence of Act of God] to be applied is whether the storm ... could reasonably have been anticipated or guarded against .... I am satisfied that the evidence shows that the storm did fall within the category of the most extreme natural phenomena and could not reasonably have been anticipated or guarded against, so that the defence of Act of God succeeds."

Statutory Authority

As with nuisance, where the activity in question takes place in the exercise of a statutory duty, this will provide a good defence in the absence of negligence. An example is *Green v Chelsea Waterworks Co* (1894) 70 LT 547. In that case, a water main belonging a waterworks company which was authorised by statute to lay the main, burst without any negligence on the part of the company. The plaintiff's premises were flooded. The company was held not liable because the company was under a statutory *obligation* to keep the mains charged at high pressure making a damaging escape an inevitable consequence of any non-negligent burst. In contrast, in *Charing Cross Electricity Co v Hydraulic Power Co* [1914] 3 KB 772, where the facts were similar to those in *Green v Chelsea Water Works Co*, the defendants were held to have no exemption under the interpretation of their statute. The distinction between these two cases is that the defendants in *Charing Cross Electricity Co v Hydraulic Power Co* were empowered by statute to supply water for industrial purposes, that is, they had *permissive* power but not a mandatory duty, and so they were under no obligation to keep their mains charged with water at high pressure, or at all.

D. Who May Sue?

Prior to *Transco*, it seemed that entitlement to sue was not limited to adjoining occupiers, but extended to any person sustaining material or personal injuries as a result of the escape. In *Transco* the House of Lords held that non-occupiers could not sue under *Rylands*. This was on the basis that the rule in *Rylands v Fletcher* should be regarded as a sub-branch of the law of nuisance which, following the House of Lords' earlier decision in *Hunter v Canary Wharf Ltd*, treated nuisance as a tort affecting property such that only those with a proprietary interest had the right to sue. The restrictions set out in *Hunter* as to who can maintain an action in nuisance have not been explicitly adopted by the Irish courts. Accordingly, in Ireland, the exact parameters regarding who may sue in *Rylands* are yet to be definitively determined.

E. Who May Be Sued?

Occupiers may be liable under the rule in *Rylands v Fletcher*. It is also probable that those on land by virtue of statutory authority (see *Smeaton v Ilford Corporation* above) or by private permission (see *Northwestern Utilities Ltd v London Guarantee and Accident Co Ltd* [1936] AC 108) may also be sued.

F. *Rylands v Fletcher* and Nuisance

Although the rule in *Rylands v Fletcher* and nuisance are both land-based torts, there are important differences between them. For example, in private nuisance the focus is on the land which the plaintiff occupies. By contrast, under the rule in *Rylands v Fletcher*, the focus is upon the land owned or controlled by the defendant. Nor is there a requirement under *Rylands* that the plaintiff have any interest in any land at all. Also, whilst the escape must come from the defendant's land in *Rylands*, there is no requirement in private nuisance that the defendant be an occupier of the land from which the nuisance emanates.

A further difference between *Rylands* and nuisance relates to the respective concepts of non-natural use and unreasonable use. A use of land may be artificial without being unreasonable. An artificial use of land will be non-natural, thereby potentially bringing it within the rule in *Rylands v Fletcher*. However, such use may not be unreasonable, thereby satisfying the unreasonable user test in private nuisance. For instance, no one would consider the construction of a reservoir to be unreasonable, given its importance to society, but the construction of a reservoir is clearly an artificial use of land. Also, in determining nuisance liability, the reasonableness of the defendant's user is a relevant factor to be taken into account, but it is not, *per se*, a pre-condition of liability because it is the unreasonableness of the *interference* that is relevant. In contrast, the non-natural use of land is a pre-condition to liability in *Rylands v Fletcher*.

G. *Rylands v Fletcher* and Negligence

Since the rule in *Rylands v Fletcher* is a strict liability tort, it follows that negligence plays no role in determining liability. Lord Goff in *Cambridge Water* make this clear when he said:

> "the defendant will be liable for harm caused to the [plaintiff] by the escape, notwithstanding that he has exercised all reasonable care and skill to prevent the escape from occurring".

Also, in *Transco*, Lord Hoffmann emphasised the fact that it was immaterial if the defendant could not reasonably have foreseen the escape. These principles, however, appear to run contrary to decisions such as *Perry v Kendricks* (see above) where it should not matter whether the defendant "could reasonably have contemplated and guarded against" the act of a third party. Such decisions, arguably, are more akin to negligence than a strict liability tort.

In *Burnie Port Authority v General Jones Pty Ltd* (1994) 179 CLR 520 the High Court of Australia considered that the analogy with negligence was sufficiently convincing for them to hold that *Rylands v Fletcher* be subsumed into the general law of negligence. In that case, General Jones Pty Ltd stored frozen vegetables in cool rooms owned by the appellant, Burnie Port Authority. An independent contractor engaged by the Authority caused a fire on the premises by carrying out unguarded welding operations in close vicinity to stacked cardboard cartons. The fire spread to the cool rooms and damaged General Jones Pty Ltd's frozen vegetables. The trial judge held that the independent contractor was negligent and that the Authority was liable for damage caused as an occupier from whose premises fire had escaped. On appeal, the Full Court of the Supreme Court of Tasmania held the Authority liable under the rule in *Rylands v Fletcher*. The matter was further appealed to the High Court of Australia which considered liability under both *Rylands v Fletcher* and negligence. That Court rejected *Rylands v Fletcher* altogether, saying that the situations envisaged by the doctrine could be dealt with by negligence. In *Transco*, Lord Hoffman said of *Burnie*:

> "In *Burnie Port Authority v General Jones Pty Ltd* (1994) 179 CLR 520 a majority of the High Court of Australia lost patience with the pretensions and uncertainties of the rule and decided that it had been 'absorbed' into the law of negligence".

All five judges of the House of Lords in *Transco* declined to follow the High Court of Australia in deciding that the rule in *Rylands v Fletcher* should no longer have a separate existence. Lord Hoffmann thought the rule worthy of retention primarily due to its longevity. Lord Goff thought it would go beyond the Court's judicial function to abolish it. Lord Walker noted that the scope of the rule had been restricted significantly by regulation of hazardous activities and the continuing development of the law of negligence, but that it would be premature to declare that it was obsolete. Lord Bingham said: "there is in my opinion a category of case, however small it may be, in which it seems just to impose liability even in the absence of fault".

Accordingly, for the time being at least, the rule in *Rylands v Fletcher* remains an integral part of the common law of England and Ireland.

Occupiers' Liability

Learning Outcomes

Upon completion of this chapter, the reader should be able to:

- Explain the position at common law prior to the introduction of the Occupiers' Liability Act 1995;
- Outline the role of the Hotel Proprietors Act 1963 in protecting visitors to hotels;
- Explain the scope of the 1995 Act;
- Appreciate the varying standards of duty owed towards particular categories of entrant by occupiers;
- Distinguish between activities on premises and dangers due to the state of premises;
- Understand the role of the Criminal Law (Defence and the Dwelling) Act 2011.

A. Overview

The liability of occupiers in respect of injury that entrants may suffer on their premises is determined by both common law and statute. Generally, the common law covers activities on premises whereas statute, the Occupiers' Liability Act 1995, covers dangers due to the state of the premises. Thus, if an entrant on another's premises is injured as a result of a careless act whilst on those premises, he or she will most likely have a remedy in the tort of negligence. If, however, the entrant suffers injury as a result of a static or structural danger on the premises, his or her remedy will probably lie under the 1995 Act. Before considering the statutory provisions, it is necessary to consider the common law rules in existence prior to the enactment of the 1995 legislation.

Figure 15.1

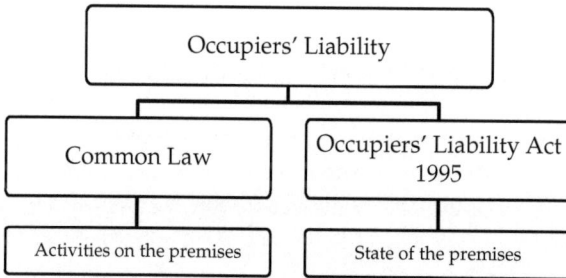

Under the common law prior to the Occupiers' Liability Act 1995, the duties of an occupier were cast in a descending scale to four different categories of entrant. These were: contractual entrants, invitees, licensees, and trespassers.

B. The Pre-1995 Common Law

Contractual Entrants

The highest degree of care was owed by the occupier to one who entered in pursuance of a contract with him: a "contractual entrant". A hotel guest or cinema patron would be examples. In respect of such entrants there was an implied warranty that the premises were as safe as reasonable care and skill could make them. Where the use of the premises was merely ancillary to the main purpose of the contract the occupier warranted that he, and perhaps his independent contractor, had taken reasonable care to see that the premises were safe.

Invitees

A lower duty was owed to an "invitee". This category of entrant was a person who, without any contract, entered on business of interest both to himself/herself and the occupier. A customer in a shop would be an example. Such an entrant was entitled to expect that the occupier should prevent damage from unusual danger, of which he knew or ought to have known: see *Indermaur v Dames* (1866) LR 1 CP 274.

Licensees

A lower duty still was owed to a "licensee". This category of entrant was a person who entered with the occupier's express or implied permission but without conferring any material benefit on the occupier. The occupier's duty towards him was to warn him of any concealed danger or trap of which he actually knew. A social guest would be an example of such an entrant.

Trespassers

Finally, there was a trespasser, whom the occupier was merely obliged not to deliberately or recklessly injure. A trespasser was (and under the 1995 Act still is) a person who enters (or remains) on property without the express or implied consent of the occupier. A burglar would be an example. But a neighbour's child who persists in coming onto the property to collect a football or a guest who refuses to leave when a party is over, could also be classified as trespassers.

This rather hard-line approach to trespassers was described in *Donovan v Landy's Ltd* [1963] IR 441 as being one where the occupier owed no duty of care to a trespasser in respect of the dangerous state of the premises, but the duty, such as it was, applied in respect of acts done on the premises with knowledge of the trespasser's presence. In other words, no liability would attach to the occupier if the trespasser fell through a defective staircase suffering injury; but liability would attach if the occupier deliberately set a trap with the wilful intention of doing harm to the trespasser. Child trespassers were treated slightly better at common law. A child's status could be raised to that of licensee if it could be shown that he had trespassed onto the premises because he was drawn there because of "an allurement". In *Latham v Johnson* [1913] 1 KB 398 the Court characterised an "allurement" in law as an object that was both "fascinating and fatal".

The position of trespassers in Ireland was improved by the Supreme Court decision in *McNamara v ESB* [1975] IR 1, following which, the duty owed to trespassers was the duty to take reasonable care. That is, the occupier owed a duty to trespassers whom he could reasonably foresee, and that the duty in such a case was to take such reasonable care as the circumstances demanded.

The Supreme Court in *McNamara* cited with approval the approach adopted by the House of Lords in *British Railways Board v Herrington* [1972] AC 877. In that case, their Lordships decided that if the occupier knows or as good as knows of the presence of a trespasser and that there is a likelihood of serious danger, then a duty of care will arise. When the duty arises, the content of the duty requires the occupier to act in a "humane manner".

The Court in *McNamara* also applied the earlier Supreme Court decision of *Purtill v Athlone UDC* [1968] IR 205. In *Purtill*, the Court said that where a danger is reasonably foreseeable, the duty to take care to avoid injury to those who are proximate, when their proximity is known, is not abrogated because the other party is a trespasser; and that this duty is based upon the duty that one person has, to those in proximity to him, to take reasonable care that they are not injured by his acts.

In *McNamara*, the Court effectively applied ordinary negligence principles to the trespasser. The Occupiers' Liability Act 1995, however, reversed this to the old (lower) common law standard. This higher standard towards trespassers, therefore, applied only between 1975 and 1995. All the common law authorities concerning trespassers in occupiers' liability, which had largely become redundant during the period 1975–1995, may be relevant once again in determining what is meant by recklessness in the context of the 1995 Act.

C. The Hotel Proprietors Act 1963

Section 4 of the Hotel Proprietors Act 1963 provides that where a person is received as a guest in a hotel, whether or not under a special contract, the proprietor of the hotel is under a duty to take reasonable care of the person of the guest and to ensure that, for the purpose of personal use by the guest, the premises are as safe as reasonable care and skill can make them.

This appears to provide a hotel guest with a statutory right of action against a hotel proprietor which is wider than an invitee's right at common law and a visitor's claim under the Occupiers' Liability Act 1995. It would also appear that the hotel proprietor would be liable for the acts of his independent contractors. The Act only protects "guests", not other lawful visitors. The 1963 Act does not define "guests", but would appear to cover persons on the premises for the purposes of consuming food and drink only.

D. The Occupiers' Liability Act 1995

The Scope of the 1995 Act

Section 2(1) of the Act provides that the duties, liabilities and rights provided for by the Act are to have effect in place of those which previously attached by the common law to occupiers of premises "as such in respect of dangers existing on their premises to entrants thereon". This provision makes it clear that the 1995 Act changes only the rules relating to the occupier's duty to entrants in respect of dangers resulting from the state of the premises. Therefore, an occupier who is negligent towards a visitor in a context other than those relating to dangers due to the state of the premises may still be sued for negligence at common law.

In *Hackett v Calla Associates Ltd* [2004] IEHC 336 where the plaintiff was assaulted by a member of security staff engaged by the occupier of premises, the Court referred to the narrow definition of "danger" in s 1(1) as meaning a danger due to the state of the premises. Peart J said:

> "It must follow from this that the plaintiff's claim is not one coming within the duty of care imposed by [the Act] as the allegations of negligence are not related in any way to the state of the premises but rather the behaviour of the [security personnel] on the night in question. It is necessary to consider this claim by reference to the more usual non-statutory criteria in relation to the possible breach of the common law duty of care owed to the plaintiff by the owners/occupier of the premises..."

Accordingly, obligations under the legislation are limited to the static condition of the land and buildings. The Court in *Allen v Trabolgan Holiday Centre Ltd* [2010] IEHC 129 made it clear that if any harm arises out of action taking place on the premises, for example sporting events, the cutting down of trees for timber, or driving vehicles on the land, liability for that harm is to be determined under the ordinary rules of negligence.

Occupiers

Section 1(1) of the 1995 Act defines an "occupier" as a person:

> "... exercising such control over the state of the premises that it is reasonable to impose upon that person a duty towards an entrant in respect of a particular danger thereon and, where there is more than one occupier of the same premises, the extent of the duty of each occupier towards an entrant depends on the degree of control each of them has over the state of the premises and the particular danger thereon and whether as respects each of them, the entrant concerned is a visitor, recreational user or trespasser."

Central to this definition is the degree of control a person exercises over the premises. In *Hackett v Calla Associates Ltd* the Court found that both the first and second defendants were "occupiers" for the purposes of the Act. The first defendant was the owner of the premises and the second defendant held the licence to operate the premises.

Premises

Section 1(1) of the Act states that "premises" include not only land, water and any fixed or movable structures on land or water but also vessels, vehicles, trains, aircraft and other means of transport. In *Weldon v Mooney* [2001] IEHC 3, the plaintiff was injured when he fell from the luggage compartment of a bus. It appeared that he had climbed into the compartment in order to "hitch" a lift home. The Court took the view that the plaintiff's injuries were the result of an activity on the premises rather than a danger due to the state of the premises. The plaintiff's claim would, therefore, have to be made in negligence as the matter fell outside the scope of the Occupiers' Liability Act 1995.

Entrants

Under the 1995 Act, persons who come onto another person's premises are divided into three categories: (i) visitors; (ii) trespassers and (iii) recreational users.

Visitors

Under s 1 of the 1995 Act, a visitor is defined as:

> "(a) an entrant, other than a recreational user, who is present on premises at the invitation, or with the permission, of the occupier or any other entrant specified in paragraph (a), (b) or (c) of the definition of "recreational user", [see below]
> (b) an entrant, other than a recreational user, who is present on premises by virtue of an express or implied term in a contract, and
> (c) an entrant as of right,
>
> while he or she is so present, as the case may be, for the purpose for which he or she is invited or permitted to be there, for the purpose of the performance of the contract or for the purpose of the exercise of the right, and includes any such entrant whose presence on premises has become unlawful after entry thereon and who is taking reasonable steps to leave."

The category of visitor broadly encompasses entrants who would formerly have been categorised as contractual entrants, invitees and licensees. But there is one exception. The Act creates a new category of entrant: the recreational user. The recreational user is an entrant who, with or without the occupier's permission, enters premises without a charge, to engage in a recreational activity, such as hiking or camping, or exploring historic buildings or sites of archaeological or architectural interest. Under the previous law, a recreational user would normally have been categorised as a licensee.

Under s 3 of the Act, the occupier owes a duty of care ("the common duty of care") to a visitor. This is defined as a duty "to take such care as is reasonable in all the circumstances ... to ensure that a visitor to the premises does not suffer injury or damage by reason of any danger existing thereon". The "common duty of care" is akin to the standard of care under ordinary negligence principles, and, as with ordinary negligence, the occupier's duty may be affected by the plaintiff's contributory negligence. Section 3 also makes clear that the occupier's "common duty of care" may be reduced where the person injured is on the premises in the company of another person who may be expected to supervise the visitor. This might occur, for example, where a child visitor is accompanied by his or her parent or supervising schoolteacher.

The distinction between visitors and recreational users was considered in *Heaves v Westmeath County Council* (17 October 2001) (CC). There, the plaintiff was injured when he slipped on steps when walking on the grounds of Belvedere House with his two children. The house was closed to the public on the day of the accident, but the gardens and grounds were open to visitors. The plaintiff parked in the car park and paid a £1 entry fee for himself and 50p for each of his children. The money was accepted by two attendants in a hut. The Court held that the payment of the entry fees made the plaintiff a visitor. If the payments were for car parking only, the plaintiff would have been a recreational user.

In *Vega v Cullen* [2005] IEHC 363, the plaintiff was a social guest at the defendant's home. The defendant went up a ladder onto a roof. The plaintiff followed him up the ladder and had a conversation with him. One leg of the ladder was on a concrete surface and the other was on a gravel surface. It was therefore unstable. As the plaintiff began to come down the ladder, it moved to the right, causing him to fall. The plaintiff was held to be a visitor under the 1995 Act: the plaintiff's injury resulted from the negligence of the defendant in leaving the ladder so positioned and by failing to warn the plaintiff not to ascend the ladder. In finding for the plaintiff, Peart J observed that there is "no meaningful distinction between the common law duty of care and the statutory duty of care under the Occupiers' Liability Act 1995".

The distinction between a visitor and trespasser was considered in *Williams v TP Wallace Construction Ltd* [2002] 2 ILRM 63. In that case, the plaintiff arrived at a building site to inspect guttering that was faulty. No one was available to bring him up onto the roof because it was break-time. It appears that the plaintiff went onto the roof to inspect the guttering by himself. He fell and was injured as he descended a ladder. The Court held that he was not a "visitor" because he did not have permission to be on the roof and was, therefore, a trespasser. Accordingly, the only duty owed to him was that the occupier/defendant not injure him intentionally nor act with reckless disregard towards him.

As we have seen, under s 3 of the 1995 Act an occupier owes what is called "the common duty of care" towards a visitor. The question then arises: what exactly is the standard expected of occupiers? In *Heaves v Westmeath County Council*, the appropriate standard was held to have been reached by the occupier. There, the plaintiff slipped on steps at a large house which was open to the public. The steps were covered in lichen and moss. The Court held that the precautions taken by the occupier were, in all the circumstances, reasonable. A satisfactory cleaning system was in place which had worked effectively for some years without any problems.

In *Coffey v Moffit T/A Moffit's Shoes* (17 June 2005) (CC), the plaintiff, a two-and-a-half year-old girl, pulled a heavy glass shelf towards herself from a display in a shoe shop which crushed and fractured her thumb. The Court held that the plaintiff was a visitor within the meaning of s 1. Accordingly, "the common duty of care" was owed to her by virtue of s 3; and the danger from which the injury arose was a danger "due to the state of the premises". However, the Court made it clear that an occupier will only be liable if he has not taken reasonable care with regard to the danger. Since the occupier had engaged competent persons to install the shelving which appeared to reach industry standards, the occupier had behaved reasonably. The plaintiff's claim was dismissed.

Prisoners are "visitors" for the purposes of the 1995 Act whilst they are in prison. In *Power v Governor of Cork Prison* [2005] IEHC 253, liability was imposed in circumstances where a prisoner slipped on the floor of a toilet which was wet following spillages of water from wash hand basins. A warning notice containing the words "danger slippery surface" was insufficient for the prison authorities to be able to claim that they had discharged their "common duty of care" to the prisoner. The Court was of the view that this danger was foreseeable and could have been remedied relatively easily and for relatively little cost. There was no contributory negligence on the part of the prisoner.

The common duty of care owed to visitors under s 3 of the Act can be extended, restricted, modified or excluded under s 5. However, the occupier is not permitted to reduce the level of his or her duty below that owed to recreational users and trespassers.

Recreational Users and Trespassers

A recreational user is defined in s 1 as an entrant who:

> "... with or without the occupier's permission or at the occupier's implied invitation, is present on premises without a charge (other than a reasonable charge in respect of the cost of providing vehicle parking facilities) being imposed for the purpose of engaging in a recreational activity, including an entrant admitted without charge to a national monument pursuant to section 16 (1) of the National Monuments Act, 1930, but not including an entrant who is so present and is—
>
> (a) a member of the occupier's family who is ordinarily resident on the premises,

> (b) an entrant who is present at the express invitation of the occupier or such a member, or
> (c) an entrant who is present with the permission of the occupier or such a member for social reasons connected with the occupier or such a member".

It will be noted that recreational users can be on the occupier's premises with the occupier's permission or at the occupier's implied invitation. But this does not make them "visitors" provided they are present on the premises for the *purpose* of engaging in recreational activity. However, if they are expressly invited onto the premises by the occupier (or a member of the occupier's family) they will become visitors.

"Recreational activity" is defined in s 1 as:

> "… any recreational activity conducted, whether alone or with others, in the open air (including any sporting activity), scientific research and nature study so conducted, exploring caves and visiting sites and buildings of historical, architectural, traditional, artistic, archaeological or scientific importance."

It should also be noted that s 8 provides that nothing in the 1995 Act is to be construed as affecting any enactment or rule of law relating to, inter alia, "the defence of property". This would appear to mean that occupiers are still entitled to exclude any entrant, including recreational users, from their property.

By virtue of s 4 of the Act, trespassers and recreational users do not receive the same level of protection as visitors. The occupier does not owe any duty of care in negligence to recreational users or trespassers with regard to dangers due to the state of the premises. All that the occupier needs to do is to ensure that he or she does not injure the recreational user or trespasser intentionally or act with reckless disregard for their safety. As mentioned above, this overturns the decisions in *Purtill* and *McNamara* in respect of all premises, urban and rural.

A trespasser, for the purposes of the Act, is an entrant other than a recreational user or visitor (s 1). An occupier may extend his or her duty towards them by express agreement or notice in accordance with s 5(1). In order to determine whether or not an occupier has acted with reckless disregard for a recreational user or trespasser (or his property), the court is obliged to have regard to all the circumstances of the case, including the nine factors set out in s 4(2). They are as follows:

(a) whether the occupier knew or had reasonable grounds for believing that a danger existed on the premises;

(b) whether the occupier knew or had reasonable grounds for believing that the person and, in the case of damage, property of the person, was or was likely to be on the premises;

(c) whether the occupier knew or had reasonable grounds for believing that the person or property of the person was in, or was likely to be in, the vicinity of the place where the danger existed;

(d) whether the danger was one against which, in all the circumstances, the occupier might reasonably be expected to provide protection for the person and property of the person;

(e) the burden on the occupier of eliminating the danger or of protecting the person and property of the person from the danger, taking into account the difficulty, expense or impracticability, having regard to the character of the premises and the degree of the danger, of so doing;

(f) the character of the premises including, in relation to premises of such a character as to be likely to be used for recreational activity, the desirability of maintaining the tradition of open access to premises of such a character for such an activity;

(g) the conduct of the person, and the care which he or she may reasonably be expected to take for his or her own safety, while on the premises, having regard to the extent of his or her knowledge thereof;

(h) the nature of any warning given by the occupier or another person of the danger; and

(i) whether or not the person was on the premises in the company of another person and, if so, the extent of the supervision and control the latter person might reasonably be expected to exercise over the other's activities.

The question of "recklessness" was considered in *Wier Rodgers v SF Trust Ltd* [2005] 1 ILRM 471. In that case, the plaintiff lost her footing at the edge of a cliff: she fell down the edge of the cliff and was injured. She sued the defendant occupier for negligence and breach of duty under s 4 of the 1995 Act. She succeeded in the High Court but the Supreme Court reversed. That Court was of the view that the Act did not require the occupier to fence off the coastline and place warning notices along it to warn against what was, in any event, an obvious danger. The Court did not express a definitive view of what was meant by recklessness in the context of the 1995 Act, but Geoghegan J did accept that, for the purposes of this case, the test of recklessness was an objective one. Geoghegan J also made it clear that even if the duty on the occupier was the ordinary *Donoghue v Stevenson* duty of care, the plaintiff, on the facts of this particular case, would not have succeeded. The plaintiff's claim was dismissed.

Under s 4(3)(a) an occupier is relieved of the obligation not to act with reckless disregard for a person who enters his or her premises for the purpose of committing an offence or a person who, while present on the premises, commits an offence — unless the court determines otherwise in the interests of justice. The occupier is relieved only of the duty not to act with reckless disregard for the entrant; he or she is still under a duty not to injure the entrant (or damage the entrant's property) intentionally (s 4(1)(a)). Section 4(3)(b) states that an "offence" includes an attempted offence.

Section 5 of the Criminal Law (Defence and the Dwelling) Act 2011 provides an additional defence for occupiers. That provision relieves a person of any liability in tort in respect of any injury, loss or damage arising from the use of such force as is permitted by s 2 of the 2011 Act (see below and chapter 10).

Under s 4(4), an occupier owes a duty to take reasonable care to recreational users where a structure on premises is provided for use primarily by recreational users. The provision specifies that reasonable care must be taken to maintain the structure in a safe condition. The kinds of structures envisaged here would include such things as benches in public parks, playground slides, viewing areas in scenic spots, and so on. It is not necessary that the occupier should have provided the structure. The duty of reasonable care regarding its maintenance attaches to the occupier.

Modification of Occupiers' Duty to Entrants

Under s 5 of the 1995 Act, an occupier, by express agreement or notice, may extend his or her duty towards any category of entrant (s 5(1)). It also enables an occupier, again by express agreement or notice, to restrict, modify or exclude his or her duty towards visitors, subject to certain qualifications (s 5(2)(a)). The restriction, modification or exclusion must be reasonable in all the circumstances (s 5(2)(b)(ii)). If not, the visitor will not be bound. Where the occupier seeks to achieve his or her objective by notice rather than by obtaining the visitor's express agreement, the occupier must then take reasonable steps to bring the notice to the attention of the visitor (s 5(2)(b)(ii)). The occupier will be presumed, unless the contrary is shown, to have taken such reasonable steps if the notice is prominently displayed at the normal means of access to the premises (s 5(2)(c)).

An occupier may not exclude liability for injuring a visitor or damaging the visitor's property intentionally or to act with reckless disregard for a visitor or the property of a visitor (s 5(3)). In other words, the occupier may not, by agreement or notice, reduce the duty he or she owes to a visitor below that owed to recreational users and trespassers. Nor is an occupier permitted to reduce the level of obligation to recreational users by agreement or notice. This may be concluded from the drafting of s 4 and s 5. Section 5 does not expressly permit such a reduction, and s 4 states that the duty to recreational users and trespassers is owed "except in so far as the occupier extends this duty in accordance with section 5".

Warnings to Visitors

Section 5(5) provides that where injury or damage is caused to a visitor (or the visitor's property) by a danger of which the visitor had been warned by the occupier or another person, the warning is not to be treated as absolving the occupier from liability unless, in all the circumstances, it was enough to enable the visitor, by having regard to the warning, to avoid the injury or damage so caused. This provision requires that a warning must be sufficiently effective in appraising the visitor of the danger such that, in all the circumstances, he or she will be in a position to avoid being injured by the danger.

Duty of Occupiers Towards Strangers to Contracts

Section 6 deals with occupiers' duties towards strangers to contracts. If an occupier enters into a contract with another person, for example a builder, the occupier will normally permit other persons, for example the builder's employees, or independent contractors engaged by the builder, to come onto his premises. The occupier will not normally be in a contractual relationship with these other persons. They will, therefore, be strangers to the contract between the occupier and the builder. Such persons will be visitors by virtue of s 1 of the 1995 Act. This is because the term "visitor" includes an entrant present with the occupier's permission or one who is present "by virtue of an express or implied term in a contract", bearing in mind that the contract need not necessarily be with the occupier.

Section 6 of the Act makes it clear that the occupier will not be permitted, by a term in the contract between him and, say, the builder in our earlier example, to exclude or modify liability that would otherwise arise under s 3 in respect of these visitors. Under s 6(1), the duty that an occupier owes to an entrant under the 1995 Act is not capable of being modified or excluded by a contract to which the entrant is a stranger, whether or not the occupier is bound by the contract to permit the entrant to enter or use the premises.

Section 6(2) provides that an entrant shall be deemed to be a stranger to a contract if the entrant is not for the time being entitled to the benefit of the contract as a party to it or as the successor by assignment or otherwise of a party to it, and, accordingly, a party to the contract who has ceased to be so entitled shall be deemed to be a stranger to the contract.

Section 6 prevents the occupier from using a contract with one person (for example, the builder) to reduce or remove his or her liability to other persons (for example the builder's employees or independent contractors). However, it does not prevent the occupier from using s 5 of the same Act to achieve the same objective. As we have seen above, this could be done by express agreement with the builder's employees or independent contractors or by notice as set down in s 5(2).

Liability of Occupiers for the Negligence of Independent Contractors

Section 7 of the 1995 Act provides that an occupier is not liable to an entrant for injury or damage caused to the entrant, or his property, by reason of a danger existing on the premises due to the negligence of an independent contractor employed by the occupier if the occupier has taken all reasonable care in the circumstances, unless the occupier has or ought to have had knowledge of "the fact that the work was not properly done". The occupier will be considered to have taken reasonable care if he or she takes such steps as ought reasonably to be taken to satisfy himself or herself that the independent contractor was competent to do the work in question.

The Saving Provision

The saving provision in s 8 of the Act provides that nothing in the Act is to be construed as affecting any enactment or rule of law relating to the following three specific areas of law:

    (i)   self-defence, defence of others and defence of property;
    (ii)   liability imposed on an occupier as a member of a particular class of persons;
    (iii) non-delegable duties.

Self-Defence, Defence of Others and Defence of Property

This area of law relates to the rights of occupiers to respond to threats to their person or property. In the context of burglary, for example, the Court in *DPP v Barnes* [2006] IECCA 165 said that such an aggressor may expect to be lawfully met with the retaliatory force to drive him off or to immobilise or detain him and end the threat which he presents to the personal rights of the householder and his or her family or guests. This is so whether the dwelling-house which he enters is, or appears to be, occupied or unoccupied when he breaks into it. The underlying principle, of course, is that of "reasonable force". What is reasonable will, most likely, be a question of fact in every case. The Criminal Law (Defence and the Dwelling) Act 2011, which was introduced in the wake of *DPP v Nally* [2006] IECCA 128, provides some refinements to the legal rights of householders to protect themselves, their families and their dwellings from trespassers.

In the *Nally* case, the defendant occupier confronted an intruder attempting to enter his kitchen at the rear of his house. In response to this, the defendant retrieved his shotgun. He accidentally (he claimed) discharged the weapon, injuring the intruder. A struggle between the defendant and the intruder then ensued. The intruder escaped to the public road. The defendant then went to a shed, reloaded his gun, and delivered a fatal gunshot to the intruder out on the road. The defendant was convicted of manslaughter by a jury. His conviction was subsequently quashed by the Court of Criminal Appeal. That Court held that the trial judge's directions to the jury on the defence of self-defence had denied the jury the opportunity of returning a verdict of not guilty (even if such a verdict would have flown in the face of the evidence). This case gave rise to considerable public debate as to the lengths householders could lawfully go in defending themselves and their homes. It was in this context that the 2011 Act was introduced.

Liability Imposed on an Occupier as a Member of a Particular Class of Persons

Section 8(b) of the 1995 Act provides that any liability imposed on an occupier as a member of a particular class of persons will be unaffected by the Act. This provision provides three examples in a non-exclusive list:

(a) persons by virtue of a contract for the hire of, or for the carriage for reward of persons or property in, any vessel, vehicle, train, aircraft or other means of transport;

(b) persons by virtue of a contract of bailment; and

(c) employers in respect of their duties towards their employees.

Non-Delegable Duties Unaffected by the Act

Section 8(c) makes plain that any liability imposed on an occupier for a tort committed by another person in circumstances where the duty imposed on the occupier is of such a nature that its performance may not be delegated to another person are not affected by the 1995 Act.

DEFAMATION

Learning Outcomes

On completion of this chapter, the reader should be able to:

- Identify the essential ingredients of the tort of defamation;
- Describe the characteristics of each ingredient;
- Appreciate the competing constitutional rights of freedom of expression and the right to a good name;
- Understand the role of the judge and jury in defamation proceedings;
- Explain the operation of the defences to defamation;
- Differentiate between the defences of absolute privilege and qualified privilege.

A. Defamation: General

The Constitutional Context

Freedom of expression is a fundamental right which is constitutionally protected. Article 40.6.1° of the Constitution provides:

> "The State guarantees liberty for the exercise of the following rights, subject to public order and morality: –
>
> > The right of citizens to express freely their convictions and opinions.
> >
> > The education of public opinion being, however, a matter of such grave import to the common good, the State shall endeavour to ensure that organs of public opinion, such as the radio, the press, the cinema, while preserving their rightful liberty of expression, including criticism of Government policy, shall not be used to undermine public order morality or the authority of the State.
> >
> > ...."

It is therefore the right of all citizens to freely express their opinions, but this right cannot be exercised at the expense of a person's good name. Article 40.3.2° of the Constitution guarantees the protection of the good name of every citizen. It states:

> "The State shall, in particular, by its laws protect as best it may from unjust attack and, in the case of injustice done, vindicate the ... good name ... of every citizen."

The reference to "good name" in this provision places an obligation on the State to ensure that appropriate laws are in place to allow every citizen to protect his or her good name. The tort of defamation fulfils this function in Irish law. It is the role of the courts to seek to ensure that the appropriate balance is struck between the competing rights of freedom of expression and a person's right to his or her good name.

Figure 16.1

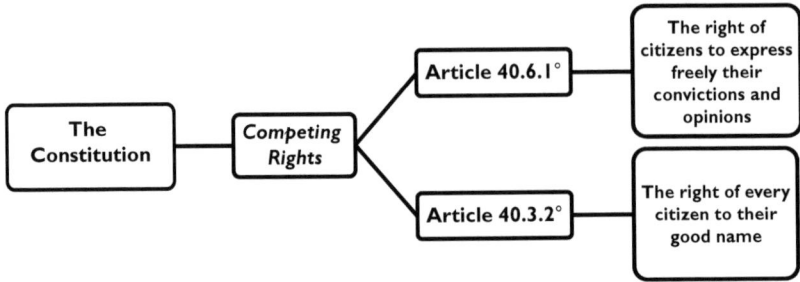

Defamation Defined

The main function of the tort of defamation is to compensate the plaintiff for his or her loss of reputation. Prior to the Defamation Act 2009, defamation, at common law, was comprised of two separate torts: libel and slander. A defamatory statement, if made in a permanent form, was libel, whereas if made in a transient form, was slander. Accordingly, a defamatory statement published in a magazine or newspaper would have been a libel, but a defamatory statement made orally in respect of the plaintiff to a third party would have been slander. The distinction between the two torts was important. First, a libel could be a crime as well as a tort. Consequently, it could have been the subject of criminal proceedings. The common law offences of defamatory libel, seditious libel and obscene libel have now been abolished by s 35 of the 2009 Act. Second, the tort of libel was actionable *per se*, so proof of actual damage was not necessary, whereas, except in exceptional circumstances, a plaintiff in an action for slander had to prove special damage. The 2009 Act subsumes the torts of libel and slander into one tort of defamation with the common law distinction between libel and slander being removed by s 6(1) of the Act.

The tort of defamation was defined at common law as the:

> "wrongful publication of a false statement about a person, which tends to lower that person in the eyes of right-thinking members of society or tends to hold that person up to hatred, ridicule or contempt, or causes that person to be shunned or avoided by right-thinking members of society": see *Quigley v Creation Ltd* [1971] IR 269; *Berry v Irish Times* [1973] IR 368.

Defamation, now placed on a statutory basis, is defined in s 6(2) of the Defamation Act 2009. It states:

> "The tort of defamation consists of the publication, by any means, of a defamatory statement concerning a person to one or more persons (other than the first mentioned person)".

The term "statement" in the phrase "defamatory statement" is defined in s 2 as including a statement which is made "orally or in writing", comprising "visual images, sounds, gestures and any other method of signifying meaning", or a statement which is "broadcast on the radio or television", "published on the Internet", or which is made by way of "an electronic communication". Thus, the 2009 Act reflects the potential for defamatory statements to be disseminated through modern electronic communication methods. "Defamatory statement" is itself defined in s 2 as: "a statement that tends to injure a person's reputation in the eyes of reasonable members of society". Therefore, it is not necessary to show actual injury, only that the defamatory statement "tends to injure" the person's reputation; nor is it necessary, by virtue of s 6(5), for the plaintiff to prove special damage to establish defamation.

Death and Defamation Actions

It is possible for a plaintiff to maintain a defamation action against a person who has died. It is also possible for the estate of a person who has died to maintain a defamation action against a person. Section 39 of the 2009 Act provides that existing causes of action for defamation survive either against or for the benefit of the deceased's estate. Accordingly, if a person has a cause of action for defamation immediately before he or she dies, that action survives for the benefit of his or her estate. Similarly, if a person who had a cause of action against him or her immediately before his or her death, that action survives against his or her estate. Section 39 also provides, however, that damages recoverable against the estate of a deceased person shall not include general damages, punitive damages or aggravated damages.

Limitation Periods and Defamation

Prior to the 2009 Act, the limitation period for defamation actions was six years. Now, under s28 of the Act, defamation actions must be taken within one year from the date on which the cause of action accrued. The court may, however, extend this period to two years if it is satisfied that:

(a) the interests of justice so require; and
(b) the prejudice that the plaintiff would suffer would significantly outweigh the prejudice that the defendant would suffer.

In deciding whether to do so, the court is required to have regard to the reason for the failure to bring the action within the one-year period and the extent to which any evidence relevant to the matter is, as a result of the delay, no longer capable of being adduced. The date of accrual will be the date on which the defamatory statement was first published, or, if published on online, the date on which it was first capable of being viewed or listened to.

B. What is Meant by "Publication"?

Publication, in the context of defamation, means that the statement is communicated to a third party. A statement is considered to be published by anyone who makes a statement, or distributes or disseminates a statement, or repeats a statement, to a third person. The term "publisher" is given a wide meaning. For example, in *Berry v Irish Times* [1973] IR 368 the defendant newspaper reproduced a photograph of a placard containing a statement which was claimed by the plaintiff to have defamed him. The words on the placard were clearly legible in the photograph. The plaintiff argued successfully that the defendant was a "publisher" for the purposes of the tort. It is clear, therefore, that a broad range of actors could be held to be publishers for the purposes of this tort, including newspaper vendors, booksellers and printers. It may also include those who send statements by way of text message or email, or who make statements at meetings or gatherings about the plaintiff to a third party.

Since publication cannot take place without communication to a third party, a statement made directly to the plaintiff, out of earshot of any other person, will not have been published. A defamation action cannot, therefore, be maintained in those circumstances. Similarly, if the statement is written in a letter addressed to the plaintiff and sent by the defendant to the plaintiff, no publication will have taken place because the statement will not have gone beyond the plaintiff. It should be noted that even if such a letter is intercepted by a third party and read by them before it reaches the plaintiff the courts will not generally consider publication to have occurred. This is because it is reasonable for the defendant to expect that the contents of a sealed letter, properly addressed, will be read only by the person to whom it is sent. In *Huth v Huth* [1915] 3 KB 32, for example, a man sent to his wife a letter which was defamatory of her and their children. It was opened and read by the butler. At that time, a wife could not to sue her husband in tort, so the action was brought by the children. At trial, the jury returned a verdict in favour of the defendant. The plaintiffs appealed. The Court of Appeal considered the question of whether evidence that the butler had opened and read the letter was evidence of publication to a third party. Lord Reading CJ said:

> "...it is no part of the butler's duty to open letters that come to the house of his master or mistress addressed to the master or mistress... No one can help a man's curiosity being excited, but it does not justify him in opening a letter, and it could not make the defendant liable for the publication to the butler of the contents of the envelope..."

However, a distinction could be made in the case of a postcard, telegram, or some other form of written communication which could quite easily be read by a third party. In such a case, because the method of communication would normally involve communication to a person other than the addressee, it would almost certainly amount to publication for the purposes of the tort. An example of this is *Theaker v Richardson* [1962] 1 WLR 151. In that case, the defendant wrote a letter containing a defamatory statement to the plaintiff who was a married woman. The letter was addressed to the plaintiff and was contained in a manila envelope similar to the kind used for distributing election addresses. The plaintiff's husband opened it: he thought (he said) it was an election address. At trial, the jury found that there had been publication of the defamatory statement. They awarded damages to the plaintiff. Their decision was appealed. In the Court of Appeal, Pearson LJ stated that the question to be asked was:

> "[Was] his [i.e. the recipient's] conduct so unusual, out of the ordinary and not reasonably to be anticipated, or was it something which could quite easily and naturally happen in the ordinary course of events?"

The jury had concluded that the opening of the letter by the husband was something that could quite easily happen in the ordinary course of events. The Court of Appeal did not disturb their decision. It is interesting to note that even up to relatively recently, an English court held that it was reasonably foreseeable that a husband would open and read his wife's post.

A slightly different question arose in *Paul v Holt* (1935) 69 ILTR. Here, a letter was addressed to "Mr Paul, Adavoyle, Meigh, Newry". The letter was a Civil Bill issued by the defendant for rent arrears. It was delivered to the plaintiff's brother who also lived at that address. The plaintiff's brother read it. He showed it to the plaintiff's wife. She then handed it to the brother's wife. The plaintiff sued in defamation and the question as to whether publication had occurred fell to be determined. The Court of Appeal took the view that publication had occurred because there was evidence that the defendant knew that there was another Mr Paul living at that address. In such circumstances, the defendant would have to prove that he did not know of the existence of the plaintiff's brother. Thus, if there is accidental publication in the communication process the defendant will, generally, not be liable. However, if communication to the third party is due to the negligence or carelessness of the defendant, then the defendant will be liable for the publication.

This position is codified in s 6(4) of the 2009 Act which states:

> "There shall be no publication for the purposes of the tort of defamation if the defamatory statement concerned is published to the person to whom it relates and to a person other than the person to whom it relates in circumstances where –

(a) it was not intended that the statement would be published to the second mentioned person, and

(b) it was not reasonably foreseeable that the publication of the statement to the first mentioned person would result in its being published to the second mentioned person."

At common law, the defendant and the defendant's spouse were treated as one entity for the purposes of publication. However, this was not the case in respect of the plaintiff and the plaintiff's spouse. Therefore, if the statement in question was communicated by the defendant to the plaintiff's spouse, communication to a third party was treated as having had occurred. On the other hand, if the statement in question was communicated by the defendant to the defendant's own spouse, communication was not treated as having had occurred: see *Wenman v Ash* (1853) 13 CB 836, 148 ER 1432 and *Wennhak v Morgan* (1888) 20 QBD 635. This common law defence of "spousal immunity" is not included in the Defamation Act 2009. Section 6(2) defines defamation as consisting of the publication of a defamatory statement "to one or more than one person (other than the [plaintiff])...". Communication by the defendant to the defendant's own spouse is not mentioned. Furthermore, s 15(1) provides that, subject to s 17(1) and s 18(1), any defence that, immediately before the commencement of Part 3 of the Act, could have been pleaded as a defence in an action for defamation is abolished.

As mentioned, publication of a defamatory statement can occur online. Statements on the Internet, by way of email or by posting on a server hosted by a third party, can amount to publication for the purposes of the tort of defamation. In *Godfrey v Demon Internet Ltd* [2001] QB 201, 3 WLR 1020 the defendants, an Internet service provider, received and stored on their news server an article which was defamatory of the plaintiff. The article had been posted by an unknown person using another service provider. The plaintiff informed the defendants that the article was defamatory and asked them to remove it from their server. The defendants failed to do so: it remained available on the server for some ten days until it expired automatically. The plaintiff brought proceedings for libel against the defendants who contended that they were not the publisher of the statement complained of. The Court held that, as a service provider who transmitted or facilitated the transmission of postings received and stored by them via the Internet, the defendants were a publisher of that posting at common law. They were not merely the passive owner of an electronic device through which postings were transmitted. They actively chose to receive and store the posting which could be accessed by their subscribers.

Repetition, linking (through hyperlinks), or transmission onwards to a large audience may also amount to publication. Section 11 of the 2009 Act provides some protection to those who repeat or transmit defamatory material by providing that there is only one cause of action in respect of a multiple publication. However, in circumstances where an intermediary, such an Internet news service, facilitates, stores, or transmits defamatory material on its website, and a defamatory statement is posted on a server but is not accessed by any person, publication will not have taken place. The onus will be on the plaintiff to show that such access took place. Consequently, it is likely to be fatal to the plaintiff's case if there is no evidence that a website containing defamatory material was ever actually accessed by any person. This would be the case if the defendant could prove that there were no "hits" to the website in question.

In relation to "blogs" placed by persons on another person's website, the English Court of Appeal in *Tamiz v Google Inc* [2013] EWCA took the view that if a defendant allows defamatory material to remain on its website in the form of a blog after it has been notified of the presence of the defamatory material, it might be reasonable for a court to infer that the defendant had associated itself with, or has made itself responsible for, the continued presence of that material. Therefore, it may have become a publisher of that material.

In many cases, such intermediaries would not be aware of all the material on their servers, much less have editorial control over it. In these cases, the intermediaries are likely to be mere facilitators or conduits through which the material passes. It could be argued that to hold such intermediaries liable in defamation would be likely to have a stifling effect on the free transfer of information in the Internet age, which may not be consistent with the public interest or public policy objectives. The amended definition of "innocent publication" in s 27 of the 2009 Act provides some protection to such intermediaries.

It is also possible, by virtue of s 12 of the 2009 Act, for a corporate plaintiff to sue for defamation where the defamation affects the corporate reputation. Special damage does not have to be proved in such an action. Section 31(7) of the Act allows the court to award damages in respect of financial loss suffered by the plaintiff as a result of defamation. This may be particularly relevant to corporate plaintiffs.

C. What Does it Mean to "Injure" a Person's Reputation?

The importance to every person of their reputation was expressed by Lord Nicholls in *Reynolds v Times Newspapers Ltd* [1999] 1 All ER 609 when he said:

> "... [r]eputation is an integral and important part of the dignity of the individual. It also forms the basis of many decisions in a democratic society which are fundamental to its well-being: whom to employ, work for, whom to promote, whom to do business with or to vote

> for. Once besmirched by an unfounded allegation... a reputation can be damaged for ever, especially if there is no opportunity to vindicate one's reputation. When this happens, society as well as the individual is the loser. For it should not be supposed that protection of reputation is a matter of importance only to the affected individual and his family. Protection of reputation is conducive to the public good... freedom of expression is not an absolute right. Its exercise may be subject to such restrictions as are prescribed by law and are necessary in a democratic society for the protection of the reputations of others."

Whether a statement is defamatory is a matter to be determined objectively. The intent of the maker of the statement is largely irrelevant. Accordingly, even if the maker of the statement intended no harm, the statement may still be held to be defamatory. It is also important to note that whether a statement is defamatory can depend on the context in which it was made and when it was made. Since social and moral values change over time, and vary from society to society, what may be considered defamatory in the nineteenth century may not be so in the twenty-first century, and vice versa. It is important to bear this in mind when considering defamation precedents.

Over the years the courts have held a wide range of statements to be capable of being defamatory. In *Fullam v Associated Newspapers Ltd* [1955-56] Ir Jur Rep 45, a statement that a well-known professional footballer had never used his right foot in kicking the ball because he was unable to do so was held, by the former Supreme Court, to be capable of being defamatory if untrue. In *Doyle v the Economist Newspaper Ltd* [1981] NI 171(HC) the defendant published a statement in an article following judicial appointments in Northern Ireland. The statement suggested that one of the appointees, a Catholic, was appointed as a token and that some Catholic QCs considered that "some of their Protestant colleagues would have been better fitted for the job". The statement was held to be defamatory. In *Curneen v Sweeney* (1969) 103 ILTR 29 a statement by an auctioneer suggesting that the plaintiff, a solicitor, had not acted in a manner consistent with the highest traditions of his profession was held to be defamatory. In *Bennett v Quane* [1948] Ir Jur Rep 28 a medical doctor suggested that a solicitor brought an action in the Circuit Court rather than the District Court to "get more costs for himself". This allegation was held to be defamatory. In *Sinclair v Gogarty* [1937] IR 377, the book *As I Was Walking down Sackville Street* by Dr Oliver St J Gogarty was held to contain defamatory statements in relation to the plaintiff by making imputations of sexual impropriety against him. One of the statements, that the plaintiff, an antique dealer, "sought new mistresses more highly than old masters", was held to be so clearly defamatory that a temporary injunction was granted to prevent the continuing sale of the book.

In *Waters v Sunday Times* (23 April 2002) HC, an allegation that the plaintiff was a bad father who might be unsympathetic to his daughter's needs was held to be defamatory. In *De Rossa v Independent Newspapers plc* [1999] 4 IR 432, the plaintiff was leader of the Democratic Left, a political party. In an article, the defendant's newspaper made certain allegations relating to the sources of support which the plaintiff had accepted when he was a member of the Worker's Party. In an action for defamation, the jury found that the statement complained of suggested that the plaintiff was involved in or tolerated serious crime, that he personally supported anti-Semitism and violent Communist oppression. The statement was held to be defamatory. Mr De Rossa was awarded £300,000 in damages. The defendant did not appeal the finding of defamation, but did appeal the measure of damages. The Supreme Court did not reduce them. In *O'Brien v Associated Newspapers* (14 February 2013) HC, businessman Denis O'Brien was accused of hypocrisy and of being motivated by self-interest when he assisted in relief efforts following a major earthquake in Haiti, a country in which he had significant business interests. The jury held that the accusation was defamatory. It rejected the newspaper's defence of honest opinion. Mr O'Brien was awarded €150,000 in damages.

Allegations of dishonesty in respect of sporting activities have been held to be defamatory in a number of cases. In *Greene v Blake* [1948] IR 242, an owner and rider at the annual point to point races at Killeagh, Co Cork, was accused of deceitfully "carrying underweight" (i.e. the horse did not carry the correct weight for the race in question). The stewards held an inquiry as a result of which they "warned the plaintiff off" all courses governed by their rules. A number of notices were published in the *Racing Calendar* making the allegations against the plaintiff. They stated that, after full investigation of the matter and careful consideration of the evidence, they had warned the plaintiff off all courses on which their rules were in force. These statements were held to be capable of defamatory meaning. Also, in *Talbot v Hermitage Golf Club* [2012] IEHC 372, a handicap certificate issued by the golf club of which the plaintiff was a member contained a suggestion that the plaintiff had engaged in "handicap building". The plaintiff claimed that these words were false and were defamatory of him as imputing that he cheated at golf. Herbert J stated that an accusation of cheating in an amateur sport has long been held to be defamatory of the person accused of such behaviour. He said that this was particularly so in relation to the game of golf which was regarded by many as an "honesty game". The statement in this case was held to be capable of defamatory meaning.

In *Quigley v Creation Ltd* [1971] IR 269, the defendants published a weekly women's magazine which contained an account of an interview that was stated to have been given by the plaintiff to the writer of the article. The title of the article was "They've left this Isle". The plaintiff's name appeared immediately below the title. No such interview had taken place. The plaintiff sued claiming damages for libel. At trial, the plaintiff contended that the ordinary meaning of certain words in the article was that he did not work in Ireland and that he chose to live and work in London because the rewards and opportunities there were better than in Ireland. The jury found that the relevant words did have that meaning, that they were untrue and that they tended to lower the plaintiff in the eyes of right-thinking members of society. The jury awarded the plaintiff damages. The defendants appealed. They submitted that the relevant words and their meaning as found by the jury were incapable of defamatory meaning because they only amounted to a statement that the plaintiff had left Ireland to improve his prospects. The Supreme Court made it clear that it would be particularly cautious in deciding whether to set aside a jury's finding of libel. The trial judge, the Court held, had acted correctly in allowing the issue of libel to go to the jury. Walsh J stated:

> "… if words only tend to lower a person in the minds of a particular class or section of society, particularly if the standard of that particular section of society is one which the Court cannot recognise or approve, the words will not be held to be defamatory. On the other hand, words are defamatory if they impute conduct which would tend to lower that person in the eyes of a considerable and respectable class of the community, though not in the eyes of the community as a whole. The test is whether it will lower him in the eyes of the average right-thinking man. If it will, then it is defamatory if untrue. It follows naturally that in an action in this country the standard would be that of the average right-thinking person in this community. The law recognises the right of the plaintiff to have the estimation in which he stands in the opinion of the right-thinking people in this community unaffected by false statements to his discredit."

The jury's finding of libel was not disturbed.

Another issue that has been considered by the courts is whether a statement describing a person as homosexual is capable of defamatory meaning. In *R v Bishop* [1975] 1 QB 274, the English Court of Appeal held that the character of a witness was impugned by an allegation of homosexual conduct made against him and that an imputation of homosexual immorality against such a witness might reflect on his reliability generally or as a witness in a criminal trial. This was notwithstanding a submission during the trial that, in view of decriminalisation of homosexual acts between men in private in England and Wales, an allegation that a man was a homosexual or practised homosexuality was not an imputation on his character.

In Ireland, the matter was considered in *Reynolds v Malocco t/a "Patrick"* [1999] 2 IR 203. In that case, the defendant referred to the plaintiff in a publication as a "gay bachelor". The defendants accepted that the plaintiff was not homosexual. Furthermore, they claimed that they never alleged he was homosexual. They contended that the word "gay", in its ordinary meaning, as an adjective, described a person who was "lively, cheerful, vivacious, light-hearted", and "fond of pleasure and gaiety". The Court rejected this argument. Kelly J stated that such an argument, if advanced 30 years earlier, might have succeeded, but, he said, "it is an absurd proposition to put to the Court in 1998". He said that, over the last 30 years or so the word "gay" had acquired a secondary meaning in that it had become synonymous with homosexuals and homosexual activity. Kelly J further stated that, in his view, the term "gay bachelor", which the defendants claimed merely described a man who was "happily unmarried", had fallen into disuse because of the secondary meaning of the word "gay". The defendants argued, however, that to say a person is a homosexual nowadays in Ireland is not, in any case, damaging to his reputation. They contended that homosexuality is accepted in Ireland and homosexuals are part of the fabric of Irish life. The plaintiff asserted, however, that an allegation of being gay is an allegation of deviant sexual practice which many people in Irish society find repellent. In finding for the plaintiff, Kelly J stated:

> "it does not appear to me to be sound to suggest that merely because an activity is no longer prohibited by the criminal law an allegation of engaging in such activity cannot be defamatory. The commission of adultery is not a criminal offence but nobody could seriously suggest that an allegation of adultery could not be defamatory. Similarly, to lie is not a criminal offence, but again can it be seriously suggested that to call a person a liar is not defamatory?"

In *Berry v Irish Times Ltd* [1973] IR 368, the Court was invited to consider whether a statement that a person had assisted in bringing wrongdoers to justice could be defamatory. *The Irish Times* had published a report on a picket mounted by Sinn Féin outside the offices of the British Overseas Airways Corporation (BOAC) in Dublin. A photograph of one of the picketers holding a placard was reproduced in the newspaper. The words on the placard were clearly legible in the photograph. They said: "Peter Berry – 20th Century Felon Setter – Helped Jail Republicans in England". The individual referred to in the placard, Peter Berry, was, at the time, Secretary of the Department of Justice. He claimed that the words were defamatory. The jury held that they were not. The Supreme Court, on appeal, refused to set aside the jury's verdict on the basis that no reasonable jury could have made such a finding. The majority of the Court made it clear that an allegation that a person who assisted in the curbing of "militant activities" would be guilty of improper conduct was not something with which ordinary right-thinking people in Ireland would necessarily agree. The jury, therefore, was entitled to hold that the words were not defamatory. Ó Dálaigh CJ did, however, suggest that if Mr Berry had been called an "informer", he might, due to the particular inferences associated with that word in Irish history, have succeeded ([1973] IR 368 at 376).

In *Berkoff v Burchell* [1996] 4 All ER 1008, Julie Burchell, a well-known journalist in England, made a number of remarks about Stephen Berkoff, the actor and film director, in film reviews in the Sunday Times. She had said, first, that "film directors, from Hitchcock to Berkoff, are notoriously hideous-looking people". Subsequently, in a review of *Mary Shelley's Frankenstein*, she had written:

> "The Creature is... rejected in disgust when it comes out scarred and primaeval. It's a very new look for the Creature – no bolts in the neck or flat-top hairdo – and I think it works: it's a lot like Stephen Berkoff, only marginally better-looking."

The English Court of Appeal considered that the assertion by the defendant that the plaintiff was "hideously ugly" was capable of defamatory meaning. Neill LJ stated that it would be

> "open to a jury to conclude that, in the context, the remarks about Mr Berkoff give the impression that he was not merely physically unattractive in appearance but actually repulsive. It seems to me that to say this of someone in the public eye who makes his living, in part at least, as an actor, is capable of lowering his standing in the estimation of the public and of making him an object of ridicule".

D. Can Vulgar Abuse be Defamatory?

Vulgar abuse may or may not be defamatory. It depends on the circumstances, context and manner in which the words are used. In *Harberagen v Koppens* [1974] 2 NZLR 597, it was held that to refer to someone as a "Dutch bastard" was mere vulgar abuse, not to be taken literally and not to be regarded as a comment amounting to a defamatory statement. In *Hickey v Sunday Newspapers Ltd* [2011] 1 IR 228, the defendant newspaper published an article quoting a wife describing the plaintiff, who had a child with her husband, as a "whore". The plaintiff claimed that she had been described as a person who engaged in sexual acts for payment or as someone who was otherwise than in a loving relationship. This, the plaintiff claimed, was defamatory. Kearns J held that the context and circumstances in which the words were used were mere vulgar abuse and not defamatory. He took the view that, although the word in question was capable of defamatory meaning, any ordinary or reasonable reader, on reading the defendant's comments, would see it simply as "vulgar abuse expressed in strong and offensive terms".

In *Brooks v Lind* 1997 Rep LR 83 it was held that it was not defamatory to suggest that the plaintiff was associated with a "Council Mafia". So, a word like "Mafia", the ordinary meaning of which would suggest a criminal organisation, can be understood to describe a close-knit group in a metaphorical, but not defamatory, sense. Indeed, in the early 1960s, President John F Kennedy's close-knit group of advisers, some of whom were of Irish descent, were often referred to in the American press as the "Irish Mafia". In that particular context, it is submitted, no reasonable person would regard such a description as defamatory.

E. Innuendo

In determining whether or not words used are in fact defamatory, the court must first consider the meaning of the words in their "natural and ordinary" sense. The whole of the statement must be considered, not just that part which the plaintiff alleges to be defamatory. Sometimes, however, the plaintiff may allege an additional "innuendo" meaning. In such cases, the plaintiff may allege that the statement is defamatory because specific facts known to the reader give to the statement a meaning other than — or additional to — its ordinary meaning. This is known as a "true" or "legal" innuendo. Here, the plaintiff must plead and prove such facts because the defendant is entitled to know the meaning of the statement on which the plaintiff seeks to rely so that he is able to argue either that the statement is not defamatory or that it true of the plaintiff.

Another possibility is that the words may have a meaning beyond the literal meaning which is inherent in them and arises by inference or implication. This is referred to as a "false" innuendo. This is something the plaintiff must plead separately. A "false" innuendo differs from a "true" innuendo in that the plaintiff pleading a "false" innuendo does not generally need to set out at any extrinsic facts in support of his plea. An example of a "true" or "legal" innuendo is *Russell v Notcutt* (1896) 12 TLR 195. In that case, the defendant engaged the plaintiff, a well-known singer, to perform a concert. The defendant printed the plaintiff's name third in the order on the programme. The Court accepted evidence that, in the world of musical performances, the best singer is always placed at the head of the programme. Those holding a lesser reputation were placed in the middle: that being so, the programme constituted a defamatory innuendo of the plaintiff.

An example of a "false" innuendo is *Rubber Improvement Ltd v Daily Telegraph Ltd* [1964] AC 234. In that case, the defendants published an article which stated that the Fraud Squad of the City of London Police were investigating the affairs of the plaintiff's company. The article was found to be capable of being defamatory in its ordinary meaning because the simple statement that the Fraud Squad was inquiring into his affairs might have damaged his reputation even though such investigation did not, *per se*, impugn his innocence. However, since the statement on its face was true, that is, the Fraud Squad *was* conducting the investigations stated, no action lay. The plaintiff also alleged that the words were defamatory in a second sense: that is, they carried with them the imputation that there was, at least, a basis for suspicion about the way in which the business was conducted. The essence of this claim was that the imputation of reasonable suspicion, although consistent with the plaintiff's innocence, was nevertheless capable of damaging the plaintiff's trading reputation. On the facts, the Court held that the words were not defamatory in this second sense. There was a distinction, it held, between, on the one hand, imputing reasonable grounds for suspicion and, on the other, simply reporting the fact of suspicion.

This distinction between a statement and an imputation of suspicion was restated by the English Court of Appeal in *Mapp v News Group Newspapers Ltd* [1998] QB 520, which held that a reference to a person being under investigation could not reasonably be read as imputing guilt, as opposed to suspicion of guilt and accordingly was not, in itself, defamatory as a matter of law. In *Griffin v Sunday Newspapers* [2011] IEHC 331 the question of whether a statement that "an enquiry or investigation was underway" was in and of itself evidence of wrongdoing fell to be considered. The Court, in that case, endorsed the approach adopted by Hirst LJ in *Mapp v News Group Newspapers Ltd*.

Two other examples of cases involving false innuendo are the cases of *Campbell v Irish Press Ltd* (1955) 90 ILTR 105 and *Fullam v Associated Newspapers Ltd* [1953-54] Ir Jur Rep 79. In *Campbell*, the plaintiff was in the business of providing billiards and snooker equipment. He organised a snooker exhibition at which a well-known snooker player, Joe Davis, was the main attraction. The following day, the defendant published an article critical of the exhibition. It said that Davis failed to make a century break because "the table told lies" — the implication being that the table was uneven. The jury held that the statement implied that the plaintiff was incompetent in the way in which he organised the exhibition. In *Fullam*, the defendant newspaper published an article which claimed that the plaintiff, a well-known and successful professional footballer, used his right foot only for balancing on. The plaintiff argued successfully that the statement implied that he was not a competent footballer and was therefore unworthy of being selected as an international player.

Two examples of true innuendo are *Tolley v Fry & Sons Ltd* [1931] AC 333 and *Cassidy v Daily Mirror Newspapers Ltd* [1929] 2 KB 331. In *Tolley*, an ostensibly innocent chocolate advertisement featuring a famous golfer, which was published without his consent, only became defamatory when his amateur status was known, thereby implying that being paid for endorsing a product would jeopardise that status. When the additional facts were pleaded of the golfer's amateur status in order to explain defamatory meaning, the Court held that the ordinary reader would assume that the golfer had compromised his reputation as an amateur. In *Cassidy*, the defendants published a photograph taken of Kettering Cassidy, also known as Michael Corrigan, and a woman. Cassidy told a press photographer that he was going to marry the woman. In the publication, the photograph appeared above the words: "Mr M Corrigan, the racehorse owner, and Miss [name omitted], whose engagement has been announced". An action in defamation was brought by Mrs Cassidy, Cassidy's lawful wife. Although they lived apart, Cassidy occasionally visited her. She argued that the words and pictures were capable of meaning that "Corrigan" was a single man and that, therefore, she was living an immoral cohabitation with him and only masquerading as his wife. At trial, three of her acquaintances gave evidence that they had in fact believed this on seeing the publication. The judge directed the jury to consider whether the publication was capable of conveying a defamatory meaning of the plaintiff to reasonably-minded people who knew the circumstances. The jury found for the plaintiff. They awarded £500 in damages. The defendant's appeal was dismissed.

F. The Statement Must Refer to the Plaintiff

Section 6(3) of the 2009 Act states: "[a] defamatory statement concerns a person if it could reasonably be understood as referring to him or her". Thus, there is a requirement of reference to the plaintiff in that the plaintiff must be identified as the person defamed. Where the plaintiff is named or clearly identified, no difficulties arise. The plaintiff need not be mentioned in the statement, nor need everyone reading it know that he was the person referred to. It suffices if ordinary sensible people, proved to have special knowledge of the facts, might reasonably believe the statement referred to the plaintiff. Where the plaintiff is not clearly named, evidence may be introduced to show that the statement in question referred to, or was capable of referring to, the plaintiff.

For instance, in *Fullam v Associated Newspapers Ltd*, the plaintiff was allowed to adduce evidence before the Court of the jeering of spectators at a football match and of some of his neighbours to show that the article in question referred to him. In *Sinclair v Gogarty*, the plaintiffs were not specifically named in the book in question; the reference was to "Two Jews in Sackville Street". In an affidavit, Mr Samuel Beckett stated that he understood the reference to be to the plaintiffs. This was considered to be sufficient evidence that the plaintiffs were the persons referred to.

In *E Hulton & Co v Jones* [1910] AC 20, Artemus Jones, a barrister, brought an action against the defendants in respect of a newspaper article which he claimed referred to him. He had previously contributed pieces to the newspaper in question. The article referred to "Artemus Jones" a churchwarden in Peckham in London and cast imputations on his moral behaviour at a motor festival in Dieppe. The words complained of were: "There is Artemus Jones with a woman who is not his wife, who must be, you know — the other thing!" The defendants argued that they had never intended the article to refer to the "real" Artemus Jones but instead had intended to create a fictitious character whom they had given a "fancy name". The plaintiff succeeded at trial. The defendant's appeal was dismissed. Similarly, in *Newstead v London Express Newspaper Ltd* [1940] 1 KB 377 the defendant newspaper published an account of the trial for bigamy of "Harold Newstead, 31-year-old Camberwell man". The reporter who wrote the story had included the address and occupation of the Harold Newstead to whom the report referred, but the sub-editor deleted it. This want of this particularity caused readers to think that the plaintiff — another Harold Newstead of Camberwell, of about the same age — was the person who was the subject of the report. It was held by the Court to be no defence that the words were true of and intended to refer to another.

A symbol could also be sufficient to associate a plaintiff with a defamatory statement. For instance, in *Byrne v RTÉ* (20 November 2007, High Court, *Irish Independent*, 21 November) the plaintiffs were a firm of solicitors. In a current affairs television programme which investigated bogus and exaggerated compensation claims, the plaintiffs' logo or letterhead was shown in the broadcast. A jury found that a reasonable viewer of the broadcast would conclude that this meant that the plaintiffs were involved in bringing bogus and exaggerated claims. They were awarded €80,000 in damages.

G. Group Defamation

Where words are spoken of a group of people or a class of persons, proof that the statement refers to an individual member of that group is likely to present difficulties. An example is the statement: "all lawyers are thieves". It has been said that this statement gives rise to no cause of action on the part of any individual lawyer (*Eastwood v Holmes* (1858) 1 F & F 347). Another example is the case of *Knuppfer v London Express Newspapers* [1944] AC 116. That case arose out of a newspaper article which was published at the time of World War II. The article claimed that a political party formed by émigrés from the Soviet Union, the "Young Russians", consisted of "quislings" with whom Hitler intended to establish a pro-German government within the Soviet Union. The party was alleged to be a "minute body professing a pure Fascist ideology". The article also claimed that "Hitler intends to nominate a puppet führer from their ranks to replace the Soviet national leaders in the Kremlin, and establish a reactionary totalitarian serf State...". The plaintiff was a Russian resident in London and was head of the British branch of the Young Russia party. He brought an action against the defendants in libel. The defendants denied that the words were reasonably capable of being understood to refer to the plaintiff. The total membership of the Young Russia Party worldwide was about 2,000, but the British branch comprised only twenty-four members. Four witnesses who knew the plaintiff gave evidence that they thought of him when they read the article. The plaintiff won at trial, but lost before the Court of Appeal. He appealed to the House of Lords but that appeal was dismissed. Viscount Simon LC said:

> "Where the plaintiff is not named, the test which decides whether the words used refer to him is the question whether the words are such as would reasonably lead persons acquainted with the plaintiff to believe that he was the person referred to."

In the course of his judgment in *Knuppfer v London Express Newspapers*, Viscount Simon referred to the Irish case of *Le Fanu v Malcolmson* (1848) 1 HLC 637. In that case, a jury awarded damages to the owners of a factory in Co Waterford against the proprietor of a newspaper published in that county. The newspaper had alleged that the factory workers were treated with cruelty, but the letterpress did not specifically refer to the plaintiff's factory. Notwithstanding this, Lord Cottenham LC and Lord Campbell held that the verdict could be upheld, on the basis, it appeared, that there were circumstances, such as the location of the factory, which enabled the jurors to identify the plaintiff's factory as the factory referred to.

This common law position is now codified in s 10 of the 2009 Act. It provides:

> "Where a person publishes a defamatory statement concerning a class of persons, a member of that class shall have a cause of action under this Act against that person if
>
> (a) by reason of the number of persons who are members of that class, or
> (b) by virtue of the circumstances in which the statement is published,
>
> the statement could reasonably be understood to refer, in particular, to the member concerned."

H. Is There a Right to a Jury Trial in Defamation Actions?

Defamation actions in the Circuit Court are heard by a judge only. High Court defamation actions are normally heard before a jury. The right to a jury trial in the High Court is not, however, a constitutional right: it is a statutory right.

The legal basis for the right originates from s 94 of the Courts of Justice Act 1924. This provision preserved, in the courts of Saorstát Éireann, the right to trial by jury in any case where a right to trial by jury in civil proceedings had previously existed. Since a right to trial by jury in defamation proceedings existed prior to the enactment of the 1924 Act it was therefore continued in force by reason of that Act. However, where a plaintiff's claim is based on defamation *and* grounds other than defamation which can be heard by a judge sitting alone, the trial judge may decide, if good reason exists, to have a single trial with no jury to determine all matters pleaded, including the defamation claim.

Clarke J, in *Bradley, practising as Malcomson Law Solicitors v Maher* [2009] IEHC 329, said that, ordinarily, a plaintiff or defendant is entitled to a jury trial in the High Court in defamation proceedings. However, that entitlement is not absolute. Where a single set of proceedings involve more than one cause of action, the court has to exercise a discretion as to the appropriate way in which all issues in the case can be disposed of. That discretion arises even in cases where no question of a right to trial by jury exists. Clarke J stated that

> "the question of whether all issues in a single case which is to be tried by a judge alone should be determined at a single unitary hearing, or in two or more separate hearings, is a matter over which the court retains a discretion which should be exercised, as should all judicial discretion, on a principled basis."

In *Kerwick v Sunday Newspapers Ltd t/a Sunday World* (10 July 2009) HC, Dunne J held that where the plaintiff sued for defamation, breach of the right to privacy and negligent infliction of emotional distress, the interests of justice required a trial of all issues and that such a trial could not be before a jury.

I. What is the Role of the Judge in Defamation Actions?

In defamation actions, the judge plays an important role in initially determining whether or not the words complained of are capable of defamatory meaning. Prior to the 2009 Act, it was for the judge to decide at the outset if the words in question were capable of a defamatory meaning in law. If the judge decided that they were, the matter was then put to the jury. The judge would only withhold the matter from the jury if he or she was satisfied that it would be wholly unreasonable to attribute a defamatory meaning to the words complained of: see *Quigley v Creation Ltd* [1971] IR 269 at 272, per Walsh J. It was also permissible for the trial judge to give a verdict by direction at the end of the plaintiff's case if he or she was satisfied that the words were not capable of bearing the defamatory meaning. In such circumstances, the matter would not be put to the jury: see *Irish Toys and Utilities Ltd v "The Irish Times" Ltd* [1937] IR 298.

Now, under s 14 of the 2009 Act, a motion may be brought at any time during the proceedings requesting the court to determine whether the statement is reasonably capable of bearing a defamatory meaning or the imputation pleaded by the plaintiff. The courts' approach to dealing with s 14 motions can vary. For example, in *McCauley v Power* [2012] IEHC 172, Kearns P approved of Gilligan J's approach in *McGrath v Independent Newspapers* [2004] 2 IR 455 where he said that the judge should put himself in the position of the trier of fact if the matter was at full hearing: the judge should determine the meaning by reference to the fair and natural meaning which would be given to them by reasonable persons of ordinary intelligence, rather than by reference to some "unusual meaning" which a particular individual with an interest in the matter might ascribe to them. However, in *Travers v Sunday Newspapers Ltd* [2012] IEHC 185, Hedigan J thought that a judge should not withdraw a question of meaning from the jury unless it was "wholly unreasonable" to leave it to the jury.

J. Defences in Defamation Actions

Figure 16.2

Part 3 of the 2009 Act places all available defences to defamation on a statutory footing. Section 15 abolishes any defence, other than those based on absolute or qualified privilege, that, prior to the Act, could have been pleaded. The available defences are summarised below.

Truth

Section 16 of the 2009 Act provides the defence of truth. This replaces the old common law defence of justification. The defendant is required to prove the truth of the alleged defamatory statement. It is a full defence. Even if the statement is made maliciously or the defendant believed it to be false when he made it, the defence can be sustained. Once the plaintiff shows that the statement is defamatory, the onus is on the defendant to prove that the statement is true. The defendant is required to prove the truth of the statement "in all material respects". Therefore, minor errors in the defendant's statement will not necessarily be "material" and will not prevent the operation of the defence. For example, in *Alexander v North Eastern Railway Company* (1865) 6 B & S 340, the defendants published a notice at their train station stating the plaintiff had been caught riding on a train without a ticket and was sentenced to a £1 fine or three weeks' imprisonment. In actual fact it was 14 days' imprisonment. The plaintiff complained that the overstatement made it appear as if the offence he had committed was worse than it was. The jury found for the defendants. The error was not sufficiently material to distort the essential truth of the statement. By contrast, in *Gwynn v South Eastern Railway* (1868) 18 LT 738, it was alleged that the plaintiff had been sentenced to a fine of one shilling or to three days' imprisonment "with hard labour" for travelling without a ticket. The allegation of hard labour was, in fact, false. The jury found for the plaintiff and awarded damages of £250. It appears that in this case the words "hard labour" gave a false impression of the gravity of the offence committed.

A more modern example is the case of *Grobbelaar v News Group Newspapers Ltd* [2002] 1 WLR 3024. In this case a former goalkeeper for Liverpool FC was covertly recorded by *The Sun* newspaper admitting to having taken money for losing matches in the past and taking money offered by the newspaper's informant in return for fixing matches in the future. When Grobbelaar was confronted by *The Sun* on the allegations of match-fixing, he denied any wrongdoing. Grobbelaar commenced proceedings for defamation against the defendants. However, before the action could proceed, he was arrested by the police in connection with the newspaper's allegations. He was charged with criminal conspiracy and accepting bribes. He stood trial twice on these charges but was found not guilty of conspiracy by a jury. In addition, he was acquitted of the count of bribe-taking after two juries were split on the issue. The prosecution decided not to pursue the matter further. Grobbelaar subsequently pleaded guilty to a disciplinary charge of assisting in betting brought against him by the Football Association. He then resumed his defamation action. At trial, he established liability before a jury and was awarded £85,000 in damages. The defendants' main defence was that of justification. They appealed to the Court of Appeal and then the House of Lords. The Law Lords thought that there were two aspects to the allegations of defamation the newspaper had made: first, that Grobbelaar had taken bribes, which could not be disputed, and second, that he had fixed or attempted to fix the results of games in which he had played, which could not be proved. The main dispute between the plaintiff and defendants was which of these aspects contained the most serious statement defamatory of the plaintiff. A majority of the House of Lords held for Grobbelaar. They held that the jury could not be criticised for taking the view that the "sting" was the accusation of match fixing. Lord Hobhouse stated (at 3043):

> "Even standing alone, it was a very serious accusation to make against a professional footballer and, if true, completely destructive of his reputation as a professional footballer. A goalkeeper who deliberately lets in goals is betraying the fans and reducing the game to a sham. For myself, I would have been surprised if the jury had come to any other verdict on the justification issue."

Where multiple distinct allegations are made, the defendant may be able to justify some but not others. In those circumstances, he will be liable only for the defamation contained in the allegations which he cannot justify. This would differ from the *Grobbelaar* case where there was one imputation albeit with different aspects. In that case, it was a matter for the jury to determine precisely where in the various statements the "sting" or "barb" actually lay.

If a defendant has made a statement that the plaintiff has committed a crime, the defendant may, by virtue of s 43(2) of the 2009 Act, prove the truth of the statement by relying on the fact of any such conviction before a criminal court. The defendant may also rely on any findings of fact made in the course of any such criminal proceedings in the defamation action.

Absolute Privilege

Article 13.8.1° of the Constitution provides for Presidential privilege. Under this provision, the President is not to be answerable to any court for the exercise and performance of the powers and functions of his or her office or for any act done or purporting to be done by him or her in the exercise and performance of these powers and functions. The general immunity contained in this provision appears to cover defamatory statements made by the President in the course of the exercise and performance of his or her powers and functions as President.

Parliamentary privilege is absolute. It applies to members of the Houses of the Oireachtas and is provided for in Article 15.12 and 15.13 of the Constitution.

Article 15.12 provides that all official reports and publications of the Oireachtas or of either House thereof and utterances made in either House, wherever published, shall be privileged. Article 15.13 provides that the members of each House of the Oireachtas are not amenable to any court or any authority other than the House itself in respect of any utterance made in either House. The modern form of Parliamentary privilege originates from s 1 of the Bill of Rights 1688. Parliamentary privilege extends also to statements made in the European Parliament and its official reports containing such statements (s 17(2)(c) and (d)).

Under s 17(2) of the 2009 Act statements made in the course of judicial proceedings are absolutely privileged. The privilege covers statements made by judges, counsel, witnesses, solicitors, parties, or jurors. It also covers statements made in preparation of the trial and to documents and pleadings connected with the proceedings. Statements made *after* judgment of the court has been given may not be privileged: see *Keenan v Wallace* (1916) 51 ILTR. The absolute immunity of a judge of an inferior court may not be relied upon where he or she acts without jurisdiction and is aware of it: see *Desmond and MCD Management Services Ltd v Riordan* [1999] IEHC 237. In relation to inquests, s 17(2)(r) provides that absolute privilege extends to statements "made in the course of an inquest by a coroner or contained in a decision made or verdict given at or during such inquest". The principles underpinning judicial privilege were famously stated by Lord Tenterden CJ in *Garnett v Ferrand* (1827) 6 B & C 611, 625:

> "This freedom from action and question at the suit of an individual is given by the law to the judges, not so much for their own sake as for the sake of the public, and for the advancement of justice, that being free from actions, they may be free in thought and independence in judgment, as all who are to administer justice ought to be".

The concept of "judicial proceedings" is given a broad meaning in s 17(2). Apart from the inferior and superior courts, the term also covers tribunals established under the Tribunals of Inquiry (Evidence) Acts 1921-2004 where the statement is connected with these proceedings: tribunals, commissions of investigation, inquests before a coroner, or various inquiries established by a minister, the government, the Oireachtas, or a court of the State. Reports of court proceedings are also subject to absolute privilege under s 17(2)(i), but they must be "fair and accurate". Public proceedings only are covered. Accordingly, *in camera* hearings are excluded. Furthermore, any reported statement must actually form part of the proceedings. Therefore, a report of a statement made by non-participant in open court will not be privileged. In *Lynam v Gowing* (1880) 6 LR Ir 259, a bystander in open court accused a witness of perjury. The Court held that the bystander formed no part of the proceedings. A report of the bystander's accusation was not, therefore, protected by privilege.

Qualified Privilege

The defence of qualified privilege is set out in s 18 of the 2009 Act. This defence may be relied upon where there is a duty to receive or interest in receiving the information and a reciprocal duty or interest in the person who publishes the statement to give it. Section 18(7) makes clear that the duty or interest can be of a legal, moral or social nature. This is a restatement of the common law position. The classic statement of the relevant principles at common law was made by Lindley LJ in *Stuart v Bell* [1891] 2 QB 341 at 350:

> "[T]he question of moral or social duty being for the judge, each judge must decide it as best he can for himself. I take moral or social duty to mean a duty recognised by English people of ordinary intelligence and moral principle, but at the same time not a duty enforceable by legal proceedings, whether civil or criminal."

Section 18(2) places the common law test of duty/interest on a statutory basis. It requires the defendant to show that the statement was published to a person who had a duty or interest in receiving the information contained in the statement and that the defendant had a corresponding duty or interest in communicating the statement to such person. The defence will be satisfied if the defendant believed upon reasonable grounds that the person had such a duty or interest in receiving the information contained within the statement. The defence can be defeated by the plaintiff if he can show that the defendant acted with malice in publishing the defamatory statement (s 19). The defence will not be lost, however, by reason only of the fact that the statement was published to a person other than an interested person if it is proved that the statement was so published because the publisher mistook that person for an interested person: see *Hynes-O Sullivan v O'Driscoll* (1989) ILRM 349.

Qualified privilege can also be claimed in relation to statements which are fair and accurate reports of certain public proceedings and which are accorded privilege without explanation or contradiction. Such statements will normally be statements of public concern the publication of which is for the public benefit (s 18(5)). Examples of such statements would be reports of proceedings in foreign courts or legislative chambers, communications from government departments and of international organisations or conferences.

The matter of qualified privilege in respect of political figures was considered by the House of Lords in *Reynolds v Times Newspapers Ltd* [2001] 2 AC 127. This case concerned an article published in *The Times* newspaper about the former Taoiseach, Albert Reynolds. Mr Reynolds claimed that the article in question alleged that he deliberately and dishonestly misled Dáil Éireann, the Cabinet and the then Tánaiste, Mr Dick Spring. Mr Reynolds sued the publishers, the editor and the author for libel. The defence of justification was rejected by the jury at trial. The matter was ultimately appealed to the House of Lords. The defendants argued that defamatory statements made in the course of political discussion should automatically attract qualified privilege. The House of Lords did not accept this proposition. Lord Nicholls sought to clarify the circumstances in which a privileged occasion would exist. He set out a list of ten factors which are important in assessing the reasonableness or fairness of the publication. They are:

1. "The seriousness of the allegation. The more serious the charge, the more the public is misinformed and the individual harmed, if the allegation is not true.

2. The nature of the information, and the extent to which the subject matter is a matter of public concern.

3. The source of the information. Some informants have no direct knowledge of the events. Some have their own axes to grind, or are being paid for their stories.

4. The steps taken to verify the information.

5. The status of the information. The allegation may have already been the subject of an investigation which commands respect.

6. The urgency of the matter. News is often a perishable commodity.

7. Whether comment was sought from the plaintiff. He may have information others do not possess or have not disclosed. An approach to the plaintiff will not always be necessary.

8. Whether the article contained the gist of the plaintiff's side of the story.

9. The tone of the article. A newspaper can raise queries or call for an investigation. It need not adopt allegations as statements of fact.

10. The circumstances of the publication, including the timing.

This list is not exhaustive. The weight that should be given to these, and any other relevant factors, will vary from case to case."

Lord Nicholls also stated that any

"court should be slow to conclude that a publication was not in the public interest and, therefore, the public had no right to know, especially when the information is in the field of political discussion".

He appeared to envisage that a liberal approach be taken in relation to defending comments made about political figures. In *Jameel v Wall Street Journal Europe SPRL*

[2006] UKHL 44, [2007] 1 AC 359 the House of Lords affirmed that it favoured greater freedom of discussion of matters of public interest. Lord Bingham emphasised that the *Reynolds* factors were not to be seen as a "series of hurdles to be negotiated by a publisher" in order for that publisher to be able to rely on the privilege. Rather, he thought, the factors consisted of "matters which might be taken into account". He also stressed the need of the court to place weight upon "editorial decisions and judgments made at the time, without the knowledge of falsity which is a benefit of hindsight".

In *Jameel* Lord Hoffmann applied the *Reynolds* test. He summarised it as two broad questions:

1. Is the matter commented upon one of public interest? In seeking to determine this, it is necessary to look at the article as a whole. The article could still be of public interest even if it contains minor inaccuracies in the narrative. Whether the matter was one of public interest was a matter of law for the judge.
2. If the answer to the first question was that a public interest existed, the following question had to be addressed: Had appropriate steps been taken to gather and publish the information in a responsible and fair manner that would be consistent with the standards of responsible journalism? If such standards had been reached, then privilege would apply to the publication. The ten factors set out by Lord Nicholls (see above) in *Reynolds* would be particularly relevant to this second question.

The defence of qualified privilege came before the Irish courts in *Leech v Independent Newspapers* [2007] IEHC 223. In that case, the defendants published a report of a statement made on a radio programme that the plaintiff had had an improper relationship with a government minister and that the plaintiff had received government work as a result of that relationship. The statement was false. The Court was required to determine as a preliminary matter whether a "public interest" defence was available to the defendant as a matter of law. Charleton J followed Lord Hoffman's approach in *Jameel*. It stipulates that "weight should ordinarily be given to the professional judgment of an editor or journalist in the absence of some indication that it was made in a casual, cavalier, slipshod or careless manner". Charleton J held that a publisher in seeking to invoke the public interest defence had to demonstrate:

1. that the subject matter of the publication was a matter of public interest; and
2. that he acted responsibly in accordance with proper standards of journalism.

Section 26 of the 2009 Act, which deals with fair and reasonable publication on a matter of public interest, appears to correspond to the *Reynolds/Jameel* defence in that it limits the defence to publication to statements published

(a) "in good faith" and
(b) "in the course of, or for the purpose of, the discussion of a subject of public interest, the discussion of which was for the public benefit".

The defendant is also obliged to demonstrate that, in all the circumstances, it was fair and reasonable to publish the statement. This is a matter to be determined by the court, taking into account Lord Nicholls' ten factors. Section 26(2) largely reflects *Jameel* to the extent that that the range of factors listed there are issues for consideration and not hurdles to be overcome. Section 26(3) makes clear that failure or refusal of a plaintiff to respond to attempts by or on behalf of the defendant to elicit the plaintiff's version of events shall not constitute or imply consent to publication or entitle the court to draw an inference therefrom.

As mentioned above, two kinds of reports are given qualified privilege by s 18 of the 2009 Act. Schedule 1, Parts 1 and 2 of the Act sets out a list of the two kinds of reports. They are:

(1) statements privileged without explanation or contradiction; and
(2) statements privileged subject to explanation or contradiction.

Statements in the second category are protected by qualified privilege except where:

> "it is proved that the defendant was requested by the plaintiff to publish...a reasonable statement by way of explanation or contradiction, and has refused or failed to do so or has done so in a manner that is not adequate or reasonable having regard to all the circumstances" (s 18(4)).

Honest Opinion

Section 20 of the 2009 Act provides the defence of "honest opinion". This defence will be available where the defendant proves that, in the case of the statement consisting of an opinion, the opinion was honestly held. Although this provision relates to opinions, it is clear that the opinion must have a basis in fact (s 20(2)). At the time of the publication the defendant must have believed in the truth of the opinion or, where the defendant is not the author of the opinion, believed that the author believed it to be true (s 20(2)(a)). Furthermore, the opinion must relate to a matter of public interest (s 20(3)(c)). Section 20(2)(b)(i) specifies that the opinion must be based on allegations of fact of one or other (or both) of the following two categories:

(i) The first category relates to facts specified in the statement containing the opinion, or referred to in that statement and which were known, or might reasonably be expected to have been known, by persons to whom the statement was published. In these cases, the defendant, by virtue of s 20(3)(a), must prove the truth of the facts supporting the opinion or, if he or she does not prove all the allegations of fact, the opinion is nevertheless honestly held having regard to the allegations of fact that have been proved.

(ii) The second category relates to facts to which the defence of privilege, absolute or qualified, would apply if a defamation action were brought in respect of the allegations. In these cases, the defendant, by virtue of s 20(3)(b), must prove either (i) the truth of the facts or (ii) that the opinion could not reasonably be understood as implying that they were true and that, at the time of publication, the defendant did not know or could not reasonably have been expected to know that the allegations were untrue.

Section 21 of the Act provides guidance to the court as to distinguishing between allegations of fact and opinion. It states that the matters to which the court shall have regard are to include the following:

(a) the extent to which the statement is capable of being proved;

(b) the extent to which the statement was made in circumstances in which it was likely to have been reasonably understood as a statement of opinion rather than a statement consisting of an allegation of fact; and

(c) the words used in the statement and the extent to which the statement was subject to a qualification or a disclaimer or was accompanied by cautionary words.

Offer to Make Amends

Section 22 of the Act provides for the defence of "an offer to make amends". The offer must be in writing. It must state that it is an "offer to make amends" for the purpose of the section. It must also state whether it is in respect of the entire statement or is a "qualified offer" only in respect of: (a) part of the statement; or (b) a particular defamatory meaning only. The offer can be made at any time before delivery of the defence. The offer can be withdrawn before it is accepted. It is permissible to then make a new offer. Section 22(5) states that "an offer to make amends" means an offer:

(a) to make a suitable correction and a sufficient apology;

(b) to publish that correction and apology in such manner as is reasonable and practicable in the circumstances; and

(c) to pay such sum in compensation or damages (if any) and costs, as may be agreed by them or as may be determined to be payable,

whether or not it is accompanied by any other offer to perform an act other than an act referred to in paragraph (a), (b) or (c).

Section 23 sets out the effect of an offer to make amends. If the offer is accepted by the plaintiff, compliance can be enforced by the High Court. Any disagreement as to how the offer is to be implemented can be determined by the court. This can include the amount of damages to be paid. If, however, the offer of amends is rejected by the plaintiff, the offer can operate as a defence against any action taken by the plaintiff, unless it can be shown that the defendant knew, or ought reasonably to have known, at the time of the publication that: it referred to the plaintiff or was likely to be understood as referring to the plaintiff; and it was false and defamatory of the plaintiff. A defendant who makes an offer of amends is not obliged to rely upon the defence in a trial of the action (s 22(4)), but where the defence is pleaded, the defendant is precluded from relying on any other defence (s 22(5)).

Apology

Section 24 of the 2009 Act provides for the defence of apology. Section 24(1) sets out the essence of the defence: the defendant may give evidence, in mitigation of damages, that he or she made or offered an apology to the plaintiff for the offending statement and published the apology or offered to do so with similar or the same prominence as the offending statement, and that it was done "as soon as practicable" after the complaint was made or after the action was brought, whichever is earlier. Section 24(3) makes clear that an apology does not constitute an express or implied admission of liability and is not relevant to the determination of liability in the action. Section 24(4) provides that evidence of such apology is not admissible in other civil proceedings as evidence of the defendant's liability.

An apology was offered in *McDaid v The Examiner* (18 November 1999) HC. In that case, the defendant newspaper published an article on its front page with the following headline: "Gardaí must get complaints before taking action. He knows who the sex monsters are, but he won't tell the Gardaí". The article alleged that the plaintiff, a government minister, would not hand over to Gardaí the details of two persons accused of sexually abusing young children. On the following day, the newspaper published an apology which said the article the previous day was inaccurate and wrongly suggested the minister was aware of the identities of the two persons in question. The defendant also acknowledged that the Murphy Report (into alleged sexual abuse of young children) did not in fact identify the alleged abusers. During the hearing, the plaintiff gave evidence that, as a result of the article, he was verbally abused in Grafton Street, Dublin, during which he was called "child abuser" and "paedophile" and was threatened at the Leopardstown Races. The judge told the jury that the only issue to be tried was how much the plaintiff was to receive in damages. The judge also told the jury that they had to be fair to the plaintiff who, without doubt, had been libelled, but they also had to be fair to the newspaper, which carried a front page apology. The jury awarded the plaintiff £90,000 in damages.

Consent

Section 25 of the 2009 Act provides for the "defence of consent". This defence is available where the plaintiff consented to the publication. Whilst consent to publication will constitute a good defence against a defamation action, the failure or refusal of a plaintiff to respond to attempts by the defendant to elicit the plaintiff's version of events will not constitute or imply consent to the publication of the statement.

Fair and Reasonable Publication

Under s 26, a defendant can rely on the defence of "fair and reasonable publication" if he or she can show the following:

(a) that the statement was published in good faith;

(b) in the course of, or for the purpose of, discussing a subject of public interest, the discussion of which was for the public benefit;

(c) the manner and extent of publication of the statement did not exceed that which was reasonably sufficient; and

(d) it was fair and reasonable to publish the statement.

In determining whether it was fair and reasonable to publish the statement, the court is required to take into consideration a number of factors. These include: the extent to which the statement concerned refers to the performance by the person of his or her public functions; the context of the statement and the attempts made, and the means used, by the defendant to verify the assertions and allegations concerning the plaintiff in the statement. These factors echo the factors listed by Lord Nicholls in *Reynolds* (see above). Again, the failure or refusal of a plaintiff to respond to attempts by the defendant to elicit the plaintiff's version of events shall not entitle the court to draw any inference therefrom (s 26 (3)).

Innocent Publication

Section 27 of the Act provides the statutory defence of "innocent publication". In order to invoke this defence, a defendant must show:

(a) that he or she was not the author, editor or publisher of the statement to which the action relates;

(b) that he or she took reasonable care in relation to its publication; and

(c) that he or she had no reason to believe that what he or she did caused or contributed to the publication of a statement that would give rise to a cause of action in defamation.

For the purposes of determining whether the defendant took reasonable care, the court will look to the extent of the person's responsibility for the content of the statement or the decision to publish it, the nature or circumstances of the publication, and the previous conduct or character of the person.

The E-Commerce Directive

In addition to the statutory defences in the 2009 Act, the Directive on e-Commerce, transposed into Irish law by the European Communities (Directive 2000/31/EEC) Regulations 2003 (SI No 68 of 2003), provides "relevant service providers" with exclusions of liability when they are mere conduits or when they are "caching" or "hosting" material. "Hosting" has been defined as an activity in which data is stored by an intermediary for a period rather than just passing through the intermediary. "Acting as a mere conduit" involves the automatic, intermediate and transient storage of information transmitted for the sole purpose of carrying out the transmission. "Caching" is defined as a process which enables Internet providers to speed up the delivery of webpages to Internet users by making a temporary copy of the webpage that is requested by a user (Clarke J in *Mulvaney v The Sporting Exchange Ltd trading as Betfair* [2011] 1 IR 85, para 12).

K. Remedies

Figure 16.3

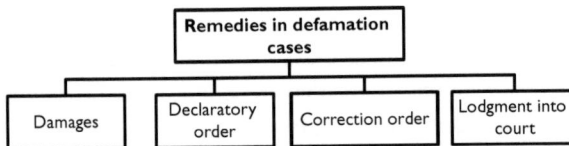

General

Monetary compensation in the form of general damages is the normal remedy available to successful plaintiffs in defamation actions. The Defamation Act 2009 has, however, made available other remedies to a successful plaintiff. These include declaratory orders (s 28) and correction orders (s 30). In addition, s 29 of the 2009 Act provides that a defendant may pay a sum of money into court (a "lodgment") in satisfaction of the claim when it is filing its defence.

Damages

Figure 16.4

```
                        ┌─────────────────────┐
                        │ Categories of Damages │
                        └─────────────────────┘
```

General	Special	Aggravated	Punitive
Compensates for injury to reputation	Compensates for financial loss	Defendant's defence aggravates injury to Plaintiff	Defendant was wilful or reckless as to publication
s 31(3), (4)	s 31(7)	s 32(1)	s 32(2)

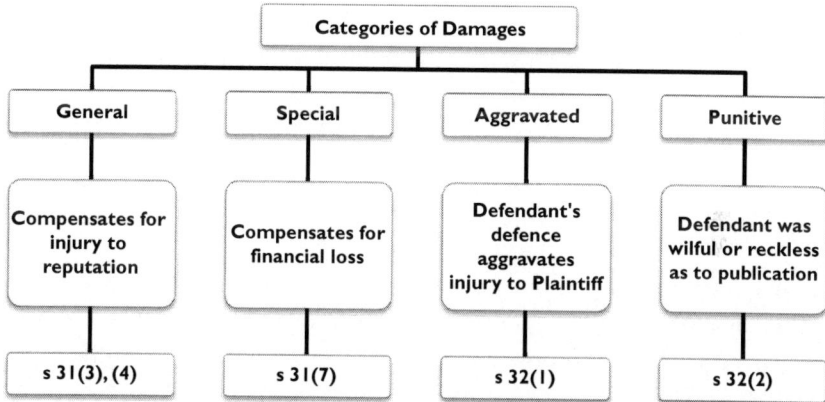

As mentioned, the normal remedy in defamation actions is damages. Section 31 of the 2009 Act allows parties to make submissions to the court in respect of the matter of damages and, where the action is brought in the High Court, the judge shall give directions to the jury on the issue. When making an award of general damages, the court is required to have regard to all the circumstances of the case. In addition, s 31(4) sets out eleven instances of circumstances that should be taken into account. Such instances include: the nature and gravity of the allegation; the enduring nature of the publication and the extent to which it was circulated; whether any apology was offered; the importance of the plaintiff's reputation in the eyes of recipients of the statement; whether the plaintiff contributed to the publication of the statement.

Section 31(5) states that if the defamatory nature of the statement is not obvious to everyone, but is limited to a small group of people who may be aware of special facts then the publication will be treated as having been published to that limited audience only. By virtue of s 31(7), the court may make an award of "special damages" to the plaintiff in respect of financial loss "suffered by him or her as a result of injury to his or her reputation caused by the publication of the defamatory statement…".

Traditionally, juries in defamation cases have been given significant latitude in determining the level of damages. This is because the jury is the representative of the community and the members thereof are best placed to determine the extent to which a plaintiff's reputation has been injured, and, accordingly, the extent of compensation payable. The role of the judge is largely confined to ensuring that the jury considers only statements that are capable of defamatory meaning. Juries do not, however, have an entirely free hand in determining the level of damages. For example, in *Barratt v Independent Newspapers Ltd* [1986] IR 13, the Supreme Court struck down as excessive a jury award of £65,000 to a politician about whom a journalist had made an allegation of a "minor unpremeditated assault" (pulling at the defendant's beard). In that case, Henchy J stated that juries had to be

> "told that they must make their assessment entirely on the facts as found by them, and they must be given such direction on the law as will enable them to reach a proper assessment on the basis of those facts."

He went on to give examples of relevant considerations the jury should take into account in determining the appropriate level of damages. These are now echoed in s 31(4) of the 2009 Act (see above). The thrust of Henchy J's judgment was that objective proportionality was a key principle in seeking to determine the quantum of damages appropriate in any given case. The Supreme Court reinforced this view in *De Rossa* when it was invited on appeal by the defendants to reduce the £300,000 in damages awarded to the plaintiff by the jury in that case. The Supreme Court declined that invitation stating that the approach of the Irish courts in respect of damages in defamation actions was consistent with Article 10 of the European Convention on Human Rights, the common law, and the Constitution ([1999] 4 IR 432 at 450).

Despite judicial guidance in relation to objective proportionality, juries have made some exceptionally large awards in Irish cases. Some examples are set out below:

Case	Award
De Rossa v Independent Newspapers plc [1999] 4 IR 432	£300,000
McDonagh v News Group Newspapers Ltd (23 November 1993)	£300,000
O'Brien v Mirror Group Newspapers Ltd [2002] 1 IR 1	£250,000
O'Brien v Mirror Group Newspapers Ltd (23 November 2003) (retrial of the above action)	£750,000
Kinsella v Kenmare Resources (17 November 2012)	€10 million
Leech v Independent Newspapers (24 June 2009)	€1.872 million
McDonagh v Sunday World (28 February 2008)	£900,000

Note: these awards were made at first instance and may have been subject to reduction on appeal.

Declaratory Order

Section 28 of the 2009 Act provides that a person may apply to the Circuit Court for a declaratory order confirming that the statement in question is false and defamatory of the applicant. If the court is satisfied that the statement is defamatory and that the respondent has no defence, and, when called upon, the respondent has failed to make and publish an apology, correction or retraction, or has failed to make an appropriate response with the same prominence as the original statement, the court "shall" make the order. Any applicant who pursues this remedy is precluded from bringing any other proceedings in respect of any cause of action arising out of the statement in question. In addition, the court is precluded from making an order for damages when this remedy is pursued, although it can make a correction order and an order prohibiting further publication.

Correction Order

Section 30 of the 2009 Act provides that, where in the course of the trial there is a finding that:

(a)   the offending statement was defamatory, and
(b)   the defendant has no defence to the action,

the court may, on the application of the plaintiff, make an order directing the defendant to publish a correction. The correction order will specify:

(a)   the date and time upon which the period within which the correction order shall be published and
(b)   the form, content, extent and manner of publication of the correction.

Lodgment into Court

Section 29(4) provides that a defendant may pay a sum of money into court in satisfaction of the claim when it is filing its defence. A lodgment can be made without admission of liability. The plaintiff may, of course, refuse to accept the lodgment and pursue the matter to full trial. However, if the plaintiff is ultimately successful at trial and any award of damages is less than the lodgment, the plaintiff will be penalised by having to pay his or her own costs and the costs the defendant has incurred from the date of the lodgment.

An interesting example of the operation of the lodgment (or "payment in") system in England is *Roache v News Group Newspapers Limited* [1998] EMLR 161. In that case, the plaintiff, William Roache, was a well-known actor in the television drama series *Coronation Street*. The defendants had published an article in *The Sun* newspaper alleging that he was boring, self-satisfied and hated by the other members of the cast. The plaintiff brought proceedings for libel. Three weeks before trial the defendants made a lodgment of £50,000 into Court in full and final settlement of the plaintiff's claim. The plaintiff refused to accept and proceeded to full trial. At trial, the jury awarded the plaintiff precisely the same sum — £50,000. A dispute between the plaintiff and defendants then arose as to whether the plaintiff had actually beaten the lodgment of £50,000. The plaintiff claimed that he had exceeded it because he had been awarded an injunction as well. Ultimately, the Court of Appeal held that the defendants had been the substantial winners at trial in that they had held the award to a sum no greater than what was already on offer. The Court of Appeal took the view that the injunction was of no significance because the defendants did not intend to re-publish anyway. In addition, the Court was satisfied that the main reason the plaintiff pursued the matter to full trial was for larger damages. Accordingly, the defendants were entitled to their costs from the date of the payment in. The plaintiff, therefore, had to pay his own legal costs of £120,000 plus the costs of the defendants from the date of the payment in. Although this case is a rather extreme and unusual one, it does illustrate the risks plaintiffs may run in not accepting payments into court in full and final settlement of claims.

Privacy

Learning Outcomes

Upon completion of this chapter, the reader should be able to:

- Identify the various legal routes available to protect privacy;
- Describe the operation of specific torts in relation to privacy issues;
- Explain the role of "breach of confidence" in the protection of privacy;
- Explain how the Constitution protects the privacy rights of citizens;
- Appreciate the role of the European Convention on Human Rights in respect of privacy matters;
- Discuss evolving rights to privacy at common law.

A. Protection of Privacy

The Irish courts have developed a constitutional right to privacy, although the precise parameters of this right have yet to be fully determined. Some protection for privacy interests is afforded by wide range of existing torts, for example negligence, malicious falsehood, private nuisance, the intentional infliction of mental suffering, trespass to the person, trespass to goods, conversion, detinue, and trespass to land. Breach of statutory duty and breach of confidence may also provide avenues for the protection of private interests.

Figure 17.1

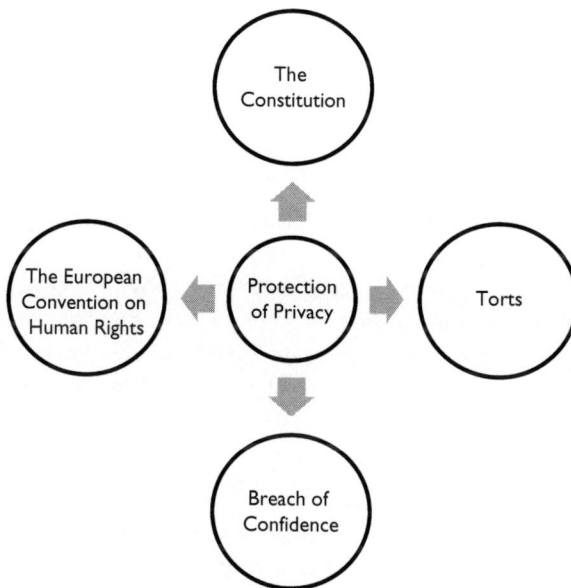

Negligence

The tort of negligence was successfully invoked to protect the privacy of the plaintiff in *Hanahoe v Hussey* [1998] 3 IR 69. In that case, a firm of solicitors was awarded £100,000 in damages in a privacy case due to the negligence of members of An Garda Síochána. The firm was due to be subjected to a search under the provisions of s 64 of the Criminal Justice Act 1994. The fact that the search was due to take place was leaked to the media by one or more members of the Gardaí. This resulted in the search taking place in the full glare of a "media scrum" which gave rise to damaging publicity for the firm. Kinlen J described the behaviour of the Gardaí as an "outrageous interference with [the firm's] privacy and their constitutional rights".

Negligent interference with a privacy interest may result in economic loss, physical or psychiatric injury. The main issue in such cases will be for the court to determine whether or not the defendant owes the plaintiff a duty of care in respect of privacy.

Malicious Falsehood

The tort of malicious falsehood may be invoked where there is the publication of intrusive personal information. The essentials of this tort are that the defendant has published about the plaintiff words which are false; that they were published maliciously, and that special damage has followed as the direct and natural result of their publication. In *Kaye v Robertson* [1991] FSR 62, the plaintiff was a well-known actor who had undergone extensive surgery on his head after an object had fallen through his car windscreen in a storm. The first defendant was the editor of *The Sunday Sport*, a tabloid renowned for "far-fetched scoops" and "advertisements for pornographic material".

While the plaintiff was in hospital recovering from his injuries, journalists from the first defendant's newspaper gained access to his private hospital room, ignoring the notices prohibiting such entry. They interviewed the plaintiff at length and took photographs using flash photography before being ejected by security staff. The Court found that the plaintiff was in no condition to give any informed consent to their interviewing or photographing him. In finding for the plaintiff, the Court held that all the elements of a claim of malicious falsehood had been made out.

Private Nuisance

The tort of private nuisance may afford a remedy against a wide range of intrusions which impact upon a person's ability to live peaceably in his or her home. But there are limits as to how far private nuisance can go in terms of protecting privacy. For example, the tort cannot be availed of to protect a resident from being overlooked by neighbouring properties. In *Fleming v Rathdown School Trust* (unreported, 6 April 1993), Denham J cited *Halsbury's Laws of England* (4th ed.), Vol 34, para 327 which says:

> "[w]here there is no infringement of a right to light, and where the act complained of is otherwise lawful, no action lies for the invasion of privacy by the opening of windows or for the destruction of a view or prospect, even though the value of a house or premises may be diminished thereby."

In *Lord Bernstein of Leigh v Skyview & General Ltd* [1978] QB 479, where the plaintiff's house was photographed from a helicopter hovering above, Griffiths J said:

"... no court would regard the taking of a single photograph as an actionable nuisance. But if the circumstances were such that a plaintiff was subjected to the harassment of constant surveillance of his home from the air, accompanied by the photographing of his every activity, I am far from saying that the courts would not regard such a monstrous invasion of his privacy as an actionable nuisance..."

Another important limitation in respect of the application of private nuisance to protect privacy is that of who may sue. In England, in *Hunter v Canary Wharf Ltd* [1997] AC 655, the House of Lords made it clear that only those with exclusive possession will be entitled to sue. In Ireland, by virtue of the decision in *Hanrahan v Merck Sharp & Dohme (Ireland) Ltd* [1988] ILRM 629, it appears that family members, regardless of legal title, may sue.

Furthermore, if the defendant interferes with the plaintiff's privacy from a neighbouring property, this may amount to a private nuisance. The defendant would not need to be in occupation of that property: see *Southport Corporation v Esso Petroleum Co Ltd* [1956] AC 218. In *Hubbard v Pitt* [1976] 1 QB 142, the Court held that picketers, who were unhappy with certain developments in an area and were watching and besetting an estate agent's premises from the pavement, were engaged in activity which could amount to a private nuisance.

Wilkinson v Downton

The tort of intentional infliction of physical or emotional harm established in *Wilkinson v Downton* [1897] 2 QB 57 has the capacity to protect privacy interests in a limited way. There, the landlord of a public house went away for the day leaving his wife behind the bar. A customer decided to play a practical joke on her by telling her that her husband had been involved in a road accident in which he had been seriously injured. The story was completely false. The landlord's wife suffered severe shock and became so ill that for some time her life was thought to be in danger. She sued and was awarded damages for nervous shock. In *Janvier v Sweeney* [1919] 2 KB 316, the tort operated to control improper methods of investigation. However, in *Wainwright v Home Office* [2003] UKHL 53, where the plaintiff's privacy had been invaded through intrusive body searches at a prison, the House of Lords took the view that the application of *Wilkinson* in such cases would not be necessary because the law of negligence would offer an adequate remedy for any psychiatric injury suffered.

The New Zealand Court of Appeal has also considered the issue of invasion of privacy in this context. *Hosking v Runting* [2004] NZCA 34 concerned the publication of photographs taken on a public street without the photographed persons, or rather their guardian, being aware of being photographed. The Court approved the lower Court's refusal to grant an injunction on a different legal basis than was chosen at first instance, though reaching the same the result. There was no binding precedent of direct relevance to the New Zealand Court of Appeal, as, up until then, invasion of personal privacy had only been dealt with at High Court level, apart the Court of Appeal in *Tucker v News Media Ltd* [1986] 2 NZLR 716. In that case, McGechan J stated that the "courts are being forced into a position where they must soon create a new law" if no legislative action is taken to protect privacy. McGechan J also said that he did not think it was beyond the common law to adapt the *Wilkinson* principles to significantly develop to meet the needs of individuals whose privacy had been invaded. He upheld an interim injunction on the grounds that the existence of a privacy tort was "a seriously arguable question".

In Ireland, in *Sullivan v Boylan (No 2)* [2013] IEHC 104, the Court opted to provide a remedy under Article 40.5 and Article 40.3.2° of the Constitution. That case concerned a debt collector who had harassed and intimidated the plaintiff in her home by repeatedly contacting her and besetting her home. *Wilkinson* was distinguished on the basis that the defendant had not made false statements and the plaintiff had suffered acute distress rather than physical injury.

Trespass to the Person

Medical intervention without the consent of the patient may intrude upon a range of constitutional rights, in particular those of personal autonomy and privacy. The effectiveness of torts falling under the rubric of trespass to the person which require physical contact or an apprehension of physical contact can limit their effectiveness in the context of protecting personal privacy.

Tort Affecting Interests in Goods

Other torts, such as trespass to goods, conversion and detinue also afford some protection against invasions of privacy. In the *People (DPP) v Morgan* (1980) 114 ILTR, an employer surreptitiously searched the handbag of an employee who was suspected by her employer of dishonesty. At the criminal trial for embezzlement, the Court excluded the evidence obtained through those searches. Sheridan J said:

> "... an examination of the private effects of another person is clearly
> an act of trespass. In the case of a lady's handbag which is often a
> receptacle for the most private documents and effects apart from
> money, I cannot think of many better examples of gross trespass..."

Accordingly, if a person takes another person's diary and reads it, the victim will be able to sue the wrongdoer for trespass and obtain damages, notwithstanding the fact that no damage will have been done to the diary. If, however, the same information is obtained simply by looking over the shoulder of the person as he or she writes in the diary, a trespass will not have occurred.

Trespass to Land

Trespass to land offers protection to privacy interests (provided the plaintiff has the requisite possession), in that wrongful entry onto property is actionable *per se*. However, the tort of trespass does not extend to surveillance activities conducted outside the boundaries of the property. That is not to say that the tort of trespass to land can never be invoked when surveillance occurs from outside the boundaries of that property. It will be recalled that in *Hickman v Maisey* [1900] 1 QB 752 an occupier of land successfully sued the defendant who was misusing the highway in spying upon the plaintiff's racehorse trials. There was no ambiguity as to the defendant's misuse of the highway because he was using binoculars, taking notes, and had spent a significant amount of time standing outside the premises occupied by the plaintiff. A misuse of the highway, however, will not occur in circumstances where passing members of the public peer into a person's living room, thus interfering with their privacy: see *Browne v Dowie* (1959) 93 ILTR 179. In *Lord Bernstein of Leigh v Skyviews & General Ltd* [1978] 1 QB 479, the plaintiff's house was photographed from the air. Although this was an incursion into the plaintiff's airspace, the plaintiff's action in this case failed because the incursion was over the maximum height "necessary for the ordinary use and enjoyment" of the property.

Breach of Statutory Duty

Under some statutory provisions, disclosure of confidential information may amount to an offence: see for example the Postal and Telecommunications Services Act, s 37; the Garda Síochána (Complaints) Act 1986, s 12; the Adoption Act 2010, s 89 (2). Whether victims of wrongful disclosure have a private right of action depends on the statute. Some statutes could be construed by the courts as providing one: other statutes expressly afford such a remedy. The constitutional right to privacy in one's private communications might be applicable in such cases: see *Kennedy and Arnold v Ireland* [1987] IR 587 (below).

B. Breach of Confidence

Breach of confidence is a wrong, based upon the breach of a duty to keep confidence arising from a confidential situation, transaction, or relationship. Originally, breach of confidence was actionable in equity and the remedy available was an injunction. In recent times, however, it is likely to result in a claim for damages. The authorities indicate that breach of confidence was not a tort, but a restitutionary claim for unjust enrichment, i.e. an action to restore a gain made by a wrongful acquisition. More recent English case law suggests that breach of confidence may have evolved into a tort of misuse of private information.

Traditionally, this action has been founded upon the unauthorised use of information of a confidential nature when the defendant is said to be under a duty of confidentiality, usually based upon a relationship. For example, in *Prince Albert v Strange* (1849) De G & Sm 652, the English royal family obtained an injunction prohibiting the unauthorised publication of family caricatures made for family and friends by Prince Albert and Queen Victoria. Here, the information was disclosed to a printer by a servant. In *Duchess of Argyll v Duke of Argyll* [1967] Ch 302, intimate aspects of a marriage were the subject of a successful breach of confidence action. There, the duty of confidentiality was seen to be intrinsic to the relationship of husband and wife. It will be noted that, in contrast to actions in defamation, actions concerning issues of privacy are not based on allegations that the subject matter concerned is untrue.

In *Coco v AN Clark (Engineers) Ltd* [1968] FSR 415 at 419-420, Megarry J stated the ingredients of breach of confidence as follows:

> "... three elements are normally required if, apart from contract, a case of breach of confidence is to succeed. First, the information itself... must have the necessary quality of confidence about it. Secondly, that information must have been imparted in circumstances importing an obligation of confidence. Thirdly, there must be an unauthorised use of that information to the detriment of the party communicating it."

In *Mahon v Post Publications Ltd* [2005] IEHC 307, the Supreme Court essentially approved Megarry J's formulation as follows:

(1) "The information must in fact be confidential or secret: it must, to quote Lord Greene, 'have the necessary quality of confidence about it';

(2) It must have been communicated by the possessor of the information in circumstances which impose an obligation of confidence or trust on the person receiving it;

(3) It must be wrongfully communicated by the person receiving it or by another person who is aware of the obligation of confidence."

Commercial Relationships

Information may be confidential as a result of a commercial relationship. This was the case in *House of Spring Gardens v Point-Blank Ltd* [1984] IR 611. There, the plaintiffs had entered into a commercial relationship with the defendants. The plaintiffs claimed that the defendants had subsequently misused information they had obtained about a product the plaintiffs had developed. The Court found for the plaintiffs on the basis that "a great deal of confidential information" which had been given to the defendants in the course of the commercial relationship had been misused by them.

In the more recent case of *Douglas v Hello!* [2002] QB 967, actors Michael Douglas and Catherine Zeta-Jones sold the exclusive rights to publish a selection of photographs of their wedding to *OK!* magazine. An unauthorised photographer secretly took photographs of the occasion, which were later published by *OK!*'s rival, *Hello!* magazine. This resulted in a series of legal actions. The plaintiffs sought to obtain an interim injunction to prevent the publication of the photographs in *Hello!* The English Court of Appeal refused to uphold the interim injunction on the grounds that the plaintiffs' interests would be adequately protected by damages, while the magazine would suffer disproportionate losses should the injunction be upheld. Since the couple had already given permission for their wedding to have a certain amount of publicity, any residual interest in privacy did not warrant an injunction. It was considered that the law of breach of confidence covered the situation. Sedley LJ said:

> "We have reached a point where it can be said with confidence that the law recognises and will appropriately protect a right of personal privacy."

However, the House of Lords in *Campbell v Mirror Group Newspapers* [2004] UKHL 22 rejected the sweeping nature of this proposition. In that case, the plaintiff, model Naomi Campbell, had publicly stated that she did not use drugs. The *Mirror* newspaper subsequently published an article describing Miss Campbell's "courageous bid to beat addiction to drink and drugs" accompanied by a photograph of her leaving a Narcotics Anonymous meeting. The plaintiff claimed damages for breach of confidence. She succeeded in the House of Lords. Their Lordships thought that, in view of the fact that her drug addiction and treatment was "open to public comment in view of her denials", the statements were not unduly intrusive. However, the disclosure of details of her treatment, accompanied by the secretly taken photograph, was more than just "peripheral" to the main story and went beyond merely setting the record straight. This could have disrupted her therapy and could not therefore be justified.

Their Lordships concluded that although "there was no overarching, all embracing cause of action of 'invasion of privacy'", they considered that there was a right against "wrongful disclosure of private information". The test was essentially subjective (based on the plaintiff's expectation), limited by the requirement that this expectation be reasonable and that the defendant knew or ought to have known about that expectation (see the recent case of *Vidal Hall and Ors v Google Inc* [2014] EWHC 13 (QB) below).

Public Interest

In *Cogley v RTÉ* [2005] IR 79, the defendants carried out secret filming in a nursing home for the purposes of a television documentary. The defendants were trespassers in doing so. The owners of the nursing home claimed that the patients' and owners' right to privacy had been breached. In refusing to grant an injunction to prevent broadcast and approving the New Zealand case of *TV3 Network Services Ltd. v Fahey* [1999] 2 NZLR 129, Clarke J held that any measures which would represent an excessive or unreasonable interference with the conditions necessary for a vigorous and informed debate on matters of public importance required very substantial justification. He also thought that a distinction must be drawn, particularly on an interlocutory application, between a situation in which the right to privacy was alleged to exist over the information in question and a situation in which the information might properly be the subject of public debate on a matter of public importance, but the manner in which it was obtained was alleged to constitute a breach of the right to privacy.

Also, in *Sinnott v Carlow Nationalist* (*Irish Independent*, 27 January 2007, *The Irish Times*, 7 July 2008), a local newspaper, the *Carlow Nationalist*, published a photograph taken of the plaintiff whilst he was playing a football match during which his private parts became visible. This was held by both the Circuit Court and the High Court on appeal to be a breach of the plaintiff's privacy. Liability was imposed and damages awarded notwithstanding the fact that the plaintiff was in a public place at the time the photograph had been taken. It is important to note that just because one is in a public place, one does not lose one's right to privacy. For instance, if a person is photographed in a state of undress in public because he or she has suffered a trauma as a consequence of an accident, such circumstances would clearly indicate that there is no consent to being photographed in that way. The expectation of privacy would remain.

C. English Developments: A "Tort of Misuse of Private Information"

The English courts have recently considered the question of tortious liability in respect of misuse of private information. This is a developing area of the law in England, which is happening in parallel with the application of the UK Human Rights Act 1998 in privacy actions. In *Vidal Hall and Ors v Google Inc* [2014] EWHC

13 (QB), a group of UK Google users called "Safari Users Against Google's Secret Tracking" claimed that the tracking and collation of information about of their internet usage by Google amounted to a misuse of personal information and a breach of the UK Data Protection Act 1998. The Court confirmed that misuse of personal information was a distinct tort. The Court held that the fact that Google had on other occasions interfered with people's privacy rights was not a basis on which the Court could contemplate issuing an injunction in the instant case. The Court also observed that there could be no real dispute that the claim for breach of confidence was not a claim in tort. With regard to the misuse of private information, the Court acknowledged that there was no general "tort of invasion of privacy" in English law. However, the Court cited Lord Nicholls in *Campbell v MGN Ltd* [2004] UKHL 22 (see above) to the effect that while the origin of the Court's protection against the wrongful use of private information lay in the equitable action of breach of confidence based on an initial confidential relationship, the "essence of the tort is better now encapsulated as misuse of private information."

D. The Constitutional Right to Privacy

There is a constitutional right to privacy, but it is not an unqualified right. It is a right which must be balanced against other constitutional rights, such as freedom of expression. It is also subject to the requirements of public order, public morality and common good. The recognition of a right to privacy can be seen in a number of cases. In *McGee v Attorney General* [1974] IR 284, the Court found that there was a right to privacy in marriage by virtue of the provisions of Article 40.3. Subsequently, in *Norris v The Attorney General* [1984] I. 36 at 71, Henchy J stated:

> "Amongst those basic personal [constitutional] rights is a complex of rights which vary in nature, purpose and range (each necessarily being a facet of the citizen's core of individuality within the constitutional order) and which may be compendiously referred to as the right of privacy."

The Court unambiguously recognised a constitutional right to privacy in respect of communications in *Kennedy and Arnold v Ireland* [1987] IR 587. There, the plaintiffs brought proceedings for damages for the unlawful tapping of their telephones by servants of the State. The Court, holding that there was a constitutional right to privacy and, though not specifically guaranteed by the Constitution, stated that it was one of the personal rights of the citizen which flowed from the Christian and democratic nature of the State. This constitutional right to privacy included the right to hold private telephone conversations without deliberate, conscious and unjustified intrusion by the State. However, the Court made it clear that this right to privacy was not unqualified but was subject to the constitutional rights of others and to the requirements of public order, public morality and the common good. In this case, the tapping of the plaintiffs' telephones was found to have been deliberate, conscious and unjustifiable and was an actionable infringement of their constitutional rights.

In *Herrity v Associated Newspapers (Ireland) Ltd* [2009] 1 IR 317, the plaintiff sought damages from the defendants who published transcripts of private telephone conversations of the plaintiff which were obtained illegally by the plaintiff's husband who had engaged a private detective to record them. The Court found for the plaintiff and awarded €90,000 in damages, holding that actions for damages for breach of the constitutional right to privacy were not confined to actions against the State or state bodies but could also be maintained against a private person or entity. The Court also emphasised that the constitutional right to privacy was not an unqualified right and might have to be balanced against other competing rights or interests. Factors to be taken into account in this regard would include the nature of the underlying information communicated and the method by which it was obtained.

Herrity also made clear that there was a hierarchy of constitutional rights and, generally, instances where the right to privacy would prevail over the right to freedom of expression might be rare. However, a breach of the right to privacy was not justified where the freedom of expression asserted was in the publication of material obtained unlawfully and in breach of legislation enacted to protect the privacy of individuals. There was a breach of s 98 of the Post and Telecommunications Services Act 1983 in this case. Overall, the Court was of the view that where there was a public interest in the information being published, that publication might outweigh another's individual right to privacy.

The activities of state security services were considered recently by the High Court in *Schrems v Data Protection Commissioner* [2014] IEHC 310. There, Hogan J found that mass and indiscriminate surveillance of communications by state security services (in this case, the USA's National Security Agency), especially of private communications generated within the home, would, as a matter of Irish law, be unconstitutional, having regard to the interaction of the guarantees of privacy and Article 40.5's protection of the inviolability of the dwelling. Hogan J observed that the

> "concept of inviolability would be wholly compromised if private communications of this kind generally made within the home were thus subjected to routine and undifferentiated surveillance by State agencies."

E. The European Court of Human Rights

The European Court of Human Rights may provide a remedy for breaches of privacy which are protected by the European Convention on Human Rights. This is subject to the "exhaustion rule" under Article 35.1 of the Convention, which states:

> "The Court may only deal with the matter after all domestic remedies have been exhausted, according to the generally recognised rules of international law, and within a period of six months from the date on which the final decision was taken."

Accordingly, if the domestic courts fail to provide an adequate remedy for a breach of a Convention right, the matter may then be brought before the Court in Strasbourg.

In *Von Hannover v Germany* [2004] EMLR 21; (2005) 40 EHRR 1, a long-standing issue with persistent paparazzi was considered by the European Court of Human Rights. Various German tabloid newspapers and magazines had published photographs and accompanying articles showing Princess Caroline of Monaco in "semi-public" places such as restaurants. Many of these photographs had been taken in France, where the legal system is generally protective of public figures, but published in Germany, where the legal system is rather more lenient towards the press.

In what has been characterised as a pro-privacy decision, the European Court of Human Rights found that the German Court, which ruled against the plaintiff's application, had failed to take the positive steps necessary to protect her Article 8 rights under the Convention. Article 8 provides:

(1) "Everyone has the right to respect for his private and family life, his home and his correspondence.

(2) There shall be no interference by a public authority with the exercise of this right except such as is in accordance with the law and is necessary in a democratic society in the interests of national security, public safety or the economic well-being of the country, for the prevention of disorder or crime, for the protection of health or morals, or for the protection of the rights and freedoms of others."

The Court noted the context, describing the photographs as having been "taken in a climate of continual harassment". The key factor for the Court lay in assessing whether the photographs could make any meaningful contribution to a debate of general interest. It was concluded that because Princess Caroline held no public office and the photographs related to her private life, there was no such justification for the intrusion. The matter was further litigated in *Von Hannover v Germany (No 2)* [2012] ECHR 228. There, the plaintiff had only limited success in preventing publication of photographs which were taken openly in public and were not regarded as being unduly intrusive. See also *Mosley v News Group Newspapers* [2008] EMLR 20.

More recently, on 13 May 2014, the Court of Justice of the European Union gave a landmark ruling that the search engine Google must amend Internet search results in order to respect the privacy of individuals. The case, *Google Spain SL, Google Inc v Agencia Española de Protección de Datos (AEPD) and Mario Costeja González* Case C-131/12, involved a challenge under the 1995 Data Protection Directive by a Spanish lawyer who objected to a newspaper reference referring to old bankruptcy proceedings against him in a Google search. The decision of the Court was given after the claimant complained that the inclusion of an auction notice for his home, which had once been threatened with repossession, on an Internet search violated his right to privacy. Essentially, it was suggested that there is a "right to be forgotten".

F. Privacy Bill 2012

A Privacy Bill is currently before Seanad Éireann. It is a Private Member's Bill sponsored by Senators Sean D Barrett, David Norris and Feargal Quinn. Its proposed long title, if enacted, will be "An Act to provide for a Tort of Violation of Privacy; and to provide for matters connected therewith". The purpose of the Bill is to provide for a new tort of violation of privacy taking into account the jurisprudence of both the Irish courts and the European Court of Human Rights. The Bill provides that it would be a tort for a person wilfully and without lawful authority to violate the privacy of an individual. The proposed tort would be actionable without proof of special damage. The Bill provides that a person's entitlement to privacy "is that which might be reasonable in all the circumstances having regard to the rights of others and to public order and the common good". The Bill provides for statutory defences and that certain disclosures will not be a violation of privacy (for example, disclosures made in good faith and in the public interest). As with all Private Members' Bills, it will be subject to the availability of parliamentary time. So, when it will be enacted, if at all, is difficult to say with any certainty.

DEFENCES AND LIMITATION

Learning Outcomes

Upon completion of this chapter, the reader should be able to:

- Understand the range of defences available in negligence actions;
- Describe the operation of those defences;
- Identify appropriate defence(s) for particular circumstances;
- Explain the role of limitation periods in civil litigation;
- Understand when a cause of action accrues;
- Explain what is meant by "date of knowledge";
- Discuss the role of judicial discretion in dismissing actions within the statutory limitation period.

A. Defences

There are three principal defences to an action for negligence: contributory negligence; voluntary assumption of risk (*volenti non fit injuria*); and illegality (*ex turpi causa non oritur actio*). All of these defences may be relevant in other proceedings. In actions for trespass to the person, trespass to goods, or trespass to land, the defence of voluntary assumption of risk tends to be treated as the defence of consent.

Figure 18.1

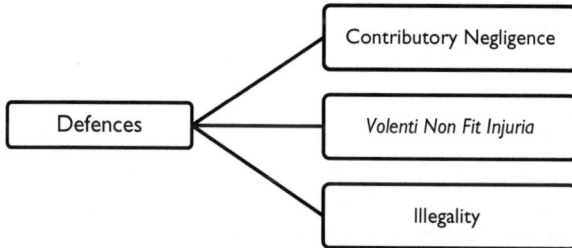

Contributory Negligence

The general rule is that, in an action for tort, where the plaintiff is at fault, damages will be reduced in proportion to his or her fault. It is not an absolute defence. Contributory negligence is essentially a lack of reasonable care for one's own safety or the safety or security of one's property or economic interests. This is in contrast to negligence itself which involves a breach of duty towards others. The law on contributory negligence is contained in the Civil Liability Act 1961. Section 34(1) provides that:

> "Where, in any action brought by one person in respect of a wrong committed by any other person, it is proved that the damage suffered by the plaintiff was caused partly by the negligence or want of care of the plaintiff or of one for whose acts he is responsible (in this Part called contributory negligence) and partly by the wrong of the defendant, the damages recoverable in respect of the said wrong shall be reduced by such amount as the court thinks just and equitable having regard to the degrees of fault of the plaintiff and defendant: provided that—
>
> (a) if, having regard to all the circumstances of the case, it is not possible to establish different degrees of fault, the liability shall be apportioned equally;
> (b) this subsection shall not operate to defeat any defence arising under a contract or the defence that the plaintiff before the act complained of agreed to waive his legal rights in respect of it, whether or not for value; but, subject as aforesaid, the provisions

of this subsection shall apply notwithstanding that the defendant might, apart from this subsection, have the defence of voluntary assumption of risk;

(c) where any contract or enactment providing for the limitation of liability is applicable to the claim, the amount of damages awarded to the plaintiff by virtue of this subsection shall not exceed the maximum limit so applicable."

So, where damage is suffered partly as a result of the plaintiff's own lack of care and partly due to the fault of the defendant, the plaintiff is liable to suffer a deduction from any compensation he or she is awarded.

General

The defence of contributory negligence will often arise in road traffic cases where a defendant may allege that the plaintiff has been guilty of contributory negligence. Generally, the defendant must show that the plaintiff's contributory negligence related to a danger which in fact transpired. So, if a plaintiff pedestrian is extremely intoxicated and is knocked down by a negligent driver, it will be irrelevant that the pedestrian was intoxicated if he would have been knocked down even if he were sober. Where a driver or passenger in a vehicle fails to use an available seat belt and, as a result, they suffer greater injury than they would have done owing to another road user's negligence, their damages will generally be reduced on the basis of contributory negligence: see *Hamill v Oliver* [1977] IR 73.

In *Boylan v Bus Átha Cliath* [2002] IEHC 135, an intoxicated passenger was struck by a bus shortly after he had alighted from it. Since he was partly at fault for his own injury, his compensation was reduced by 25%. In *Gammell v Doyle T/A Lee's Public House* [2009] IEHC 416, the plaintiff was struck and injured by the second defendant. The plaintiff had provoked the second defendant by making lewd comments and poking him: on the grounds of contributory negligence, the plaintiff's compensation was reduced by 50%.

Emergencies

A plaintiff who is confronted by an emergency caused by the defendant's negligence will generally be treated leniently by the courts. In *Jones v Boyce* (1816) 1 Stark 493; 171 ER 540 (CCP), the plaintiff was a passenger in a horse-drawn coach. He reasonably believed that the coach was about to overturn owing to the negligent driving of the defendant. The plaintiff therefore jumped off, breaking one of his legs. As it turned out, the coach did not overturn, but the plaintiff was adjudged not to be contributorily negligent. This is sometimes referred to as the "agony of the moment" principle.

A more recent example is *Moore v Hotelplan Ltd* [2010] EWHC 276 (QB). There, the plaintiff was riding a snowmobile on holiday. She was not given proper instructions in the use of the snowmobile by the defendants who were leading the plaintiff's ride. The plaintiff mistakenly believed that the snowmobile's brakes had failed. She panicked and accidentally depressed the throttle. The snowmobile ran into a car park and collided with a vehicle. The plaintiff was catastrophically injured. She was found not guilty of contributory negligence. The question for the Court, as it is in all such cases, was whether the plaintiff had behaved reasonably in the light of the dilemma in which the defendant's negligence had placed her.

In *Sayers v Harlow UDC* [1958] 2 All ER 342, however, a woman, who was locked in a public lavatory and was injured when trying to escape, had her damages reduced by 25% on the grounds that she had adopted an unduly hazardous method of escape. In the Canadian case of *Holomis v Dubuc* (1975) 56 DLR (3d) 35, the defendant landed a seaplane in which the plaintiff was travelling on a remote lake in British Columbia. The plane hit a submerged object. Water began to pour into the passenger compartment. The plaintiff jumped out and was drowned. Had he remained in the plane he would have been safe, as the plane was successfully beached. However, the plaintiff was held to be 50% responsible for his own death, not for jumping out, but for jumping out without a lifejacket.

Imputed Contributory Negligence

Sometimes, the plaintiff, in a tort action, can have the negligence of another person imputed to him or her by virtue of some special relationship between them: Civil Liability Act 1961, s 35. This can arise in cases of vicarious liability. For example, just as an employer may be answerable for the negligence of his employee, so too may the contributory negligence of an employee afford a defence to one who is sued by the employer. Suppose A drives B's car for B and is struck by C's vehicle due to C's negligence. If A is contributorily negligent, his carelessness may count against B in proceedings against C in respect of the damage to his vehicle.

Volenti Non Fit Injuria

Volenti non fit injuria is the ancient doctrine of voluntary assumption of risk. The defence operated where a person consented to the negligent act which injured him. He could not then complain when the injury occurred. This defence has changed significantly over the years and is now on a statutory basis in s 34(1)(b) of the Civil Liability Act 1961, which provides that:

> "… this subsection [dealing with contributory negligence] shall not operate to defeat any defence arising under a contract or the defence that the plaintiff before the act complained of agreed to waive his legal rights in respect of it, whether or not for value; but, subject as aforesaid, the provisions of this subsection shall apply notwithstanding that the defendant might, apart from this subsection, have the defence of voluntary assumption of risk;"

The effect of s 34(1)(b) is as follows:

The defence of *volenti non fit injuria* is effectively abolished in its old common law form, but a defendant can escape liability where:

(a) he shows that by virtue of a contract he is not liable; or

(b) he shows that the plaintiff before the act agreed to waive his legal rights in respect of it.

In either case the burden of establishing the defence falls on the defendant. In *O'Hanlon v ESB* [1969] IR 75 at 90, the Supreme Court said:

> "… what used to be called the defence of *volenti non fit injuria*… can now properly be described in the words of that… Act… as a 'defence that the plaintiff before the act complained of agreed to waive his legal rights in respect of it'."

Contract

Where the plaintiff and defendant enter into a contract which exempts the defendant from liability for negligence, the courts tend to construe such contracts strictly. In *O'Hanlon v ESB* [1969] IR 75 at 91, Walsh J said:

> "… Such contracts are construed strictly against the party claiming the benefit of the exception and there are instances where such contracts are actually prohibited by statute."

Agreement

Where the plaintiff has assured the defendant that he or she has waived any right of action that he or she might have in respect of the negligence of the defendant, that defendant will have a defence. The communication between the plaintiff and defendant must be clear. Where unambiguous language is used, no particular problem should arise. But where there is non-verbal communication, it may be more difficult for the court to infer that an agreement exists. Each case will be determined on its own facts.

In *Morris v Murray* [1991] 2 QB 6, the plaintiff and defendant spent the afternoon drinking, during which time the defendant consumed the equivalent of 17 whiskeys, the alcohol concentration in his blood being more than three times that permitted for a car driver. The defendant then suggested that they go for a flight in his light aircraft for which he held a pilot's licence. The defendant took off downwind rather than upwind which he should have done. The plane climbed to 300 feet. It stalled and dived into the ground. The pilot was killed and the plaintiff passenger was injured. The Court held that the defendant was not liable as the plaintiff had consented to the risk.

As mentioned, the Civil Liability Act 1961, s 34, requires agreement between the parties to waive the right to action. The courts have interpreted this provision as meaning that an agreement will only exist where there is proof of communication between the parties from which that waiver can be inferred. This approach was adopted in *Hussey v Twomey* [2009] IESC 1. There, a passenger travelled with a driver when she was "well aware" that the driver was intoxicated. She was injured in an accident caused by the driver's negligence. The Supreme Court held that the defence of *volenti non fit injuria* was not available, though a reduction of 40% in compensation for the plaintiff was imposed to take account of the plaintiff's contributory negligence.

Cases, such as *Hussey v Twomey*, where a passenger elects to get into a car with a driver who is intoxicated, will generally be dealt with under the principles of contributory negligence. That is not to say, however, that such a passenger will never be found to have waived his or her right to sue. It all depends on whether there has been communication between the plaintiff and defendant from which such a waiver can be inferred. Consider the following example. A asks B, a driver, for a lift. B explains to A that he is a bad driver, but that he will give A a lift if A agrees not to sue him if he crashes and injures A as a result of his negligent driving. A thinks about it for a moment, and then gets into B's car without saying anything. In this case there may be sufficient communication between A and B for the court to be able to infer that A has waived his legal right to sue B. However, in *McComiskey v McDermott* [1984] IR 75, the Court held that a notice in the front window of a car stating: "All passengers travel at their own risk", was not sufficient to bind the passenger.

Rescuers

As we have seen in the context of contributory negligence, in most common law jurisdictions, when the defendant has put someone in an urgent or dangerous situation, the law is reluctant to penalise that person. This principle also applies to rescuers. Accordingly, if the defendant's negligence results in peril to another which induces a rescue attempt by a third party, the defendant will also be liable to the rescuer. Liability to rescuers must be distinguished from contributory negligence. If I negligently undertake a dangerous activity, and someone is injured trying to rescue me, I will be liable to the rescuer for my breach of duty of care to him.

The Civil Law (Miscellaneous Provisions) Act 2011, s 4, inserts Part IVA into the Civil Liability Act 1961, a provision whose effect is to render "good samaritans" and "volunteers" immune from liability in negligence (though they may be liable for gross negligence or for acting "in bad faith") in certain circumstances. A "good samaritan" is defined as:

"a person who, without expectation of payment or other reward, provides assistance, advice or care to another person in an emergency, but does not include a person who does so as a volunteer".

Accordingly, professional workers in the emergency services do not fall within this definition.

Good samaritans are immune where, in an emergency, they provide assistance, advice or care to:

(i) persons who are, or appear to be, in serious and imminent danger of being injured or further injured;
(ii) persons who are injured or apparently injured, or
(iii) persons who are suffering, or apparently suffering from an illness.

This immunity will apply even where the emergency has been created by an act of a good samaritan. Under s 4, a volunteer will not be personally liable in negligence for any act done when carrying out voluntary work, save when the act was done in bad faith or was grossly negligent, or the volunteer knew or ought reasonably to have known that the act was outside the scope of the voluntary work authorised by the volunteer organisation in question, or was contrary to its instructions. Volunteer organisations remain subject to a duty of care in negligence.

As mentioned, once a person is classified as a rescuer, the courts tend to be more indulgent towards him or her. In *Turner v Iarnród Éireann* (unreported, 14 February 1996), a six-year-old child got on to a railway track through a gap in a fence. The child's mother, whilst frantically looking for the child, tripped on the railway track and suffered an injury. Liability was imposed on the defendants on the basis that the plaintiff's injuries were "a direct consequence" of the failure to provide adequate fencing. Also, in *O'Neill v Dunnes Stores* [2010] IESC 380, the plaintiff was injured when, shopping at the defendant's shopping centre, he was attacked by one of two shoplifters after having gone to the assistance of a lone security guard who had apprehended the other shoplifter. The security guard had sought the assistance of the plaintiff. Liability was imposed on the defendants because the Court considered that there ought to have been in place a more effective system of alerting other security staff at the shopping centre.

Volenti Non Fit Injuria in Other Jurisdictions

In *Baker v TE Hopkins & Sons Ltd* [1959] 3 All ER 225, two employees of the defendant were working in a well when they were overcome by carbon monoxide fumes. A doctor climbed down into the well and tried to save them despite the fact that the fire brigade was on its way. All three men died. The defence of *volenti non fit injuria* was argued by the defendant. The English Court of Appeal said it would be "ungracious", and neither "rational" nor "seemly" to say the doctor freely and voluntarily accepted the risk of the rescue.

A number of States in the United States have legislation which prohibits fire officers or other emergency personnel from bringing an action in negligence for injury against a party whose negligence is responsible for the emergency to which they were responding i.e., the very thing which they are employed to do. It appears that in Ireland and England there is no such "fireman's rule": see *Phillips v Durgan* [1991] ILRM 321 and *Ogwo v Taylor* [1988] AC 431.

Illegality (*Ex Turpi Causa Non Oritur Actio*)

The Latin phrase, *ex turpi causa non oritur actio*, can be translated as "No action can be founded upon a shameful act". This principle means, for modern purposes, that the law will not assist a plaintiff who has based his claim on an illegal act. For example, if an injured burglar tries to sue another burglar for the negligent use of explosives in seeking to "blow a safe", he is unlikely to succeed in his action. On the other hand, if that same burglar is on his way by bus to carry out a burglary and is injured by the negligent driving of the bus driver, there is no reason why his claim should not succeed.

Section 57(1) of the Civil Liability Act 1961, provides that:

> "[i]t shall not be a defence in an action merely to show that the plaintiff is in breach of the civil or criminal law."

Section 57(1) does not abolish the defence of illegality — it simply ensures that the mere fact that the defendant can show that the plaintiff is in breach of the law will not, in and of itself, be a defence. The section gives no guidance as to the circumstances in which the defence might be engaged.

In *Ashton v Turner* [1981] QB 137, the plaintiff was one of three men involved in a road traffic accident whilst driving at speed after committing a burglary. His claim in negligence failed owing to the defence of illegality; the Court found that no duty of care was owed to him in those circumstances. In *Pitts v Hunt* [1991] 1 QB 24, the plaintiff had been a passenger on a motorcycle. He was injured when it crashed after he had knowingly encouraged the driver to race, while drunk. His claim failed on the grounds of illegality. The English Court of Appeal held that it was not possible to set a standard of care. The plaintiff was also held to have been contributorily negligent.

In these two cases, the plaintiffs were involved in joint illegal enterprises. But the defence can also operate in circumstances where the plaintiff has acted alone. This occurred in *Clunis v Camden and Islington Health Authority* [1998] QB 978. There, the plaintiff had been detained in hospital for treatment of a mental disorder. On 24 September 1992 the hospital discharged him and 17 December 1992 , in a sudden and unprovoked attack, the plaintiff stabbed and killed a man. He pleaded guilty to manslaughter on the grounds of diminished responsibility and was sentenced to be detained in hospital for an indefinite period. The plaintiff sued the Health Authority, alleging that it had been negligent in discharging him and not providing adequate after care. He also claimed damages for his loss of liberty. The Health Authority applied to strike out the action on the ground that, even assuming that it had been negligent and that the plaintiff would not otherwise have committed the homicide, damages could not be recovered for the consequences of the plaintiff's own unlawful act. The Court accepted this submission.

In *Gray v Thames Trains* [2009] 1 AC 1391, the plaintiff was injured in the Ladbroke Grove rail crash in London in October 1999 which was caused by the negligence of the defendant. He suffered post-traumatic stress disorder. Whilst suffering the effects of this condition he stabbed and killed a pedestrian. He was convicted of manslaughter on the grounds of diminished responsibility and was ordered to be detained in a secure hospital indefinitely. He claimed for loss of earnings, damages for his detention and for his loss of reputation, and also an indemnity against any claims by dependents of the person he had killed. The Court held that whilst the defendant was liable to the plaintiff, that liability was limited and excluded any loss (such as loss of earnings after the conviction, or the indemnity) which flowed from his killing of the pedestrian. Although the plaintiff was successful in respect of general damages for loss of liberty and reputation derived from his original injury, he failed in the aspects of his loss which were derived from his crime. Lord Hoffmann said that the justification for accepting the defence of illegality in this case was that it would be inconsistent for a court to compensate a plaintiff for a sentence imposed owing to a criminal act for which he was responsible.

B. Limitation

Limitation periods have been laid down by statute to restrict the amount of time within which a plaintiff can begin his action. It would not be workable, fair, or convenient, if plaintiffs had an unlimited time within which to bring their tort claims. Evidence would be lost, memories would fade and insurers would never be able to update or close their books.

The General Rule

By virtue of s 11(2)(a) of the Statute of Limitations 1957, the general period of limitation for an action founded in tort is six years from the date on which the cause of action accrued. However, the period for an action claiming damages for negligence, nuisance or breach of duty or if the plaintiff claims damages for personal injuries is two years from the date of accrual or the "date of knowledge", if later than the date of accrual.

Accrual of a Cause of Action

The limitation period begins to run from the "date on which the cause of action accrued" (s 2). Accordingly, where a wrongful act is actionable *per se* (without proof of actual damage) the period begins to run from the time when the act is committed. In cases of continuing trespass or nuisance, or where the plaintiff is falsely imprisoned for a number of days, a fresh cause of action arises *de die in diem* ("from day to day"). Where a tort is actionable only on proof of damage, time does not begin to run before some damage actually occurs. This may be many years after the tort is committed.

In some cases, damage may occur before it is discovered. Consequently, if the cause of action accrues when the damage occurs, but is not discovered by the plaintiff until after the limitation period has run out, that plaintiff could find himself statute-barred in relation to that tort. This was the effect of s 11(2)(b) of the Statute of Limitations 1957. That provision was challenged in *Cahill v Sutton* [1980] IR 269 on the grounds that it killed off an action before an injured person might reasonably have become aware that he had one at all. The claim failed on the basis of *locus standi*.

In *Morgan v Park Developments Ltd* [1983] ILRM 156, the Court was of the view that a "discoverability" rule should apply to the interpretation of s 11(2) in view of the fact that a plaintiff could have his action statute-barred before he knew he had one. This, according to the Court, was "indefensible in the light of the Constitution". That issue was subsequently considered by the Supreme Court in *Hegarty v O'Loughran* [1990] 1 IR 148. There, the plaintiff underwent surgery to her nose. It was performed by the first defendant in 1973. This surgery was unsuccessful. So, in 1974 the second defendant performed a remedial operation which began to deteriorate by 1976. Proceedings were instituted against both defendants in 1982 claiming damages for personal injury due to medical negligence. Section 11(2)(b) of the Statute of Limitations 1957 provided that an action in tort for damages for personal injury had to be brought within three years from the date of the accrual of the cause of action. The plaintiff contended that under s 11(2)(b) a cause of action only accrued when the injured party could, by the exercise of reasonable diligence, have discovered that the injury had been caused by the wrongful act complained of. The defendants pleaded that the claim was statute-barred. The Supreme Court rejected the plaintiff's contention holding that, on the facts, her cause of action against the first defendant accrued in 1974 and against the second in 1976 and, accordingly, both claims were statute-barred.

The Court made it clear that the cause of action accrued at the time when *provable* personal injury capable of attracting compensation occurred to the plaintiff which was the completion of the tort alleged to have been committed against her. The tort of negligence was complete when damage had been caused by the defendants' wrongful acts. The Court considered that this was the appropriate interpretation given the effect of s 71 of the 1957 Act. Section 71 provides that, in the case of fraud, time does not begin to run against a plaintiff until the fraud is discovered or could, with reasonable diligence, be discovered. By implication, therefore, in cases where there was no allegation of fraud, time began to run whether or not the damage could have been discovered. In other words, any other interpretation of s 11(2)(b) would mean that s 71 was an entirely superfluous section.

In *Irish Equine Foundation v Robinson* [1999] 2 ILRM 289, the Court interpreted *Hegarty v O'Loughran* as authority for the view that

> "the cause of action for personal injury did not arise until the injury was manifest but it did then arise irrespective of whether it ever occurred to the party injured or could ever have reasonably occurred to the party injured that it resulted from the negligence of somebody else."

Accordingly, time starts to run when the injury is manifest in the sense of being reasonably capable of being discovered by the plaintiff. It does not matter if the plaintiff is not reasonably capable of attributing the injury to the negligence of the defendant. Once the physical injury is manifest, time begins to run.

Following the decision in *Hegarty v O'Loughran*, the Oireachtas enacted the Statute of Limitations (Amendment) Act 1991. This statute introduced a special limitation period for personal injuries actions. Section 3(1) provides that an action claiming damages in respect of personal injuries to a person caused by negligence, nuisance or breach of duty shall not be brought after the expiration of two years from the date on which the cause of action accrued or the date of knowledge (if later) of the person injured. The period was originally three years but was reduced to two by the Civil Liability and Courts Act 2004, s 7. The introduction of a "date of knowledge" means that plaintiffs are not prejudiced by a delay in their capacity to discover personal injuries that they have suffered or, where they are aware that they have suffered an injury, there is a delay in their ability to appreciate that it is a significant one. Personal injuries caused by intentional torts, such as trespass to the person, remain subject to the longer six-year limitation period provided for in s 11(2)(a) of the 1957 Act.

Date of Knowledge

According to s 2(1) of the 1991 Act, a person's date of knowledge is the date on which he had knowledge of the following facts:

(a)   that the person alleged to have been injured had been injured;
(b)   that the injury in question was significant;
(c)   that the injury was attributable in whole or in part to the act or omission which is alleged to constitute negligence, nuisance or breach of duty;
(d)   the identity of the defendant; and
(e)   if it is alleged that the act or omission was that of a person other than the defendant, the identity of that person and the additional facts supporting the bringing of an action against the defendant.

Knowledge that any acts or omissions did or did not, as a matter of law, involve negligence, nuisance or breach of duty is irrelevant: s 2(1). Thus, if a person knows that he has suffered a significant injury as a result of another person's act or omission, time will run against him even though he may not appreciate that he has been the victim of a tort. By virtue of s 2(2), a person's knowledge includes knowledge which he might reasonably have been expected to acquire—

(a)   from facts observable or ascertainable by him, or
(b)   from facts ascertainable by him with the help of medical or other appropriate expert advice which it is reasonable for him to seek

By virtue of s 2(3)(a) a person is not fixed under s 2 with knowledge of a fact ascertainable with the help of expert advice so long as he has taken all reasonable steps to obtain (and, where appropriate, to act upon) that advice. In addition, a person injured is not fixed under s 2 with knowledge of a fact relevant to the injury which he has failed to acquire as a result of that injury. Accordingly, a plaintiff who ignores symptoms will not be able to prevent time running against him if he would have discovered reasonably ascertainable facts relevant to his condition if he had investigated the symptoms. For example, if a person does not take reasonable steps to acquire medical advice, he will be considered to know the facts that would have been ascertainable with the help of that advice. However, if the person does take all reasonable steps to obtain and, where appropriate, act upon that advice, and that advice does not make that person aware of the relevant facts (for example, because the advice was negligently given) those facts will not be deemed to be known by the injured person. This means that a plaintiff who takes reasonable steps to inform himself of his condition will not be prejudiced if he is the victim of bad advice. It appears, however, that if the bad advice comes from his own lawyer, this will not prevent time running against him: see *O'Driscoll v Dublin Corporation* [1999] 1 ILRM 106. In those circumstances, a claim for negligence may lie against the lawyer.

As mentioned above, a person may have suffered an injury without being aware of it. The question of what "injury" means in this context was considered in

Gough v Neary [2003] 3 IR 92. In that case, the plaintiff had a hysterectomy in 1990 which was performed by the first defendant which he had said was necessary. Complaints from the first defendant's other patients began to appear in the media in 1998. The plaintiff then began to suspect that the hysterectomy that she had back in 1990 may have been unnecessary. She instituted proceedings that year: 1998. The Supreme Court held that her claim was not statute-barred. The Court held that the relevant knowledge was that the operation had been unnecessary: knowledge that an operation was unnecessary was not the same thing as knowledge that in proceeding to carry out the operation, the tort of negligence had been committed.

In *Behan v Bank of Ireland* [1998] 2 ILRM 507, the plaintiff farmer, who was in financial difficulties, claimed that he had been negligently advised by his bank manager in 1981 not to sell part of his farm. He claimed that the bank manager promised him the appropriate financial support if he did not sell. In the years which followed, the plaintiff's financial position worsened which, it was alleged, led to a nervous breakdown in 1982. The plaintiff's debts had to be restructured in 1983. Further financial accommodation was refused. The plaintiff issued proceedings in 1990. The Supreme Court held that the plaintiff's cause of action accrued in 1982 when the nervous breakdown had occurred and, accordingly, the claim for negligence was statute-barred.

In *McCoy v Keating* [2011] IEHC 260; [2012] 9 ICLMD 71, the plaintiffs suffered post-traumatic stress disorder following a road traffic accident in which children were trapped in a car, one of whom died. The plaintiffs issued proceedings more than two years after the accident. They argued that the relevant date from which the time started to run was the date of knowledge that their injuries were significant, which was the date on which each were diagnosed by their psychiatrist. The Court held, however, that their symptoms arose in the immediate aftermath of the accident and that:

> "...they all ought to have known from facts observable or ascertainable by each of them that they had suffered a significant injury. The diagnosis by the psychiatrist merely named the condition from which they were each suffering; they knew they had a condition before that, even if they had not known the medical term for it."

The plaintiffs had failed to establish that the applicable date of knowledge was the date on which they were each diagnosed by their psychiatrist. If they had, they would have been within the limitation period.

In *Whiteley v Minister for Defence* [1998] 4 IR 442, the plaintiff was subjected to excessive noise without adequate protection over a period of 21 years in the Army.

He left the Army in 1978 and afterwards began to suffer from deafness and tinnitus. He instituted his claim in 1995. The Court held that his claim was statute-barred on the basis that he would have considered his hearing loss and tinnitus sufficiently serious to justify instituting proceedings as early as 1978 or 1980.

Another Army deafness case is *Gallagher v Minister for Defence* (unreported 25 February 1998). There, the plaintiff had been in the army for 38 years. In November 1989 he had an audiogram, "the result or the significance of [which] was not explained to him". He instituted proceedings in February 1993. On the question of what constitutes "knowledge" for the purpose of s 2 of the 1991 Act, the Court applied the test adopted by Lord Donaldson in *Halford v Brookes* [1991] 1 WLR 428 at 443. He said:

> "In this context knowledge clearly does not mean 'I know for certain and beyond possibility of contradiction'. It does, however, mean know with sufficient confidence to justify embarking on the preliminaries to the issue of a writ, such as submitting a claim to the proposed defendant, taking legal or other advice and collecting evidence. Suspicion, particularly if it is vague and unsupported, will indeed not be enough, but reasonable belief will normally suffice."

The question of whether the plaintiff was aware of a "significant" injury for the purpose of s 2(1)(b) was considered by the Supreme Court in *Bolger v O'Brien* [1999] 2 IR 431. The plaintiff was injured in an accident in March 1990. He claimed that he only realised that the injury was significant when he had the result of x-rays almost two and half years later. He issued proceedings a further year after this. The Court held that his claim was statute-barred: the fact that he did not fully appreciate the full extent of his injuries did not mean that he was not aware that he had suffered a "significant" injury at the time.

In *Boylan v Motor Distributors Ltd* [1994] 1 ILRM 115 the plaintiff suffered a serious hand injury in the door of a van on 7 May 1986. It was not until 18 January 1989 that the plaintiffs received an engineer's report which said that the injury may have been caused by a design defect in the hinge mechanism of the van door. The Court accepted that the delay in getting the engineer's report was reasonable. The plaintiff's action against the manufacturers of the van was not commenced until 14 January 1992, some five years and eight months after the injury. The defendants claimed that the plaintiff's action was statute-barred by virtue of s 11(2)(b) of the Statute of Limitations 1957. The Court held that plaintiff's date of knowledge was not earlier than 18 January 1989 (the date the engineer's report was delivered) and, accordingly, the plaintiff's action, which was commenced by the issue of a plenary summons on the 14 January 1992, was not barred by s 11(2)(b) of the 1957 Act as amended by the Statute of Limitations (Amendment)

Act 1991. The 1991 Act became law on 10 July 1991 which, as we have seen, introduced the "date of knowledge". The plaintiff was therefore able to rely, by virtue of s 7, on the amendment introduced by the 1991 Act.

The identity of the defendant, knowledge of which is required to activate the "date of knowledge", can be an issue in some cases, in particular where the injured person is the victim of an environmental tort or a defective product. The precise source of the injuries in such cases may not be easy to determine. In addition, the "date of knowledge" will not be activated until the injured person knows the identity of a person other than the defendant in cases where it is alleged that the injurious act or omission was that of such person, as well as the additional facts supporting the bringing of an action against the defendant. This will typically arise in vicarious liability cases. Accordingly, if a person injured by another was acting within the scope of his employment, time does not begin to run in respect of the victim's claim against the employer until the victim knows the identity of the employer, the nature of the employment relationship with the employee and the other circumstances that support the bringing of an action against the employer. In such a case, this will include the fact that the employee was acting within the scope of his employment.

Persons under a Disability

The law affords persons under a disability special protection in respect of limitation periods. There are four categories of persons under a disability:

(a) an infant (a person under the age of 18 years);
(b) a person of unsound mind;
(c) a convict subject to the operation of the Forfeiture Act 1870, in whose case no administrator or curator has been appointed under that Act;
(d) a victim of sexual abuse who was suffering from consequent psychological injury.

Section 48(2) of the 1957 Act provides that a person detained "in pursuance of any enactment authorising the detention of persons of unsound mind or criminal lunatics" is conclusively presumed to be of unsound mind, the presumption being without prejudice to the generality of the term. Lord Denning MR in *Kirby v Leather* [1965] 2 QB 367 interpreted "person of unsound mind" as meaning a person who "is by reason of mental illness, incapable of managing his affairs in relation to the accident as a reasonable man would do". In the Irish courts, Murphy J in *Presho v Doohan* [2009] IEHC 631 thought that the test was "whether or not the plaintiff was capable of managing his affairs in relation to the alleged wrong. Managing his affairs includes the protection of his legal rights".

In general, if, on the date when the right of action accrued, the person to whom it accrued was under a disability, the action may be brought at any time before the expiration of six years (two years in personal injuries cases) from the date on which the person ceases to be under a disability or dies, whichever event first occurs, notwithstanding that the period of limitation has expired: Statute of Limitations 1957, s 49(1)(a). Accordingly, where a person of unsound mind has a right of action, the relevant limitation period will not begin to run until he regains his sanity or until he dies, whichever is the sooner. Or, where a minor has a right of action, the relevant limitation period will not begin to run until he reaches the age of 18 or until he dies, whichever is the sooner. This position is subject to two main exceptions:

- where the right of action originally accrued to some person not under a disability through whom the person under a disability claims, no extension will be permitted;
- where a right of action, which has accrued to a person under a disability, accrues, on his death, while still under a disability, to another person under a disability, no further extension of time is allowed by reason of the disability of the second person.

The Statute of Limitations 1957, s 49(2)(a)(ii), which offered a more a favourable limitation period to minors not in the custody of a parent was found to be constitutionally invalid in *O'Brien v Keogh* [1972] IR 144.

Judicial Discretion and the Effect of Undue Delay

The court has inherent jurisdiction to dismiss proceedings on the grounds of inordinate or inexcusable delay in their prosecution. This occurred in *O'Domhnaill v Merrick* [1984] IR 151. There, proceedings were instituted long after an accident occurred, but within the statutory limitation period by virtue of the extension for minors. The proceedings were dismissed after the progress of the case had slowed considerably once the writ was issued. The delay in prosecuting the case would not normally have been sufficient to warrant dismissal, but it became so when the long extension for minors was taken into account.

There was a similar outcome in the *Toal v Duignan* [1991] ILRM 135. In that case, the plaintiff, who was born in 1961, claimed that he learned in the summer of 1983 (when he was 22 years old) that he was sterile due to an undiagnosed undescended testicle at the time of his birth. He sued a number of defendants, including the doctors attending his birth and the maternity hospital in question. He claimed that the doctors should either have prescribed remedial treatment or warned his parents of the need to obtain remedial treatment. The plaintiff instituted proceedings in October 1984 within 15 months of discovering his condition.

However, the Supreme Court affirmed the High Court decision to strike out the plaintiff's claim on the basis that the defendants would be unable to properly defend proceedings by reason of lapse of time. In this regard, the Court specifically referred to the absence of detailed clinical notes and records and the deaths of the gynaecologist and paediatrician concerned.

Toal v Duignan, therefore, operates as a qualification to the discoverability principle. Even though the plaintiff could not reasonably have learned of his right of action any earlier than he did, and even though he may have taken all reasonable steps to commence proceedings once he learned of his right of action, his claim could be killed off by the exercise of judicial discretion before it begins.

In *Rainsford v Limerick Corporation* [1995] 2 ILRM 561 and in the Supreme Court's decision in *Primor plc v Stokes Kennedy Crowley* [1996] 2 IR 459 greater certainty was brought to this area of the law. In *Primor*, Hamilton CJ set down the various factors which the court will take into account in determining where the balance of justice lies in cases where there has been a long delay in instituting proceedings. These factors include such matters as the extent to which the defendant is prejudiced through the passage of time; the availability of witnesses or documents; the impact prolonged litigation may have on the reputation of the defendant as long as the matter is undetermined (for example if the defendant is a doctor or lawyer), or where the defendant, because of the passage of time, is no longer covered by insurance. On the other hand, if liability has already been admitted, the defendant's claim to be prejudiced would be weakened. Any dilatoriness on the part of the defendant would also be taken into account.

The Effect of Fraud

Section 71(1) of the Statute of Limitations 1957 states:

> "Where, in the case of an action for which a period of limitation is fixed by this Act, either –
>
> (a) the action is based on the fraud of the defendant or his agent or of any person through whom he claims or his agent, or
> (b) the right of action is concealed by the fraud of any such person, the period of limitation shall not begin to run until the plaintiff has discovered the fraud or could with reasonable diligence have discovered it."

In paragraph (a) the word "fraud" refers to the tort of deceit in that such fraud will of itself give rise to a right of action. In paragraph (b) the word "fraud" is taken to have the same meaning as fraud in the Real Property Limitation Act 1833: see *Beaman v ARTS Ltd* [1949] 1 KB 550 at 567, Court of Appeal, Somerville LJ.

It is clear from the authorities that "fraud" for the purposes of s 71 does not involve "moral turpitude". In *Kitchen v Royal Air Force Association* [1958] 1 WLR 569, Lord Evershed, referring to an equivalent English statutory provision stated:

"... the word 'fraud'... is by no means limited to common law fraud or deceit. Equally, it is clear... that no degree of moral turpitude is necessary to establish fraud within the section...it is, I think, clear that the phrase covers conduct which, having regard to some special relationship between the two parties concerned, is an unconscionable thing for the one to do towards the other."

"Fraud" in this context can arise where one party, for example a solicitor, conceals from his client that he, the client, has a cause of action against him, the solicitor.

Lord Denning MR in *Applegate v Moss* [1971] 1 QB 406 considered that the statutory provision relating to "fraud" applied whenever the defendant's conduct had been such

"as to hide from the plaintiff the existence of his right of action, in such circumstances that it would be inequitable to allow the defendant to rely on the lapse of time as a bar to the claim."

Later, Lord Denning MR in *Keane v Victor Parsons & Co* [1973] 1 WLR 29 said that in order to show that a right of action was concealed by fraud, it is not necessary to show that the defendant took active steps to conceal his wrongdoing. Saying nothing would be sufficient. However, if the defendant was quite unaware that he was committing a wrong, then that would be different. If, by an honest blunder, the defendant unwittingly commits a wrong, then he could avail himself of the Statute of Limitations.

Hedigan J in *Sullivan v Rogan, practising as Rogan and Morgan Solicitors* [2009] IEHC 456 cited the English authorities above. In that case, the plaintiff, a retired farmer aged 90, claimed damages from his solicitors for negligence, misrepresentation, breach of contract, breach of duty and breach of statutory duty, arising from a transaction involving the sale of lands in 1999. He claimed that the defendants had failed to advise him properly in respect of a transfer of his property at undervalue, which amounted to divesting himself of his entire property. Proceedings were instituted in 2008. The defendants invoked the Statute of Limitations 1957 claiming the plaintiff's action was statute-barred. The plaintiff in reply sought to rely upon s 71 alleging that the failure of the defendants to advise him in March 1999 that he had a cause of action against them due to their failure to advise him properly on the transaction in question amounted to a fraudulent concealment. The Court declined the defendants' invitation to dismiss the proceedings. The matter was remitted to a plenary hearing.

Special Limitation Periods

Some statutes set down special limitation periods which deal with particular categories of tort claim. This section summarises some of the more important ones.

Claims Relating to Child Abuse

Under the Statute of Limitations (Amendment) Act 2000, s 2 inserts a new s 48A into the Statute of Limitations 1957. It provides that a person bringing an action founded on tort in respect of an act of sexual abuse committed against him or her during minority is to be treated as being under a disability while he or she is suffering from any psychological injury caused by that act or any other act of the transgressor and the psychological injury is of such significance that his or her will, or his or her ability to make a reasoned decision, in bringing that action is substantially impaired: s 48A(1).

An "act of sexual abuse" is defined in s 48A(7) as including:

(a) "any act of causing, inducing or coercing a person to participate in any sexual activity,

(b) any act of causing, inducing or coercing the person to observe any other person engaging in any sexual activity, or

(c) any act committed against, or in the presence of, a person that any reasonable person would, in all the circumstances, regard as misconduct of a sexual nature:

Provided that the doing or commission of the act concerned is recognised by law as giving rise to a cause of action;"

Accordingly, the act must constitute a tort.

It will be noted that this provision applies not just to claims against the perpetrators themselves, but also against those alleged to have been guilty of negligence or breach of duty in respect of the personal injuries caused by the act of sexual abuse: s 48A(1)(b). Hence, if a victim takes a claim against an institution, a school, or, for that matter, the State, contending that the defendant negligently facilitated or failed to prevent the abuse, the Act of 2000 applies to that claim.

This provision seeks to address concerns that victims of child sexual abuse would not, due to psychological injury sustained as a consequence of that abuse, be in the position to initiate proceedings against the perpetrators of that abuse. They are to be treated as being under a disability for the purposes of limitation, during which, time will not run against them in respect of their claims.

It should be noted that s 3, in mirroring *Toal v Duignan* [1991] ILRM 135, states that nothing in s 48A of the Statute of Limitations 1957 (inserted by s 2 of the 2000 Act),

> "is to be construed as affecting any power of a court to dismiss an action on the ground of there being such delay between the accrual of the cause of action and the bringing of the action as, in the interests of justice, would warrant its dismissal."

Therefore, the court's power to dismiss an action on the ground of delay where this would be in the interests of justice is expressly preserved.

Defective Products

The Liability for Defective Products Act 1991 provides a statutory remedy for injury or damage caused by defective products (see chapter 9). This statute supplements the common law right of action in negligence. The legislation prevents an action from being brought more than three years after the date that the cause of action accrued or the date (if later) that the plaintiff became aware, or should reasonably have become aware, of the damage, the defect and the identity of the producer: s 7(1).

Although s 7(5) of the Civil Liability and Courts Act 2004 reduced the limitation period for personal injuries actions in negligence from three years to two years, the three-year limitation period in the Liability for Defective Products Act 1991 is unaffected. This is because that limitation period is contained in the product liability directive (Council Directive 85/374/EEC), a European law provision (which the Liability for Defective Products Act 1991 transposes into Irish law) which, by virtue of the doctrine of supremacy of EU law, takes precedence over all domestic law.

In addition, s 7(2)(a) of the Liability for Defective Products Act extinguishes a right of action, regardless of any question of discoverability, on the expiration of 10 years from the date on which the producer put into circulation the product that caused the damage — unless the injured person has in the meantime instituted proceedings against the producer.

Defamation

Section 38 of the Defamation Act 2009 amends s 11 of the Statute of Limitations 1957, by providing that a defamation action shall not be brought after the expiry of one year or such longer period as the court may direct not exceeding two years from the date on which the cause of action accrued: s 38(1). The courts are precluded from giving such a direction unless they are satisfied that it is in the interests of justice and the prejudice that the plaintiff would suffer if the direction were *not* given would significantly outweigh the prejudice that the defendant would suffer if the direction *were* given. The courts will also have regard to the reason for the failure to bring the action within the shorter period and the extent to which any evidence relevant to the matter is by virtue of the delay no longer capable of being adduced.

In defamation proceedings, the date of accrual will be the date when the defamatory statement was first published; or if published on the Internet, the date on which it was first capable of being accessed.

Survival of Actions

Section 9(2) of the Civil Liability Act 1961 provides:

> "No proceedings shall be maintainable in respect of any cause of action whatsoever which has survived against the estate of a deceased person unless either—
>
> (a) proceedings against him in respect of that cause of action were commenced within the relevant period and were pending at the date of his death, or
> (b) proceedings are commenced in respect of that cause of action within the relevant period or within the period of two years after his death, whichever period first expires."

Accordingly, if a negligent motorist dies shortly after a road traffic accident in which he has injured a cyclist, the cyclist has no more than two years after the motorist's death in which to take proceedings. Due to the wording of s 50 of the Personal Injuries Assessment Board Act 2003, it would appear that the extension normally allowed to persons who make an application first to InjuriesBoard.ie (formerly known as the Personal Injuries Assessment Board or PIAB), will not be available in such cases: see Canny, *Limitation of Actions* (Round Hall, 2010), para 12.05.

The constitutionality of this two-year limitation period was challenged unsuccessfully by a minor in *Moynihan v Greensmyth* [1977] IR 55 on the basis that it was repugnant to Article 40.3 of the Constitution where the State guarantees by its laws to "protect as best of may from unjust attack and, in the case of injustice done, [to] vindicate the... property rights of every citizen". The Supreme Court, accepting that the right to sue is a property right, took the view that the period of infancy should not form part of the limitation period because the danger of stale claims being brought would be increased and could constitute a serious threat to the rights of beneficiaries of the estate of a deceased. The Court thought that the two-year limitation period was a necessary imposition, as no compromise appeared possible bearing in mind the State's duty to others, in particular those who represent the estate of the deceased and beneficiaries.

Maritime Cases

Where there is a collision between vessels at sea, special limitation periods apply to claims in respect of any resultant damage. These limitation periods are set out in s 46 of the Civil Liability Act 1961. Section 46(2) prescribes a general limitation period of two years from the date of damage, death or injury in actions to enforce a claim for damages or lien in respect of damage to a vessel, cargo or property or the loss of life or personal injury suffered by a person on board a vessel, caused by the sole or concurrent fault of the defendant vessel: an action for contribution in respect of any overpaid proportion of any of these damages must be commenced within a year from the date of payment. The court has discretion under s 46(3) to extend this period to such extent and subject to such conditions as it thinks fit. If the plaintiff is suing in respect of injury suffered whilst on a vessel, but in circumstances where no other vessel is involved, s 46 does not apply: see *McGuinness v Marine Institute* [2009] IEHC 177.

Actions for Contribution under the Civil Liability Act 1961

Where there are concurrent wrongdoers, and one wrongdoer is ordered by the court to pay damages to the plaintiff, that wrongdoer may be able to claim a contribution from a second wrongdoer in respect of the damages he, the first wrongdoer, has to pay. That second wrongdoer may or may not have been sued at the same time as the first wrongdoer. Section 31 of the Civil Liability Act 1961 sets down the limitation period within which such claims must be made by one wrongdoer against another wrongdoer. Section 31 provides:

> "An action may be brought for contribution within the same period as the injured person is allowed by law for bringing an action against the contributor, or within the period of two years after the liability of the claimant is ascertained or the injured person's damages are paid, whichever is the greater."

Where an action for contribution and/or indemnity is made by a first defendant against a second defendant who is the personal representative of a deceased person, the relevant limitation period is that which is set down in s 9(2) of the 1961 Act, which is two years from the death of the deceased, not the period in s 31: see *Keane v Western Health Board* [2007] 2 IR 555.

REMEDIES AND PRINCIPLES OF COMPENSATION

Learning Outcomes

Upon completion of this chapter, the reader should be able to:

- Understand the separate roles of damages and injunctions as remedies;
- Distinguish between the various categories of damages;
- Identify the circumstances in which the courts will award specific categories of damages;
- Appreciate the role of s 26 of the Civil Liability and Courts Act 2004 in the dismissal of fraudulent or exaggerated claims;
- Explain the roles of prohibitory, mandatory and *quia timet* injunctions.
- Explain the roles of perpetual, interlocutory and interim injunctions.

A. Overview

The main remedies in tort actions are damages and injunctions.

Damages

Damages can be defined as money compensation for loss suffered by a person due to the tort, breach of contract, or breach of statutory duty by another person. Damages are compensatory and are intended to restore to the plaintiff what he or she has lost. There are also heads of non-compensatory damages: contemptuous, nominal and exemplary or punitive damages.

Compensatory damages can be divided into pecuniary and non-pecuniary damages. Pecuniary damages would cover such things as loss of earnings and medical and care expenses incurred up to the date of trial. For example, owing to disability, the plaintiff may have to have his or her home adapted. Non-pecuniary damages will include such things as compensation for pain and suffering, and loss of expectation of life.

A more problematic aspect of pecuniary loss is that which must be anticipated for the future, but must be awarded at the time of the trial. This is due to the "once and for all" nature of damages payments which must be made as lump sum awards. This means that plaintiffs must sue in one action for all loss: past, present and prospective. If the plaintiff's life expectancy has been shortened, damages may include loss of earnings in those "lost years". Mental suffering as a consequence of awareness of shortened life expectancy could be awarded under "pain and suffering".

Injunctions

An injunction is a judgment or order of the court restraining the commission or continuance of some wrongful act, or the continuance of some wrongful omission. Injunctions are usually sought against torts such as nuisance, or continuing or repeated trespass. An injunction is a discretionary remedy and cannot be demanded as of right.

B. Types of Damages Awarded

Nominal Damages

In some cases, the plaintiff will be held to have had his or her legal rights violated but will not have actually suffered any loss. In such cases, the plaintiff may be awarded nominal damages. He or she will be "vindicated and not blameworthy".

Contemptuous Damages

Contemptuous damages are awarded in some cases, commonly defamation, to indicate that although the plaintiff has been successful technically, the court feels that the action should never have been brought. The plaintiff will usually receive the smallest coin in circulation at the time and is unlikely to have a costs order made in his favour. For example, in *Reynolds v Times Newspapers* [2001] 2 AC 127, former Taoiseach Albert Reynolds was awarded one penny (and was ordered to pay the newspaper's costs) when he won his libel action in London.

Special and General Damages

Special damages are damages which the law does not presume to flow from the defendant's act and which must be expressly pleaded and proved. These might be for example, loss of earnings or medical expenses. The term special damages is used to denote damages which are capable of exact calculation, as distinct from those not capable of being so calculated, which are known as general damages. General damages, therefore, are damages which the law presumes to flow from the defendant's act. These might be damages for pain and suffering in personal injury actions. In *Wise v Kaye* [1962] 1 QB 638, a victim who had been unconscious continuously since the accident was presumed to have experienced nothing of her injuries and, therefore, received nothing for pain and suffering.

The courts seek to ensure finality in litigation. For this reason, lump sum awards of damages are made. It is important that damages are adequately assessed at trial because awards cannot be changed later. Periodic payments are made in some jurisdictions and this approach is being considered in Ireland.

Restitutio in Integrum and Compensatory Damages

Restitutio in integrum ("restoration to the original position") is effective in cases where the plaintiff has suffered pecuniary loss. However, in cases where it is difficult to make a reasonably precise pecuniary assessment, the principle is not entirely effective. Clearly, where the plaintiff has lost a limb as a result of the defendant's negligence, he or she can never be put into their original position. An award of money damages is manifestly insufficient, but is the only thing that the law can give.

Restitutionary Damages

Restitutionary damages have recently been described by Lord Kerr in *R (on the application of Lumba) v Secretary of State for the Home Department* [2012] 1 AC 245 para 254 in the UK Supreme Court in the following terms:

> "[t]raditionally, the primary function of damages has been to compensate the individual for the loss that he or she has suffered ('compensatory damages'). More recently the concept of restitutionary damages has been recognised where damages for the tort are

measured according to the gain that the defendant has obtained or the value that the right infringed might have had to the claimant where, for instance, unknown to the claimant, the defendant has used the claimant's property".

It is possible, therefore, for damages to be assessed by taking into account the possible profit or gain that the defendant has made at the expense of the plaintiff and not basing the award simply on the loss suffered by the plaintiff. In *Hickey v Roches Stores* (14 July 1976), Finlay P said that where a wrongdoer has calculated and intended by his wrongdoing to achieve a gain or profit which he could not otherwise achieve and has in that way acted *mala fide* then irrespective of whether the form of his wrongdoing constitutes a tort or a breach of contract, the Court should, in assessing damages, look not only to the loss suffered by the injured party but also to the profit or gain, unjustly or wrongly obtained by the wrongdoer.

Exemplary Damages

Exemplary damages, sometimes referred to as punitive damages, are imposed over and above any compensatory damages. Historically, this will occur where there was an unconstitutional or wanton interference of the plaintiff's rights; "punitive" (or "exemplary") damages could also be awarded. This shows that one of the functions of the tort system is deterrence. In *Rookes v Barnard* [1964] AC 1129 the House of Lords enumerated the restricted situations in which exemplary or punitive damages would be appropriate:

- Oppressive, arbitrary or unconstitutional actions by servants of the government. This includes not only local or central governmental bodies but, significantly, the police and prison officers. The tort in such cases would typically be trespass to the person or malicious prosecution. In *Thompson v Commissioner of Police for the Metropolis* [1997] 3 WLR 403, some judicial limits were placed on exemplary damages awarded against the police in the UK. The usual minimum in cases where such damages are appropriate is £5000, and £25,000 would be the usual maximum, up to £50,000 only when high-ranking officers are implicated.
- Where the conduct has been calculated to make a profit. This typically applies in some defamation cases. For example, in *Elton John v MGN* [1997] QB 586, a well-known singer won a libel action in respect of an article in the *Daily Mirror* which claimed that he had adopted a bizarre weight loss strategy. The jury awarded him damages totalling £350,000 but this was reduced to £75,000 on appeal. The English Court of Appeal endorsed for the first time that the judge may indicate to the jury appropriate guidelines

of the range of appropriate damages in the case; and furthermore that it may be appropriate for a judge to draw comparisons with levels of damages in personal injuries cases.

The Irish courts have not definitively endorsed the policy of *Rookes v Barnard*, although some judges, up to the Supreme Court, have expressed support for the approach in individual cases. It can be said that there is no Irish decision which definitively rejects the *Rookes v Barnard* limitations as its *ratio decidendi*. Moreover, some judges have expressed the view that Irish law is not subject to the *Rookes v Barnard* limitations: see *Conway v Irish National teachers Organisation* [1991] 2 IR 305. Exemplary damages have, of course, been awarded by the Irish courts in a number cases: see *Garvey v Ireland* [1981] ILRM 266; *Crofter Properties Ltd v Genport Ltd (No 2)* [2005] 4 IR 28.

Aggravated Damages

Aggravated damages are compensatory in nature but indicate that the plaintiff's position has been made worse because of the defendant's malice or bad motivation. In assessing the level of aggravated damages, the courts will take into account the manner in which the wrongs have been committed, involving such elements as oppressiveness or arrogance, and the wrongdoer's conduct after the commission of the wrong, such as a refusal to apologise or a threat to repeat the wrong.

In *Shortt v Commissioner of An Garda Síochána* [2007] 4 IR 587, the plaintiff had been "set up" by members of An Garda Síochána. This resulted in his wrongful conviction for a drugs offence, a sentence of three years' imprisonment, and the loss of his business. The Supreme Court awarded him substantial aggravated damages as well as exemplary damages.

In *Connellan v St Joseph's Kilkenny* [2006] IEHC 119, the plaintiff had been subjected to serious assaults and ill-treatment at an orphanage. He was awarded €50,000 in aggravated damages. In *Swaine v Commissioners of Public Works in Ireland* [2002] 1 IR 521, the plaintiff had been exposed to asbestos in his workplace for an extended period of time which could have resulted in fatal injury. The High Court characterised the defendant as being guilty of "negligence of the grossest kind". The plaintiff was awarded €45,000 plus €15,000 aggravated damages.

In *Philp v Ryan* [2004] 4 IR 241, the Supreme Court awarded €55,000 in aggravated damages in a professional negligence claim where a doctor had altered his clinical notes on a critical issue, thereby misleading his own legal advisers and expert witnesses by making his defence seem stronger than it actually was. The Court deprecated this "truly appalling feature" of the case where the defendants' advisers had been told of the doctor's alteration over a week before the commencement of the action but had not informed the plaintiff's solicitors of the truth (though they did not seek to rely on the notes in cross-examination of the plaintiff or his advisers).

Figure 19.1

Nominal

Aggravated

Contemptuous

Exemplary/punitive

Types of Damages

Special

Restitutionary

General

Restitutio in Integrum

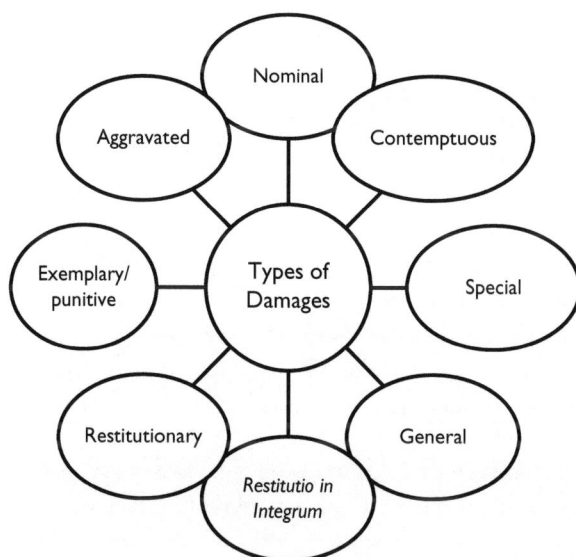

Fraudulent or Exaggerated Claims

Section 26 of the Civil Liability and Courts Act 2004 places an obligation on the court to dismiss the entirety of a claim, even where legal liability is established or not contested, once the defendant proves the relevant falsity or misleading character of the evidence or affidavit and the fact that the plaintiff knew of such falsity or misleading character, unless dismissal would result in injustice being done. Any falsity or misleading evidence must relate to the proceedings in question. If the plaintiff has lacked candour or made false statements relating to his health or physical capacity in his dealings with others not directly related to the litigation in question, this will not be a reason to invoke s 26. In *Mulkern v Flesk* [2005] IEHC 48, the plaintiff untruthfully told her employer that she did not have any back trouble when she sought employment. In legal proceedings against the defendant concerning injuries she sustained following a road traffic accident, the defendant sought to invoke s 26. The Court held that although she had been untruthful to her prospective employers, she had not been untruthful to the Court. Accordingly, s 26 had no application.

C. Injunctions

Prohibitory, Mandatory and *Quia Timet* Injunctions

Figure 19.2

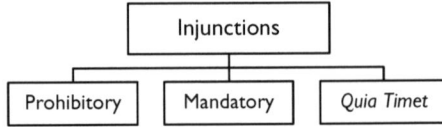

In some cases, damages will be an insufficient remedy. In such cases, an injunction may be sought. An injunction is an order of the court requiring the defendant either to do something (mandatory injunction) or to cease doing something (prohibitory injunction). A *quia timet* injunction may also be issued. This is an injunction that restrains wrongful conduct that has not yet been committed but is merely apprehended. One such injunction was issued in *Whelan v Madigan* [1978] ILRM 136, where the defendant landlord was likely to continue a campaign of intimidation to force his tenants to leave the premises. Injunctions, therefore, are appropriate in cases in which the tort is of an ongoing nature: for instance, nuisance caused by noise.

The High Court and the Circuit Court have power to issue an injunction wherever it appears "just or convenient" to do so: Courts (Supplemental Provisions) Act 1961, s 8; Supreme Court of Judicature (Ireland) Act 1877, s 28(8). Because an injunction is an equitable remedy, it is not available as of right, but rather at the court's discretion. The factors which influence how this discretion is exercised are determined by the type of injunction being sought.

Injunctions will be ordered in relation to a wide range of torts including public and private nuisance, trespass to land, defamation, trespass to the person, trespass to chattels, injurious falsehood. Injunctions may be sought against the commission or continuance of any tort, but, their equitable and discretionary character inevitably means that they will not be granted in every case.

Perpetual, Interlocutory and Interim Injunctions

Figure 19.3

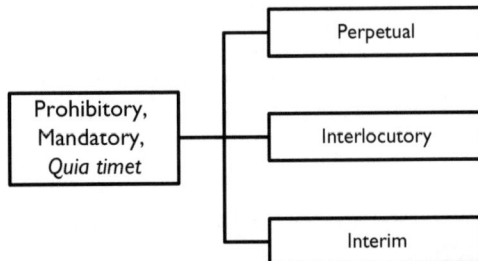

Injunctions, whether they be prohibitory, mandatory or *quia timet*, are of three kinds:

- *Perpetual injunction* — a permanent injunction after hearing of the action;
- *Interlocutory injunction* — a temporary injunction pending trial of the action;
- *Interim injunction* — an injunction restraining the defendant until some specified time.

A perpetual injunction is issued at the end of the trial of the action on its merits. This is when the judge has heard all the relevant facts and both parties have had their say in court. An interim injunction may be granted to restrain the defendant until a specified time determined by the court. It is an injunction of an interlocutory nature granted by the court on the application to it *ex parte* by the plaintiff. It is very much an emergency "holding position" until proceedings with both parties can take place. An interlocutory injunction may be sought where the tort may already have been committed and the plaintiff will urgently want to prevent damage until such time as the merits of the dispute can come to trial. In these cases, the court will be concerned to balance the rights of both parties, on the basis that the plaintiff could ultimately lose. To secure an interlocutory injunction, the plaintiff must pass three tests. He or she must show:

(1) that there is "a serious question to be tried";
(2) that the balance of convenience lies in favour of granting an interlocutory injunction; and
(3) that irreparable harm would follow if the injunction were refused.

In *American Cyanamid v Ethicon* [1975] AC 396, the House of Lords set down the requirement that there be a "serious question to be tried". That test was endorsed by the Supreme Court in *Campus Oil Ltd v Minister for Industry and Energy (No 2)* [1983] IR 88.

Interlocutory injunctions are commonly applied for in respect of torts where the plaintiff contends that the state of affairs resulting from the defendant's act is sufficiently serious that the defendant ought not to be allowed to continue that state of affairs. Examples might be trespass to land, nuisance, or alleged defamatory material on the Internet. So far as the court is concerned, it is entirely appropriate, where possible, to consider the respective strength of both parties' cases and, if the plaintiff has a strong *prima facie* case, to go ahead and grant the injunction. However, where an interlocutory injunction would effectively ruin the defendant's livelihood, the court would be very slow to grant it without a full hearing having taken place.

Sometimes an applicant for an injunction may be required to give an undertaking as to damages. This means that if the injunction is later found to have been wrongly granted, the applicant may have to pay damages to the party against whom the injunction was granted to compensate him for losses occasioned by the granting of the injunction.

Damages in Lieu of an Injunction

When an application has been made for an injunction, the defendant may try to persuade the court that damages would be a preferable remedy. In *Shelfer v City of London Electric Lighting Co* [1895] 1 Ch 287, an injunction was granted to an occupier to prevent continued noise and vibration caused by the defendant despite its significant impact upon the local electricity supply. It was held that "damages in lieu" of an injunction would only be justified if the injury to the plaintiff's legal right:

- is small;
- is capable of being estimated in money;
- can be adequately compensated by a small money payment; and
- where it would be oppressive to the defendant to grant an injunction.

In Ireland, the courts have had, since the The Chancery Amendment Act 1858 (Lord Cairns's Act) (21 & 22 Vict. c. 27), untrammelled discretion to award damages either in addition to or in lieu of an injunction. The courts may choose to exercise this discretion where there are exceptional circumstances. For example, if the granting of the injunction would be oppressive to the defendant and damages would be a perfectly adequate remedy for the plaintiff, damages in lieu of an injunction may be appropriate. Also, the conduct of the plaintiff may be such as to disentitle him from an injunction or the conduct of the defendant may be such as to disentitle him from seeking the substitution of damages for an injunction. The mere fact that a wrongdoer is able and willing to pay for the injury he has inflicted is not a ground for substituting damages: see *Patterson v Murphy* [1978] ILRM 85 per Costello J at 99-100 citing *Shelfer v City of London Electric Lighting Co* [1895] 1 Ch 287.

Index